FAMILY
MATTERS

365 DAILY
DEVOTIONS
FOR FAMILIES

KYLE & SHARON DODD

FAMILY
MATTERS

365 DAILY DEVOTIONS FOR FAMILIES

KYLE & SHARON DODD

FAMILY MATTERS

Kyle Dodd, Family Matters

ISBN 978-0-9845750-3-9

Cross Training Publishing
P.O. Box 1874
Kearney, NE 68848
(308) 293-3891

This book is manufactured in the United States of America.

Library of Congress Cataloging in Publication Data in Progress.

DEDICATION

"An excellent wife is THE crown of her husband." Proverbs 12:4

This book is dedicated to my crown...Sharon Elizabeth Dodd. While attending Baylor University, I was told by friends, "when you found her...you out-punted your coverage." So why would I dedicate a "devotional" book to her? Because she is the greatest example of "devotion" I have witnessed. First she is devoted to her Savior, Jesus Christ. I have watched her rise before the sun rises and spend countless mornings reading her Bible and praying. She has been 100 percent devoted and dedicated to me as her husband since May 18, 1985. She is devoted to her four sons and training them up as to the way they should go and lastly, she is devoted to her friends [in that order]. Don't ya think that's a good reason to dedicate this book to her? I am blessed beyond measure!

FOREWORD

When it comes to issues surrounding marriage and family, Kyle Dodd is one of the "go to" communicators of our day. He is practical, authentic, and relevant as he speaks and writes to the needs of marrieds and families. You'll laugh, cry and be convicted as he shares his passion for families in a contagious and compelling way.

Dennis Rainey
President of FamilyLife Ministries
FamilyLife Today Broadcast

DISCIPLESHIP

UNDISCIPLED DISCIPLES

*Go therefore and make disciples of all nations, baptizing them in the name
of the Father, Son and Holy Spirit.*
Matthew 28:19

☆ ☆ ☆

In 1937, Dietrich Bonhoeffer used several terms in his book, *The Cost of Discipleship*, to describe our social rendition of faith in God as "easy Christianity" and "cheap grace." The word disciple is used 269 times in the New Testament while the word "Christian" is only found three times to refer to the disciples. The New Testament is written by disciples, about disciples and for disciples. Our contemporary churches today are filled with members who have not yet decided to follow Christ. The above verse has been rewritten in our western culture to read more like "make converts and baptize them into church membership." Why? Where has our alignment gotten out-of-line in our understanding of our purpose and responsibility for being a disciple and then making a disciple? A disciple is not some heavy duty model of a Christian. Discipleship was and is being with Christ and today is not something one can do through a correspondence course. The cost of not having discipleship is a lack of abiding peace. The results of discipleship are a life penetrated with love, faith that sees as God does, hope in the middle of chaos and power to do what's right!

In 1973, a guy named Aaron Fleming came to my high school to take 12 guys and disciple them through their senior year. I was fortunate to be one of those 12 guys, and today I attribute my being in full-time ministry to God and Aaron. You see . . . being a disciple who passed on his life to others cost Aaron a lot, yet true discipleship is forfeiting the things normally sought in human life for a worthy cause. The cost of discipleship is exactly that abundance of life Christ said He came to bring (John 10:10). My question to you is this . . . are you an Apostle Paul and if so, who is your Timothy? This world lacks our ultimate calling to "plant trees (disciples) that we will never sit under for shade (no hidden agendas)." Be a fisher of men (or women), cuz the fish "shore" are bitin'. So as you start the new year, remember "we are called to be fishers of men, not keepers of the aquarium."

☆ ☆ ☆

Further Study: Read Luke 14:26-35 and discuss the cost of discipleship. Does God call the qualified for His service or does He qualify the called?

OVERCOMERS

Whoever wishes to be great among you must first be a servant.
Matthew 20:26

☆ ☆ ☆

For years now you will find at the bottom of every letter that goes out of my office two powerful words . . . "Press On." No one exemplifies this phrase more than a guy named Doug Blevins. At the beginning of the 1997 NFL season, you found him not on a sofa with remote in hand, but on the sidelines of the Miami Dolphins at Pro Player Stadium with stopwatch in hand. Doug is the kicking coach for the Dolphins, and his knowledge of the art of punting, kicking off and field goal attempts leads one to believe he must be a retired NFL kicker himself. False. Doug was stricken with cerebral palsy at birth and is confined to a motorized wheel-chair. You might be asking yourself, "What does he know about kicking a football?" The answer: physically and experientially nothing, but mentally a lot. Physical handicaps affect your body, but not your mind and will. Doug isn't new at this; he coached in college and for the New York Jets and New England Patriots. The head coach of the Dolphins is no merciful man and hired Doug because he can help the Dolphins win games, not because he felt sorry for him.

What a tremendous story of a man who has an "iron will" to succeed despite his obvious handicap. You don't have to be crippled or mentally handicapped by your mind's limitations, sin, lack of motivation or past mistakes. In the above passage, Jesus didn't get mad at James and John for wanting to aspire to greatness; He just said to do it His way. We walk by folks every day who are disabled in one form or another, yet the power of God and their willingness to serve allow them victory over setbacks. My high school coach used to say, "Make a setback be a comeback." How true it is that all of us (you included) have the capability to do all things through Christ who fuels our tanks with that high octane (Philippians 4:13). God wants to lead us to personal victories and greatness on this planet far more than we want to follow. Look at the example Doug and so many others have set. Don't forget we also have a Savior who goes exceedingly, abundantly, beyond our every expectation (Ephesians 3:20). Go get it!

☆ ☆ ☆

Further Study: What do you feel are your own personal handicaps or disabilities that hinder you? How can you and God overcome those?

COMMITMENT

Finish Well

Then I (Isaiah) said, "Lord, for how long must I do this?" and the Lord said, "Until cities are devastated and without inhabitant, houses are without people and the land is utterly desolate (until it is finished!)."
Isaiah 6:11

☆ ☆ ☆

In our society, the employee, family, coach or youth pastor that finishes with the same intensity he/she started with is a rare breed. Now, I'm not saying that God can't call you to another occupation, but what happened to the good, old "loyalty" thing? Why is it so hard to find people sticking with a job until it's finished? People hop from job to job, spouse to spouse like a cricket on the hood of a car on a hot summer day. This scary pattern not only penetrates into marriages, but into a person's relationship with Christ. Did you know that out of all the Bible characters who started the race with a personal relationship with God, 400 in all, only 80 (1 in 5) finished well? No, I'm not saying they lost their salvation, but 320 out of 400 went astray. Why? What causes the human being to become so fickle? What did the 80 who did stick-it-out all have in common to "press on" till the end? Let's take a look at some qualities needed to finish well:

#1 All 80 were humble at heart.
#2 All 80 had an intimate relationship with God.
#3 All 80 were obedient to God's standards.
#4 All 80 had child-like faith in God.
#5 All 80 were able to receive counsel without taking offense as they grew old.

Wow! Is that interesting or what? Folks like Noah, Moses, Abraham, Sarah, Abel, Isaiah, Micah, Samuel, Paul and Jesus finished the job. I could mention others, but they wouldn't fit on this page. The real issue is . . . will you be able to add your name to this list, or are you developing a quitter's pattern today that will prevent a strong finish? "Winners never quit and quitters never win." Be the one out of five who finishes well!

☆ ☆ ☆

Further Study: If someone were to ask whether or not you finish what you start, what would you say? Do you possess any of the five qualities it takes to finish? Why or why not?

SOLOMON SYNDROME

*If any of you lacks wisdom, let him ask of God, who gives to all men generously
and without reproach, and it will be given to him. But let him ask in
faith without any doubting, for the one who doubts is like the
surf of the sea driven and tossed by the wind.*
James 1:5-6

☆ ☆ ☆

It's called "recovery time" in sporting events, but I call it "getting your clock cleaned." This devotion comes on the heels of my best effort, at the young age of 38, trying my hand at "boogie-boarding" on the beach at New Smyrna, Florida. We were there on a family vacation in early August, and I was trying to teach my oldest son, Daniel, how to ride the pipe of a breaking wave about 100 feet off-shore. This hip form of "baby boomer" surfing is harder than it looks, especially when your timing is off and your coconut (head) gets cracked by the power and weight of an 8-foot wave. The power of the surf is unbelievable, and trust me when I say it can make ya' see double if you're not careful.

In the above passage of scripture, James (half brother to Jesus) speaks from his experience as a fisherman. To be in a boat on the ocean during a storm is a bit more stressful than me on a mini-surfboard facing a 6-foot wave. The issue he deals with is wisdom. People are spouting all kinds of wisdom being used in the world today. James is speaking here of Godly wisdom, with a Divine source. King Solomon, considered the wisest man ever, got all his wisdom from God, and so can you. We all need heavenly wisdom to make it day to day. We need extra eyes to see situations from a Godly perspective. How do you get this set of spiritual eyes? The same way Solomon did; he asked God. The key number in this formula is that you must have faith (Hebrews 11:1) in God to ask. I can speak from experience that a lack of faith leads to a tumble you don't want to take. Don't doubt for one minute that God doesn't get excited with goose bumps to give you, yes you, a large dose of wisdom. Trust me . . . the ride will be a lot smoother.

☆ ☆ ☆

Further Study: Why is wisdom important? Read Hebrews 11:1 and talk about what faith really is. Now take a minute and ask God to give you heavenly wisdom.

OBEDIENCE

THE PLAGUE OF DISOBEDIENCE

The locust covered the surface of the whole land so that the land was darkened;
they ate every plant and all fruit, nothing green was left through all of
Egypt. Then Pharaoh hurriedly called for Moses and Aaron.
"I have sinned against the Lord your God; please forgive
my sin and make an appeal to the Lord to
remove this death from me."
Exodus 10:15–17

☆ ☆ ☆

In our generation, areas having the potential for a locust outbreak are monitored by international agencies using satellite reconnaissance and other technology. The swarms of locusts are met by aircraft and trucks carrying powerful pesticides to stomp out their plague. However, if the locusts are not destroyed quickly after they hatch, control efforts are minimally effective. An example of this was in 1988 during the civil war in Chad. The fighting prevented help in attacking the hatch, and a destructive swarm spread throughout North Africa. Some of the poorest nations were devastated, and Europe was threatened. It's difficult for us in the western world to appreciate the threat of a locust plague in earlier periods of time. Locusts were the eighth plague on Egypt, and images of locusts were carved in sixth-dynasty tombs at Saggara over three-quarters of a millennium earlier. Locusts can migrate great distances and have even been observed 1,200 miles at sea. In 1889, a swarm across the Red Sea was estimated to cover 2,000 square miles, containing up to 120 million insects per square mile.

So why am I on this bug binge? To point out the severity of disobedience to God. No, I'm not saying that the next time you make a mistake God is going to send down a swarm of locusts to take up residency in your hair. I am saying there were in Old Testament times, and still are today, consequences for our actions. I know this tarnishes the "God is Love" image you may have locked in your mind, but it is the truth of Scripture and of the character of Yahweh (God). God is going to bless us when we obey Him or judge us with consequences when we don't. No, no, no . . . we are not talking about a perfect Christian here, just one who "presses on" towards being as much like Christ as possible. Through God's grace and a lot of divine help we can please our Lord.

☆ ☆ ☆

Further Study: Why does God want you to obey Him? What was the purpose of the locust plagues or any other plagues?

YOU NEED A RITUAL

Thus says the Lord, "The fast of the fourth, the fast of the fifth, the fast of the seventh, and the fast of the tenth months will become joy, gladness, and cheerful feasts for the house of Judah; so love, truth and peace."
Zechariah 8:19

☆ ☆ ☆

At the finals of the Compaq World Putting Championship held at Walt Disney World in Florida, the contestants had different styles, different strokes and different degrees of success. However, they all had something in common–time after time, every player made a consistent series of movements before each putt, a "ritual." The rituals were not the same. In fact, with 200 players reaching the final stage of the tournament, there were 200 different ways of settling in and setting up for a putt. All 200 contestants took this tourney seriously with a $250,000 purse going to the winner.

Other sports are not unlike golf in the sense of rituals or habits. Consider basketball players at the free-throw line, a gymnast during warm-up, pitchers on the mound, swimmers before a meet and so on. We are all creatures of habit, yet it seems we lack ritual in our spiritual lives. The purpose of a ritual in the athletic arena is to better prepare yourself for your event. We need rituals in our personal and family lives as well, like daily prayer and scripture reading, sit-down mealtimes as a family and family devotions around the table. What is your personal and family ritual? What helps you daily to compete in the game of life? Without rituals you usually find your game is off and you fail at those simple putts in life. The greatest journeys in our history began with one single step. If you have no ritual, begin today. Spiritual rituals far surpass any putting championship purse you'd ever win, and the trophies last through eternity.

☆ ☆ ☆

Further Study: Why are rituals so important in sports? What are some of your consistent family rituals? What new rituals could you begin this week?

FALSE PROPHECY

TRUE OR FALSE

Do not quench the spirit; do not despise prophetic utterances. But
examine everything carefully; hold fast to that which is
good, abstain from every form of evil
1 Thessalonians 5:19-22

★ ★ ★

They're all found in the Old Testament, and they went by names like Hosea, Joel, Amos, Obadiah, Jonah, Micah, Nahum, Habakkuk, Zephaniah, Haggai, Zechariah, and Malachi, just to name a few. They were often called Seers, Servants, Messengers, Men of God and Sons of Prophets. Their purpose was to "edify" the people to whom they spoke. Proofs of a true prophet were: (read Deuteronomy 18:15-22).

#1   Speak in the name of Yahweh
#2   Speak by revelation or inspiration
#3   Moral character of the prophet
#4   A true call of God
#5   A message authenticated by signs
#6   A message in agreement with previous revelation
#7   The fulfillment of predictions

What I don't want to get into during this devotional time is trying to answer the question, "Is there modern day prophecy?" or "Are there modern day prophets?" What I do want to touch on is verifying the true from the false. The list from Deuteronomy 18 makes clear what constitutes a true prophet of God. But we must beware because a false prophet doesn't prophesy in the name of a pagan god, but under the name of Yahweh (the only God). Although this false prophet claims to speak in the name of Yahweh, he/she will not hold up when compared to the above proofs of a true prophet. The New Testament continually warns us of "wolves dressed in sheep's clothes," and "good and bad trees." Be careful what you take as fact and learn to discern truth from error. As James warns us in chapter 1 verse 16, "Don't be easily deceived fellow believers!" Remember that everyone on earth is fallen (Romans 3:23) and needs the power of God and the accountability of the scripture. Make sure you test what people teach from the Bible. False teaching leads to false theology, which ultimately leads to a false religion. Take heed!

★ ★ ★

Further Study: How do you separate biblical truth from secular theology? Where can you always find truth? Where can false prophets claiming false doctrine lead you?

THE LION IN DANIEL'S DEN

*Then the king was pleased and gave orders for Daniel to be taken
up out of the den, and no injury whatever was found
on Daniel because he had trusted in his God.*

Daniel 6:23

☆ ☆ ☆

My wife and I named our oldest son Daniel for a reason. I love the story of a man in the Bible named Daniel who stood strong in the midst of great adversity. To fully appreciate the story of how Daniel escaped unharmed from the lions' den, you must first know a few facts about a lion. Contrary to how Simba was portrayed in Disney's movie, *Lion King,* a lion in the wild is a predator and aggressor, the dominator of his land. Lions have a keen sense of hearing and eyesight and are quick as a snake and strong as Hercules. Lions will only attack their prey from behind, not straight on. That's why they feed at night and rest during the hot African days. Surprise is their greatest asset, and they use it regularly to maintain their "King of the Beasts" title.

Daniel was wise beyond his years and needed that wisdom as he interpreted the dreams of Nebuchadnezzar (how is that for a long name?), the bad king of a bad place called Babylon. This king wanted everyone to worship a gold image or statue, but Daniel wouldn't because he had a different belief.

The world in which you and I live is always asking us to bow down and worship images in the form of money, appearance, where we live, power, lack of integrity or dishonesty. We, like Daniel, will be tested to see whose god we will follow. The real question is, do we believe so much in Christ that we are willing to take on any lion in our lives to show His faithfulness? Do we trust in God so much that we are more willing to stand alone for the truth than with the crowds in a lie? You will have these "tests of trust" throughout your life where you will have an opportunity to prove once again, as Daniel did, "Our God is an awesome God and He reigns in heaven and on earth."

☆ ☆ ☆

Further Study: What does the world offer you as "good" that ultimately robs you of what's "great" with God? What did Daniel do to survive in the lions' den? How can you trust God in the face of adversity? What does trusting God mean to you?

TIME

*And he will speak out against the Most High and wear down the saints of the
Highest One, and he will intend to make alterations in times and in law;
and they will be given into his hand for a time, times, and half a time.*
Daniel 7:25

☆ ☆ ☆

God created time and humans invented the watch. For thousands of
years, human beings have been anxious about the time they have on earth.
We all have a desire to live long and prosperous lives, yet there are no guarantees on how long our time will last (James 4:14). I love this life as much as
the next person, yet the older I get (which is happening way too fast) and the
more I read the scriptures, I realize this life is not gonna be a walk in the lily
field. A life lived being a follower of Jesus Christ is gonna get tougher and
harder the longer you walk. I admire men and women of God who started
their journey at a young age and got up and kept going when they stumbled
along the way. We here in America don't feel or see the persecution that so
many brothers and sisters across the ocean feel daily. Our lives in the "Good
Old U.S. of A" are pretty insulated from such aggression, yet I believe the
scriptures indicate that "time" will come before Christ does.

Now this is not a devotion about a pre, mid or post-tribulation that
believers will encounter, but it is a reality check on what we can expect.
Daniel's interpretation of a vision was alarming to him and should be a wake-
up call to us. We will, if we are producing spiritual fruit (Galatians 5:22-23),
be persecuted for our faith in one form or another. It may be mental persecution rather than physical persecution, but mental persecution is painful, too.
Daniel warns us that we will hear those who speak out against God and will
experience a wearing down effect. Our country will be run by leaders with a
game plan that is opposite ours and the journey will be long and weary. Enjoy
the journey and cling tightly to righteousness. Live life with the realization
that we will have an afterlife of hope without pain and sorrow. Keep your eyes
on the prize.

☆ ☆ ☆

Further Study: How do you feel when a non-believer makes fun of you for your
faith? How can you remain strong? What is the purpose of trials and tribula-
tion? How do they affect you? How do they affect your family?

SHOULDER TO SHOULDER

It is not good for man to be alone.
Genesis 2:18

☆ ☆ ☆

For South African President Nelson Mandela and his prison mates, keeping dignity intact required shared vision, commitment to bear one another's burdens, and strength to stand in unity no matter what the opposition. In *Time* magazine (Nov. 28, 1994) Mandela wrote, "The authorities' greatest mistake was keeping us together, for together our determination was reinforced. It would be very hard, if not impossible, for one man alone to resist. I do not know if I could have done it had I been alone. Whatever we learned, we shared, and by sharing we multiplied whatever courage we had individually. The stronger ones raised up the weaker ones and both became strong in the process."

What a powerful story, don't you think? What a tremendous lesson (and one we can learn without taking up residence in the pen) about staying shoulder to shoulder with other Christians in the midst of adversity. If God wanted us to be loners and have no fellowship, I think He would have put us each on our own planet to sit and rotate on our axis all our lonely lives. A ton of strength lies in those "friends that stick closer than any brother." Don't be fearful that it may take time to develop a shoulder-to-shoulder relationship with someone. Don't put off until tomorrow what can help you today. Don't make yourself out to be some super hero with an emblem on your chest. Don't be a cowboy (or girl) riding into the sunset alone, acting tough. Don't you hate reading the word "don't" 10 times straight? Okay, then just do it!

☆ ☆ ☆

Further Study: Write down a list of your top 10 best friends (I'll wait). Okay, now which of these folks do you stand shoulder-to-shoulder with? Why or why not? How can you develop this today?

RIGHT TOOL, WRONG WAY

Come let us worship and bow down; let us kneel before
the Lord our maker for He is our God.
Psalm 95:6 7

☆ ☆ ☆

In an issue of *Meat & Poultry* magazine, editors quoted *Feathers*, the publication of the California Poultry Industry Federation, telling the following story. It seems the U.S. Federal Aviation Administration has a unique device for testing the strength of windshields on airplanes. The device is a gun that launches a dead chicken at a plane's windshield at approximately the speed the plane flies. The theory is that if the windshield doesn't crack from the carcass impact, it will survive a real air collision with a bird during flight.

It seems the British were very interested in this and wanted to test a windshield on a brand new, speedy locomotive they were developing. They borrowed FAA's chicken launcher, loaded the chicken and fired.

The ballistic chicken shattered the windshield, broke the engineer's chair and embedded itself in the back wall of the engine cab. The British were stunned and asked the FAA to recheck the test to see if everything was done correctly.

The FAA reviewed the test thoroughly and had one recommendation: use thawed chickens!

What a hilarious story (true) of having the right tool, but using it the wrong way and the results thereof. This devotion is going to address the subject of "worship" both personally and corporately. The first question I have for you is "Do you worship God?" And my second question is "What are the motives behind your worship?" Contemporary churches today are really turning up the music in terms of bands and modern day lyrics to songs during singing at church. The meaning of worship is to "find worth in" what you're worshiping. In the Old Testament, believers worshiped through blood sacrifices and offerings. Today we seem to be falling into more of a "feeling" rather than a "realization" of worship. I'm not saying feeling is wrong, yet I am saying we need to come into worship with a sense of reverence and honor of the Holy One rather than only a "buddy" or "pal" mentality. Use your time alone or with others in worship as a personal time to honor and glorify your Savior and Lord, not as a time of false feeling and public display. Make sure you're living out privately what you're worshiping publicly.

☆ ☆ ☆

Further Study: What does worship mean to you? Do you prefer to worship publicly or privately? Why do you think worship is such a big deal to God? What does the motive behind that worship need to be? Is your motive pure?

GOD'S CHARACTER

In wrath remember mercy.
Habakkuk 3:2

☆ ☆ ☆

Do you come from the same type of family I came from, where your mother represented TLC (Tender Loving Care) and sugar and your dad represented the heat and vinegar? Now I say that in all due respect, yet to prove a valuable point. Most of our parents served in a specific role in our growing up years. That role influenced how we think of our parents today.

We also have a particular view of God that has been influenced by our upbringing and culture. The problem is that the view we have may not be the complete truth. We don't often hear in our contemporary, padded pew churches that the God (Yahweh) of scripture is a God of, yes, love and mercy, but also of judgment and consequences. Now the reason we don't hear that much today is that it doesn't enlarge church attendance or make a good fundraising ploy. The true character of Yahweh is all four of those characteristics. Those qualities didn't change from the God of the Old Testament to the Jesus of the New Testament. In Revelation 5:5, Jesus Himself is called the "Lion of Judah." Correct me if I'm wrong, but I don't think lions make cuddly pets. Instead, they are well respected for their power and position.

Here's my point . . . we have a hard time in our western culture seeing or knowing of anyone who could possibly be tender yet firm. Usually people are seen as loving and merciful or as judgmental and abrasive, but not both. God's character is one to love and fear because He will either bless you because you obeyed or judge you with consequences because you disobeyed. That is the God of the Bible. Obedience to His Spirit and Holy Word are key to our future and happiness on this earth. Understanding fully the true character of God helps us to love, worship, pray to and obey Him more.

☆ ☆ ☆

Further Study: Describe your mother, then your father. How does your view of your parents influence your view of your heavenly Father? How can God be so balanced? Why does the Old Testament use the phrase "fear the Lord?"

WHO AM I, LORD?

*Now as they observed the confidence of Peter and John and understood that
they were uneducated and untrained men, they were marveling,
and began to recognize them as having been with Jesus.*
Acts 4:13

★ ★ ★

Verbal slams on intelligence are as common as flies on a cow. Check out
a few bumper stickers I've seen recently that prove my point:

Your kid may be an honors student but you're still an idiot.
Forget about world peace . . . Visualize using your blinker.
We have enough youth, how about a fountain of smart?
He who laughs last thinks slowest.
Lottery: A tax on people who are bad at math.
All men are idiots and I married their king.
The more people I meet . . . the smarter my dog is.
I took an I.Q. test and the results were negative.

Fewer students graduate from college in only four years, and when they
do get out . . . they go right back in to get that masters. Our society puts a
very high value on education and intelligence, which is not necessarily wrong.
However, it is wrong when society places a lower value on morals and values.
I have been taking classes at a local seminary and noticed a spiritual arrogance
among the students and teachers. I'm not bashing the purpose of education
or the value of learning, but I do know that God and His divine intervention
in a person's life through faithfulness and obedience is really what needs to be
looked up to and admired. In the above scripture, here are Peter and John,
two fishermen who didn't get an MBA or a masters degree in theology or
fishing, yet were chosen as two of twelve to "be" with Christ. Why? Because
they were willing and obedient to their call (Luke 5:11). God's eyes search
near and far for those under-qualified, under-gifted, under-achievers to live
out His glory and power through them. Are you someone who feels God is
lucky to have you on His team or are you the one questioning if God could
ever use someone like you? I'll let you do the math and figure out which one
He'll choose. Until next time . . . keep walking in His Spirit and spending daily
time in His Word.

★ ★ ★

Further Study: Why does our culture put such a huge emphasis on education
and not Christ-like qualities? How can God still use you if you don't have a
seminary degree or can't quote the whole New Testament? Are you willing to
trust and obey?

GLEANING

He who is faithful in a very little is faithful also in much.
Luke 16:10

☆ ☆ ☆

Webster defines gleaning as "gathering grain (leftovers or scraps) or other produce left behind by the reapers." I saw peasants gleaning in the fields in the third world country of Haiti. You don't have to go far in our country to find street people or beggars gleaning for a morsel of food or left-over soda in a thrown away fast food container.

The book of Ruth tells a great story. The scene begins with Ruth, the Moabitess, asking Naomi (her mother-in-law) for permission to be "lowly" and go to the fields to glean a meal. To make this story short and get to the application, Ruth, by her willingness to be lowly and work hard, meets a wealthy man named Boaz, who ends up marrying Ruth. Together they have a son and live happily ever after.

Now my point here is not to show you an early "Leave it to Beaver" family, but to outline how Ruth got from point "A" of gleaning to point "B" of happiness and fulfillment. Let's take a quick look at how this progression was achieved by Ruth:

verse 2:1 Ruth had a proper perspective of God and His faithfulness to us.
verse 2:2 Ruth was faithful in the small areas and respectful to others.
verse 2:3 Ruth was obedient and worked hard at what she could do.
verse 2:4 Ruth was faithful (loyal) for as long as God wanted her to glean.
verse 2:7 Ruth's faithfulness and hard work opened doors.

You see, God is more willing to lead you and me as we follow Him. God's work can be slow for a long time, then suddenly it can move quickly. God doesn't elevate foolish people to high positions. He won't guide you until He breaks you. The process can be ugly, but the results are beautiful. If you're lowly now and gleaning for all you can . . . press on, God is close by.

☆ ☆ ☆

Further Study: Have you ever had to be lowly for a long period of time? How did you respond? Why does God really need to "bruise you before He can use you?"

PEER PRESSURE

UNCHANGING WORD IN A CHANGING WORLD

*Who will dwell on Thy holy hill? He who walks with integrity and
works righteousness and speaks truth in his heart.*
Psalm 15:1-2

☆ ☆ ☆

I absolutely love the way biblical accounts play out to a plot, as well as
the lessons you and I learn from them and can apply today. Take a minute
and read the story found in 1 Kings 22:1-38 and I'll be here when you come
back . . . go on. Welcome back. Now was that awesome or what? Did Micaiah
the prophet go into this scene lookin' foolish and come out smelling like a
rose or what? Today, politicians say whatever they need to get the votes;
media plays to the audience and our culture applauds. Where are those few
who are willing to "stand alone" in the midst of the firing squad? There is a
country song that says, "You've got to stand for something or you'll fall for
anything." Micaiah had Ahab, the king of Israel, and Jehoshaphat, the King of
Judah, along with 400 prophet puppets breathing down his neck to prophesy
falsely and fold under the pressure. Did he, though? No! This man of God
was willing to take verbal, physical and mental abuse for the cause of Yahweh
(God). He knew his role and continued to play the lead until his prophecy
came true in verses 37-38. Here are a few lessons I personally learned from
this nugget of scripture. Feel free to add to them:

#1 It is better to be divided by the truth than be united in compromise.
#2 It is better to speak biblical truth that heals than lies that kill.
#3 It is better to be hated for standing for truth than embraced for telling
a lie.
#4 It is better to be lonely in the truth than with the multitudes in a lie.
#5 It is better to ultimately succeed with truth than temporarily succeed
in a lie.

Don't forget that Noah went into the ark a minority with only his family, but 40 days later . . . he came out a majority. You and I need to be the ones
that stand firm (and sometimes alone) for what's right. This world needs to
see disciples of Christ standing for Christ-like principles in a world that
approves of abortions, ungodly movies and music, broken commitments and
promises. The scriptures are full of men and women who held tight to truth
in the midst of turbulent tests and trials, and that legacy can continue if you
choose to be a modern day Micaiah.

☆ ☆ ☆

Further Study: What's the scariest part about standing alone? What makes
your knees buckle in a truth and lie struggle? Are you willing to do the five
things listed for God?

ENTHUSIASM

FIRE IT UP!

Finally Christian, we request you in the Lord that as you received from us instructions as to how to walk and please God that you may excel still more.
1 Thessalonians 4:1

☆ ☆ ☆

Catch the jingle of this tune: "Enthusiasm, it's the bread of life, like protoplasm, one, two, three, four, five, it's great to be alive because I've got . . . enthusiasm." (catchy, ain't it). Dale Carnegie said, "A person can accomplish almost anything for which he has unlimited enthusiasm." Thomas Edison was quoted, "If all we leave to our kids is enthusiasm, we've left them an estate of incalculable value." It won't be education, connections or the way you dress that get you there . . . it will be those who are excited about something who will go farthest in life. When you become an excited person, you will have an exciting life. When you actually get excited about your career, marriage and/or friendships, you will have an exciting career, marriage and/or friendships. To change your attitude, which is the ignition of enthusiasm, you start with a change in behavior. Begin to act the part of the person you'd rather be or become and gradually the old person with no spark will fade out of the picture.

A couple of key points to remember as you become more excited about life!
- #1   Change your bad attitude
- #2   Fake joy is better than genuine depression
- #3   Claim victory and take ownership
- #4   Don't let your feelings become facts
- #5   Winners never quit and quitters never win

Four beliefs worth believing as you go:
- #1   Belief in God gives you a sense of purpose
- #2   Belief in yourself gives you confidence
- #3   Belief in others gives you relationships
- #4   Belief in what you do gives you enthusiasm

Life really is, when you think about it, so simple. Life is energy. It is our use of that energy that influences the circumstances and situations of our lives. If you want to change the direction of your life, all you need to do is change your energy level. So . . . "get fired up!"

☆ ☆ ☆

Further Study: What gets you excited about life? How do you maintain a high level of enthusiasm throughout the day? What about being a member of God's family gets you fired up? Why?

GOD-GIVEN GIFTS

A man's gift makes room for him and brings him before great men.
Proverbs 18:16

▲ ▲ ▲

A raccoon is equipped with special reflective cells which are located at the rear of his eyes. This apparatus allows the coon to see in partial darkness. Light enters the eyes of the animal and is absorbed. The light that is not absorbed is reflected by these "mirror cells" and it again passes through the retina, giving this light another chance to be absorbed. Through this mirroring device, "tapetum lucidum," the raccoon is able to use what limited light the night has to hunt and move around.

I lived in southwest Missouri for 13 years where a popular pastime is coon huntin' in the wee hours of the morning. The coon dogs are let go by their owner (the hunter) to track and tree the raccoon (the hunted). The whole time you hear these huntin' dogs yelping in the hills and woods, telling their master the location of the coon through the pitch of their howls (bark). Once the coon is treed, the hunter can quickly locate the animal up in the giant oaks by shining a flashlight up into the tree and picking up the reflective glow off the eyes of the coon.

One of the best tips of marital wisdom I ever got was at a FamilyLife Conference. It was this, "What lures you (attracts) to your spouse during courtship can repel (separate) you during marriage." So the reflective eyes of the raccoon, an obvious gift of nature, end up being the very thing that leads the raccoon to its death. How can a strength become a weakness? How can a gift become a gag? I'll tell ya' what this old cowboy thinks . . . worldliness and darkness take control instead of the Spirit of righteousness and light. A good tool for you becomes a weapon for the enemy; ironic, ain't it? Beware, my friend, and take warning . . . Satan is out to kill and destroy you in whatever deceptive way possible.

☆ ☆ ☆

Further Study: What do you feel are your greatest gifts personally? Have you ever used them for dishonest gain? How can you use your God-given gifts and talents only for the Kingdom?

PREPARE THE WAY

"What do I have to do with you, Jesus, Son of the Most High God? Do not torment me!" And the demons entreated Him saying, "Send us into the swine."
Mark 5:7, 12

✱ ✱ ✱

It was probably early the next morning that they came to see; by this time, the Gadarene had dressed and gotten cleaned up and was sitting with Jesus and the disciples (Mark 5:15). The men were fearful and asked Jesus to leave, maybe because of a lost herd of pigs, maybe because of someone possessing supreme power in their midst. In this Greek city of Decapolis they were ignorant of spiritual truth and infested with pagan superstition. There is a contrast here between the attitude of the men and the attitude of the one who was rid of his demons. They begged Jesus to leave, while the healed man begged to stay with Jesus and was refused. He probably feared that if Jesus left him the demons would enter his body again, or he felt acceptance and safety with his newfound master. Understand this, he had been an outcast from his friends for such a long time, and it was tough for him to be denied fellowship with the One who made him whole and happy again. The reason Jesus told him "no," but to go home and tell his friends of what great thing had happened to him (Mark 5:19), was that these folks needed evidence that the Lord would not only do miracles, but could permanently transform a life.

It seems like a great story with a rotten punch line. Why so mean, Jesus? Let the guy stay with ya', Jesus. He had been healed, yet Jesus did with him what He did with the demons . . . cast em' out. The reality of this story is that there was much more to be done than casting out demons into some smelly swine herd. The real story was just about to begin, as this Gadarene man was commanded to spread the good news in a Greek area where Jesus was not very welcome. When the Lord returned to that area later, He was warmly received because of the footwork this man had done. Why? The Gadarene had prepared the way for Him and now Jesus was able to go to work in their midst (Mark 7:31-37). Maybe it's a club, team, business, social group or peer clique that God is asking you to go into and proclaim truth. Then His Spirit can go to town transforming lives. Are you willing to take that step of faith to see lives saved and changed, or are you scared of losing face in front of your peers and friends? Go ahead . . . make that move!

✱ ✱ ✱

Further Study: Are you, like the Gadarene, willing to go into uncomfortable areas to proclaim good news? Why do we fear rejection more than lost souls to the devil? Think about it.

PASSED DOWN

This I command you, that you love one another just as I (Jesus) *have loved you.*
John 15:12

ʌ ʌ ʌ

It has the same potential for destruction as any of the terrorist bombings in Beirut, Manhattan or Oklahoma City. It's a bomb all right, hidden in the heart of a majority of the world's population. If not defused, it could send us all flying from an explosion of domestic violence and inherited anger. This bomb is called racism. The blood-poisoning of ignorance, misinformation, hate and anger has been passed down from generation to generation. White, black, yellow or brown—we must forget the past and stop using that as fuel for our present beliefs. God put us all on one planet for a reason. Let me inject this vaccine into your thinking. You won't overcome the hate and anger stemming from racism without a strong dose of Jesus in your heart. I direct an inner-city camp called "The Sky's the Limit" in the five points region ("the Hood") of Denver. It has been a huge education for me to get involved with "the Hood" and the youth who live there. Love is the bridge that allows all colors to come together before anger, hate and revenge take the spot. No matter your background, you have the capability to stop the thinking passed down from generations past. Open your heart to Christ's renewing love and educate yourself. Cross-cultural friendships can be some of the most rewarding you'll ever make. Serving a minority, feeding the poor and hungry, volunteering your time and labor to a cause is what Christianity is made of. Be a part of the solution, not the problem, and be a catalyst (leader) in putting an end to racism.

☆ ☆ ☆

Further Study: Do you think that racism is a problem? Why? Why not? Do you see yourself as a racist? Do you have friends of another color? What can you do to be a part of the solution, not the problem, of racism?

Keep on Keeping on

Beloved, do not be surprised at the fiery ordeal among you, which comes upon you for your testing, as though some strange thing were happening to you.
1 Peter 4:12

✲ ✲ ✲

I've been on a horse at the middle fork of the Salmon River, northwest of Challis, Idaho, in the Salmon National Forest. The Salmon River empties into the Snake River, which then flows into the Columbia River that empties into the Pacific Ocean just north of Portland, Oregon. The king salmon (fish) begins its journey from the ocean and salt water to the place it hatched years before in freshwater rivers. Facing overwhelming odds, this fish doggedly fights its way upstream, returning to its original spawning grounds. The salmon will travel some 25 miles each day, fighting a rough current and predators, while relying on rays of the moon and sun to navigate. This trip can take up to six months and many missed meals. When the salmon arrives, the males battle against each other for territorial rights. Each February, pale orange eggs hatch after lying on the bottom of the riverbed during the winter. Lying along the gravel of the river bottom, eggs are vulnerable to other fish and birds. Only about 10 percent end up hatching and beginning their journey back to the ocean, repeating this incredible cycle.

This natural struggle and determination is what make king salmon (all 50 to 100 pounds) one of the most highly prized game and commercial fish in North America. The struggle and barriers along this migratory journey serve as a way to strengthen the fish for tougher battles and obstacles ahead. You and I tend to view tough, turbulent times as unfortunate or inconvenient, yet God's plan is to test us so we and He can see what we need to work on and what areas need improvement. Christ never said that following Him was gonna be a walk in the park. Just as taking a test in school helps you and the teacher find out how many of the lessons are learned, so it is in God's classroom, which can't be taken via correspondence or by using Cliff Notes. The upstream waters in our life will be turbulent with trials, but the destination is heavenly.

✲ ✲ ✲

Further Study: Why are endurance and perseverance as important for believers as they are to the migration of the king salmon?

CONFLICT

DUELING

Be angry yet don't sin; Don't let the sun go down on your anger, and don't give the devil an opportunity.
Ephesians 4:26-27

☆ ☆ ☆

It took place on a hill overlooking the Hudson River between two statesmen (politicians) on July 11, 1804. Both represented our political system, one an honored Democrat, the other a noble Republican. They differed in their personal ways of handling conflict, yet this meeting on July 11th proved fatal. Their names: Aaron Burr and Alexander Hamilton. The straw that broke the camel's back was a letter that Hamilton published in a newspaper in New Jersey to air out his distrust and dissatisfaction of the job Burr had been doing on Capitol Hill. Burr read the article and became furious, challenging Hamilton to a pistol duel. Hamilton was a church-going, Bible-believing Christian whose character wouldn't allow him to handle disagreements in this manner, especially a shoot out. Just three years earlier, Philip, Alexander's son, was killed in a duel because of his beliefs. At the duel in 1804, Alexander was killed by Burr because Alexander shot his pistol in the air, not at Burr.

Not much has changed in almost 200 years. Many still resolve differences with violence. Television programs, movies, gangster rap and militia magazines all try to sway us towards violence. Our inner cities are war zones of fist fights and drive-by shootings. Our "right to bear arms" has turned into a "license to kill." Jesus had, and still has, another means for His followers to resolve disagreements. How? Read Ephesians 6:13-17. Notice that of all the armor only one piece is offensive; the others are defensive (or to protect us). God's Word is our weapon, not a rifle, pistol, bomb, fist, knife, or sharp tongue. Jesus exemplified this tactic when He Himself was in arms against the devil's temptations. God's Word and His Spirit are all we have, but they are also all we need. A word of caution about our tongues . . . it's the only instrument that the more you use it, the sharper it becomes!

☆ ☆ ☆

Further Study: How do you and your family resolve conflict? Is your first instinct to lash out with your tongue? How do you handle your anger? Snap? Hit? Backbite? Stuff it? Run? How can you and your family handle arguments better? Will you?

SIGNIFICANCE

SEARCH FOR SIGNIFICANCE

*You made all the delicate, inner parts of my body
and knit them together in my mother's womb.*
Psalm 139:13

✫ ✫ ✫

Why do we search for our personal significance through places, positions and people? We base our value and our worth on everything but truth. I sure don't want to sound preachy, but we need to get back to the basics. We need to let truth grab our hearts and change how we act and think! If we can change the way we think, we will act differently.

Let's go over some basics. Did God need humans? Absolutely not! But He obviously thought there was some worth in our existence because He chose to use us. Did God have the ultimate veto power in deciding if you should have been born, no matter what the circumstance? You had better say, "Absolutely!" Okay, through the process of elimination, there is a very good reason for you being born. You are significant, and there is a reason for you being on this earth and/or in your particular family.

If you said "yes" to God needing humans or "no" to God being able to veto our births, then you are saying something very serious about God–that He is a liar! The Book of John tells us that He is Truth. God is completely incapable of lying. He has no ability in any way to lie! And if you don't believe the Word of God, then pray! God says that if we seek the truth, we will find it.

God has created us with the ability to get to know Him intimately, but we need to read His love letter. Psalm 139 reminds us that He knows everything about us . . . and He still loves us (you). That's a forgiving God. The Living Bible says, "How precious it is, Lord, to realize that you're thinking about me constantly. I can't even count how many times a day your thoughts turn towards me." That is awesome. Search Him, and let Him remind you how very precious you are to Him.

✫ ✫ ✫

Further Study: What does the world say about you and your worth? How does this contrast with what God says? Which will you choose and why?

GOD WORKS DESPITE US

If I have all faith, so as to remove mountains, but do not have love, I'm nothing.
1 Corinthians 13:2

※ ※ ※

Does God place an unbelievable amount of significance on love or what? Wow, take a look at 1 Corinthians chapter 13. These aren't things like taking the trash out for your mom, or helping grandma across the street. These acts are monumental; for example, verse 1, "speaks with the tongues of men and angels;" verse 2, "prophecy;" verse 3, "know all mysteries and all knowledge, faith to remove mountains;" verse 4, "give everything to the poor, sacrifice my body." Can you believe what God is saying?! He is making a very strong point. He wants us to exemplify that same kind of love!

What is amazing about these verses is they prove to us that God is going to work despite what we do or don't do. He is a sovereign God; what He wants done, He will get done with or without us! And isn't it awesome that He does work despite us. If God really needed us, we would mess up all kinds of projects (not to mention what it says about God if He needs us. If God really needs us, then He is not all powerful, all knowing, sovereign and many other things that God says He is!)

Okay, so let's get practical. God is probably not going to ask us to move a mountain, or speak with the tongues of angels (although nothing is impossible with God). What does God ask of us? He asks us to be patient, kind, not jealous, not arrogant. He asks us not to be unbecoming, not to seek our own desires, not to take account of a wrong, etc. Truth be known, a lot of times these things are extremely difficult. We might rather have God ask us to move a mountain than not seek our own desires or not remain angry at something someone did to us.

Paul's point is clear in 1 Corinthians 13: show your love not in huge and great acts, but in everyday acts with kindness and patience to those with whom you are surrounded. "The greatest of these is love."

★ ★ ★

Further Study: What kinds of things have you done out of selfishness and not love? Are you taking account of any wrongs suffered that you need to forgive? Why is it harder to show 1 Corinthians 13 love to our families than to anyone else?

A Final Farewell

I know you will bring me down to death a place appointed to all the living.
JOB 30:23

☆ ☆ ☆

In the game of life we must all make many important choices. There is one door that we all will go through without a choice . . . death. I think the "reality check" we all feel when we go to a funeral is that at some unannounced moment in our lives, we too, will pass through that door. In a world of advancing technology, medicine and cultural predictability, we haven't quite figured out God's timing. Whether we're young and full of energy like Princess Diana, who died unexpectedly at age 36, or like Mother Teresa, who had lived a fulfilling life to age 87, death is unpredictable. Death seems to surround itself with friends like grief, mourning, tears, questions, nervousness, anxiety, surprise and hopelessness, yet it shouldn't if eternal life is the big picture. Death of a pagan and death of a believer in Jesus Christ are on separate ends of the emotional scale. They both include loss and sorrow, yet only one has inner peace and eternal hope.

I heard a quote one time that said, "hell, some people believe in it, some people don't; someday they will." You don't hear much these days being taught on the subject of heaven and hell. Upon entering the tunnel of mortal death, we all will come out in either of those two final resting places. One will be a destination of eternal pain, torment and unrest called hell. The second being a divine paradise, lacking pain and sorrow, yet consisting of peaceful joy, happiness and eternity with the God of the Universe called heaven. Gang, no one has the corner on the market of time, nor a guarantee of length of life. Once you pass through those unappeasable doors, you live with the decisions of belief you came in with. There will be no turning back; the hands of time and life will continue on. Cultivate daily your faith in Christ, your friendships in the faith and your family. Leave a legacy of heavenly love that will endure long after you leave. All our clocks are ticking, and when God your Father decides your clock should stop, either slowly or suddenly, and you have your final farewell . . . will you be ready? Will your death signify the beginning of a better life ahead? Invest in the present, and don't bank on your future. It won't be what you did outwardly, but who you are inwardly that will count at your final farewell.

☆ ☆ ☆

Further Study: How does talking about death make you feel? If you were to die suddenly today like Princess Diana, where would you go . . . heaven or hell? Why? How do you know you will go to heaven? Read John 4:14.

FOLLOWING JESUS

YOKE FELLOW

Jesus said to the twelve, "You don't want to go away also, do you?"
John 6:67

✯ ✯ ✯

What a question to ask your teammates. Jesus has such a way of simplifying the process and getting to the point. The disciples knew who Jesus was, yet He wanted to know . . . would they leave? Peter saw Christ as someone to give eternal salvation to him and the world, yet Jesus wants us to see Him as more than a savior. He wants to be yoke fellows with us. Ironically, after Jesus asked this many of His disciples went back and walked no more with Him.

So many folks today focus so much of their attention on doing "things" and "services" for the cause of Christ, yet they don't walk with Him. God desires that we be one with Christ, not only in deed, but in passion and dependence. Don't try to live life with God on any other terms than His terms.

So what? How do we truly learn to walk with Jesus on a daily basis? What do we need to give up to do so? Our Lord wants us to let go before He can lay hold. He doesn't want our goodness, honesty or good deeds, but our sin. That's right, the sins we all possess so He can exchange them for real righteousness. Are you willing to relinquish all pretense of being anything or of deserving God's love? God's Spirit will guide us to which sin we need to give up. It may come in the form of possessions, power or position. There is always a painful disillusionment we go through before we do the relinquishing. When we see ourselves as the Lord sees us, it's not the abominable sins of the flesh that shock us, but the awful nature of pride in our own hearts against Christ. That's when conviction takes place. Be a follower of Jesus who will stick with Him through the good and bad times. Do you want to be a true "yoke fellow" and join up with Jesus on your journey through life? It will cost you today, but pay big dividends in the future. It may seem like it's costly today, but believe me, the dividends in the future are worth it.

✯ ✯ ✯

Further Study: Why is it so hard to walk daily with Christ? How does sin hinder our walk like a nail in the bottom of our hiking boot on a campout? Today, what would be the hardest thing for you to relinquish to God in order to walk closer with Him?

THE LONG HAUL

He was faithful to Him who appointed Him, as Moses also was in his own house.
Hebrews 3:2

☆ ☆ ☆

Moses was born in a country that had banned his own birth. His mother, to protect him, floated him down the Nile River. Moses was found by Pharaoh's daughter, and she adopted him as her own. Ironically, Pharaoh's daughter hired Moses' birth mother to nurse him, not knowing Moses was her son. Moses was raised like a king in soft beds, eating royal food, yet in a palace void of spiritual influence. In spite of this environment, he learned skills of military science, useful in organizing a group of slaves into an army. Years in the desert of Midian taught Moses to serve sheep, his family and father-in-law, and deepened his communion with God. He learned the skills of nomadic survival which helped him as he led three million slaves in the Sinai Peninsula for 40 years. Now he was ready for the task God had called him to after 80 years of training. In Exodus 14:16 we read how God used Moses to divide the Red Sea and lead the Israelites to safety while watching the Egyptian army all drown. Moses was to lead these people to the Land of Milk and Honey (Promised Land), yet he was forbidden by the Lord to enter the land and see his goal achieved. He died in the land of Moab, disappointed. He pleaded three times for this not to happen, yet was told by God not to mention his request anymore (Deuteronomy 3:26). More than a thousand years later, however, his request was granted on the Mount of Transfiguration when two men talked with Jesus whose glory had been unveiled. One was Elijah, the other Moses (Luke 9:31). Moses had been divinely escorted into the Promised Land at last.

You see, Moses was one of the first to know about the Lord's plan of redemption through the death, burial and resurrection of Jesus. Moses had led the hard-to-manage, whiny-baby Israelites out of Egypt's slavery and now knew how Jesus was gonna lead others out of the bondage of sin into His Promised Land called heaven. God's timing is perfect yet unpredictable. We want to get instant gratification for a life lived in faithfulness to God! We have a tendency to believe that if we don't get rewarded today for our efforts, God will forget or overlook us. I tell you the truth, if you live a life of sincere faith and trust in Christ, your rewards will come in time, just maybe not on your time-table. Rewards will come; press on.

☆ ☆ ☆

Further Study: Why did Moses have to go through so much training? Do you think Moses was frustrated with God's timing? How did Moses' faith (Hebrews 11:23) help him? How can faith in God help you today?

HUMILITY

JUST FORGET IT!

Forgetting what lies behind and reaching forward to what lies ahead.
Philippians 3:13

☆ ☆ ☆

It wouldn't be a true family devotional book unless I included a devotion about the family I grew up with in Dallas, Texas. You could describe my family as extremely athletic and pedigree potent. My mother (half Native American) was an all-state basketball player in high school. My father grew up in Oklahoma (he's an Okie) in a very poor family. His room was a screened-in porch (got cold in the winter, I bet) and he picked cotton and worked at his dad's feed store to help make ends meet. The only way he would get to go to college was if he earned a football scholarship out of Norman High School. My father did just that; he was a high school football star and signed with the University of Oklahoma to play for legendary coach Bud Wilkinson in 1954. My dad was a running back his first two years, then moved to starting quarterback his junior and senior years. Now get this, from the time my dad started his career at Oklahoma to the time he ended his career there, his record was 47 wins in a row and 1 loss. That final loss came in the last game of his college career against Notre Dame in the Orange Bowl in 1958 . . . 7–0. All along the way he won tons of honors, not to mention two national championships. This record of 47–1 still stands today as the longest winning streak in college football history. My dad went on to a professional football career in Canada, Dallas and Kansas City with the NFL.

Today, in my father's hay barn in Weatherford, Texas, you'll find boxes of dusty trophies, medals, ribbons and certificates; piles of sports pages honoring him; two solid bronze national championship trophies and his dinged up Oklahoma helmet, all with bird dung on them. Why? My dad is extremely humble and takes to heart not living in his past. My dad has every earned right to display his honors and hang out at the athletic departments in Norman and check out all those pictures of him and his team. Their record will never be beat. Carl Ray Dodd is a legend in football history, yet he doesn't know it. I'm not saying it's wrong to display your accomplishments or feel proud of your honors, but it's nice to know that there are some folks (few) out there not signing their own autographs, living in their past or reminding you just how great they are or were. I'm proud that one of those few is my dad.

☆ ☆ ☆

Further Study: Why does scripture tell us to forget the past? Do you? Why is humility so meaningful to God? What does it mean to you to be humble?

THE PROMISE

I set my bow in the cloud, and it shall be a sign
of a covenant between me and the earth.
Genesis 9:13

✯ ✯ ✯

I don't know if we can ever really understand what Noah must have gone through with the flood, followed by God giving him the promise "that all flesh shall never again be cut off by the water of the flood, neither shall there again be a flood to destroy the earth" (verse 11). That promise was not only for Noah and his family, but for us as well.

Do we really comprehend how much God loves us that He might give us promises? One of Webster's definitions of promise is: "a legally binding declaration that gives the person to whom it is made a right to expect or to claim the performance or forbearance of a specified act!" Hence, the person on the receiving end will benefit from the person making the promise. However, the person giving the promise has a huge responsibility to uphold his legally binding declaration. If God is who He says He is, He cannot come back on His word; that's not a part of His character.

Meditate on these promises and take God at His word . . .

- Do not tremble or be dismayed for the Lord your God is with you wherever you go. (Joshua 1:9)
- The Lord will accomplish what concerns me. (Psalm 138:8)
- And in Thy book they were all written, the days that were ordained for me, even before there was one of them. (Psalm 139:16)
- Train up a child in the way he should go, even when he is old he will not depart from it. (Proverbs 22:6)
- My sheep hear my voice and I know them . . . no one will snatch them out of my hand. (John 10:27-28)
- Walk by the Spirit and you will not carry out the desire of the flesh. (Galatians 5:16)
- Consider it joy when you encounter trials, knowing that the testing of your faith produces endurance and its perfect result . . . perfect and complete lacking in nothing. (James 1:2-4)

There are thousands more promises . . . so get in the Word and search for His promises. They will lift your spirit . . . .. I promise!

✯ ✯ ✯

Further Study: Which promises do you dwell on the most? Why? Why do we need to be reminded of God's promises? What will you do to practice these promises?

FALSE PRETENSE

And God saw all that He had made, and behold, it was very good.
Genesis 1:31

☆ ★ ☆

I know you don't care about this ancient history, but I need you to read on in order to make a spiritual point. When I was playing basketball at the University of Oklahoma, I was almost treated as a god in that state. I know that the only claim to fame for the state of Oklahoma was generated out of the musical starring Gordon McCrae and Shirley Jones, so it doesn't take much in the state to get attention. My point is this . . . it was fun to be so popular and high profile at the age of 20, but those feelings are fleeting and life goes on. The problem comes when most of my teammates who are now around 40 moved back to Norman, Oklahoma, to try and dip back into the past. It's tough to move away from those "Utopia times" when life seems to be a continual mountain top experience. The apostle Paul said, "Forget what lies behind and press on into the present and future" (Philippians 3:13). There is something in all of us, a longing, that we try to fill with a false pretense that there really is a "Garden of Eden" in a remote location somewhere in the world.

The beef I have about old teammates not moving on coincides with Christians in our culture pretending that a utopia exists somewhere in this world when it doesn't. There is not today, nor will there ever be, a perfect garden with no weeds this side of heaven. heaven is our hope and the gate we arrive at when we leave this world. Why in the world is everyone trying to get back into Genesis chapters 1 and 2 before sin enters the scene and destroys the plot of humanity? We desire a garden with no weeds. However, our job today is to face up to the fact that there are and always will be weeds (sin); we need to stop wishing and start pulling weeds in our world. Christians need to come back to the reality of a fallen world and a future place of hope, and not confuse the location of each. The reality of it all is that as bad as the world is, heaven looks better and better.

★ ☆ ★

Further Study: Read Genesis 3:1-19 and discuss its ramifications. Why will this world today not ever be heaven? What should your job be while on earth? (Read Genesis 3:23.) What are the weeds in your own garden?

RESOLVING CONFLICT

FAMILY FEUD

By wisdom a house is built, and by understanding it is established.
Proverbs 24:3

✩ ✩ ✩

The sun was warm as it shone on the red, orange and brown leaves of the trees along the Tug River separating Kentucky and West Virginia that Indian summer day in the 1800s. It was a day that started like many other days when two families, one from Kentucky and the other from West Virginia, got together to share friendship, food and drink. However, the jubilance of the day turned into anger and mistrust when they started eating and a member of the host family informed their guests (maybe after a bit of moonshine) that the roast pig set before them had been rustled (stolen). That was the day the Hatfield clan, headed by "Devil Anse" Hatfield, informed the McCoy clan, headed by Ole Ran'l McCoy, that they were eatin' one of their own prized pigs. The feud intensified when several of the Hatfields, who had been drinking, disrupted an election party. Ellison Hatfield was stabbed and two McCoy youngsters were killed in retaliation. What followed was one of the longest, bloodiest feuds on record that our country has ever remembered . . . even today.

The old Hatfield vs. McCoy feud has been a legend that has lived on forever. It's like the family that never lets it die. Living in a society where the "fast lane" seems to be getting "stressed" up with no place to go, it's no wonder we live in conflict. Marriages and families are falling apart because the participants don't want to work through disagreements or misunderstandings. Pseudo listening and misunderstandings can develop when two people are at opposite ends of the continuum. We have got to realize we are all fearfully and wonderfully made (Psalm 139) and allow freedom for differences in styles and expressiveness. Our personal programming, self-images, false concepts and distrust hinder our relationships. We need to learn to appreciate differences; listen better; respect others' thoughts, feelings and needs; and realize communication is a life-long process. There are no quick fixes or simplified formulas, just a willing heart and an understanding of God's grace. Don't let ant hills of conflict become mountains of separation. Be bound and determined to do whatever it takes to end the feud.

✩ ✩ ✩

Further Study: Why does God desire we live in harmony? What is the source of most of your family's feuds? How does your family peacefully resolve a feud? Take a look at the following scriptures and discuss each one of them: Ecclesiastes 3:1, 7 and James 1:19.

IDOLATRY

PAGAN ADORATION

Therefore, my beloved, flee from idolatry.
1 Corinthians 10:14

ʌ ʌ ʌ

The best definition I have heard to describe an idol would be "anything that demands and gets their adoration." In lay terms . . . anything you or I adore above God is an idol. This form of false idol worship didn't just jump into our culture recently like a new fad. The Old Testament is full of kings like Nebuchadnezzar, the commander and chief of the Babylonian army, who was used as an instrument of judgment by God for His chosen disobedient people (Israelites). King "Neb" wanted his people to bow down to a god of gold. In our society today we don't have to look hard, or far, to see idolatry. In our western civilization we worship things like cars, houses, power, people (movie stars and athletes) and places. We see it in our world as countries still worship military power; pagan gods, such as those in the Hindu religion; dead gods, like Buddha; or stars in the sky.

We have become obsessed with all other gods rather than the true God. Why? Because the adoration of a false, pagan god requires no change or commitment. Yahweh doesn't choose to deal with idolatry lightly or overlook this sin. If we study the Old Testament, we'll see God judged harshly this type of worship with death, natural disasters and plagues. The idols may have changed, but the method behind the means hasn't. God is and will continue to judge our nation for its idolatry, and you and me, too, in order to bring us to a point of repentance (back home to Him). Take a look at your personal life and see what people, places or things have moved Jesus down on the priority pole (Matthew 6:24). Do you struggle with adoring and worshiping your job, money, appearance, body, children, spouse, friends, house, car, intellectual capabilities, an animal, sports, nature and celebrities more than your Savior? If so, you need to prioritize your adoration. Our God is a jealous God and requires all time, talents and treasures (Joshua 24:19). He will use whatever means He must to get your attention and adoration back.

✫ ✫ ✫

Further Study: In view of historical biblical accounts of idolatry, why does scripture say, "a dog will return to his vomit?" Read Galatians 5:20-21 and see the importance of staying away from idol worship. What do you personally struggle with as an idol? Are you willing to change? When?

GOD'S LOVE

LET GO AND LET GOD

She came to Him and began to bow down before Him, saying, "Lord help me!"
Matthew 15:25

✫ ✫ ✫

You've heard the phrase "let go and let God" for years. I never really understood that principle until the summer of 1970 on a small island in the middle of Lake Texoma where some friends and I would go hang out during the summer. I was only 12 at the time and about as smart as a box of rocks. My three friends, Bobby, Jeff, Billy and I were doing our best to recreate an old war movie we saw the night before. I remember a large mound of sand that must have piled up from high water which we decided would be great to tunnel through to make a series of connecting fox holes. My buddies were gathering some tree limbs while I, the macho nacho, was digging this termite tunnel. As you have probably figured out by now, sand is the worst to try to dig in, because it has no strength to hold up walls. The tunnel collapsed on me, so all that was left showing was my Chuck Taylor basketball shoes. Immediately my vision became blackness and the oxygen became non-existent. I'm sorry to say I lost it and panicked. I began to kick, scream, twist and turn like a wind-up toy gone mad. My friends returned to find me trapped and tried to grab my feet and pull me out backwards. There was only one small problem . . . they couldn't catch my feet, because I was kicking like an Olympic swimmer. Finally, after I had used all the air left in that pocket, I passed out, at which time my friends could free me from the hole.

How many times in our lives do we kick, twist, rant and rave in a situation before we finally let go and let God? God seems to always be there at the right time, but we seem to think we wear an "S" on our chest and can "get out of this ourselves." Why is it that there are always two ways to do things, our way and the right way? Allow God to take control of your life in chaos without kicking Him away. All He wants to do is help us out of our holes, and all we need to do is relax and let Him. Take it from an ex-foxhole digger . . . it sure is good to see the light at the end of the tunnel.

✫ ✫ ✫

Further Study: What holes have you dug yourself into lately? Are you kicking God or allowing Him to free you? Why or why not?

COUNSEL

VERBAL ROAD SIGNS

Without consultation, plans are frustrated, but with many counselors, they succeed.
Proverbs 15:22

ʌ ʌ ʌ

If I had one dollar for every piece of false counsel I've received in my lifetime, I'd single-handedly make Fort Knox go belly-up. Seeking guidance, direction, opinions or advice on matters of importance in one's life can be a dangerous adventure. As you travel along life's journey of rock slides, sharp turns, steep grades, and uneven ground, you will value verbal road signs. Whether it's advice on a career change, marriage partner, financial investment, or simply a recommendation for a movie, you'll need direction. But be careful; when the wrong folks give counsel, it can cause real problems. Here is a quick lesson from people who are wise enough to give counsel–don't give it until asked (and then they'll probably get back to you after some thought and prayer). Wise counsel is not the answer to every problem, but good, thought-provoking questions cause you to re-evaluate a situation and think through the process.

This information is probably not news to you. I do think that we all should be very selective of those we choose to guide and direct our decisions. Set up a "personal advisory board" made up of three people. The following is a check-list of qualifications for your board members:

Must be over 40 years old.
Must be a Christian-Servant.
Must seek God daily through scripture study and prayer.
Must have at least one male and two females or two males and
one female on the board.
Must have known you for at least five years.
Must use scripture-based precepts as basis for counsel.

Use this group (board) as a sounding board for all your major decisions. Pray about who should be on your board, then call and ask them to participate. Good luck!

☆ ☆ ☆

Further Study: Ready to assemble a board? Who qualifies that you know? How can you go about asking them? What's the hold-up?

INTO-ME-SEE (INTIMACY)

Jonathan was knit to the soul of David, and
Jonathan loved him (David) *as himself.*
1 Samuel 18:1

☪ ☪ ☪

It makes our lives happier, improves our daily productivity, boosts our confidence level and self-worth, and most importantly, strengthens our walk with God. This endangered species in the wilderness of words is intimacy, or into-me-see. Intimacy is the ability to experience an open, supportive, compassionate relationship with another person without fear of condemnation or loss of individual identity. Men seem to struggle most with this lost art to masculinity while women appear to come by it naturally (there are exceptions to both). Men need to be more like Esau, who grieved when he lost his birthright. David mourned the death of his blood covenant friend, Jonathan, whom he loved like a relative. Women, this devotion is targeted at encouraging men to dive into the unknown and unlikely–to begin the pursuit of quality relationships with men in an accountable scriptural fashion.

To put it in clear form, I will list the five levels of a relationship, then follow them with barriers to intimacy:

Level 1 is talking about the weather or other vague subjects.

Level 2 is offering an opinion about the weather.

Level 3 is expressing a belief or conviction.

Level 4 is when others share their dreams, fears and emotions with me.

Level 5 is when I share my dreams, fears and emotions with others.

Note: Many men can get to Level 3, but true relationships take place on Levels 4 and 5.

Barriers for men include:

Men don't give each other affection.

Men don't nurture each other.

Men don't talk to each other about intimate things.

Men don't befriend other men just to enjoy their friendship.

Listen up! Before you dive into this unnatural episode you should know that this formula leads to intimacy and includes solid identity, empathy, loyalty, basic trust and delay of gratification. Do yourself a favor and realize that with this type of relationship you'll become vulnerable and Christ-like.

☆ ☆ ☆

Further Study: What does intimacy mean to you? Is your answer sexual? Why is friendship's worldly definition wrong?

FINDING THE REAL ME

But we all, with unveiled face beholding as in a mirror the glory of the
Lord, are being transformed into the same image from glory
to glory just as from the Lord, the Spirit.
2 Corinthians 3:18

☆ ☆ ☆

Every time I pick up a magazine or scan the bookstore shelves these days, I find several publications that try (key word in sentence) to decipher the "real" me.

It appears we all give ourselves away psychologically every time we choose Pepsi over Coke or eat cold Wheaties instead of hot Cream of Wheat. One article I read counseled me on how the colors I choose could tell me what sort of mood I was going to be in that day (go figure). Never mind wasting all that time in a shrink's office on a couch, just let someone interpret your wardrobe. I never clued in that maybe wearing a red T-shirt could strip my emotions bare to the world . . . awesome dude! On one of those classy (yeah, right) talk shows the other day, they had as the guest a "mood evaluator" who told the audience you can give your life-long secrets away by what you wear, drive, buy or sell (sounds a little "iffy" to me).

I'm not so sure that this practice of "finding one's self" isn't an age old tradition. The ironic thing is that the book I've been reading (the Bible) tells me to "deny self" in order to find it . . . get it? You know . . . lose to find, die to live, bury to resurrect? Wait a minute–this thinking goes against every concept or theory known to modern man. You will not, I repeat, will not find the "real you" until you get rid of self for the cause of Christ. The "real you," by nature (the sin one), has the capability to murder, lie, cheat, steal, hate, boast . . . need I go on? The Christ in you, after you remove self and replace it with Him, has the capacity to experience real peace, love an enemy, have compassion for the hungry and forgive the unforgivable. Sound like you? No, because it's not the "real you," it's the "transformed you." Now that's one transformation even the crew of the *Starship Enterprise* couldn't figure out.

☆ ☆ ☆

Further Study: What is it that makes us want to find (like it's hiding) the "real me?" Why do you think Jesus wants us to die to self? Why is that process so hard? How can you deny yourself in the next hour? Go do it, okay?

GRADUATION DAY

*Yet you do not know what your life will be like tomorrow. Your life is but
a vapor that appears for a little while and then vanishes away.*
James 4:14

☆ ☆ ☆

Graduation day, whether it be from high school or college, is not only
an accomplishment, but for some, a relief. The tougher the studies get, the
harder the diploma comes. To set out on this adventure is more than taking
a course in math or science. To arrive at the final destination in a gym or audi-
torium dressed in a cap and gown, lookin' like an ordained minister is exciting. To walk down the aisle in front of beaming parents and gloating in-laws
to receive a certificate of graduation evolves into a memorable moment.
Realize it or not, this event is a mirror of real life experiences. It starts in elementary school and ends at death. We all go from the bottle, to crawling, to
walking, to talking, to riding a bike, to kindergarten, then elementary school,
to junior high, onward to high school, to driving, to college, to career, to marriage, to kiddos who call you mommy or daddy, to retirement, then to the life
hereafter. That's the question . . . what is the hereafter? It will be the ultimate
graduation ceremony we all will be a part of. When does it happen? The book
of James says like a vapor or mist. The common world can't predict it nor
schedule its arrival time.

How do you handle death when it passes by your house? It may come
knocking on the door of a parent, coach, friend or sibling first. It's been said
that there are two things we all must do . . . pay taxes and graduate (die). The
purpose of this devotion is not to start your day out on a down note, but to
get you to thinkin'. Death doesn't have to be sad when you know where
you're graduating to. Jesus is the ultimate commencement speaker who holds
the certificate of heaven in His, and only His, hands. Do you have family,
friends, or others who you know won't be a part of the happy graduation
experience? Are you sure that you are ready today, at a moment's notice, to
walk the aisle of eternity with Christ? If yes, then your degree is gonna' take
you farther than just a career. If not, maybe you should consider what you're
graduating into.

☆ ☆ ☆

Further Study: What scares you most about death? Are you sure you're gonna'
receive a diploma of life? If not, how can you get on the right course?

BITTERNESS

KILLER WEEDS

See to it that no one comes short of the grace of God, that no root of bitterness springing up causes trouble, and by it many be defiled.
Hebrews 12·15

✷ ✷ ✷

It was hotter than chili peppers in mid-July. I would make a gentleman's wager that the soles on my sneakers were melting like butter on a hot frying pan. I had this idea (a real brainstorm) which was about as bright as a two-watt lightbulb. How in the world I let my mom talk me and my dad into planting a garden is beyond my capacity to comprehend. I have a new-found respect for the farmers of America who actually enjoy this voyage of vegetation and can make an honest living at it. Now, if you've never had the pain . . . ah, I mean privilege of gathering groceries from the green earth, let my feeble mind take you through the process, one corn row at a time. Okay, I'll go real slow so I don't lose ya' along the way. First, you till the ground under. Second, you plant seeds of whatever your little heart desires to grow. Finally, you water the little suckers. Now, was that tough? (You'll be tested on this Monday.) Oooh, yes, there is one small detail I forgot to tell you about: Weeds can grow up around your vegetables and choke them to death so all that's left are a few hard-as-rock peas.

Now, you must be asking yourself at this point, "Self, what the heck does a garden with weeds have to do with life?" Weeds are like bitterness that left unattended (and not dealt with) can grow up and choke out all the life in your life. Lots of folks carry around the excess baggage of bitterness and it robs all their joy and happiness like a slick shoplifter. The way to deal with bitterness is weed it out–get to the root of the issue and pull it out. In other words, the best way to deal with it is to deal with it! Don't let your garden of life be over-taken with the worldliness of weeds. Communicate, deal with it, root it out and then walk away from it. Make sure you weed your life of bitterness on a daily basis so that you, in due time, will reap a good harvest.

✷ ✷ ✷

Further Study: What is bitterness? How does it spring up in your life? Do you have bitterness toward anyone today? How can you root it out of your life? Are you? When?

DISCIPLESHIP

GO FIGURE

No one can be my disciple who does not give up all his own possessions.
Luke 14:33

☆ ☆ ☆

It was one of those errand things that sent me into the jaws of the grocery store at rush hour. Granted, most men are banished from these "malls of meals" for the simple reason they haven't a clue what to buy, what aisle to search, or what has any nutritional value. My wife had endured one of those L–O–N–G days with the kids, so I thought (I always get into trouble when I start thinking) I would win the "Husband of the Month" award by volunteering to pick up a few items at the grocery store for her. My motive was good, but this chore would soon turn into a nightmare when I realized (after waiting through the check-out line) that I only had a $20 bill and no checks with me. My calculator mind set immediately into action, figured up the cost of the items in my cart, and guess what? My total was $39.25, which by my calculations, left me in a real pickle of a position—and $19.25 short.

I'll never forget the humiliation as I stood there, trying to seek a quick line of credit in front of a mob of mad mothers. My problem wasn't necessarily bad shopping skills, as much as it was not counting the cost of my purchases. Many Christians today walk around doing what I did—not counting the entire cost of being a disciple of Christ. Jesus figured it up before He took on the job of Savior, and realized it would cost Him His life. In this passage of scripture, Jesus is explaining that a possession is anything that detours you from total commitment to Him. Don't get into the thick of this Christian stuff and then calculate the cost of being a real follower of Christ. Trust me—being short of the cost can bring on a whole lot of embarrassment.

☆ ☆ ☆

Further Study: How much has being a follower of Jesus cost you? What possessions must you give up to be a disciple? Why is Jesus so jealous of all our attention?

EMOTIONS

CRY BABY

Then all the people (Israelites) lifted up their voices
and cried, and the people wept all night.
Numbers 14:1

☆ ☆ ☆

I remember learning in a high school health class how good crying is for us. It serves many purposes such as relieving stress, washing out foreign debris from the eye socket and unclogging the tear ducts of babies and probably adults, too. No matter how tough someone may seem, we all have cried at some point or another in our lives. Crying can be a part of a mourning process after the loss of a loved one, or a reaction from lack of sleep, or a release of too much stress. Whatever the cause, crying is a God-made way of dealing or coping in life.

Moses and Joshua dealt with a different kind of crying as they led a whole mess of people (Israelites) out of slavery, across the desert and through the Red Sea (sounds like over the river and through the woods to grandmother's house we go), and put up with a whole bunch of whining. This crying (whining) didn't stem from pure motives or sincere faith, but the lack of both of these. You see, this is a great example of how not all expressed emotion such as crying and weeping is sincere. At times, people shed tears that are not valid. Some moments you can see that the tears are of anger or lack of faith (God failed them), and they are wrong. Don't take a God-given emotion and use it as a mortal manipulation. You can see in this example that God allowed these people to wander in the wilderness until all of them died off because they were wrong in their ways. Go ahead, cry all you want to; just make sure it's not a fake.

☆ ☆ ☆

Further Study: When was the last time you cried? What caused it? How did you solve the situation that provoked it, or did you? Have you ever cried insincere tears? Why?

SECOND WIND

Do all your work heartily for the Lord rather than for men.
Colossians 3:23

☆ ☆ ☆

It was a hot August day, and I happened to be wearing a hot football uniform under the guidance of a hot-tempered coach. These three did not go well for my health during two-a-day workouts preparing for the coming season. I remember how that day's practice schedule went about as slowly as a duck swimming in oil. It dragged on and on and on until I heard my coach say, "Boys, everyone on the line for some pukers." Sorry for the graphic language, but that meant we now had to run sprints until we dropped. I felt like this would be the perfect time to get run over by a steamroller, just to extinguish my pain. I was on the line ready to drop when out of the corner of my helmet, between the face guard bars, I saw . . . beauty in the bleachers. Yep, my girlfriend had come to watch her sugar plum, sweetie pie, honey muffin practice. Hot dog, did I perk up, pooch out my chest, stand up tall and begin to clap and cheer up my teammates who were ready for a stretcher. It was like a second wind (maybe just puppy love) came over me, and you'd think I'd been shot out of a cannon the way I ran those sprints. Miracles still happen.

We are a people who are in the "do" mode most of the time. We go, go, go like a hamster on a treadmill, day in and day out. We work, serve, slave throughout our lives, but for whom? Are we trying to earn our ticket aboard the heavenly Airways Express? To do whatever we're doing for our Creator rather than a crowd will take a new perspective, since we live in a world that bases acceptance on performance. God is more than happy to help in this process that starts in a prayer. Give God your glory, and see if your reward isn't relished more. Imagine God in the bleachers, cheering you on in your daily tasks, and see if you don't find a second wind.

☆ ☆ ☆

Further Study: Do you do all you do for you, or who? What kind of work do you do daily? How can you give the glory to God?

FESS UP

*Then the King said to him, "How many times must I tell you to speak
to me nothing but the truth in the name of the Lord?"*
2 Chronicles 18:15

* * *

One of the favorite pastimes at our ranch while growing up was to shoot water moccasin snakes in our pond. They were a hazard to our bullfrog population, not to mention they could bite the fire out of ya'. These slithery, slimy, scum surviving snakes were best seen sunning on the shore on a hot summer's day (say that sentence fast 10 times). We would drive our tractor to the edge of the bank, raise up the bucket full of friends, guns and plenty of ammo to its full extension for maximum viewing, then commence to firing away at will. One day, our routine snake hunt turned into an unplanned nightmare. We accidentally drove the $40,000 tractor into the pond. Man, oh man, did I know that I was gonna' get it. My dad wasn't with us; in fact, no parent was, and we all knew if he found out, we would all hang at high noon. We got a neighboring farmer to pull out the submerged submarine, cleaned it up, raked the tire tracks leading into the pond and got it running again by 2:00 a.m.

How many times have you been in a pure pickle that you knew would spell out pure trouble? The real question is, did you ever get away with it scot-free? Did you lie or just not tell at all? How characteristic that in story after story we see biblical characters doing the same? You know, hey . . . what they don't know can't hurt them, or one white lie never killed anyone. The problem comes when we start small and it becomes a common routine in our lives. God, whether you know it or will admit it, is everywhere at once and is all knowing. He sees deceit, cheating, lying, stealing, hating and defiling even when common folks don't. He is faithful and just to forgive us of these, yet we are called also to make it right with the person(s) we victimized. Keeping a clean slate is tough, yet our conscience is relieved when we do. I know you're wondering what I did. Yes, I did conceal the truth, and yes, my dad did find out. How? . . . (suspense is building isn't it?) the neighbor told him and yes, I did get it!

* * *

Further Study: When was the last time you lied? Did you confess or conceal? How will you handle it differently next time?

MENTOR ME

*And the things which you've received from me, entrust these
to faithful men who can teach others also.*

2 Timothy 2:2

★ ★ ★

Let me set the scene, 1988, 4 X 100 relay in the Summer Olympics
equipped with a peerless group of sprint champions, and it was inconceivable
that the United States team could lose the gold medal. Yet, as the final leg of
the relay approached, the unbelievable happened. The Americans dropped
the baton, the crowd moments earlier electrified, became mute.

This disastrous scene aptly describes the essence of loss that "Generation
X" feels as they enter adulthood. Searching desperately for godly mentors to
teach and model, they feel like runners stranded at the starting blocks with no
baton. Our country is teeming with young men and women who have little
identity or direction, missing a sense of continuity with our heritage. This fact
underscores our need for mature, growing older men and women to pull up
along side these young folks and hand off the baton of godliness and leadership to equip the next generation. Mentoring is a relational experience
through which one person empowers another by sharing God-given
resources. The resources will vary but mentoring is a positive dynamic that
enables people to develop their potential. Observing someone's growth, struggles, responses and decision-making process can change the perspective of a
mentoree forever. Mentoring can reduce the probability of leadership failure,
divorce, provide accountability and empower a responsible, potential laborer.
Mentoring is as old as civilization itself. The Old Testament showed this with
Eli and Samuel, Elijah and Elisha, Barnabas and Paul. These days the human
touch has been replaced with computers, videos, books and classrooms.

Many years ago my wife and I began taking young men and women into
our home to live for a year. Yes, it's like living your life in a fish bowl and
demands a higher energy level, but the rewards will be eternal. These folks
become a part of our family, and we don't even realize how profound our
words and actions really are. People were and still are God's method for making disciples. The self-made man or woman is a myth and, though some claim
it, few aspire to it. You, yes you, have what it takes to mentor if you see potential in others, are flexible, patient, and are experiencing continuing growth
toward holiness. If you're willing . . . there's someone out there waiting to
receive the baton and continue the race; don't drop it.

★ ★ ★

Further Study: Who could you mentor? Pray specifically. Are your character
qualities at a Godly standard? What are your fears?

Personal Touch

Let the one who is taught the word share all good things with him who teaches.
Galatians 6:6

✩ ✩ ✩

One of the all-time greatest on the gridiron is a guy named Jerry Rice. He plays for the San Francisco 49ers' football team and is considered by most experts the best wide receiver in the history of the NFL. Once, Jerry was asked why he attended such a small, obscure university like Mississippi Valley State University in Itta Bena, Mississippi. Jerry's response was, "Out of all the big-time schools (like UCLA) that recruited me, MVSU was the only school to come to my house for a personal visit." The big-time powerhouse universities send out generic letters, cards and advertisements, but only this one showed Rice personal attention and sincere concern.

When I heard this story it brought to mind just how important personal outreach is. Here is a guy who few thought valuable enough to recruit personally, but now he's a superstar in the sports world. Gang, people, no matter what color or size or nationality, are valuable. How much more important is the personal touch in matters concerning the heart, soul and spirit of a person. If you're in the business market and you don't extend a personal touch to your clients, then get ready to go belly-up (broke). Wal-Mart would not be the nation's number one discount center without friendly smiles, warm handshakes, (low prices) and personal demeanor. Every Wal-Mart store in America has a greeter at the door to offer you their services. Christians need to learn from old "Wally World" and make evangelism personal and more practical. Each person you meet deserves your personal best, not your bulk mail worst. Do God, and yourself, a favor and put a personal touch into your outreach formula.

★ ★ ★

Further Study: Are you giving your best? Do you have a tendency to be generic instead of personal in sharing with others? How valuable do you see those who are different from you?

THREE SIMPLE WORDS

Love never fails.
1 Corinthians 13:8

☆ ☆ ☆

February 14 is Valentine's Day, a time set aside for lovers of all ages. This day for romanticism was created, no doubt, by florists, candy makers and greeting card companies. Businesses rake in big-time cash simply by offering folks a creative way to say, "I love you," at that special time each year. Despite the hoopla and commercialization, I think Valentine's Day is a great idea, and the male species needs all the help it can get. Perhaps you're asking yourself why I've included a valentine devotion on February 13 rather than February 14. Why? Because it is never too late or too early to tell someone you love them. Love is the high octane fuel that powers our engine and keeps us going. Relationships, whether with the opposite sex or not, need to be nurtured so they don't wither like a plant without water.

Unfortunately, millions of marriages, friendships and working relationships are in trouble today because of the inability of those involved to get along. Maybe the fundamental problem is selfishness. We are so intent on satisfying our own needs and desires that we fail to recognize the longings of others. Relationships always work best when we think less about ourselves and more about another. True agape (unconditional) love is hardly a new concept. In fact, it's ancient. Jesus not only told us, He modeled for us, the way to develop, build, nurture and sustain a valuable relationship. Whatever our height, weight, color, or shoe-size, we all have two basic needs–to love and be loved by someone. Begin today to humble yourself (even if you've been wronged) and mend an old relationship, work to maintain a current one, or develop a brand new relationship. Make Jesus the real cupid, a model for what it really takes, and what it really means to say three simple words–I . . . love . . . you!

☆ ☆ ☆

Further Study: What does love mean to you? Why is it so hard to maintain a relationship? How are you nurturing your relationships today?

GOD'S LOVE

VALENTINE'S DAY

*Love is patient; love is kind, is not jealous, does not brag, isn't arrogant,
doesn't act unbecomingly, does not seek its own, is not provoked,
doesn't take into account a wrong suffered, doesn't rejoice in
unrighteousness, but rejoices in truth, bears all things,
believes all things, hopes all things, endures
all things. Love never fails.*
1 Corinthians 13:4-8

✯ ✯ ✯

There aren't many typical days lived experiencing the love which is
exchanged on this day. Cupid starts firing arrows in the direction of our tender hearts, moving us to share this day with someone we love. The card
shops, flower nurseries and candy stores make a killing each year on this day.
It seems like the collars tighten up around the male sex to first, not forget
February 14th, but even more impressive, to try out those creative skills and
come up with a day she won't soon forget. I'm no expert on understanding
the opposite sex, but I have learned that it's the little things that really matter.
You don't have to be married or have a relationship going on to have a sweetheart. It could be that a sister, mom or another female relative falls into the
category of a valentine. The cards are cute, the flowers are favorites and the
candy dandy, but Valentine's Day is love God's way.

When you read what Paul wrote to the church in Corinth, he defines
what we should be wrapping up in our actions to give to our sweeties. This
love is a written description of what God's true love is to you as a child of
God. God celebrates this special day year-round. Do you know how people
would view you if you really took to heart (pun) these verses in your life daily?
Give a gift today that won't wilt without water, that doesn't melt under heat,
or end up in a scrapbook. That gift is applied scripture. Look out cupid, this
is one arrow that shoots long and deep into our hearts.

✯ ✯ ✯

Further Study: What ways can you show your sweetheart you really value
him/her?

EMPATHY

Carry each other's burdens, and in this way you will fulfill the law of Christ.
Galatians 6:2

☆ ☆ ☆

Mr. Alter's fifth grade class at Lake Elementary School in Oceanside, California, included 14 bald-headed boys. Only one had no choice in the matter. Ian O'Gorman was losing his hair in clumps as the result of the chemotherapy used to fight lymphoma. So Ian wouldn't feel out of place in the classroom, all 13 of his buddies shaved their heads, too. If they all were bald, no one could point out the one who had cancer. A 10-year-old boy named Kyle started it all as he proposed the plan to the group, then marched them all down to the barber. Ian's father, touched by the gesture of compassion, was in tears as he told them how he appreciated their kindness and good deed.

What an awesome example of carrying a burden for a friend. You don't often see such a sense of compassion. Take a look sometime at the words that precede an act of healing by Jesus in the gospels. They state, "He felt compassion, so . . .." So what? Sew buttons on your underwear? No. So, He did something about it by expressing empathy for the afflicted and became part of the solution, not the problem. There is probably no better way to show how much Jesus you have living in your heart than by carrying someone else's burden(s). Our second greatest commandment is, "Love your neighbor as yourself." Do you realize just how much you love yourself? Let me answer that, and I don't even know you . . . a lot! Tune in to the spirit of Christ and see where He leads you and what cross (burden) He leads you to carry for a friend. You'll feel good about yourself, and this selfish world will know that you are different.

☆ ☆ ☆

Further Study: How compassionate are you? Have you ever acted on that sense? Why or why not? Who could you help today? What are you waiting on?

LANDING LEADERS

*Let not many of you be leaders because you know that
we who lead will be judged more strictly.*
James 3:1

★ ★ ★

Flight No. 401 on Eastern Airlines was making a routine approach at the Los Angeles airport. Throughout the journey there had been little or no turbulence and preparations were being made for landing. The crew was made up of five stewardesses, a captain, first assistant and a flight navigator. After making final contact with the tower in L.A. and being cleared for landing, the captain flipped the switch to engage the landing gear and noticed that the indicator light didn't come on. The crew did a quick visual check and found the landing gear was down, which indicated that the light itself must be burned out. To make sure that the bulb was the problem, the plane continued to circle the airport while the navigator tried to remove the bulb from the instrument panel, but couldn't. The first assistant also tried, then the captain. Little did they realize that while the entire cabin crew was messing with one little bulb, the plane was losing altitude and ultimately crashed in a swampy area miles from the airport, killing hundreds. This tragedy was caused by a bulb valued at 75 cents. That's right . . . a cheap bulb was the root cause of a multi-million dollar plane crash that cost hundreds of lives. Why? Because the captain took his eyes off the big picture, his main responsibility, to deal with a meaningless job of no value.

We, as leaders, need to keep flying the plane, not dabbling with dinkies. As a leader you must maintain a focus on what really matters or what doesn't at the time of decision making. We need to learn to "choose our mountains" to climb in life. There is always gonna' be tons of stuff to do, events to volunteer for, committees to serve on and meetings to attend, but there are really only 24 hours in a day (that I can tell). Learn to see (through God's eyes) what is a priority and what can wait. Learn to say no to some things and guard your time with your family and God. Learn to delegate to others so they can learn and you just take the priority lists. Leadership isn't a title, it's a learned skill.

★ ★ ★

Further Study: Who is the best Christian leader you've ever seen at work? What made them so good at leading others? How can you be an effective leader? How do you learn to prioritize?

A TONGUE LASHING

They set their mouth against the heavens and
their tongue parades loose through the earth.
Psalm 73:9

⋇ ⋇ ⋇

Take a look at the human anatomy for a moment. Look specifically at the head (neck up). Have you noticed that we all have two ears, a mouth and one nose (I hope)? Do you see that you can close and open the mouth but not the ears? Why? Do you think it's just an assembly line mistake and God is soon to have a factory recall on everyone's face any day now? Growing up, I'm sure you hummed the tune of "sticks and stones may break my bones, but words can never hurt me." I bet the guy who wrote that must have been a hermit in a cave on a deserted island to have made up such a lie. Untruthful words can probably do more damage to a person than diving into an empty pool. The tongue has done more damage to the human race than the black plague or polio. With it we praise our friends then turn around and stab them in their backs. Why, oh why?

The Bible says the tongue is the bit in a horse's mouth, the spark that sets off a forest fire and the poison of a cobra. To realize its power one must first realize its whereabouts and where it hides . . . in your mouth. Self-image, reputation and potential can be all but destroyed by a few words of gossip. What defines the word gossip? Speaking to anyone about another person's business that is neither part of the solution or problem. It's trying to knock someone down a notch for selfish reasons. This is why God tells us to be quick to listen and slow to speak. Today's galloping gossips seem to have this verse flipped around. Learn to tame your tongue and put out rumors when they come to you; don't fuel their fire. Listen to yourself in a conversation with others and see if you're spreading a rumor, or stating a fact or fiction. Do yourself and others a favor by being a different breed of person and not letting that muscle in your mouth exercise on someone else's life.

☆ ☆ ☆

Further Study: Do you gossip? Do you say things to others in order to demean someone else? How can you begin to tame your tongue? How can you train it to speak the truth?

GRACE

STOOPING

But God demonstrates his own love for us in this:
while we were yet sinners, Christ died for us.
Romans 5:8

☆ ☆ ☆

A vivid picture exists in my brain of a ritual which seems to take place annually in March. If you know anything about horses or horse breeding, you know that March is the "foal" time of the year. That's the time when pregnant mares have their colts out in pastures on ranches across the south. There is nothing quite like seeing a newborn colt trying with all its four-legged might to stand up and walk for the first time. It's amazing how soon after birth and the mom licking the colt clean that it learns to maneuver. I remember my dad, upon sight of a newborn colt in one of his pastures, crawling for up to a half mile on his hands and knees toward the mare and colt. It's the first time the colt would have ever seen a human before and should be scared, but it's not. The fact that with no rope or halter or feed bucket, my father could stoop up to this colt and begin to rub its legs, back, belly, and head without scaring it is amazing. The key element to this is never allowing your head to be taller than the colt's head.

The Hebrew meaning of the word "grace" is to stoop or bow. Have you ever realized that the Creator of this world crawls to you for miles (humbly) and comes to you to get to know you? (Remember, He humbled Himself.) Listen . . . God could have walked up to you all proud and tough, but He knew you would run (like the colt) if He did. Remember, He knocks gently at the door to our hearts; He doesn't kick it down (Revelation 3:20). What a unique sight it was to see my dad humble himself to a horse to get to know it, but what an awesome picture it is to see the God who holds each star in place crawl to us in order to save us from eternal death.

☆ ☆ ☆

Further Study: What does grace mean to you? How have you seen God humble Himself or stoop in your life? How did you respond? What does grace do to you and for your relationship to Christ?

DON'T SWEAT THE SMALL STUFF

*Yes, woe upon you, Pharisees, and you other religious leaders–hypocrites!
For you tithe down to the last mint leaf in your garden, but ignore
the important things–justice and mercy and faith. Yes, you
should tithe, but you shouldn't leave the more
important things undone . . . You strain
out a gnat and swallow a camel.*
Matthew 23:23-24

☆ ☆ ☆

As a child on my grandparents' farm, I spent time "putting by" (as the farm folks say). "Putting by" means preserving farm produce so it can be stored to use later. The method of the day was canning. My grandma was good at it. She canned everything, but my favorite was jelly.

We were so proud of the jelly we entered it in the fair one year, sure the judges would agree it was worth the effort it took to produce. But victory was not ours. A piece of peel had made it through the strainer and got wedged between the judge's teeth, so the prize went to someone who had made jelly from commercial grape juice, smooth and peel-less, but not "homemade."

Often in life we struggle so with insignificant (in the context of eternity) blips that we completely miss the genuine intent, then turn our backs and let a humongous injustice stomp right past us. Just prior to this verse Jesus spoke to the crowds concerning Jewish law in Jerusalem, after He'd booted the money changers out of the Temple. Angry at His acceptance from the crowd, the Pharisees tried to trip up Jesus with trick questions about God's laws.

If we're constantly searching for the smallest flaw, the least mistake, the one place where we colored outside the lines, we're liable to miss the grand design, the big picture (catchin' on?). Jesus said that if you follow the first and greatest commandment to love the Lord your God with all your heart, soul, and mind, you'll find you are obeying all the others (Matthew 23:37-40). Keep Jesus in your heart, your eyes on God and don't sweat the small stuff. Gnats go down a lot easier than camels . . . one hump, or two?

☆ ☆ ☆

Further Study: What chokes you that really is insignificant in the light of eternity? Why?

GIFTS

GIFT OF GIVING

When He (Jesus) ascended into heaven, He led captive a host of captives and, He gave gifts to men (women).
Ephesians 4:8

☆ ☆ ☆

You're gonna' love this devotion if you're one of those who wakes up early and runs with happy feet downstairs before dawn to open up presents on Christmas and to see if Santa stuffed your stocking. One of the greatest seasons we have on this planet is the celebration season of Jesus' birth when we get presents, too. When was the last time you went to someone's birthday party and received more goodies than the birthday boy or girl? (Party favors don't count). If and when you have children, you will know what I'm talking about when I say the kiddos get "excited!" If you're not planning to get married, you can relate because you were a child once. Christmas and all the festive frenzies that go along with this spirit are too few and far between. Wouldn't it be great to have this celebration of joy when everyone's happy, caring and full of turkey, each month? I'll take that idea back because I'd be broke and weigh two tons if we did. So record over that message, will ya'? Jesus really is the reason for this spectacular season, and isn't it fun to be invited each year? There's nothing quite like giving and receiving fun things.

Jesus really does, through His Spirit, allow us to open gifts. His gifts. He has graciously given some to you (with no take-backs) to enjoy daily. What gifts am I speaking of? Spiritual gifts. In His family room He leaves, nicely wrapped for you to open and use daily, divine gifts for His glory. Your present may be the gift of giving, so give. The gift of mercy, so care. The gift of teaching, so train. The gift of exhortation, so encourage, or the gift of discernment, so choose. Whatever you find under God's giving tree, open it, use it, and be thankful. These gifts are like the EverReady Bunny . . . they keep going and going and going.

☆ ☆ ☆

Further Study: Do you open up your divine spiritual gift daily? Why or why not? How can you use it today?

STANDARDS

A Standard of Quality

*In those days Israel had no king, and everyone did
what was right in their own eyes.*
Judges 21:25

☆ ☆ ☆

The sport of track is one of history prior. It is amazing how endurance, speed and quickness play such a pivotal role in this competition between individuals. It is one of these sports that at the end of the race, you can't blame coming in last on another teammate for missing the shot, fumbling the ball, duffing a serve or whiffing a pitch. As this sport evolved, new events were added to enhance the viewing and generate some flare for the public and the participants. The event . . . high jumping. I ask you, who would be creative enough (if that's what you'd call it) to come up with a sport where a person bounces over a bar, Fosbury Flops and then pile drives themselves into a pit? Have you ever noticed that the way the winner is determined is by the continual movement of the bar up in height and the weeding out process of the jumpers not being able to jump over the advancing bar? What would happen if the bar wasn't needed and everyone was scored by their own standard? Talk about chaos, talk about disagreements. The bar is the standard which the participants have to shoot (jump) for in order to test themselves. As the bar moves up, the standard to conquer becomes more difficult to achieve, yet more rewarding to attain.

Can you imagine a world without a standard and a society without a Savior? You should, you're living in one as we speak. Our society seems to have drifted onto the rocks of destruction without notice. The Bible is full of past civilizations who seem to have come up with their own rules and ended up failing the test. Jesus is our standard, our world record holder, our model of excellence we are shooting for. Without Him going before us setting the scale, walking beside us, helping us compete, following us up, and holding us accountable, we wouldn't make it. Don't get mad at the standard. It's there for you to shoot for. Never lose hope in the King, He's the record holder. So what are you waiting on? It's your jump next!

☆ ☆ ☆

Further Study: How much do you prepare daily for attaining His standard? How much did you prepare today? (If not, then get after it!)

STEPPIN' OUT

*And He said, "Come" and Peter stepped out of the boat and
walked on the water and came toward Jesus.*
Matthew 14:29

☆ ☆ ☆

Have you ever been summoned to step out before? How about at a
track meet when the coach tells you, before the final race, to step out? What
about when a friend encourages you to step out of your comfort zone and try
something different? How about on the dance floor? When does someone
describes you as steppin' out of your normal ways and doing something totally out of character?

I love the story of Peter (the disciple) being scared from sailing in the
storm. He looked off the port side (just a guess) and saw someone apparent-
ly walking on top of the rough seas. He rubbed his red eyes and did a double
take. It was at that moment he realized it was his hero, Jesus, and then he was
asked to come along for a casual walk on the water. Sure! Right! Can't you
just hear old Pete saying to himself, "Jesus, you must be crazy . . . me, walk on
that water? I don't think so."

The ending to this scene in scripture is worth reading again. Peter, Mr.
Aggressive, jumped out of the boat (his comfort zone) and began walking on
the water toward Jesus. He must have felt pretty powerful and cool until that
moment he took his focus off Christ. Reality set in, and when he looked
down, he began to sink like a brick. I'm not sure about this, but I'll bet ya' that
Peter was no All-American swimmer and wondered if he wasn't about to
become shark bait.

Jesus calls us daily to walk away from security blankets and step out in
faith to follow Him. Walking on water is not easy, but neither is having total
faith in the Master's plans. Faith is the assurance of things hoped for (fear of
not drowning) and the conviction of things not seen (waves of turbulent
tough times). Go ahead . . . step out. Jesus won't let you sink.

☆ ☆ ☆

Further Study: Has God ever called you to step out of your comfort zone and
do something totally radical for Him? Why is it so tough to step out on unsure
waters and follow him? When will you step out of your boat?

CONFIDENCE CREATOR

And Elijah answered and said, "If I am a man of God, let fire come down from
heaven and consume you and your fifty." Then the fire of God came
down from heaven and consumed him and his fifty.

2 Kings 1.12

* * *

Confidence is something to be compared with bravery in a war. Some call it reliance, assurance, certainty and faith, but scripture calls it faith, trust, hope, conviction, belief and dependence. My father used to tell me, "If your ability was half of your confidence, you'd be dangerous." The problem we humans seem to have with confidence is that we have it in the wrong things. We tend to put all our cards on our business brains, athletic attributes, luxurious looks or witty way with words. This is why so many have such low self-image–because we fail in areas that we rely on self, not God, to be successful.

Elijah, as you probably know, was a great prophet. He was called upon by God to be a communicator and public address system of the truths to come. He was obedient to his calling which allowed him to have divine confidence that his Master's messages would not be mocked and would "hold water," so to speak, when tested. Elijah had the confidence (faith) that when he picked up the phone to call upon the Creator, he would not get a busy signal. What trust it must have taken to stand in front of a bunch of doubting dummies and put his God (the Almighty) to the test. It was kinda like a youngster saying, "My dad can beat up your dad." God the Father has not, nor will He ever be made out to be a joke (mocked). Elijah called down the fire from heaven, and at once (not a moment's notice) his wish came true in full force. You see, God doesn't do anything halfway, and this includes showing His power over a false god. Learn from this and know that you worship this same God who shows Himself the all powerful, yet knows how many hairs you have on your head. Have your confidence (faith) in the right thing, not things. Remember, they will someday all burn.

* * *

Further Study: Where does your confidence come from? How confident are you in the flesh? Is God the power in your strength?

DISGUISED

*In order that no advantage be taken of us by Satan,
for we are not ignorant of his schemes* (disguises).
2 Corinthians 2:11

☆ ☆ ☆

One of my favorite friends also happens to be a big animal lover. He has four children who know their father has a soft spot for critters. On one occasion, he caught a baby raccoon and brought it home for the kids to see. At a family dinner meeting that night, they came up with a name for the new arrival—"Bandit." One fact about raccoons they seemed to overlook is that as they mature, these animals go through a glandular change and often become aggressive to the point of attack. Since a 30-pound raccoon can equal a 100 pound dog in a fight, they can be the source of extensive hospital bills. I recall talking to the nine-year-old daughter about the dilemma, and her response was, "Bandit wouldn't hurt me . . . he just wouldn't!" But, after several friends of the family and their own kids suffered puncture wounds and face lacerations, they released the beast back to the wilderness.

I'm reminded how sin often comes disguised (dressed) in an adorable appearance, and as we play, it becomes easy to say, "It will be different for me," but the result of this type thinking is predictable. Sin is like fire—if you mess with it, you will get burned. Don't be taken in (lured) by Satan's appearance as a harmless creature, but be wise to his power and schemes to destroy you . . . the wounds can be fatal!

☆ ☆ ☆

Further Study: Are you deceived by sin's disguise? Do you ever think you are superman or superwoman, capable of taking on sin? How can you wise up to sin's game?

No Guts, No Glory

The proof of your faith, being more precious than gold which is perishable, even though tested by fire, may be found to result in praise, glory and honor to Christ.

1 Peter 1.7

☆ ☆ ☆

Close your eyes (no dozing off now) and say to yourself the title of this devotion and see what visions dance in your head. No fair seeing sugar plums either. This kind of line is called "baiting" if you want to know the street name for it. You use this "one-liner" when you want to coax, or persuade, someone to do something they probably wouldn't do on their own. It's kind of a "guts" check on the spot, you might say. You'll hear it on the ski slopes, on the 20 foot bluffs of a lake, in the athletic arenas and at the late night parties. Sometimes it's a sincere effort to motivate, and other times it's to set someone up for failure or destruction. No matter where you call home, or what your age is, this phrase chooses no favorites and knows not of the consequences.

You hear this lingo in the secular world more than you will in the Christian circles. I offer you a suggestion. We need to hear it more on the God Squad, too. Isn't it true we are athletes, warriors, risk takers in this forgiven family? Are we not called to run in such a way that we may win!? Doesn't it take guts to receive the crown of eternal life called heaven? You bet your sweet potatoes it does! This Christian stuff is no walk through the lily fields or a yellow brick road (sorry Dorothy). Folks without guts in this league (Christianity) won't last too long. I would much rather be considered a risk taker in my faith, than a bench sitter. It's a heck of a lot better to have tried and failed, than never to have tried at all. Failure helps us realize that we are human and we do need a Savior. Step up to the plate and take a 100 percent swing. Remember, home runs in this league are always preceded by a few strikeouts, but that makes the successes for Christ all the more to celebrate about. Have some guts and see some glory. Go God's way.

☆ ☆ ☆

Further Study: Why do you shy away from uncertain situations in your faith? How can you have God's guts?

GOALS

PERFECT PRACTICE

*The goal of our instruction is first love from a pure heart,
good conscience and sincere faith.*
1 Timothy 1:5

☆ ☆ ☆

There is a famous NBA basketball star who played for the Boston Celtics throughout the '80s. His name is Larry Bird. He was a star forward for Indiana State and fueled his college team to the 1979 NCAA National Championship showdown with none other than Michigan State, whose star was Magic Johnson. Larry then went on to a star-studded, all-star career with the Celtics and led them to several world championships in the late '80s. The story is told of a pre-game warm-up session in which Larry was alone, shooting baskets at the Boston Garden a few hours prior to a playoff game with the L.A. Lakers. After shooting several shots and missing all of them, Larry called upon the arena manager to check to see if the basket was at the standard height of 10 feet. The arena manager, proud of his dependability for doing things right the first time, was disgusted with Larry's questioning his capabilities, but measured the basket a second time. Much to his surprise, the basket was a half-inch low (hence the reason for the missed shots).

The point of this story is to show you the importance of knowing exactly what the goal is that you're shooting for. Larry Bird's goal was a circle of metal attached to a glass backboard 10 feet from the floor. Our goal as a Christian is to love others with a healthy heart, a clean conscience and a flawless faith. We, too, should know in our spirits when the goal is a bit off and we are probably missing our mark. To love others is not only to share Jesus with them, but to follow up with discipleship. In other words, you will be striving after this goal for the rest of your life so don't expect to stop anytime soon. Larry Bird didn't get all his recognition and rewards in the sport of basketball by missing his mark often. Christians likewise don't see the fruits of their labor by failing to follow through with specific instructions. Perfect practice makes perfect. Hey, and in the end, we'll all be all-stars in heaven!

☆ ☆ ☆

Further Study: How does this scripture apply to your daily life? What makes athletes good at what they do? How does that differ from what allows Christians to excel in their faith? Do you know your exact goals as a believer? Where are the measurements found? (Hint: the Bible)

CHRISTIAN RACE

FLEET OF FEET

Therefore, since we have so great a cloud of witnesses surrounding us, let us also lay aside every encumbrance and the sin which so easily entangles us, and let us run with endurance the race that is set before us.

Hebrews 12.1

* * *

If you go to many track meets or cross country events, you will find competitors who are basically made up of only two body parts . . . legs and lungs. My hat is off to those courageous souls who brave the weather and the big neighborhood dogs running loose, to call themselves runners. America is full of pavement beaters who rise up from slumber daily to get the old ticker (heart) in shape for those later years of life. I, for one, standing 6 feet 5 inches tall, weighing in at 220 pounds and accompanied with a flat size thirteen fleet of feet, am not one of that species. When I run, it sounds like a wild herd of elephants escaping from the city zoo and stampeding loose on the streets.

The Bible, over and over, uses the words run and race. The Christian life is compared with a race and the Christian person with a runner who can enter as a participant because of Christ's payment at the cross. The author of Hebrews tells us that in order to succeed in this event, we need to throw off two things: every encumbrance and the sin that trips us up. The sin, in this context, is lack of faith, and the encumbrance is defined as excess weight. In other words, to finish you need faith in God's way and prior training that will allow the weight of worldliness to be burned off like calories.

How are you training today to be a competitive runner for God? How deep is your faith in your Savior, that this race is the most important race of your life? Do yourself a favor and get training for this one because the reward you will receive beats the heck out of any medal or trophy earned today.

* * *

Further Study: What worldly weight are you carrying with you? How can you lose it?

DAILY PHONE CALLS

As Jesus approached the town gate, a dead person was being carried out, the
only son of his mother, and she was a widow. And a large crowd from
the town was with her. When Jesus saw her, his heart went out to
her, and he felt compassion, and he said, "Don't cry."
Luke 7:12-13

✯ ✯ ✯

On March 12, 1994, I received a phone call while in Telluride, Colorado, that won't quit ringing in my mind for a long time. The call was from my wife, to inform me of a very close friend of mine who died of a heart attack in Houston, Texas. Wow . . . did this news stop me in my tracks. It was weird how I almost didn't seem to believe her (my own wife) and continued to interrogate her on the validity of the news. Death comes so quickly, yet it doesn't play favorites or give much warning of its arrival time. Throughout the entire funeral I noticed the joy on the some fifteen hundred faces attending. It was like those in attendance weren't as concerned with the loss of a friend as they were with the future of the hope. The tears came from loss of a friend, not from having to guess where he had gone. They knew . . . heaven.

If you notice in the scripture, Jesus tells the mother of the deceased son not to cry. Why? Doesn't that seem a little harsh to stomach? After all, He had just stated that He felt compassion for her, right? I believe the reason for this statement by the Savior was because He was in total control. Have you ever noticed the ones who don't get tangled up in the turbulence of the times are those with a heavenly perspective? Remember, the vantage point which overlooks situations from above can be yours also. Now I'm not saying that crying is wrong, and neither is God, as long as your heart realizes that Jesus cares for you and your situations and He holds the future. Hey, it's not bad having a Savior who exemplifies compassion and knowing my friend is residing with his Creator . . . what a set up!

✯ ✯ ✯

Further Study: If you were to lose a friend today, how would you react? How does this scripture apply today?

CONTENTMENT

THE TESTING TREE

And God saw all that He had made, and behold it was very good.
Genesis 1:31

☆ ☆ ☆

Picture the most beautiful place you've ever been or seen. Can it even compare with the first place ever created? The Ultimate Artist put His brush and paint to the sky and to the water and to the ground, and at the mention of a word the most exquisite place was formed. My four year old will look at a sunset and say, "Mommy, God painted that."

But what about this perfect garden . . . what was so special? Larry Norman, one of the early rock'n'roll Christians, says in one of his songs, "So long ago the garden." What is his point? I think he means the garden is a place in which we all long to live. No ugliness, no perversion, only complete perfection with purposeful fulfillment. One man, one woman . . . each obviously made for the other.

Isn't it odd that God would have put a very unique tree in that perfect place? My nephew, when at church, was asked, "What was the name of the tree that God forbid Adam and Eve to partake of?" He answered, "The testing tree." It was exactly that, a tree that tested Adam and Eve. They did not do very well on that test, but what would we have done on the very same test? Today we are still trying to reverse the curse of that test. No work for men, easy money, no pain in childbirth and no consequences for our sins.

Well, the ending of that story can be found in Genesis, and it is still happening today. The fact is, until Jesus comes back and we all return to heaven, we will never be in a perfect place with perfect people. But God has given us good instruction and promises concerning what to do until that time occurs. Put His Word to the test . . .. Love when it hurts to love, heap burning coals and remember . . . He will never leave or forsake us, and He will never give us more than we can handle.

☆ ☆ ☆

Further Study: How have you tried to reverse the curse? What place or person do you wish was perfect? Not one of us is perfect, so how do we handle imperfect people and places?

PLAYING FAVORITES

RED CARPET TREATMENT

*But if you show favoritism, you are committing sin
and are convicted by the law as transgressors.*
James 2:10

☆ ☆ ☆

A couple of snow-to-snows ago (that's American Indian talk for "years"), I had the opportunity to see the President of the United States, George Bush, when he came for a campaign speech at a local theme park. Talk about an event of the century! Talk about rolling out the red carpet for someone! Oh my! I could not believe what a big to-do it was just for a guy to talk to a few thousand folks. Streets were blocked off for miles, Secret Service agents swarmed like bees, a fleet of limos cruised in, and presidential helicopters filled the airways like a flock of geese. Come on, I mean how many folks does it take to protect one guy, and how can the President fly in all those "copters" at once? (Split personality, maybe?) I was amazed at how people from all around the community basically laid down everything to be of service to a guy who would make a speech, then jet set off to four other cities to repeat this brouhaha again.

We seem to live in a world that will only roll out the red carpet to those who are in high places. We idolize politicians, doctors, lawyers, movie stars and athletes, but seldom do you see someone ask the grocery store bagger for an autograph. The reason, a lot of times, that we play favorites is in hopes we will get a perk, a bonus, a break, a loan from our efforts. God doesn't show favorites in whom He loves and whom He doesn't, does He? Can you imagine a Savior who would only die for those who would pay Him back later? Our light shines brighter when we treat everyone the same—the class clown or the superstar. It's not hard to treat the gifted with special effort, but how about those who aren't the socially accepted types? Then you need God's help. Come on, take a gamble and treat the peons like a president.

☆ ☆ ☆

Further Study: Find someone who'd never expect it, and roll out the red carpet for them today. How does it feel to love the unloved?

GIFTS

ANATOMY

For the body is not one member but many.
1 Corinthians 12:14

☆ ☆ ☆

A little boy was asked to write an essay on the different parts of the human body (anatomy). Here is what he wrote:

"Your head is kind of round and hard, and your brains are in it and your hair, too. Your face is the front of your head where you eat and make faces. Your neck is what keeps your head out of your collar and it's hard to keep clean. Your shoulders are sort of shelves where you hook your suspenders on. Your stummick is something that if you don't eat often enough it hurts, and spinach don't help none. Your spine is a long bone in your back that keeps you from folding up. Your back is always behind you no matter how quick you turn around. Your arms you got to have to pitch with and so you can reach the butter. Your fingers stick out of your hands so you can throw a curve and add up rithmetick. Your legs is what if you have not got two of, you can't get to first base. Your feet are what you run on, your toes are what get stubbed. And that's all their is of you, except what's inside, and I never saw that."

Just as the human earth-suit has many parts with specific functions, so do we as a Christian family. The problem seems to be that we function more as individuals than as a family. We seem to have inserted the letter "I" in the word team. We all are different in the way we look, talk, act and function, but we have a common thread that is supposed to sew us together–Christ. Each one of us brings to the table a whole new set of goals and gifts used to further the kingdom as a body of believers. Think about it (I'll wait here!) . . . the hand has a separate function from the foot, the foot is different than the knee, the knee does not perform as an eye, and so on. As you look around, you'll notice that each Christian brings a different gift or talent to the family and together we mount a mighty force for the Kingdom. Now let's go team!

☆ ☆ ☆

Further Study: What do you feel your gifts are? Are you, at times, intimidated by others' gifts? Why? Do you function as a part or separate from the body?

LAUGHTER

WAYS TO HANDLE STRESS

A time to weep and a time to laugh.
Ecclesiastes 3:4

☆ ☆ ☆

We all need to grab a break from this treadmill of life from time to time. Since we are such creatures of habit, we need to break the mold, spread our wings, and just be strange for a minute . . . totally out of character. The following list is an example of some strange things we can do to handle those tough times in life. You can add to this list or take away, but hopefully, it will get your creative juices flowing down the funnel of fun. Take a look:

Pop some popcorn without putting the lid on.
Use your Mastercard to pay your Visa (just kidding).
When someone says, "Have a nice day," tell them you have other plans.
Forget the diet center and send yourself a candy gram.
Make a list of things to do that you've already done.
Dance in front of your pets.
Draw underwear on the natives in *National Geographic.*
Drive to work in reverse (a joke).
Reflect on your favorite episode of "The Flintstones" during class.
Refresh yourself: put your tongue on a frozen steel guardrail.
Start a funny rumor and see if you recognize it when it comes back.
Write a short story using alphabet soup.
Stare at people through a fork and pretend they are all in jail.
Make up a language and ask people for directions.
Put your clothes on backwards and pretend nothing's wrong (walk backward).

Note: these ideas are not to taken literally; they're just thought provokers. You make up your own list. Live a little!

☆ ☆ ☆

Further Study: How often do you laugh? How do you handle stress? Do you take yourself too seriously at times? Why?

PEACE OF GOD

PEACE TREATY

He will stand and shepherd his flock in the strength of the Lord, in the majesty of the name of the Lord his God. And they will live securely, for then his greatness will reach to the ends of the earth. And He will be their peace.

Micah 5:4-5

☆ ☆ ☆

Since George Washington's first inauguration in April of 1789 through Bill Clinton's reign, we have had wars and rumors of wars to live with. For the past 200 years of America's history, we have survived World War I and II, Korea, Vietnam, and most recently the Gulf War. The war that seems to have left its mark in our history books is the Civil War era. It was four years of vicious, devastating warfare that cost hundreds of thousands of lives, divided families and friends, and left half the country smoldering. The war was between the North's commercial economic structure (railroads, canals, steamships, etc.) and the South's agrarian slave-based economy, which provided cotton, tobacco, rice and corn. The simplest explanation for the war might be that the Southerners didn't want to be told how to live their lives. The struggle for control was a powder keg with a long burning fuse that ultimately exploded with horrifying results which we still see today.

As long as we all live on the same planet, there will be rumors of war. Where you have people, you have a difference in philosophies, ideas, and ways of doing things. Everyone always thinks his/her way is best and holds the mentality "my way or the highway." Take a look back since the division of Cain and Abel, and you'll see two paths, two ways. We all are looking for that plot of peace to seek shelter and refuge in, a quiet spot which is secure for ourselves and our families removed from the violence and destruction. Let me tell you that the only peace we'll ever have in this lifetime is with our Lord. He is the producer of peace, Savior of security and the refuge of redemption. He will stand between us and an angry world. He will fill the gap of peace and war, and finally, He will return to take us to that shelter in the sky we call heaven. He is the Prince of Peace, you know.

☆ ☆ ☆

Further Study: If Webster's dictionary called you to define peace, what would you tell them? Where do you seek peace? Why do we want peace so badly?

PEACE OF GOD

PEACE TREATY

He will stand and shepherd his flock in the strength of the Lord, in the majesty of the name of the Lord his God. And they will live securely, for then his greatness will reach to the ends of the earth. And He will be their peace.

Micah 5:4-5

☆ ☆ ☆

Since George Washington's first inauguration in April of 1789 through Bill Clinton's reign, we have had wars and rumors of wars to live with. For the past 200 years of America's history, we have survived World War I and II, Korea, Vietnam, and most recently the Gulf War. The war that seems to have left its mark in our history books is the Civil War era. It was four years of vicious, devastating warfare that cost hundreds of thousands of lives, divided families and friends, and left half the country smoldering. The war was between the North's commercial economic structure (railroads, canals, steamships, etc.) and the South's agrarian slave-based economy, which provided cotton, tobacco, rice and corn. The simplest explanation for the war might be that the Southerners didn't want to be told how to live their lives. The struggle for control was a powder keg with a long burning fuse that ultimately exploded with horrifying results which we still see today.

As long as we all live on the same planet, there will be rumors of war. Where you have people, you have a difference in philosophies, ideas, and ways of doing things. Everyone always thinks his/her way is best and holds the mentality "my way or the highway." Take a look back since the division of Cain and Abel, and you'll see two paths, two ways. We all are looking for that plot of peace to seek shelter and refuge in, a quiet spot which is secure for ourselves and our families removed from the violence and destruction. Let me tell you that the only peace we'll ever have in this lifetime is with our Lord. He is the producer of peace, Savior of security and the refuge of redemption. He will stand between us and an angry world. He will fill the gap of peace and war, and finally, He will return to take us to that shelter in the sky we call heaven. He is the Prince of Peace, you know.

☆ ☆ ☆

Further Study: If Webster's dictionary called you to define peace, what would you tell them? Where do you seek peace? Why do we want peace so badly?

STUBBORNNESS

MALE MENTALITY

But these people are stubborn and have a rebellious heart.
Jeremiah 5:23

☆ ☆ ☆

Between two farms near Valleyview, Alberta, you will find two fences running parallel for half a mile, only two feet apart. Why two fences when only one is necessary? Two farmers named Paul and Oscar had a disagreement that erupted into an all out feud. Paul wanted to build a fence between their land and split the cost, but Oscar disagreed and refused to contribute. Paul wanted to keep cattle on his land, so he went ahead and built the fence on his own. Afterward, Oscar said to Paul, "I see we have a fence now." "What do you mean we?" Paul replied. "I had the property line surveyed and built the fence two feet inside my property line, which means some of my land is outside the fence. Now if any of your cows step foot on my property, I'll shoot 'em for trespassing." Oscar knew this was not a joke, so when he eventually decided to use the land adjoining Paul's pasture, he was forced to build a second fence only two feet from the first. Oscar and Paul are both gone now, but their double fence stands as a monument to the high price paid for stubbornness.

It's amazing just what sparks a "tiff" between people. Often folks are all out to win with no regard for the feelings or concerns of others. It's the "my way or the highway" mentality that gets most of us in trouble. Why can't we have a servant's attitude and heart when it comes to dealing with each other? Don't you realize we were all placed on the same planet for a reason? "Getting along" is only difficult when we create an environment (with attitude and behavior) that makes it difficult. What if Christ had an attitude that only exalted Me, Myself and I? (Answer: We'd be in a pickle about now!) Learn to live in harmony, not harassment. Give a little, and you'll get a lot.

☆ ☆ ☆

Further Study: Are you a stubborn person? What makes you want to be stubborn (specific areas)? Does having a "my way" attitude make life easier or more difficult? How can you work on that area?

THE BOA CONSTRICTOR

Now the serpent was more crafty than any beast of the field which the Lord God had made.
Genesis 3:1

☆ ☆ ☆

I have a big problem with reptiles that slither on their bellies and scare the pants off people. In college my bright roommate decided life wasn't exciting enough, so he purchased a rather large boa constrictor snake. That's right . . . a third roomie–one that eats people and never sleeps. My roommate (not the slimy one) fed his new found companion (named Bert) rats for an afternoon snack. Yuck-eee! You talk about gross! Can you believe you can actually purchase rats to use for snake food? Don't rats have a humane society to protect them? (Guess not . . . who has a rat for a pet anyway? Don't answer that!) Let me get to my point. I always thought that constrictors squeezed their prey to death, then ate it whole. Not true–these snakes wrap their slithery bodies around a victim, wait for them to exhale and squeeze down. Wait for an exhale, squeeze down, another exhale, squeeze tighter until the prey can't inhale again and finally dies.

Do you recall anyone in the Bible who could possibly go by the code name "Serpent?" I believe he first made his debut on stage in the Broadway hit, "In The Garden." Satan is (notice I didn't say was) a constrictor of life who squeezes the joy out of life when we fall prey to sin. Whether pre-marital sex, compulsive dishonesty, bitterness, or hatred, sin will choke you out like a candle with no oxygen. Steer clear of the serpent and his deceiving tactics of tightening that will result in death (physical and spiritual). Believe you me, having a snake as a roommate was bad, but as a master, it would be worse.

☆ ☆ ☆

Further Study: Why was Satan called a serpent? What does it mean in the verse above that the snake was more crafty than any beast of the field? What does Satan tighten down on in your life to squeeze the joy out of being a Christian?

GET READY

Be ye therefore ready also.
Luke 12:40

☆ ☆ ☆

One of the greatest needs today is to be a Christian ready to face Christ at any turn. This is about as easy as eating soup with a fork. The biggest battle in our journey is not against sin, difficulties or circumstances, but against being so wrapped up in what we do in our daily trek that we aren't ready to face Christ around the next corner. Our one great need is not for a defining creed or figuring out if we are of any value to God, but to be ready to face Him. The funny (mostly scary) thing about this subject is that Jesus rarely comes when or where we expect. Rather, we find Him when we least expect and always in the most illogical situations and circumstances. The only way a believer can keep true to our Lord is by being ready for His surprise visits. It's not what we are doing, but who we are in the deep closets of our soul that is important. He wants our lives to reflect the attitude of child-wonder. If we honestly want to "be ready" for Jesus, we must stop being religious and be spiritually sincere. Our culture will stereotype you as impractical and dreamy if you live out a life of "looking off to Jesus," but when He does appear in the midst of a trial, or when the heat is turned up in your life, you will be the only one who is ready. Don't trust, obey, follow or listen to anyone, even the finest saint who ever walked this planet, if they hinder your sight of Christ. Get ready today, don't wait for tomorrow . . . it could be too late.

☆ ☆ ☆

Further Study: If Christ were to come today, this very minute, would you be ready? What do you need to do to get yourself ready? What does "ready" mean? Describe who you know that you feel is ready.

JESUS

SEEKING YOUR SAVIOR

There is no Savior besides me.
Isaiah 43:11

⋏ ⋏ ⋏

The sun had just risen over the small village of Plelo in German-occupied France on a hot summer day in 1944. A 15-year-old boy didn't understand why he and his community had been brought before a firing squad in the town square. Maybe it was because they had hidden out from a unit of Marquisards (French underground freedom fighters), or perhaps merely to satisfy the blood-thirsty German commander's need for revenge. No matter the reason, they knew they were about to die. As the young boy stood in front of the firing squad, memories of childhood began to pop into his mind–running around the French countryside, playing in the streets, kick-ball games. Most of all, he feared the feeling of bullets entering his body. He hoped no one would see his tears or hear his cries, so he exhaled and closed his eyes. Suddenly, he heard exploding mortar behind the building, tanks rolling into town. The German firing squad ran for cover and the boy saw a unit of U.S. tanks led by Bob Hamsley. After three hours, 50 Nazis were dead and another 50 were taken prisoner. In 1990 the town of Plelo honored Captain Hamsley on the very spot (town square) where dozens of village residents were nearly executed. The man who initiated the search for Hamsley and the ceremony honoring him was the former 15-year-old boy. He was determined to find the man who saved his life and honor him.

This is a touching story about remembering and honoring a savior. What a neat testimony of a man who was indebted to a savior (Captain Hamsley) and refused to go through life without recognizing him. Never forget the Savior (Jesus) who rescued you.

✫ ✫ ✫

Further Study: Do you forget your Savior? Why? How can you honor Him? Will you? How? When?

I GIVE YOU MY WORD

Let your yes be yes and your no be no.
James 5:12

☆ ☆ ☆

The Boy Scout Oath: "On my honor I will do my best to do my duty to God and my country and to obey the Scout Law; to help other people at all times; to keep myself physically strong, mentally awake and morally straight."

There it is, just as easy to quote now as it was when I was younger. This oath is what every Boy and Girl Scout promises to live. This life in which we live is full of oaths. You see it when the President of the United States takes office, you repeat it before you take the witness stand in a court of law, you'll be in awe of it when two people are exchanging rings at the altar for marriage, and you read it when Moses came down from Mt. Sinai glowing after his encounter with God Almighty. I realize that saying and living are on two sides of the freeway. It's one thing to put your hand up or mumble the words, but following through and committing to what you just said is tough.

We seem to have lost something other than our wallet or car keys from prior generations. I'm not sure if they forgot to teach us, we didn't listen or maybe we just don't see the value in it. What? Your word. It's a rare quality to see surviving today when someone gives you his word and also follows through with the commitment. When someone says he will be there at 2:00 and he arrives 10 minutes early, you can bet on it. In a society of red tape and paper work, we could sure do ourselves a favor by closing out business contracts with a handshake and a verbal commitment instead of a novel of words. How about teachers giving you a test and letting you take it home on your word that you won't cheat, or committing to your date's parents that you will go where you promise to go? Promises and oaths are interchangeable words, and whether you're a Scout or a Christian, they are worth taking and keeping for the rest of your life.

☆ ☆ ☆

Further Study: How good is your word? Why is it so tough to commit to a promise? Is your word good today?

A COACH'S PERSPECTIVE

That they (people of Israel) *may see and recognize, and consider and gain insight as well, that the hand of the Lord has done this.*
Isaiah 41:10

☆ ☆ ☆

It was the summer of 1970, and I was playing for the Dallas Little League All-Star team under Coach Hayden Fry, now coach of the University of Iowa football team. Coach had a rule that no one could steal a base unless he first gave the sign. This upset me a lot because I felt I knew the pitchers and catchers well enough to tell when I could and couldn't steal. In one game I decided to steal without a sign from Coach (mistake). I got a good jump off the pitcher and easily beat the throw to second base. After I shook the dirt off my uniform, I smiled with delight, feeling proud of myself. After the game, Coach Fry took me aside and explained why he hadn't given me the sign to steal and why what I did was foolish. The batter behind me was Eddie, the homerun slugger. When I stole second, first base was left open, so the other team walked the slugger intentionally, taking the bat out of his hands. The next batter hadn't been hitting the ball well, so Coach intended to send in a pinch hitter to try and drive in the men (me) on base. That left Coach Fry without bench strength later in the game when he needed it.

The problem was, I saw only my capability to steal. Coach Fry was watching the whole game, not just one inning. We too, see only so far, but God sees the bigger picture. When He sends us a signal, it's wise to obey, no matter how much we may think we know. God is the coach in the game of life because we aren't capable. Listen and obey, it's the only way.

☆ ☆ ☆

Further Study: Have you ever done anything on your own call despite warnings from your authority? Did you blow the game for your team, family, friends?

FALSE PROPHECY

How Do You Know?

But the prophet who shall speak a word presumptuously in My name which I have not commanded him to speak in the name of other gods, that prophet shall die.
Deuteronomy 18:20

✩ ✩ ✩

What comes to your mind when you hear the word "prophet?" Do you think of someone of high intelligence, royal or divine insight; someone who is over qualified and underpaid? If you were to die today, go to heaven and find yourself sitting down at a table next to or across from Habakkuk, Amos, Zephaniah, Haggai, Malachi, Obadiah, Zechariah, Hosea, Joel or Ezra, would you ask them . . . "Now who are you guys?" The other two-thirds of your Bible is filled with former or latter prophets who were appointed by Yahweh to be spokespersons for Him. They may have come under the title of seer, servant, messenger, man of God or sons of prophets. The proof that they were legitimate was if they spoke in the name of God, spoke by revelation or inspiration, had high moral character, had a true call of God, if their message was authenticated by signs, if their message was in agreement with previous revelation and if there was fulfillment of predictions. Their goal was to edify and encourage the believers in God into a deeper, more obedient relationship with Him.

It is important to distinguish between popular conceptions of who were prophets and those who were truly chosen by God. Jesus demonstrated prophetic characteristics in His message, predictions of the future, being sent by God, speaking only words of the Father, and in His ministry. 1 Corinthians 13:8 says that prophecy will cease, but it doesn't say when. A false prophet was not the same as a pagan prophet because false prophets were and are prophesying in the name of God (Yahweh). My purpose here is not to figure out if there are or are not modern day prophets. It's to get you excited about the prophets in your Bible so you will study them and to educate you on who they are. I want you to have a foundation of knowledge to call their "bluff" when someone you see or hear claims to be a prophet, yet his/her qualifications don't match up to those in Deuteronomy 18. Beware!

✩ ✩ ✩

Further Study: Read the qualifications to be a prophet of Yahweh in Deuteronomy 18:15-22. How can you tell in our culture today if someone is a "true" or "false" prophet? What are you to do if you find yourself being led by a false prophet?

DECISIONS

HALF FULL OR HALF EMPTY

*Caleb quieted the people before Moses and said, "We should by all means go up
and take possession of it, we shall overcome it." But the other men had
gone up with him too and said, "We are not able to go up against
the people for they are too strong for us."*
Numbers 13:30-31

☆ ☆ ☆

A great test to see if people are optimists or pessimists is to show them
a clear glass containing water up to the half-way point. Now ask if the glass
is half empty or half full. You will find most of the time that the majority will
view the glass of water as half empty. This is not wrong, just a fact. Most people always see situations in life as half empty, too. The masses will, most of
the time, see life's negatives far before they see its positives.

If you have ever read the story of Joshua and Caleb, you have read a story
of two perspectives. In a nutshell God has told the people of Israel that the
"Land of Milk and Honey" is theirs for the taking. A bunch of spies (or scouts)
are sent into the land of Canaan to check it out and bring back a report of its
condition. They were to find out if the land was safe, had good pastures, grew
good vegetation and would be a good home for three million new Israelite
residents. Of all the scouts only two came back positive; the rest saw a glass
half empty. Yes, the land was perfect, but it did have a few bugs to work out,
namely, mean thugs called Amelikites who could be dealt with. God calls you
daily to go into your home, school, clubs, team, or circle of friends and take a
stand, take up residency for Him. Yes, it will be tough, and there will be opposition, but remember He took care of them on the cross at Calvary. Will you
return to Him as the majority with a half empty report or a Joshua and Caleb
report of half full? Think about it.

☆ ☆ ☆

Further Study: How do you view the cup? Do you see more negative in God's
plans or positive? Do you feel you are an overcomer and capable of accomplishing anything with Him? Why or why not?

WORLDLINESS

ASSOCIATE STAFF

For all that is in the world, the lust of the flesh and the lust of the eyes and the boastful pride of life, is not from the Father, but is from the world.
1 John 2.16

☆ ☆ ☆

The more you look like Christ, the more the world is gonna' treat you like Him. It is a frightening thing when you arrive at the point in your spiritual journey that you decide to truly be an ambassador for Jesus. The scary part about it is that when you pledge allegiance to the flag of America, you live and associate as a citizen of America. However, when you pledge allegiance to Christ, you disassociate yourself from the world and proclaim heaven as your homeland. Being a Christian is more than walking down the aisle, attending church or wearing a cross. The price Jesus paid was a heavy one. You may not get ridiculed and alienated when you associate with a church, youth group, Bible study or religious movement, but you do when you say, "I'm a follower of Jesus Christ." The penalty (really a privilege) is when you finally come to that point of locking arms with Christ.

Years ago a country song summed up what being a real Christian in a real hurting world is all about . . . "If you don't stand for something, then you'll fall for anything." The "something" has got to be Jesus. The "anything" might be sex, money, status, cults, and so on. Ask God to plant deep in the chambers of your heart a soul of passion to follow Him, knowing that the cost will include pain and suffering. I don't know where folks get off on all this hoopla that Christianity is a total joy ride. Either I am reading a different Bible, or they are not hearing the truth that the adventure, called Christianity, takes endurance and perseverance. Pain is a part of the curriculum of God's classroom, so prepare for a tough test, but one worth passing.

☆ ☆ ☆

Further Study: Why is association with Christ so costly? To whom do people say you are pledged? How can you handcuff yourself to Christ from now on? Why is ridicule a part of Christianity?

A FASHION STATEMENT

Likewise I want women to adorn (dress) *themselves with proper clothing, modestly and discreetly.*
1 Timothy 2:9

★ ★ ★

Look no further than your local newsstand to see the latest styles trickling down the fashion pipe of the world. *Vogue, Seventeen, GQ, Glamour, Self, Fashion & Design, Elle,* and of course, *Cosmopolitan* to name a few. Fashion in this world of ours changes as often as weather patterns. One minute you're making a fashion "statement," and the next you're frowned upon as being out-of-date. If I have this figured out, the way I see it is that if you just hang on to the same clothes for a few years, they'll come back in style (i.e. bell bottoms, neons, wide ties, etc.). Now don't get me wrong, some things will never be out-to-lunch, but that's not the norm. Psychologists claim that there are several ways people show their inward desires in an outward expression. For example, what we desire can be seen in the sort of car we drive, hairstyle we sport and clothes we wear. The only problem with this "expression" is that it seems to be moving in the "less is better" direction. The shorter the dress or shorts, the tighter the pants, the more high cut and revealing the swim-suit the better . . . for who?

I know about right now you have decided this whole devotion is targeted at the female and yep, that's a good guess. Why? Because women are like a crock pot (heat up slowly), and men are like a microwave (heat up fast). In other words, men are turned on by sight much easier than women. So when they see a "cute young thing" running around half clothed, they get aroused quickly, which in turn leads to lustful thoughts (Philippians 4:8). Please, I beg of you, from the knees of all men trying to seek God's ways on everything, watch what you wear and how you present yourself to men. I don't know of anything that can steal a man's heavenly perspective quicker than a worldly outfit. I'm not telling you to buy all your clothes at the local Thrift Store, but I am asking you to ask yourself one question before you step into your closet or throw down the credit card . . . how comfortable would you feel if Jesus stepped into the room while you were wearing what you had on? Make a fashion statement for Jesus . . . dress modestly.

★ ★ ★

Further Study: Do you dress modestly or risky? How does this affect the opposite sex? What does Luke 17:2 mean?

GROWTH CHART

I planted, Apollos watered, but God causes the growth.
1 Corinthians 3:6

✳ ✳ ✳

Growing up can be one of the most fun experiences in life. Three sons fill our house with wrestling, war, GI Joe's, monster grocery lists, scabby knees, dirty clothes and intense competition–you can imagine the total chaos. We measure the boys each month on a growth chart attached to the wall. One day, the chart slipped from the wall, and my oldest son, Daniel, tried to re-hang it. As he did, the chart slipped off the nail and rested flush with the floor . . . about four inches short of the real height. Daniel got his brother, Dustin, up against the chart the next day, then came running into the room yelling, "Mommy! Mommy! Dustin grew four inches this month." My wife responded, "That's impossible, he's only two years old. Let's go see." They walked up to the bedroom where suspicions were confirmed–the chart was set at an improper height.

We can easily repeat Daniel's mistake in gauging our spiritual growth. Compared to a shortened scale, we may appear better than we are, or more mature in Christ. It is only when we stand against the cross, that "great leveler of men" (as A.T. Robertson called it), that we cannot think of ourselves more highly than we should. Jesus must be the standard against which we measure ourselves. When we stand against friends or society, we elevate our spiritual mentality. Match up with Christ, and you'll remain focused and on track. Growth is a slow, steady, daily process that takes time and effort through Christ to accomplish.

✩ ✩ ✩

Further Study: Do you compare yourself to others? To what standard do you compare yourself? How do you match up? What is the danger of comparing yourself to worldly standards?

A CHAIN REACTION

Pilate had a notice prepared and fastened to the cross. It read:
"Jesus of Nazareth, King of the Jews."
John 19:19

☆ ☆ ☆

It took place in Los Alamos on May 21, 1946, and it involved a young scientist performing an experiment necessary for testing the atomic bomb in the waters of the south Pacific at Bikini. He'd successfully completed the experiment several times before, but this test would be different. In an effort to determine the amount of U-235 needed for a chain reaction, he would push two hemispheres of uranium together. Then, just at critical mass, he would push them apart with his screwdriver (sounds real hi-tech to me), instantly stopping the chain reaction. As he was about to separate the masses, the screwdriver slipped and the hemispheres of uranium came too close together. Instantly, the room was filled with a bluish haze. Young Louis Slotin reacted and instead of diving for cover and maybe saving himself, he tore the two hemispheres apart bare-handed, thus stopping the chain reaction. By this heroic act, he saved the lives of seven others in the lab, but exposed himself to the dangerous radiation of Uranium 235. Nine days later, he died in agony, but his colleagues survived.

Nineteen centuries ago the Son of the living God walked directly into sin's most concentrated radiation and willingly allowed Himself to be touched by its curse (death). But get this, by this heroic act of courage on the cross, He broke the chain reaction of a sinful world with no hope for a future and broke the power of sin that began in the laboratory of Eden. He died so that you and I might walk away unharmed into the glory of heaven–what a deal!

☆ ☆ ☆

Further Study: What do you feel is the most significant event in the Bible? Why? Is what Christ did on the cross important in your life? Do you see Jesus as a modern-day hero, or a forgotten fable?

WIZARD OF OZ

And the God of peace will soon crush Satan under your feet,
and the grace of our Lord Jesus will be with you.
Romans 16:20

☆ ☆ ☆

They seem to be household names in all generations. Dorothy, Toto, Scarecrow, Tin Man, Cowardly Lion and the Wicked Witch are the familiar characters in *The Wizard of Oz*, along with scenes of flying monkeys, dark and mysterious castles, a city of emerald green, bright red slippers, the yellow brick road and a farmhouse spinning up to heaven. My personal favorite adventure in Oz is the way Dorothy got back to Kansas. The intimidating Wizard first required items scavenged from the Wicked Witch. The gang returned with the items, but the big Oz reneged on the deal and tried to run them off. It looked as if there'd be no brain for the Scarecrow, no courage for the Lion, no heart for the Tin Man, and definitely no plane ticket for Dorothy and Toto . . . that is, until the little rat-dog went around back and pulled back the curtain to expose a harmless, little, gray-haired man, claiming to be the Wizard of Oz.

Satan, the fierce lion that roams the earth stalking his victims, is in reality a pussycat. Yes, he does have a lot of tricks up his sleeve, but he was defeated once and for all on a hill called Calvary. The crucifixion of Jesus proved Satan's lack of power and exposed him for what he is . . . a wimp of a wizard. As a Christian, you are capable of disarming this enemy and his ragged brigade of blundering bean-headed demons at any given moment. You have no need to fear the enemy, but you must be wise to his deceiving smokescreens. No matter your age, size or years you have been a believer (Toto was a small dog, notice), you can defeat this enemy with a wave of your Christlike wand. Click your heels together and say, "I am a winner" three times. You will eventually go home, not to Kansas, but heaven.

☆ ☆ ☆

Further Study: Are you aware of Satan? Are you scared of him? Think about all the power of Christ you have in your life to defeat and expose him.

DISCIPLE

PRUNING

Those whom I love, I rebuke and disciple; be excited and therefore repent.
Revelation 3:19

✦ ✦ ✦

Growing up in an area with lots of trees, many of which planted themselves right smack in the middle of my frontyard, was fun but exhausting. As you know, where trees abound, so does a multitude of leaves each fall. People visiting our home used to make this awful big deal about the beautiful fall foliage, but it foreshadowed raking and bagging to me. Every year, like a tradition, my father and I would recover out of storage the chainsaw and go to pruning the monster pecan trees, all 21 of them. Talk about a task that seemed endless! It was almost like we were creating more of a mess than making an improvement. Consider the viewpoint of the tree also. Man, did I think that all that cutting and cracking would produce some awful pain (if trees do feel). My dad could make a 30 foot high massive tree look like a nub in just a matter of a few coarse cuts. Little did my feeble mind know that this whole process was for the benefit, not the harm, of the trees' future growth. God, too, periodically goes and gets His spiritual saw and begins to trim off areas in your life that don't look like or act like His Son Jesus. Once as I watched a woodcarver chisel on a block of wood, another observer asked him what he was making. "An Indian warrior," the woodcarver replied. "How do you know which parts to carve away?" the onlooker then asked. "Everything that doesn't look like an Indian," said the carver.

God's purpose in discipling you is to make you better, not to kill or destroy you. Realize He only does this pruning because He loves you. Your parents only put parameters and rules around you because they care, not because they want to hurt you. God only wants you to succeed in this journey we call Christianity, and one way is to prune off the dead or heavy branches which could eventually destroy the tree (you). Next time your God or your loving parents prune away on you, look past the momentary pain and see the benefits that will come . . . a person who looks more like Jesus.

✧ ✧ ✧

Further Study: How has God pruned you lately? Did you feel His love? How do your parents show they care?

BACK TO THE BASICS

In those days there was no king of Israel; everyone
did what was right in their own eyes.
Judges 21:25

☆ ☆ ☆

Americans have been slow to see that as the old moral map fades, we won't be left with another alternative, but with no map at all. "Sin" by the end of the 19th century was fading as a belief, and how could it be otherwise. After all, sin means transgression against God. In our culture God has been replaced by fortune, and fortune makes no moral judgments. Evil has turned into bad luck, and good luck became the new benediction. To pray for the grace of God has become more embarrassing than to hope for luck. This way of thinking has changed the meaning of death, since there is no one to whom the dying are going. People are so busy "doing" that they forget why they are doing; we have become occupied with routine pleasures that are fading fast. We are a people who are going, but are not sure where. We are a culture with no rules, guidelines, morals, values, virtues, standards, law and no god.

We as a body of believers need to get back to the basics. Vince Lombardi, the diciest coach of the Super Bowl champs, was famous for coming into the locker room after a Green Bay Packer loss, tossing a football in his hand and explaining to his pro athletes that "this is a football." In other words, we are gonna' have to get back to the basics if we are to win for Christ in our culture.

#1 Sola Scriptura : scripture alone
#2 Solus Christus : Faith alone
#3 Sola Gratia : Grace alone
#4 Sola Fide : To Him be all the Glory!

If we as believers will get back to the foundations of our faith in God and live out these four points, people will be in awe of our Savior. People in our society see so much hypocrisy, deceit, failure and wishy-washy standards it's no wonder they aren't impressed by us or our God. God's Word and our faith, grace lived out in T-shirts and tennis shoes in our earth suits, will bring glory to our Lord and Savior. This sort of lifestyle will bring repentance and national reformation, which is much needed at this stage of the game . . . don't ya' think?

☆ ☆ ☆

Further Study: Why do we as a whole make our faith so complicated? How can you live out the Bible, your faith and grace? Why are these areas so important?

SEARCH AND RESCUE

For the Son of Man has come to seek and to save that which was lost.
Luke 19:10

✝ ✝ ✝

On the night of April 15, 1912, the Titanic sunk to the floor of the Atlantic, some two and a half hours after hitting an iceberg that tore a 300 foot gash in her starboard side. Although 20 life-boats and rafts were launched, they were too few and only partially filled. Most passengers ended up struggling in the icy seas while those in the life boats waited a safe distance from the sinking vessel. Lifeboat #14 did row back after the "unsinkable" ship slipped from sight to chase cries in the darkness, seeking to save a precious few. No other boat joined #14 for the rescue mission (even though they were only about half full), fearing that a swarm of unknown swimmers might flip their safe boat and swamp them in the frigid seas. Members of the rescue mission that eventually found the life-boats never quite understood how fear (selfish fear) could prompt the survivors to not help as they watched hundreds die in the violent sea that night.

In His mission statement, Jesus says that He has "come to seek and save" and has commissioned us to do the same. I find that most Christians have good hearts and a willing spirit, but they often go down in defeat to the arch rival, fear. While people drown in the treacherous waters around us, we are tempted to stay all safe and dry and make certain no one rocks our security boat. What we don't understand is that the life boats aren't our own, so safety comes only at the expense of the One who overcame His fear with love to save us. Don't let the security and safety of your present position as an heir to the Kingdom, and the fear of rejection, stop you from throwing a life-line to the lost souls bobbing around your daily life. Paddle, boy . . . paddle!

★ ★ ★

Further Study: Do you fear sharing Jesus with someone else? Are you sitting in your nice, safe, cozy world watching and hearing the cries of the drowning victims? Make it your goal to tell a lost person about the love of Jesus today? (Fear later!)

EXAMPLE OF CHRIST

CHRIST IN THE CRISIS

Show yourself an example of those who believe.
1 Timothy 4:12

☆ ☆ ☆

There's an interesting account of a lady named Judy Anderson, who grew up as the daughter of a missionary in Zaire. As a little girl, she went to a day-long rally celebrating the 100th anniversary of Christian missionaries coming to Zaire. After a long day of speeches and festive music, an old man came out of the crowd and insisted that he be allowed to speak. He told the crowd that he soon would die and that he alone had some important information to share. He explained that when the missionaries came 100 years before, his people thought they were strange and their message unusual. The tribal leaders decided to test the missionaries by slowly poisoning them to death. Over a period of months and years, all the missionaries and their families died one by one. The old man said, "It was as we watched how they died that we decided we wanted to live as Christians."

That story had gone untold for 100 years. Those faithful followers died and never knew why they were dying. They stayed true to their tasks and loyal to their Lord, not knowing what an impact, even to their last few breaths, they made on thousands of viewers who saw Christ in the crisis. You don't have to be in Africa or a missionary for folks to see the Christ in you. It's easy to be a Christian during those high times, but what about when you're in the valleys of life? Are you gonna' be one of those followers who takes Christ with you, even to your grave? I hope and pray so!

☆ ☆ ☆

Further Study: Do people see Christ in the middle of your crisis? How much impact does your every reaction have on others? How many eyes watch you even though you're not aware of them?

CHRISTIAN RACE

SHINE JESUS SHINE

The lamp of the body is the eye, if therefore your eye is clear,
your whole body will be full of light.
Matthew 6:22

⭐ ⭐ ⭐

Talk about an outdoor experience! Little did I know when I accepted an invitation to go on an elk hunting trip in a five-million acre wilderness in Idaho, it would be such an adventure! Our trusty guide led us for five days over 9,000-foot mountain tops and through pine forests in search of the "Big One." The lessons about life in general and the parallels of my Christian life were as plentiful as mountain daisies in the springtime.

Our home was a tent, our water from a spring, our food . . . home cooked, and our transportation . . . horses and mules (look out wagon train!). Little did I know I would only get four to five hours of sleep a night and be on the back of a horse five hours a day. Each morning at 4:00 a.m. we would ride out of camp straight up the mountains in pitch dark on a 12 inch wide trail next to thousand foot cliffs where only the horse could see, searching for the bugle of a bull elk, relying solely on the eyes of our horse and guide. Never before have I depended on one of the five senses so heavily for my safety and my success in a hunt.

In one of the greatest sermons ever accounted, Jesus refers to the eye in a unique manner. Matthew 6:22 tells us that the "lamp of the body is the eye." The verse goes on to say "if your eye is clear, your whole body will be full of light." What worldly items clog our vision of God? What can you do at home to keep your eye clear? What does the lost society in which we live see if we shine for Christ? During a ride on my horse "Jock," I realized how much we rely on our eyes (the hot-line to our hearts) to guide us toward our goal . . . not elk, but living for Christ. I understood how TV, movies, books and magazines can cause us to be spiritually blind, making us vulnerable as prey. Take a minute to look in a mirror at those beautiful eyes and see if the lamp is lit. If it's dim in there, do what it takes to get it shining brightly again.

⭐ ⭐ ⭐

Further Study: Have you had an eye exam from the Savior lately? How's your light burning today?

ALCOHOL MARCH 25

DRINK FOR THOUGHT

Be not drunk with wine but, be filled with the Spirit.
Ephesians 5:18

✦ ✦ ✦

It can spell T-R-O-U-B-L-E for all of us, and it is the most dangerous drug in general use in our culture today. Pay close attention to this. I am by no means insinuating or tying to "make" you believe one way or another, yet I feel convicted to share this knowledge with you. The Bible gives 637 references to drink or drinking. In those references there are a number of different words which are translated "wine." To fully understand ancient Jewish culture, versus our contemporary western culture, we need to take a look at some of these words.

In the Old Testament there are three key Hebrew words: 1) "yayin," 2) "shekar" and 3) "tirosh." The first word occurs 140 times and is a general term for all classes of wine, alcoholic, and non-alcoholic fermented or unfermented grape beverages. These are mixed or diluted with water. The second word occurs 23 times and is in reference to "strong drink" or unmixed with water. The third word is used 38 times and is often called "sweet wine" or "grape juice." In the New Testament you find 3 Greek terms: 1) "oinos," 2) "sikera" and 3) "gleukos." "Oinos," counterpart to the Old Testament "yayin," is used 33 times; in the process of fermentation it was diluted with water. "Sikera," whose counterpart in the Old Testament was "shekar," means strong drink or unmixed wine. "Gleukos," whose counterpart is "tirosh," refers to "new wine."

O.K. . . . now, what does all this have to do with anything? Distillation was not discovered until about 1500 AD. You can't get around the fact that scripture condemns drunkenness, yet the question arises: "Are today's beer and wine alcohol levels considered to be strong drink?" Biblical "wine" was 2.5% to 2.75% after a 3 to 1 water to wine mixture. "Strong drink" in Biblical times was from 3% to 11% and those who consumed it are described in scripture as "barbarian." All of this is to say that it's your responsibility and personal spirit-felt convictions (via scripture) that need to guide you, not a devotion. Obviously being under age and consuming alcohol is illegal and wrong, along with getting drunk. After that, you make the call. I am not trying to be your holy spirit or sway you, just get you thinking and studying.

✦ ✦ ✦

Further Study: Read: Proverbs 23:20, Romans 13:13, Galatians 5:19 & 21, 1 Corinthians 6:9-11, Proverbs 20:21 and 23:29-31, John 2:10, Luke 1:15, Proverbs 31:6 and Proverbs 3: 9-10.

TRAINING

LET THE GAMES BEGIN

I give you this charge: Preach the word; be prepared in season and out of season; correct, rebuke and encourage with great patience and careful instruction.
2 Timothy 4:2

☆ ☆ ☆

When September rolls around and there is a cool, crisp, nip in the air, the smell of football season is a reality. Friday night football heroes begin to shine under the stadium lights like stars on a dark night. Where I grew up in Texas, the only thing that was worse than missing Sunday church was failing to make it to the hometown high school football game (and that was serious).

We seem to live our lives from season to season, waiting for the next sporting event to transpire. As an athlete competing in these events, you know the time, sacrifice and dedication it takes to pull off a victory on Friday night. Spectators only see a small percentage of what it takes to compete at a winning level and miss the months and hours of prior-to-season preparation training. Paul (the head coach) teaches his player (Timothy) a few lessons and game plans which he, through his years of experience as a competitor, learned about being a Christian player. The book of 2 Timothy is the last book that the apostle Paul wrote before his death. Can you imagine, as his pupil, how you would hang on every last word of wisdom? One of the last gold nuggets of truth given to Timothy was to train, not only in season, but also during the off-season. Championships are won, not during season, but in the off-season training in the weight rooms, on the track and in the gyms after hours. Anyone can be motivated when there are people in the grandstands. Anyone can draw strength from within when the crowd roars with encouragement. But what about when there are no stands and no noise? We, as Christians, always need to be in spiritual training. We continually need to be using God's game plan (His word) to encourage and lead our friends down the narrow path of a championship life walking close to the Savior. If you think that a good cross-town rivalry game is exciting, try God's game . . . it's the best game goin'.

☆ ☆ ☆

Further Study: What ways can you train today for God's game in the upcoming season?

COMMITMENT

COACH BUMBLEBEE

*You became obedient from the heart to that form
of teaching to which you were committed.*
Romans 6:17

☆ ☆ ☆

He was like no man I'd ever seen or been around in all my years. If you looked up the word self-discipline in the dictionary, you'd find his picture next to it. He was a boxing coach for a youth club out of Seattle, Washington, and was training two teenage boxers for a national match that could lead to the 1996 Olympics. The tournament was scheduled to take place in Colorado Springs at the Olympic Training Facility where 350 young boxers were trying to be the next Foreman, Frazier or Ali. This coach went by the name "Coach Bumble-Bee," because aeronautically, bumble-bees shouldn't be able to fly, since their wings are too small for the size of their bodies. But the bees don't know that, so they fly anyway.

Coach Bumble-Bee, now 50 years old, was the driver in a serious bus accident that left him paralyzed from the waist down. For five and a half years he managed his life from a wheelchair until one day, after years of prayer and exercise, Coach began moving his legs again. Today, Coach Bumble-Bee is walking, running, lifting weights and jumping rope with his team members as he works out daily with them in vigorous training.

What faith! What determination! What discipline! What a deal! Told he would never walk again by physicians, but today not only walking, but running. I learned just through watching him work out with his boxers what it means to "never give up on God." The key ingredient to faith is commitment. Trust in God that He is bigger than theories, doctors' analysis and scientific data. You can be a bumble-bee too if you will turn a deaf ear to the crowd of doubters and focus on the Savior. God is and always will be bigger than any problem or situation you get yourself into. If you don't believe me . . . just go watch the bumble-bee fly.

☆ ☆ ☆

Further Study: What does it mean to you to never give up? What makes you want to give up in tough times? What could you do to deepen that never-say-die attitude? Who could help you? Call 'em.

RULES

FENCE WALKERS

Where will you be stricken again, as you continue in your rebellion?
The whole head is sick and the whole heart is faint.

Isaiah 1:5

☆ ☆ ☆

Growing up on a ranch all my life sure didn't make me a cowboy or farmer by any stretch of the imagination. One thing it did do is educate me in a few areas that I most likely would have slept through if it were taught in a classroom. One of my father's adventures was in the cattle ranching industry for a "short" while. I learned a few interesting tidbits about the nature of a cow. First of all, while buying cows at an auction barn (a real adventure), you can't tell which ones will turn out to be producers and which ones may be a problem. The first test comes when you first turn out the new cows into the pasture they'll soon call "home on the range." One of two things will happen. They'll either adapt to the new living arrangements, or they'll begin to walk the fence line to find a hole and escape captivity. I recall my dad just waiting there the first few hours to see which ones would run through the fence. He would immediately trailer those cows back up and take them to the slaughter house for processing into hamburgers and steaks. Once a fence walker, always a fence walker, and they're not worth the trouble of keeping.

Some folks are no different than a cow in that they always look for ways of breaking the barriers (fences) of life, Christian or not. Some folks walk the fences instead of roaming freely in the pasture God has given them. They look for loopholes in scripture, school, sports, business, family, and commitment. We as Christians can be different. We can live freely and enjoy all that we do have, instead of focusing on the few areas of no-no's we have been warned to stay clear of by God and His Word. Rebellious attitudes and behaviors do nothing but get us in trouble which eventually lead to destruction of our own lives. Don't be a fence walker, but be a pasture dweller for God. It's that one loophole that will eventually strangle us and send us to the packing plant.

☆ ☆ ☆

Further Study: What areas of your walk with Christ do you try to escape? Why do you do it? What perspective can we have that will allow us to see all the positives of fences (rules) and not focus on the few negatives?

BROKEN SPIRIT

SIFTED

Simon, Simon, behold, Satan has demanded permission to sift you like wheat.
Luke 22:31

☆ ☆ ☆

Take a moment to read in your Bible the verses prior to this one, beginning at verse 24. Do you see it? Do you see a gold nugget of scripture? What rich verses, full of knowledge and wisdom! We are all trying to make it to the top. We are all striving after a goal or reward that we think (false security) might fill the void in the pit of our stomachs. The problem is that to go up we must first go down, to win we must lose, to gain we must die . . . be sifted. The word sifted means to be separated, strained, screened and sorted out (doesn't sound like fun). If you think about it for a minute, there are only three things we bring to the table—time, talent, and treasure. That's it. No more, no less. Today we are either building upon our kingdom or God's kingdom. When we build on ourselves, we show the world statues in our memory, trophies accepted on our behalf. What is amazing about these treasures of self is that we aren't going to take them with us in eternity. God treasures those who are selfless, those who leave behind a Godly heritage, not an inheritance. Here is a little insight . . . you will not build a treasure for God until you have been "sifted" like wheat. Why? Because the process of sifting out self includes pain and suffering. Sifting is good for our maturing process and can only be accomplished by a divine God who knows what needs to be sifted out of our spiritual lives. Dying to self is a long, hard, process, but worth it when it comes to harvesting a good product.

☆ ☆ ☆

Further Study: What are your talents? How are you using them today? Who gets the credit? Have you ever been sifted before? Was it a good or bad experience? Why or why not? What selfish desires do you think God needs to sift out of your life before He will use you?

DREAMING

DREAM TEAM

Where there is no vision, people perish.
Proverbs 29:18

☆ ☆ ☆

You're never too old for a trip to see Mickey and Minnie Mouse. No place on this planet, I believe, has more fun rides, atmosphere or a better theme than Disney World. There's a story that when Walt Disney purchased the cheap swamp land in Orlando, he first held a huge party and invited everyone who would be a part of building the park. Electricians, plumbers, carpenters, welders, bulldozer operators, concrete layers, painters, designers, engineers and technicians all were included. An architectural firm built a model of the theme parks, and Walt had it displayed at the cook-out so workers could see the dream they were building. His desire was that workers would devote not only their labor to the project, but also their hearts.

Soon after the completion of Disney World, someone said, "Isn't it too bad that Walt Disney didn't live to see this?" Mike Vance, creative director of Disney Studios replied, "He did see it—that's why it's here." People need to dream more and learn to instill their dreams in others. When you stop dreaming, you start dying. Let your uninhibited creative juices flow and dream a little. Catch the vision that God has for you as His child. Dream of a place called heaven where there will be no pain, hate, sorrow, or tears—a place of joy, love, peace, and eternity with your Savior. Be a member of the "Dream Team!"

☆ ☆ ☆

Further Study: What is your biggest dream? Do you share your dreams with others? What stops you from sharing your dreams? Take a 30 minute walk alone this week to dream a little.

SACRIFICE

HECATOMB

*Even if I am being poured out as a drink offering upon
the sacrifice and service of your faith,*
Philippians 2:17

☆ ☆ ☆

Father Maximilian Kolbe was a prisoner at Auschwitz in August, 1941. Another prisoner escaped from the camp, and in reprisal, the Nazis ordered 10 prisoners to die by starvation. Father Kolbe offered to take the place of one of the condemned men. The Nazis kept Kolbe in the starvation bunker for two solid weeks and then put him to death by lethal injection on August 14, 1941. Thirty years later, a survivor of Aushwitz described the effect of Father Kolbe's sacrificial action:

It was an enormous shock to the whole camp. We realized that someone among us in the spiritual dark night of the soul was raising the standard of life on high. Someone unknown, like everyone else, tortured and bereft of name and social standing, went to a horrible death for the sake of someone not even related to him. Therefore it is not true, we cried, that humanity is cast down and trampled in the mud, overcome by oppressors, and overwhelmed by hopelessness. Thousands of prisoners were convinced the true world continued to exist and that our torturers would not be able to destroy it. To say that Father Kolbe died for us or for that person's family is too great a simplification. His death was the salvation of thousands. We were stunned by his act, which became for us a mighty explosion of light in the dark camp.

What an incredible story of self-denial. How our world marvels at such an act of sacrifice. What an impact it would make on you and I to exemplify such sacrificial love for those with whom we have no relation. Jesus started the way for us to follow. It's easy to sacrifice for those we love, but how about those we don't care for or don't even know? Sacrifice with no recognition is only done by divine intervention.

☆ ☆ ☆

Further Study: What is the biggest sacrifice you ever made? When did you do this? What does hecatomb mean? (Look it up.) What is the greatest example of sacrifice you've ever seen or heard of?

JOKE'S ON THEM

We are fools for Christ's sake, but you are prudent in Christ; we are weak, but you are strong; you are distinguished, but we are without honor.
1 Corinthians 4:10

✩ ✩ ✩

I know you've been on one end or the other of this beast before. What might we be talking about here? Look what day it is. Either you are planning or permitting (probably not by choice) a joke for today, and you may not even know you are the victim. If you are the culprit, be nice and do not embarrass the receiver. If you are the receiver . . . take cover. Far too many times it seems that the good guys always lose in this scene, and the bad guys (not really bad) are the ones riding off into the sunset grinning on their trusty horse.

All too often as Christians we appear, from our perspective, as the ones who look the fool in so many cases. Not cheating on a test when everyone else is, not chiming in on a gossip session, not going places we know will get us in trouble, not taking what is being stolen, not acting on a date like what seems to be the norm, and obeying our parents on curfew times, all can get us ridiculed. I'm sure nine out of 10 times the secular world looks at all this Christian commitment and just snickers like the roadrunner after a Wile Coyote flub. We may look like fools today, friend, but we're not living for the moment; we're living for the kingdom to come. Take notice, and notes (if you must), and realize that your Savior Jesus looked like a fool, too. He came into the world in a barn and went out on a mountain of trash called Calvary while hanging on a cross. Guess what? He also ascended into heaven to prepare our beds in His house for our coming . . . now, that's what I call a happy ending.

✩ ✩ ✩

Further Study: When did the world last view you as a fool for Christ? How are you gonna' be seen today?

LOSING YOUR SHELL

"Have faith in God," Jesus answered.
Mark 11:22

✫ ✫ ✫

From time to time a lobster (you know the red creatures with clamps for hands) leaves its shell as part of the growth process. The shell means protection, but when the lobster grows, the shell must be abandoned; otherwise, it would soon become a prison, and eventually a casket. The tricky part for the lobster is the period of time between discarding the old shell and forming the new one. During this vulnerable time, the lobster must be scared to death, as the ocean floor currents cartwheel it from coral to kelp. Hungry schools of fish are ready to make it a part of their dinner. For a while at least, the old shell must look pretty good–even if it had begun to feel a little like a girdle. Sometimes the unfortunate lobster dies between shells, but perhaps that's not as bad as suffocating in a shell that no longer fits. So it is with the life of a growing lobster in the ocean blue.

We aren't much different when it comes to growth. If we didn't have a shell (structure and framework) within which to grow, then I doubt if any of us would have made it this far. Even so, change and growth (maturity) are necessary for survival as a Christian. We don't often see the value at the time of change because it forces us out of our comfort zone and into our faith zone. The only way maturity can take place is to step out into faith and away from security and comfort. Discipleship means being so committed to Jesus that when He asks us to follow Him, to change, to ditch the security and comfort for a ride on faith, to risk it all, to grow, to leave our shells behind and be vulnerable and naked in a tough old world, we answer, "I'm yours, Lord!" Be prepared for anxious (up-tight) moments, fear, doubts, strange looks, and skepticism from others. You know . . . faith doesn't always make sense, but it doesn't have to.

✫ ✫ ✫

Further Study: What is your shell (i.e. comfort zone, security, stronghold)? Why does God call you to leave your shell and become vulnerable? Is that comfortable? Why not? Why are change and maturity two key ingredients to spiritual growth?

BEING DEFINED

Since you died with Christ to the basic principles of this world, why,
as though you still belonged to it, do you submit to its rules.
Colossians 2:20

✭ ✭ ✭

To be defined means to be calculated and prescribed for a stated meaning or purpose. I've never been one to spend free time reading the dictionary, but this thick book contains the meaning of every word in the English language. Even if you never knew a word existed, you'll find it in good old Webster's.

Our society defines thoughts, beliefs, theories and standards through the avenues of music, radio, television, newspapers and magazines. Billions of dollars are made each year by exploiting viewers and readers. These media vessels have also clued in that they can teach and mold a generation's way of thinking. What was considered vulgar and pornographic 30 years ago is now acceptable. Sex, violence, homosexuality, abortion, extra-marital activity and a long list of other things can be seen on prime-time TV, or in million-subscriber magazines. Best selling books and albums (music) are at the top, not because of their brilliance, but because of their corrupt content. Why? We have been trained to listen to, read and watch things that are appealing to our flesh. Pigs love to wallow in the mud and so does a culture living in sin. We must stop defining ourselves and let God, through His Word, remold and reprogram our way of thinking. These worldly vessels (media) should be downright offensive to our spirits and repulsive to our minds. Stop it! Stop letting some guru at the controls of TV, record labels, publishing and so on, define your convictions. Take an active stand against such evils and boycott what's not right. Don't go to bad movies, don't buy CD's that have negative lyrics, don't buy pornographic publications, don't subscribe to liberal newspapers. No, you won't put them out of business, but you will not help fund their efforts, and that is doing something about it.

✭ ✭ ✭

Further Study: Do you feel you are exploited by the media in any way? Are your thoughts, beliefs, and standards being defined by them? What should be defining you? How can you be redefined?

THE HEAT IS ON

And don't be conformed to this world, but be transformed by the renewing
of your mind, that you may prove what the will of God is,
that which is good and acceptable and perfect.
Romans 12.2

✶ ✶ ✶

Can you feel it? It starts with a few butterflies, graduates to sweat, then comes in the form of a knot deep in the pit of your stomach and finally climaxes with short breaths and tight muscles. What is this disease we are talking about? Pressure. It comes in all shapes and sizes and doesn't choose favorites for its victims. We find it around every corner of our lives. Through sports, education, business, medical fields, families and friends, we feel it. One way or another, sometime in your life, you will meet this beast, and you'll either defeat the foe or become clutched in its painful jaws. Pressure is something we all wish we could avoid, but when encountered and victoriously conquered, we realize the process feels better than winning any championship or earning any "A." Realizing that pressure can be a verb, not just a noun and is a state mind, is winning half the battle.

When God created the heavens and the earth, there probably weren't too many pressures that existed other than volcanic. That is until people were painted into the picture. He knew that people would pressure others into situations they wished had never existed. We call it "peer" pressure, but I call it "conforming" pressure. Nobody turns the heat up in our lives to conform to another image worse than friends. True friendship is a sacrificial love, not a conditional one. You were created in God's image, not the world's, and you do live in the world, but you're not of the world cuz' you're a new creature, remember? The best and only way to defeat the pest of pressure is to exterminate with God's purifying Word daily.

Not too long ago Michael Jordan did a commercial that was really fun for Gatorade (which I love to drink), and the slogan was "Be like Mike!" With no disrespect to Michael, I personally think I'll keep trying to be like Christ. It may not allow you to dunk, but it will win you victory in life.

✶ ✶ ✶

Further Study: What pressure do you face today? How are you going to defeat it?

THE CROSS

T.G.I.F.

God demonstrated His own love for us, in that while
we were still sinners, Christ died for us (you).
Romans 5:8

☆ ☆ ☆

We hear it all the time . . . T.G.I.F. . . . . thank God it's Friday! Most folks throw this term around like a monkey does a banana peel and don't have a clue what it really means. Most use it without any reverence to or for God, and they are just bustin' at the seams because it signals the last of the work week. It allows folks to go ballistic for two days each week when they can relax, play, take a nap, and basically just "do their own thing." The Friday before Easter, you know chocolate bunnies and sugar eggs, is called Good Friday. It's a day where millions of believers in Christ all over this planet are mindful of what God did for them through Christ, His Son, 2,000 years previously. Why is it so good, when it marks a dreadful day when a blameless lamb was sent to slaughter on a cross at Calvary for you and me? That sure doesn't sound like my definition of good by any stretch of the imagination. Sounds more like a "day that Jesus went down in defeat" than it does a day we should celebrate each year.

The apostle Paul gives us the answer in an nutshell. The love here is too profound for any Einstein to grasp, yet so simple that any little child could accept. No doubt, T.G.I.F. by all means. This truly is a day which sets the tone for a happy Easter and excitement to be worshipping a living (not dead) God. Next time you hear the disc jockey on the radio use that phrase, T.G.I.F., maybe you can be thankful for one particular Friday in history . . . it will bring more joy than finding some old hard-boiled egg, I bet.

☆ ☆ ☆

Further Study: What is the significance in Good Friday to a Christian? What does Easter mean to you? How can this one Friday in history change someone's life? Why do other religion's worship a dead god? How cool is it that Jesus is alive today?

UNDERDOG

*Encourage one another day after day as long as it's still called today
lest your heart be hardened by the deceitfulness of sin.*
Hebrews 3:13

☆ ☆ ☆

The Nickelodeon channel has a cartoon on each Sunday morning that is a stitch. This goofy little dog in a superman outfit comes out and says, "There's no need to fear, Underdog is here," then flies off to fight crime on the streets. I've personally always been the type to root for the person or team who is supposed to lose. Somebody once asked President Eisenhower why he ever bought that farm of his located in Gettysburg, Pennsylvania. He told them that all of his life he wanted to take a piece of ground which really hadn't been cared for (cultivated or fertilized or watered) and work with everything he had to leave it in better condition than he found it, and that's exactly what he did.

You know, that is such a simple principle, yet it is loaded with truth. Many folks in life, regardless of what they do or where they're from, have that inner urge to make a winner out of a loser. We are always looking for a big challenge, and there is really none too big with God as our source of power and motivation. William Barclay wrote, "One of the highest duties is to encourage others . . . it is easy to laugh at men's ideals; it is easy to pour cold water on their enthusiasm; it is easy to discourage. The world is full of discouragers. We have a Christian duty to encourage one another. Many a time a word of praise or thanks or appreciation or cheer has kept a man on his feet. Blessed is the man who speaks such a word."

Jesus was the underdog by the world's standards yet became the victor and now sits at the throne of God. With a simple wink of an eye, smile, soft word or serving hand, you can encourage someone to be or do better and follow Christ's example. Don't expect a lot of praise or to sign any autographs for encouraging others because it's definitely not the norm. Don't be one of those folks in life who rains on everyone else's parade . . . be there with ticker-tape and banners waving high for encouragement.

☆ ☆ ☆

Further Study: Do you ever feel like an underdog? How do you treat the world's underdogs? Are Christians really the underdogs, or ultimate victors?

Pods

If any widow has children, let them learn to practice piety in regard to their own family, and make some return to their parents for this is good in God's eyes.
1 Timothy 5:4

☆ ☆ ☆

Recently, I was watching one of those educational shows which come on late Sunday evenings. This particular show was a documentary on those zany creatures of the sea (no, not the Little Mermaid), the killer whale. These enormous conglomerations of blubber, fins and teeth have intrigued me since I visited Sea World in Florida and got spit on by Shamu. I did learn though, that these predators of the sea seem to have the personality of a puppy and the family standards we ought to have. Their family is correctly called a "pod," and they stay together at all times. Starting at the moment of birth, the calf (baby whale) and its mommy will always breath in unison . . . the mom surfaces for air at the same time as her young. The families of whales can be as large as 50 and stay together until death. They hunt, swim, play and learn from each other throughout their life-span. So, the next time you see one at an aquarium, look past the flips and stunts and notice the loyalty that runs deeper than any ocean.

We've lost the art of "pod" making. In human terms, we don't value the family unit like we should and God intended. Our number one focus here on earth is to build a structure (like the three little pigs) that can't be blown down by the wolves of time. Alcohol, divorce, drugs, anger, rebellion and sex outside marriage are a few weapons of wind the wolves huff and puff to try to blow down our homes. To change the trends we have got to put a huge value on the family fortress and never give in to the armies of hell. Satan would like nothing more than to destroy our lives through a dysfunctional family. A family needs to be a refuge, haven, security blanket and living quarters of love, therein serving its chosen purpose. We need to take a lesson from the untainted lifestyle of the killer whales of the sea and get our family back swimming together. Realize that Christ is and will have to be the glue which holds your pod together. Begin by eating one meal a day, praying one time a day, serving once a week and encouraging once an hour.

☆ ☆ ☆

Further Study: What is your definition of a family? Does it jive with the biblical one? Are you glue in your home? How?

JESUS THE C.E.O.

*In everything you do put God first, and He will direct
you and crown your efforts with success.*

Proverbs 3:6

☆ ☆ ☆

Okay, here's a wacked-out thought for you to compute in your cranium. Can you imagine if Jesus came back to earth today dressed not in a cloak and sandals, but in pinstripes and wingtips? What if He drove a Lexus downtown to a sizable skyscraper and took over as "the boss" (Chief Executive Officer) of a major investment firm on Wall Street? Could He succeed? Let's just see . . . in only three short years Jesus defined a mission and formed strategies to carry it out to completion. He had a small staff of 12 unlikely, unqualified, unruly disciples. With that staff He organized Christianity, which today has branches in all corners of the world and a 32.4% share of the population–twice the size of the closest rival's. His salesmen (disciples) took all they learned and utilized it in everyday life. Jesus (the marketing master) developed original material to market eternity to a broad-based region of purchasers. His salesmen learned sizzlin' sales-pitches like salvation, love, joy, healing, heaven and guaranteed success.

I think it would be interesting to compare today's tycoons' self-help strategies with Christ's divine one-liners. Catch this idea–if people in the corporate world would review the real book of success (the Bible), I think they might learn something. (scripture is, was and always will be a landmark for you and I, no matter what career path we choose.) Don't slough off that thick, dusty, unused book on the piano (the Bible) as just a fable of fiction, value it as words of wisdom. Jesus' way to climb the corporate ladder might surprise you.

☆ ☆ ☆

Further Study: Ask your father (or any business man) what his secret to success is, then compare that with Matthew 5:1-10.

TRILS

UNDER THE SEA

He rebuked the wind and the surging waves of the sea,
and it became perfectly calm.
Mark 4:39

☆ ☆ ☆

My feelings on the subject of scuba diving are pretty simple . . . if God wanted us to breath underwater, He would have given us gills. It was totally against my better judgment to try my hand at this sport, but peer pressure overtook me. I first had to go through the difficult procedure of obtaining a license and certification, which I thought was enough. After graduating from scuba school, I was then permitted in the big pool–the ocean. Open water is a lot more different than a pool or lake. Why? 'Cuz there are animals that don't take kindly to us blowfish humans trespassing on their territory. We paid our fee, loaded the giant scuba boat and drifted out to sea. We headed out to a reef that was home to all kinds of marine life, including sharks (I'd be happier with "Flipper"). The boat tossed around like the S.S. Minnow, and I'd swear the crew included Gilligan and the Skipper. Talk about motion sickness (better known as ocean sickness while at sea). I'd never seen waves 20-feet tall or that rough. That all changed once we strapped on our gear and took the Nestea plunge.

The surface seemed out of control, yet below it was calm, quiet, and peaceful. Amazing . . . how could it be so bad from one perspective and so peaceful from another? It's a lot like God's perspective. We see the craziness, yet God sees the peace. He controls both sides, but from a human's vantage we think God has left us. The turbulent waters that Jesus and Peter walked on were calm below the surface. No matter how tough life may seem, God keeps it all under control if we only dive into the divine. God never leaves us; we leave Him. God's faithfulness is always just a prayer away. We have not (His peacefulness) because we ask not. Dive in!

☆ ☆ ☆

Further Study: How peaceful is your life? How much peace do you have in the midst of turbulent trials? How much do you seek God's peace in the midst of your trials?

GOD'S WORD

LAMP LIGHTER

Thy word is a lamp unto my feet and a light unto my path.
Psalm 119:105

☆ ☆ ☆

When most of us hear this verse, we immediately recall Amy Grant singing the song. You've heard if for years in church, youth groups and on the radio, but have you ever stopped and looked at it? It comes off as a pretty simple set of divine words which have a nice ring to them, and they fit well with musical notes. Read it one time through, and your report would be that the Bible is like a light to my steps along this Christian journey, right? Well, pretty close, but look again . . . notice a key word in this verse? No, it's not lamp or light, but "feet." Check this bad boy thought out for a minute. God's word is a light, but its halo only surrounds your steps. Get it? Okay, I'll explain further . . . when you are walking down a narrow path at night with a flashlight pointed downward, you can only see a few feet (no pun intended) ahead of you at a time. In other words, you still need to walk with care (slowly, one step at a time) or you'll run into a tree, or stumble on an unnoticed boulder. I mean, if God wanted to, He could light up the country side with His word so you wouldn't even need a lamp. Come on now, this is God who can do it all, right?

The Bible is the flame in the lamp that gives light to every step our feet walk on this thin, windy pathway we call Christianity. I believe God is telling us that hey, the Bible is great, but it's not enough to make this journey . . . we still need His Spirit to guide us, too. He's telling us we must still carry faith in the Father accompanied by a lamp (not a spotlight) to find our way through life's dark, messed-up world in which we all travel. Study the Word of God daily to keep that flame from going out, and also keep the faith which compliments His word. Don't be afraid of the danger which will lie   ahead . . . you forget, Jesus made the path and has been on it several times before you.

☆ ☆ ☆

Further Study: How often do you read the Bible? Do you believe it is a lamp to your feet? How can you get excited about God's Word? How can you make Bible study a habit?

ACCOUNTABILITY

CALLED TO ACCOUNT

Now we know what the law says; it speaks to those under the law, that every mouth may be closed and the world may be held accountable to God.
Romans 3:19

☆ ☆ ☆

This word will not come up in casual conversation at dinner. It won't appear on the prime time nightly news. It's not a category on the popular game show Jeopardy. You'll have to run with a different pack of folks to even use this word, yet it's essential to the survival of a concrete Christian today. What is this word? Accountability. The old dictionary defines it as "liable to be called to account for your action(s); responsible; capable of being explained."

About three years ago I realized at a ripe age of 32, how weak I was alone in my walk with Christ (I learn quickly, don't I?). The older I get, the less confidence I seem to have in myself for fighting this battle called faith, alone. Late one night I was watching one of those educational television shows on the Discovery channel, and I saw how packs of wolves would patiently wait until their prey, a thousand pound caribou crossing the frozen terrain of northern Canada, would file off alone. It was at that moment, like the wolves knew they were on camera, that they would charge the victim, like bugs to a light and take it down suddenly, without remorse. What a scene to show on the tube (I bet the animal rights folks were ticked). How sudden, how pre-planned, what violence, yet how true even in our own lives. Satan is the wolf (dressed in disguise) who waits for us to single ourselves away from the fellowship of other believers in the herd and bites to kill. Accountability keeps us out of the jaws of consumption and into the fearless hands of our Father in heaven. We are first called to be held accountable to God then to our agape friends daily. Accountability means having someone ask you the tough questions which matter in our walk with Christ. We need someone to not let us slack off and hold us to a standard we can't always hold ourselves to. Try it . . . I promise it's better than being prey in the jaws of sin.

☆ ☆ ☆

Further Study: Who can hold you accountable today? How will you be consistent? When will you start?

CHRISTIAN RACE

SETBACK BE A COMEBACK

Fixing our eyes on Christ, the author and perfector of our faith.
Hebrews 12:2

☆ ☆ ☆

Eamonn Coghlan was the Irish world record holder at 1,500 meters and was running in a qualifying heat at the World Indoor Track and Field Championships in Indianapolis, Indiana. With two and a half laps left in the race, he was accidentally tripped and fell to the track surface. Eamonn didn't get to be a record holder by having a quitter's attitude, so he pulled himself up to his feet, and with incredible effort, managed to catch up to the leaders in the race. With approximately 20 yards left to the finish line, he was in third place–good enough to qualify for the finals. Eamonn looked over his left shoulder and saw no one even close to him, so he let up to coast the last 10 yards. What he hadn't seen was a runner charging up over his right shoulder with the momentum to pass him at the finish line, thus eliminating him from the finals. His great comeback after a fall was rendered worthless by taking his eyes and heart off the finish line.

In today's world of chaos and fast lanes, it's tempting to let up when it looks like things around us are favorable. We feel comfortable the way we are and the way life is going for us, so we coast. We take it out of four-wheel drive and put it in neutral. The problem comes when our wheels begin to slip, we lose our momentum, and risk losing the race. I have always admired those few individuals that finish the race as excited and determined as when they started. Be the runner on God's track team that stays focused on the goal, purpose and reason (Jesus). You may get tripped up during this race, so have the mindset going into it that you will not quit and you will get up. Make a set-back be a comeback.

☆ ☆ ☆

Further Study: What conditions cause you to take your eyes off Christ? When are you tempted to just coast instead of press on? How can you become the type of Christian that finishes as strong as you start?

CONTENTMENT

THIS NEW AGE

Let no one be found among you who practices divination or sorcery, interprets omens, engages in witchcraft or one who casts spells, or who is a medium, or spiritist, or who consults the dead. Anyone who does these things is detestable to the Lord.
Deuteronomy 18:9-12

☆ ☆ ☆

I heard a saying one time that said, "If you don't know where you're going, you'll probably get there." Our world is falling all over itself with people going nowhere. Daily you can read about someone on this planet who tries his/her hand at being or coming up with a new way of doing things. The New Age Movement is a rapidly growing cult of followers who at first glance seem to have the winning ticket for happiness. Words spill from their mouths like psychic, Nirvana, astrology, self-realization, reincarnation, pantheism, out-of-body experiences, transformation, channeling, ESP, karma and Shirley MacLaine. They practice their religion with tools such as crystals, yoga, ESP, Ouigi boards and tarot cards. The reason this cult has taken off like a bullet out of a barrel is it requires no sacrifice at all, and it's a tremendous self-image builder. Their doctrine is "if everything is god, then I am god."

The movement is all about no higher moral absolutes and that truth is perceived individually. The New Age Movement derides the biblical doctrine of sin and substitutes reincarnation as the means of atonement. They believe there is no reality; therefore, all deaths lead to another life on earth in another form (who knows, maybe you'll return as a cockroach).

Realize that this is one of many types of cults in today's world, and they all are dangerous to tangle with. You'll see where Christians have retreated in society (i.e. Hollywood, politics, music, etc.) as this movement has advanced. The goal of new agers is to change "how I feel" (it's all a feeling). How can we help in throwing a wrench in its gears? First, pray. Then, be a light in a dark world. Love your enemy. And finally, wear your armor daily (time in the Word).

☆ ☆ ☆

Further Study: Have you been approached or seen this movement in your community? How can you better prepare yourself today for this battle?

HUMAN BEING OR HUMAN

The Lord God formed the man from the dust of the ground and breathed into his nostrils the breath of life, and the man became a human being.
Genesis 2:7

☆ ☆ ☆

One of the greatest books of the Bible lies within the first several pages where God shows off His awesome power and creativity. When we read the book of beginnings, God seems to show us how all this began. When God created you He intended you to be in a relationship with Him from day one. There is a reason we were made human beings and not human doings. A human being what? In love with its Creator! Yep, you read it right, a human selling out his heart and soul to the Master mechanic of two-legged folks. Our greatest commandment that Moses brought back from the mountain is to "love the Lord God with all your heart, soul and mind." It seems like in this day and time, we tend to think we can actually pay God off with cheap works (doings) to get us to, or keep us in, those golden gates called heaven.

We are a society saved by grace, not by works (Ephesians 2:5). The word grace means to stoop or bow. You cannot earn the right to go to heaven, just accept the ticket (salvation through Christ) and say "thank you" for the cross of calvary. My dad is a horse rancher. For years I have watched him walk stooped-over across a pasture, never standing higher than the horse, right up to a newborn colt, who has never seen a human before, and begin to rub and pet this colt. The colt doesn't run away. Why? Because my dad humbly stoops (with grace) in order not to intimidate the baby colt by his size or stature.

Take this to the bank and deposit it. You are called first to love God and develop a relationship, then the fruits of faith will follow. Try being what you were created to do and that's "be."

☆ ☆ ☆

Further Study: How intimate is your relationship to the Creator? How can it be better?

ANGER

TICKED OFF

Be angry, and yet do not sin; do not let the sun go down on your anger.
Ephesians 4:26

✶ ✶ ✶

Have you ever had any of the following thoughts before? It's a sin to get angry. Don't share your angry feelings with anyone. God doesn't understand anger. Hold all anger inside. The best way to deal with anger is to ignore it. Jesus never got angry. Anger is only an outward feeling. Anger shows spiritual immaturity. God doesn't forgive anger. Christians just don't get angry.

Well, if you chimed right in on this "top 10" list, then listen up because what you see is not necessarily what you get. In this day and time, it's easy to get ticked off when you've been done wrong: cut off by another car, butted in front of in the checkout line, called something you're not, felt like you've been dealt a bad hand in the game of life. Jesus Himself felt these same emotions 2,000 years ago. A common Bible story tells how an angry Jesus turned over mega tables set up by tax collectors in His Father's temple. What about Mark 3:5 or John 3:36? These recorded instances were true expressions of anger by our Savior, and when looked intently upon, equate to a slow rising type of anger in which Jesus is displeased with the situation, but handles it like it should be handled, without violence or destruction. There are two types of anger (news to me) that are defined, one which is Christ-like, the other which is man-made. One is targeted at the disobedience and defiance of God's word, and the other contains jealousy and bitterness (Galatians).

You see, anger, handled as Jesus did, is not wrong if its pure motive is to correct and set back on the right path to Christ. The other is purely of the world and results in violence and uncontrolled outbursts that stem from desires of the flesh. Make it a point to check the reason behind your anger first, then deal with it directly in accordance to scripture before the sun goes down that day.

✶ ✶ ✶

Further Study: What ticks you off the most? Why?

EASTER

THE HUNT

*So the other disciple who had first come to the tomb entered
then also, and he saw and believed.*
John 20.8

★ ★ ★

I wasn't quite sure if I was attending a concert or an early morning Easter service. The location was "Fiddler's Green," and the attendance was somewhere around 10,000. It was an outdoor amphitheater, and you couldn't have painted a more beautiful day or a more scenic backdrop than the Colorado Rockies (and I don't mean the baseball team). I was amazed at the number that showed up, yet I question some motivations for attendance. Did they come because of ritual, guilt, status or conviction, or was it for celebration? Well . . . only God knows, but the worship service was awesome.

Easter is far more than a time to hunt for colored, hard-boiled eggs or dress up in a festive new outfit. It's above all the hype, yet down to earth enough to understand. Easter is the celebration following Good Friday which separates Christianity from many other religions. You see those who worship another god honor a dead god that didn't die specifically for them. We get so excited about the empty tomb, because our future lies in a risen Lord. When Peter and the other disciples saw the empty tomb, they realized what Mary knew as she sat outside the tomb and wept. As believers in Christ, we don't worship a grave, bronze statue or a past legend, but a risen, living, breathing, omnipresent God. Now, if that thought doesn't get your blood flow movin', then I'm not sure you are alive (take a moment and check your pulse). Gang, who gives a rip about the tomb? He's alive!

★ ★ ★

Further Study: Why should you be more excited about a living Jesus than an empty tomb? Why is it so important to our faith that we worship and follow a L-I-V-I-N-G Savior?

EXERCISE

EXTENSION

Which one of you by worrying can add a single cubit to his life?
Matthew 6:27

☆ ☆ ☆

Jane Fonda, Richard Simmons, Kathy Smith, Cindy Crawford and Bruce Jenner have all made thousands of dollars selling not only machines or techniques, but a false concept. Info-commercials are packed with trim and tight, fit and fancy, sexy and skinny models peddling products like Nordic-Trac, Ab-roller, Life-cycle, Gut-buster or Thigh-Master. Health clubs are packed with exercise fanatics with one goal in mind, to look good and feel good with the hope of living longer. Hear me out here, I am not down on anyone or any product, but I am down on the concept of extending one's life through the vehicle of workouts and exercise. scripture is very direct and clear that your body is the temple of our Lord. I personally believe our Savior shouldn't have to live in the ghetto (1 Corinthians 6:19). The serious issue here is trying to play god and actually thinking for one second that by weightlifting, aerobics, stair masters, stationary bikes, jogging, swimming or whatever you can actually add a few more years (cubits) to your life. God is in charge of our life expectancy (James 4:14), and when He says it's time to go (die) . . . you're gone! God invented time; even though health studies show the average American lives to be 75, there are no guarantees. In the above scripture, I think Jesus is saying, "Your destiny lies on your choosing Me or not choosing Me." A cubit is a measurement in Jesus' culture which was from the end of your elbow to the tip of your middle finger; now that varied a bit, but it equated to be around 18 inches. Isn't that a sarcastic comment when Jesus says, "Which one of you by worrying can add a single cubit to his life?" So, next time your "sweatin' to the oldies" or working on those "buns of steel," do it to enhance your quality of life . . . not quantity of years. Sweat on!

☆ ☆ ☆

Further Study: Do you exercise? Why? What is the "real" reason to exercise?

DOULOS: A BOND SERVANT

*If you point these things out to the brothers, you will be a good minister
of Christ Jesus, brought up in the truths of faith and of the
good teaching that you have followed.*

1 Timothy 4:6

☆ ☆ ☆

In the summer of 1989, Mark Wellman, a paraplegic, gained national recognition by climbing the sheer granite face of "El Capitan" in Yosemite National Park. On the seventh and final day of his heroic climb, the headline of the Fresno newspaper read, "Showing a Will of Granite." Mark's partner, Mike Corbett, who is not paralyzed, received little recognition. With the article was a picture of Mike carrying his companion on his shoulders, subtitled, "Paraplegic and partner prove no wall is too high to scale." The ironic thing about this event is that Mike scaled (climbed) the granite face of El Capitan three times in order to help Mark pull himself up once.

You won't find many articles, pictures, broadcasts or praise going out for a servant. You don't see people flocking around a servant, badgering him for an autograph. To be a servant means to serve when you're not cast in the lead role (the star). Servanthood is a lost art. To be a servant is to exemplify humility and selflessness in its truest form (be like Christ). No standing ovations or syndicated TV shows await a humble servant. In fact, servants are looked upon as the lowest member of the food chain. A Doulos (bond-servant) is as low as a snake's belly, seldom recognized, promoted, or viewed very highly by anyone . . . except God Almighty! God will (not might) exalt you over any mountain (like El Capitan) when you serve others. Serving reveals the Savior. Without it, you'll never accomplish great things for God's Kingdom.

☆ ☆ ☆

Further Study: Are you a server or a servee? Do you think serving means giving or getting? Why do you see few Doulos bond-servants in society today? Why do you think Jesus asks you to be one? Will you? Why or why not?

GIVING

FLY AWAY HOME

Each man should give what he has decided in his heart to give, not reluctantly or under compulsion, for God loves a cheerful giver.
2 Corinthians 9:7

☆ ☆ ☆

Birds of the air are interesting to watch. Now, I don't I consider myself a real bird watcher, but you can learn a lot from them. There is a lesson in watching a swallow teach its young to fly. The mother bird gets the chicks out of the nest, high atop a tree and starts shoving them out toward the end of the branch. Before the chicks do a nose-dive into the pavement, they learn to fly. If a chick tightens its talons (claws) on the branch and refuses to jump, the mother will peck at its feet. When the chick can't stand the pain anymore, it lets go and flies. Birds have feet and can walk, talons that can grasp a tree branch tightly, but flying is their heritage. Not until they fly are they living at their best and doing what they were intended to do.

You know, giving is what Christians do best. It is the air into which we were born. It is the action that was designed into us before our birth, yet sometimes we desperately try to hold on and live for self. We look bedraggled and pathetic doing it, hanging on to the dead branch of a bank account, afraid to risk ourselves on the untried wings of giving. We don't think we can live generously because we've never tried it before. The sooner we start, the quicker we find the joy that accompanies giving and letting go for God. God will peck at the closed hands of our heart until we stop feeling, or let go and let God work. Flying is more fun than watching anyway.

☆ ☆ ☆

Further Study: Are you a giver? To what do you give? Are you a hoarder? Why? Did you come into this world with money? Are you gonna' leave this world with money? How can you become a better giver?

CONTENTMENT

A LEARNED TRAIT

For I have learned to be content in all circumstances.
Philippians 4:11

✫ ✫ ✫

One of the hottest behind-the-counter drugs that Americans use today is Valium. It's kind of a mind tranquilizer that allows oneself to have the attitude of "let well enough alone." Call it what you want, take your pick of adjectives like complacent, peaceful, satisfied, at ease, sans souci, not particular, resigned, unaffected, serene, unmolested, comfortable (tired yet?) or unperturbed (whatever). We have a tendency in our terrain to always be wanting on the other side of the fence. The reason that we pop Valium in our diet is the pressure to escape our present situation. Why is it that we're always looking for something better like the newest car, computer, job, house, lingo, style of clothes, hairstyle or spouse? What happened to loyalty and contentment with where we are at the moment? No, I'm not saying that we are not to strive for perfection or push ourselves, but come on . . . we've lost that balance. When it begins to be like a game of Monopoly where you're continually trying to get more and more, then there is a problem. The apostle Paul speaks louder than a tornado siren when he (of all people) states that he has become content in all things. I mean, this guy hasn't had much to brag about to his neighbors in a while. He has been beaten, blamed and posted bail for being a disciple of Jesus for years. His home has been a jail cell, his life persecuted and his body beaten to a pulp, and he says he is content no matter if he's in the club house or outhouse. We can learn a huge lesson in life . . . if we learn to be content in whatever circumstances our sovereign God has placed us. You know, if we could learn this lesson in God's classroom, we wouldn't need the school nurse for aspirin (or Valium) nearly as much. Then, our local drugstores could be selling more cold medicine than pain pills.

✫ ✫ ✫

Further Study: What always makes you want to retreat from a situation? What exactly is contentment? How can you obtain more of it? Is contentment a way of thinking or a place we all come to?

LOVING OTHERS

SIRENS

His calamity will come suddenly, and instantly he will be broken.
Proverbs 6:15

⋏ ⋏ ⋏

Growing up in a big city, they were as normal as flies at a picnic, but now living in a small country town, they are as noticeable as a ketchup stain on a white shirt. I'm talking about the scream of sirens. When you hear one while in a car, you're supposed to pull over and give right of way, but when you're on a street corner, all you do is stop, look and wonder. Sirens only show up in our lives when something bad is in the process of happening. It may mean a fire, wreck, heart attack, shooting or funeral procession, but you can bet it's not for a birthday party. Usually the people who become directly involved with a siren are either scared, mesmerized, hysterical, crying, confused or just plain terrified. Count on it, you will hear one or more in due time with the direction our country is headed. The final destination of the siren won't be a chill-out moment in time. Rest assured that the folks involved need more than a fire hose or paramedics . . . they need God.

Whether you hear them as loudly as you do those on top of a police car or not, they are still there. Siren sounds come dressed in a little different shape and are presented in random packages. They may sound like an outburst of anger or a cutting remark. You may see them drunk or high at a party, or they may reveal themselves by leaving a 20-year marriage with a wife and two kids, but they are sirens. You see, sirens are nothing more than attitudes which emit actions as warning signals. You hear and see them far more than you do the flashing lights. We have become so callused to them we have grown accustomed to their ways and accept them as a "norm." False! Wrong answer . . . we need to realize they are cries for help, and we need to be of assistance as much as we would if we were performing CPR. Be alert at all times for people sirens in your life. Be attentive to what is going on in the arenas in which you live. Be a useful hand of God to a world falling apart. And the next time you hear a siren, I hope your eyes and ears perk up like a dog's to a signal of help needed.

☆ ☆ ☆

Further Study: What are the siren sounds you hear the most? How do your friends cry out for help? Are you willing to help?

BAD HABITS

Do you not know that your body is a temple for the Holy Spirit
who is in you whom you have received from God?
1 Corinthians 6:19

☆ ☆ ☆

The "he-man" rugged model for the macho nacho cigarette power-house, Marlboro, succumbed to cancer at age 51. You may remember him as the weathered cowboy, marked with tattoos and chapped lips, who rode the range punching cows like the men of the Old West. What he did for the manufacturer was lead consumers to believe the stud thing to do was to smoke. What we didn't see on the billboards was that he spent the last three years of his life warning others of the dangers of smoking. Though it was too late for him, he thought if he could keep just one youth from starting, or help one smoker to stop, it would all be worth it. He was a convincing spokesperson because he knew all too well the price to be paid for becoming enslaved to this habit. You'll never see a magazine ad or billboard poster showing a smoke-filled room of emaciated hackers throwing up their offerings to the god of tobacco. The lesson can be learned that all of us can be overtaken by a habit which owns our lives and body.

My personal belief is that if God intended us to smoke we would all be born with exhaust systems. Granted, this is just one of many bad habits that we bow down to. We are to worship no other god than the Creator of the universe. Another god could be classified as anything that takes jurisdiction in our lives and fights for the number one spot in our hearts. Bad habits develop simply from lack of self-control. Take control of those areas that have escaped from the corral and are now running wild in your life. Seek help from other supporting believers by confessing the habit and the need for their prayers and accountability. Don't forget there is a big God who loves you, and all He desires is to be asked for His help to make you more like His Son, then look out! Bad habits are like a comfortable couch, easy to get into and hard to get out of.

☆ ☆ ☆

Further Study: What bad habits do you have that have taken over in your life? Do you desire to quit? Do you want to quit badly enough to seek help? When are you gonna' start?

SOCIAL TRENDS

Glorify God in your body.
1 Corinthians 6:20

✮ ✮ ✮

A trend is defined as a social movement or surge in a specific area in our culture. Noticed recently is the adornment trend of tattoos and piercing. It doesn't take an investigative journalist or a fashion consultant to see just how (no pun intended) ingrained these fashion statements have become. Crossing mono-sexual boundaries, these trends are now unisex. Tattoos show up on ankles, arms, hands and places too risky to discuss. Piercing takes place not only in the ears, but the naval, nose and lips. Such adornments are not a new idea to civilization, but the recoil of these trends is strong. It boils down to how can followers of Christ keep the balance? When is it proper to follow a trend?

Now, I realize that this is a controversial issue. I think scripture gives us the parameters to decide how Christians are to conduct themselves. The question one needs to ask is why? Why do I feel the need to partake in the trend? The answer may lie in individual insecurities, rebellion or expression of a particular image. On the other hand, the motive may be pure and undefiled. You need to do some soul searching and motive meddling to find the personal inner-answer for yourself. Ask yourself, no matter what the trend of the year is:

Why am I participating? (Motive)
What does scripture say about it? (Means)
What would Jesus do? (Mentor)
Who am I honoring? (Method)

Now, rely on the Holy Spirit and your conscience to direct your decision in the matter. Oh yeah, you probably noticed that I didn't really answer the question. You're right, Sherlock . . . that's because the decision is yours . . . I've already made mine.

✮ ✮ ✮

Further Study: So how do you feel about these two issues? Are you participating in either of them now? Why or why not?

TRILS

WINE PRESS

I now rejoice in my sufferings for you, and fill up that which is behind of the afflictions of Christ in my flesh for His body's sake.

Colossians 1:24

☆ ☆ ☆

We continually strive for those mountain top experiences of life. Prior to conversion to Christ, you may have lived daily on the top, yet after this experience you learn a revolutionary lesson. God can allow life with Him to rivet us with pain that is more intense than anything we might have dreamed. One moment we are lost, then after a radiant flash, we see what He is really after and say, "Lord, here I am. Do what needs doing to make me more like you." This event has nothing to do with personal sanctification, but instead being made broken bread and poured-out wine. God can never make us into wine if we object to the fingers He uses to squeeze the grapes (you and me). If God would only use His own fingers, we would feel special. But when He uses someone we don't like or a set of difficult circumstances as the crushers, we hate it. We must never choose our own martyrdom (pain). If we want to be made into wine, we will be crushed because no one can drink grapes. Grapes only become wine when they're crushed.

If by chance the grapes of your spiritual walk are not ripe, then the wine would be bitter if God squeezed you. You have to be totally in tune with God before the squeezing and pouring-out process can take place. Keep your life "right" with God and let Him have His way with you, and you will see that He is producing the kind of bread and wine that will benefit His Kingdom. The older you get the sweeter the wine will become in life . . . you'll see.

☆ ☆ ☆

Further Study: What kind of finger and thumb of God has been squeezing you? Why is pressure so important on the wine press? If you're not getting squeezed, then what do you see as the problem? When will you be ready?

BEING A CHRISTIAN

SCARRED FOR LIFE

You have been bought with a price; don't be the servants of man.
1 Corinthians 7:23

☆ ☆ ☆

If you're ever doing the "traveling thing" and your journey happens to take you across the western plains of Texas, you'll see tumbleweeds, windmills, miles of pasture, fields of bluebells, old postcard gas stations and the state bird of Texas–the cow. That's right, there are more of those lonesome doggies (cows) per square mile in the area around Hereford, Texas, than anywhere else in the world. You'll find every make of cow imaginable from Black Angus to the white-faced Hereford. In the late 1800s the cattle industry experienced a surge in what they commonly called, "cattle rustlin'," which was really just plain stealing. The thieves rustled up someone else's herd and took it to market to sell for themselves. With so many large herds of cattle coming in each day, it was difficult to identify one rancher's cow from the next. Little could be done to stop the thieves unless they were caught red-handed. That was true until the invention of the "branding iron," which permanently marked livestock with the custom brand of the owner's ranch name, like JH, T-Bar-M or Bar-K.

Believe it or not, you, as a follower of Christ, have been branded (spiritually, not physically). Remember that the brand symbolizes ownership and loyalty to a particular person and place of residence. As a Christian your owner (Jesus) paid the debt on the cross, and now your future pasture of peace is heaven. Isn't that cool, to think you are scarred with the mental brand of Calvary, setting you apart from the others you rub shoulders with every day? Be proud of your owner, yet humble to your position here on earth. The hot branding iron process that marked the rawhide of a cow was a painful procedure, but your pain was borne by your Savior. What a deal!

☆ ☆ ☆

Further Study: What does being bought with a price say about Christ's love for you? Are you proud to be a member of the heavenly herd? How can you help others know about your future pasture?

Prayer on Proposal

*For those things which you pray, believe that you have
received them, and they shall be given to you.*

Mark 11:24

✲ ✲ ✲

Now this is not gonna' be one of those devotions on "name it, claim it." This devotion is on a kind of prayer warrior who has the right perspective and procedure. I'll begin with a true story I heard in a small farming community in western Iowa. As usual, the good ol' American farmer was being dealt another bad hand in the weather department. Not a drop of rain had fallen for a total of 31 days, so a town meeting was called. The location was the local church with the preacher presiding. The gathering was basically a prayer meeting to ask God to show favor on their dry, scorched farm land and crops so they could have a good harvest to pay some bills. The reason this meeting and story are so interesting is that all the locals who attended the meeting came with umbrellas. Now that's what I call an expectant prayer meeting.

We, as Christians, only have one road to travel to see the Savior, and that's on "Highway Prayer." The only communication we have with the Creator is through the two-way radio we call prayer. With all that in mind, isn't it important that we know how to pray? God will always answer your requests with either yes, no or wait. What we need to do more of is keep our tuner tuned to God so finely that our prayers match His way of thinking. This way, when we pray, we are so deeply into God's will and looking out for His best interest, all our requests and petitions are right on. Now what this does is give us the liberty to pray boldly through faith that we will receive His will for the particular situation we're praying for. Whether it's a need for healing someone sick, a material matter, guidance on a decision, or wisdom in our thinking, He will come through . . . bank on it.

So, be like that group of believers in Iowa and pray to God with results in mind . . . cuz' when it rains, it pours!

✲ ✲ ✲

Further Study: Who or what can you pray for today? When you pray, do you pray believing God is listening? Do you pray consistently? Do you doubt you're righteous enough for God to listen?

HERO SHOPPING

Everyone, after he has been fully trained, will be like his teacher.
Luke 6:40

☆ ☆ ☆

It doesn't take long in the riches of society to find poverty in the hero profession. The problem is that there are not many folks interviewing for this job because of the incredible amount of experience needed. One must be willing, honest, loyal, unselfish, humble, dedicated, caring, self-disciplined and intent on one purpose (I could go on). Wow! What a resume would be needed in this job search. Isn't it funny that the profession we're talking about is the endangered species of real life, red, white and blue "heroes?" Isn't it ironic (look closely) that the qualities mentioned don't deal with head knowledge but heart knowledge? Believe it or not (no, it's not Ripley's), very few heroes or mentors are around to be followed. In this profession, the title must be earned; it's not just freely given. Worthiness must be proven on the playing fields of family relationships, battle grounds of business, spectrum of sports and the stadiums of society.

As you grow older, you will observe that trying to find this mentor is like trying to find a penny in the Grand Canyon. They come around about as often as a total eclipse of the sun, but guess what? They are out there in small numbers and not where you expect to see them. They carry no flash (they're humble); they wave not their own banner (unselfish), nor do they advertise their position (folks of integrity). The truth is, the position can only be held by a sincere follower of Jesus. Why? Without Him there is no divine strength to pull off walking upright day after day, year after year. If you want to find a hero, start first, not by looking for one, but by praying for one. God wants us all to have a mentor to teach us (like Paul did Timothy), and then wait on the Lord.

Let me offer a brief suggestion as you climb this mountain in search of a glimpse of this endangered species. See if they can say these simple, yet convicting words, "you can do as I do." Make sure they are an original and not a cheap replica of a real, live, modern day "hero."

☆ ☆ ☆

Further Study: Who is your hero today? Can you do as they do? Is what they do honoring to God?

Turn Down the Volume

Be still and know that I am God.
Psalm 46:10

☆ ☆ ☆

In this civilization of chaos with so many living frantically on the fast track, few times in daily schedules could be classified as quiet, still times. Don't you feel like you're the hamster in the cage on a wheel going like mad, and you're on display for others to see? An article in the Boston newspaper tells how after Lenny Bias, first round draft choice of the Boston Celtics, was found dead of an overdose of cocaine, reporters questioned his high school coach, who said, "It looks like life in the fast lane got even faster." The pace of society doesn't exactly promote or applaud times of stillness and silence. Ever been in a conversation, or with a group of people, when all turned silent? Man, do the body languages start speaking, as heads start bowing, fingers and toes go to tapping with nervous gestures. Let's face up to it, we don't like quiet or the fact that we're still because we feel like time is passing us by without anything productive happening. Just the opposite is true to God. Be sure you don't let your feelings become fact in this situation.

God, being a caring Creator, doesn't want to try to speak above the volume of society. You and I both know when God needs to get our attention, He can. But He chooses not to, unless we want Him to. Learn, while you're young, to find a consistent quiet time daily in a specific location, which is like a secret hide-out that only you and the Savior know about. When you're at that spot and begin to read His word, study it. When you pray for guidance, listen to His answer. You can't do all this while on the treadmill of life. Who knows, you may begin to glow after meeting with God each day . . . Moses did.

☆ ☆ ☆

Further Study: Did you find a still, quiet place today to visit with Jesus? Why not? How can you?

FLICKS

Your eyes will see strange things, and your mind will utter perverse things.
Proverbs 23:33

☆ ☆ ☆

Summertime is definitely the bread-and-butter of Hollywood. According to *Movieguide* magazine there is a little different twist to the reports coming out of movie land. Despite Hollywood's insistence that it is making more movies for the American family, less than half of 1994's releases were rated acceptable for teenagers or for children. The report went something like this:

NC-17 rated movies	1%
G rated movies	3%
Not rated movies	14%
PG rated movies	19%
PG-13 rated movies	22%
R rated movies	41%

Now, there is no one who loves a good flick (movie) more than me. Buttered popcorn, 32-ounce soda pop, Junior Mints and Gummy Bears are as mandatory at a movie as hot dogs and soft pretzels are at a baseball game. The problem is the standards of the movie rating system. Violence, sex and offensive language are huge box office draws. You can't tell me you can watch a two-hour movie infected with nudity (or sexual connotations), excessive violence, and offensive language, and not be swayed by these brain-branding scenes. These impure movies are easily accessed at theaters, in hotel rooms, or on your home TV set. Whether you see it or not, your character, beliefs, standards and rationale is persuaded to agree with Hollywood's philosophies. Every time you buy a movie ticket, you are supporting the production of another movie. My plea to you is send a message to movie-land, loud and clear, that you are not (as a Christian) going to lower your integrity or standards to this filth any longer. You can't turn off your mind or shut your ears, so flee (run or avoid) from this junk. Next time you're watching a movie, ask yourself if Jesus were to appear in physical form next to you, would you still watch it?

☆ ☆ ☆

Further Study: What rating do you go to? R? PG-13? Are PG movies free of sex, violence or offensive language? Are the movies you watch acceptable by Jesus' standards?

SEXUAL PURITY

SEMESTER THINKING

To the pure, all things are pure.
Titus 1:15

☆ ☆ ☆

The *Wall Street Journal* reports that in a recent study, one of the reasons the deadly virus HIV causes AIDS is because it is a tenacious opponent. An infected person produces a billion (that's right–billion) particles of the virus daily. This is a ton more than anyone had previously believed true. The body's immune system fends off many of these particles, but over time, it's overwhelmed by the attack. The disease's proclivity for mutation has been recognized for quite some time. This, together with the newly discovered productivity, caused a researcher named David Ho (director of the Aaron Diamond AIDS Research Center in New York where HIV's multiplying power was discovered) to state that no drug currently under testing can eradicate the virus in a patient. Even small amounts are capable of eventually producing mutants that can resist any drug. There may be little hope in the medical field, but there is in the spiritual field–purity.

Now, I realize that a percentage of people get this virus through impure blood transfusions, needles and odd means. I also know, however, that by and large, this deadly disease is transferred through sexual activity. AIDS is not going to be cured by man's hand, but from his heart. Purity is a word seldom heard in casual conversation, but found often in scripture. AIDS is, for the most part, a consequence of immorality. Yes, tons of Christians are cleansed mentally of immorality, but not from its physical consequence. Medical science hasn't created a condom for the conscience yet. Realize that what you do today can and will affect your tomorrow. Stop living your life in semesters, thinking that you can play around sexually now, and then settle down when you get older. God's grace is the only cure for this sickness. It starts by purifying our hearts, which leads to purity of our bodies.

☆ ☆ ☆

Further Study: Does what you do now affect your future? How? Are you pure? Why does God tell us to live pure and undefiled lives?

THE IMMORAL MAJORITY

*All will be condemned who have not believed the truth
but have delighted in wickedness.*
2 Thessalonians 2.12

★ ★ ★

It was a news flash that stunned the world. Any international event took a back seat to the billion people who viewed the funeral at the 13th century church in London, England, on September 6, 1997. At 12:30 a.m. in Paris, after leaving dinner at the Ritz, the Princess of Wales, Lady Diana, and her wealthy boyfriend, Dodi al Fayed, jumped into a chauffeur-driven Mercedes and eight minutes later died in a sudden car crash.

Ironically, on the eve of the funeral, a friend of the princess, Mother Teresa of Calcutta, India, died of heart problems at the age of 87. Mother Teresa was called "mother to the poor" and felt called by God for life to minister to the poor, sick and needy on the streets of India. The media frenzy couldn't find any more room in their papers or on their broadcasts for her.

The thing that hit me was how the media, which was a speculated cause for the crash along with drug and alcohol use of the driver, had such unbridled power–power to manipulate and turn feeling into facts and literally persuade the world to change their set of standards and beliefs. The Queen and Royal Family were not allowed to mourn and grieve their way, they had to do it the media's way . . . publicly. I truly believe that freedom of speech has been taken to the extreme and now dictates actions and attitudes. The media of today is a powerful, effective tool in the hands of darkness. My point is that most TV shows, magazines articles, radio broadcasts and newspaper columns come to you with a secular, humanistic slant. Mother Teresa once said, "I am a little pencil in the writing hand of God." The opposite can be said about this world's media avenues. In the Old Testament they had prophets, in the New Testament they had Jesus, and now you and I have God's Word and Spirit to guide us and teach us the truth. I truly believe that in a deceitful, lawless world, we need to cling to God's sovereignty and ways, not what we are getting fed by the media. Be careful what you take in as facts. Filter every word you hear or read through scripture and the Spirit of God who lives inside your heart and steers your mind, will and emotions. If you really think about it, the media situation is an important international moral problem; the media and press are fueled by the readers, watchers and listeners who have acquired a taste for immorality and continue to buy the junk and fuel the fire for the media to stay in business.

★ ★ ★

Further Study: How much media teaching do you take in daily? Do you screen what you watch, read and take as fact? How can you purify your heart and mind daily?

WORRY

Excess Baggage

*For my iniquities have gone over my head; As a heavy
burden they weigh too much for me.*
Psalm 38;4

☆ ☆ ☆

It had been one of those days from the moment I got up at 7:00 a.m. I
nearly melted my eyebrows with a hair dryer, and my shirt had a giant grape
juice stain on the back. I was scheduled to be in Denver by 1:00 p.m. for a
connecting flight through Dallas/Ft. Worth Airport with a 35 minute lay-
over. I opted not to check any bags below the plane for fear the airlines would
pull a bonehead stunt and lose my luggage. My flight came in late to Dallas,
not to mention that I almost had to use the barf-bag, and I was left with about
10 minutes to catch the Denver plane five miles from the place where we'd
arrived. I ran down the terminal like a crazed halfback headed for the goal-
line with four big bags flopping like crazy. Boy, did I nearly steamroll about
three children, two old people, a poodle and a policeman (oops)! Needless to
say, I missed my flight by about 30 steps, and on top of that, one of my bags
broke open sending socks and underwear flying all over the terminal floor
(how embarrassing).

As Christians we have times we carry excess baggage such as worry,
anger, envy, jealousy and bitterness while racing through the terminals of
time. They become a heavy burden and at times too much to bear. Our knees
buckle, our tempers go ballistic, and our attitude stinks, simply because we
don't allow God to carry them for us. A lot of times people have adverse reac-
tions like depression, violence or even suicide as a release valve. Don't let your
baggage encumber you to the point of wanting to quit. Cast your worries and
all your troubles (bags) on Him because He cares. Believe me, bags not only
slow you down, they are a down right pain to deal with and could cause you
to miss your flight to happiness.

☆ ☆ ☆

Further Study: What bags are you carrying around with you through life? How
can God help relieve you of the heavy burdens society weighs on you? Will
you let Him today?

GOD'S LOVE

A TASTE TEST

Taste and see that the Lord is good.
Psalm 34:8

✩ ✩ ✩

One of the fondest memories I have from my childhood is Thanksgiving at my grandparents' house in Norman, Oklahoma. We would load up the old station wagon with my sisters' and my bikes on the roof and head across the Red River into Sooner country. Riding on the tractor with Grandpa, feeding the cows and eating tender smoked turkey are vivid memories, but not so much as Grandma's homemade peach pies. I recall her spending hours working the crust, skinning the peaches and churning the ice cream. The phase I drooled over the most was the just-cooked pies in the window sill. Now to give you an idea of my situation, I was always about a smell away from those pies, but they were too high up in the window to reach. I remember getting a good swat (spanking) for stacking two barrels on top of each other and taking a pie (before dinner) and eating it all by myself. I might have been little, but I could eat. You better believe I knew how good they were, but my tastebuds had to taste and see for themselves to make sure.

You see, we all know that God is loving, powerful, merciful, gracious, protecting, tender, accepting, sacrificial and almighty, but do we really know? The only way to know if He really is all He says He is, is to taste of Him and experience the satisfaction. Just as I knew Grandma's pies were good, I had to make the extra effort to go to them and try 'em out. The same is true with our God. You must taste and see of God's love, mercy, faithfulness, compassion, grace and power. Take it from an expert in eating, taste and fulfillment definitely hold up to their billing.

✩ ✩ ✩

Further Study: When did you last taste of God? How do you really taste of Him? What desires will be satisfied when you do? Taste and see for yourself today.

PROMISE REAPERS

*Do not be deceived, God is not mocked; for whatever a
man sows, this he will also reap.*
Galatians 6:7

☆ ☆ ☆

What began in 1990 as the dream of Bill McCartney, former head coach of the University of Colorado Buffaloes football team, is today the fastest growing men's movement in the United States. Coach "Mac," who led his team to the national title in college football, resigned his $325,000-a-year job to practice what he preached and devote his full time and attention to his wife, kids and the Promise Keepers' movement. Prior to this radical move, his life had been a blur of off-season recruiting, late afternoon practices and weekend college road trips, with little time for his family. Coach Mac was led by his commitment to Christ to gather seventy men together for the purpose of encouragement and support in their roles as husbands and fathers. Today, supporters number in the hundreds of thousands, packing stadiums in major cities each year. This movement calls men of integrity back to their responsibility without encouraging a harsh, authoritarian leadership. Commitment to the family should not be one of control, but of research and development.

Of late, the family has been spiritually led by the woman. Our society needs to see what spiritual men, as husbands and fathers committed to Christ, look like. The Promise Keepers' movement is an attempt (it's working) to reverse this trend and encourage men to be involved at home with their time and spiritual input.

What does this movement mean to you today? Tons! You can start now to develop the qualities necessary to be a Promise Keeper. You won't just wake up transformed, or take a magic pill that turns you into a committed man of integrity and conviction. Don't think for one minute that what you are doing won't affect your tomorrow. It will! The choices and decisions you make now will in turn make you better, later. Be a man of your word; be a leader through Christ; be a man of high values; be consistent with your talk and walk. Be all you can be! You will reap what you sow. Be a Promise Keeper.

☆ ☆ ☆

Further Study: Write down five goals you wish to attain in five years. How do you plan to attain them? When do you start pursuing?

TELLING FRIENDS OF CHRIST

HIDE AND SEEK

This son of mine was dead and has come to life again; he was lost,
and has now been found. And they began to be merry.
Luke 15.24

☆ ☆ ☆

It's one game we've all played before, yet as we get older and graduate from childish games, it's still good for some fun watchin'. Ponder with me as we descend upon a game of hide and seek with a bunch of five-year-olds. The group selects the gullible one of the bunch to be the seeker, as the rest scatter like flies to their secret hideouts. The seeker begins to count to 10 (by thousands) then shouts out, "ready or not, here I come!" Remember how you would always go to the obvious spots first and come up empty handed, so then you would resort to phase two of the search and rescue mission? Finally, after a few minutes, your Sherlock Holmes investigation tactics were successful. The part I never liked about this goofy game (you too, I'll bet) was when you did such a good job of hiding that you never got found. You were the one who wasn't told the game was over, so you stayed in the stinky, dirty, laundry basket camouflaged in socks, underwear and shirts with armpit stains. The object of that game is to eventually be found, not remain concealed forever.

Everyone, and I mean everyone, you pass on the streets each day is still, in one form or another, playing hide and seek. The sad thing is that we all really want to be found because that means we matter. The incredible thing about God is He entered His Son (Jesus) into this game of life to find those who are lost with no hope. No matter how macho, tough, independent, self-reliant a soul may appear to be, it's all a front. In their own way they wiggle and make high-pitch noises and sounds to draw attention from the seeker. As Christians, we need to listen for those noises, gestures, comments, attitudes and outbursts which are really saying, "I'm over here. . . come find me." The prodigal son was lost, living in a pig pen and returned to an inaugural ball reception from his father. The same will be true for those lost souls on earth . . . ready or not, here He comes!

☆ ☆ ☆

Further Study: Who do you know that is lost in the game of life from Jesus? Can you help find them?

FORGIVENESS

MIND OVER MATTER

There is forgiveness with Thee.
Psalms 130:4

☆ ☆ ☆

It's like a steel trap that snares its victims with little hope for release. Your mind and your memory can either provide freedom, or lock you in an emotional prison. Chuck Swindoll said, "Life is 10% what happens and 90% how you react to what happens." That's the key. Okay, so you don't deck someone for treating you unfairly, or practice tit-for-tat strategies either. Not so fast though! Retaliation will often take a more subtle form. The best way to ensure true forgiveness is to be aware of the sly ways people don't forgive each other, like:

Gossip–We make negative reports about someone else, driving a wedge.
Criticism (without constructive advice)–We complain and nag the people who offend us until they are as hurt as we think we are.
Withdrawal–We avoid, deprive or exclude from our plans and company those people who hurt us.
Self-appointed martyrdom–Using a real or imagined injury, we manipulate people into feeling sorry for us.
Constructive criticism–While helpful criticism encourages and corrects, even good advice becomes "poison" when it's motivated by disappointment and resentment.

Humility is the key to this whole forgiveness issue. Phillips Brooks wrote, "The true way to be humble is not to stoop until you are smaller than yourself, but to stand at your real height against some higher nature that will show you what the real smallness of your greatness is." Forgive and forget . . . it's the ultimate in abundant living and freedom.

☆ ☆ ☆

Further Study: Are you a forgiving person? Do you feel that you have any bitterness towards anyone? Do you forget easily? Do you hold grudges?

PRIVILEGE NOT PROGRAM

Our Father who art in heaven hallowed be thy name.
Matthew 6:9

☆ ☆ ☆

I wrestled over the decision to include a devotional expounding on this bit of scripture. Why? Because Christians seem to have lost their grip on the purpose of prayer designated by God. I am not a "name it, claim it" Christian (don't tune me out . . . I'm not done). Yes, yes, yes, I do believe that our God is bigger than any sickness, any financial debt, or any situation we might get ourselves into, but I don't believe we can ask God for selfish things or ones that are incompatible with scripture and expect to receive them. Take a look at how Jesus taught His disciples to pray with the Lord's Prayer. See if materialism rears its ugly head anywhere in this prayer. Instead, it teaches us to recognize God's position as God, praise His majesty, ask for daily survival tools, forgive us our mess-ups, and provide us strength to lessen our mistakes in the future.

My philosophy may appear to be that if I can't convince you, I'll confuse you, and I see by that look on your face, you're confused. Put it this way–prayer is a privilege, not a program. Prayer is an awesome moment when we enter into God's presence and communicate spiritually with Him face-to-face. Why do we let worldly thoughts enter our faith and convince us that the purpose for prayer is to gain acceptance or get our way? Don't forget that communication is not a one-way street where we talk and God listens. Part of an effective prayer life is that we "be still and know that I am God." Listen. You won't be able to hear Him in the midst of chaos. Find a Bethel (Old Testament place of worship) and be consistent in meeting your Savior on a regular basis. Make your prayer life as practical as eating and breathing . . . it's a lot more fulfilling, too! (No pun intended.)

☆ ☆ ☆

Further Study: How often do you pray? What gets in your way of having an effective daily prayer time? Do you see prayer as a privilege? How do you pray?

HERITAGE OR INHERITANCE

Indeed, my heritage is beautiful to me.
Psalm 16:6

☆ ☆ ☆

Moses trained Joshua for leadership; Paul modeled church-planting to Timothy; Abraham exemplified sacrifice to Isaac; Noah proved obedience has its rewards to his family; Naomi mirrored care to Ruth. There are so many benefits that leaving a legacy can bring. Passing down a heritage demands character, commitment, love, staying power and a heavenly perspective. The institute called the family is God's smallest yet most productive battle formation. God's plan for parents in passing down a godly heritage or legacy requires first developing a strategy in opposition to the world's plan. scripture is packed with examples of obedient godly followers who continued the cycle through mentoring. Our world today is more concerned with trust funds and savings accounts to be passed down to ensure financial stability for their kids than a heritage of godliness. I think we could say here that "we got the cart way before the horse." Jesus modeled best for us the passing of a heritage to His twelve disciples. He was there for and with them, and left them to carry out the orders after He was gone from earth.

I realize the overwhelming reality of actually passing down character traits, beliefs and traditions, not to mention the family name. I realize that as a dad and husband your daily responsibilities are enough to drive you over the edge. I understand the war against the persistent attacks of Satan, the flesh and the world are enough to make you wanna' throw your hands up in disgust. My encouragement to you as a parent and spouse is to push through the discouraging times, which are caused in part by a lack of immediate results due to unrealistic expectations. God will honor your faithfulness (read Matthew 25:23) and your labor. Your children need a heritage far more than they need an inheritance, and the cash will run out long before the legacy. The world's plan results in a tribute to self surrounded by turmoil and division, while God's plan honors God and rests in peace and harmony. Don't give up; leave behind something of eternal value. True laborers or families can't be mass produced; they are raised up through life on life experiences.

☆ ☆ ☆

Further Study: How would you define a legacy? How does someone pass down a heritage today? What obstacle will you encounter in the process? Are you more concerned about the heritage or inheritance? Go ahead . . . hand it off.

THE ART OF DELEGATION

Furthermore, you shall select out of all the people able men who fear God,
men of ruth, those who hate dishonest gain, and you shall delegate
to them and place them as leaders over thousands, hundreds,
fifties and tens. So it will be easier for you, and they
will bear the burden with you. If you do these
things and God so commands you, then
you will be able to endure.
Exodus 18:21-23

☆ ☆ ☆

Working with people, which all of us are doing or will be doing, is a fun task. One lost art that I see missing from the centerpiece of the godly living room is delegation. Webster's defines delegation as "to commit or entrust authority to another person as an agent." We have far too many people who need to do it all, all the time. The word "training" (teaching) comes to mind here for the simple reason that those folks who have the philosophy "if you want something done right, do it yourself" seem to have lost sight. Granted, you want your trainee (pupil) to fall on his/her face, but not lose face in a project. You see, Jesus used another word for training and that is discipleship.

In this passage, Moses takes a little advice from his father-in-law. Moses is to answer all questions, meet everyone's needs and play referee too? Not alone, he's not. This is the scene where the pop-in-law flies onto the set and sheds a little wisdom of prior knowledge to the formula of leadership/delegation (they go hand-in-hand, you know). The formula for successful delegation of a project, or task, is to find folks who possess the character qualities listed in scripture, create the vision for them, then ask the "delegate-to-be" to tell you what you told him before setting out on this voyage. First, make sure you don't set someone up for failure by delegating to him a task that you know he doesn't have the skills to pull off. You must know your people, as Jesus did. Second, the proper steps to training are as follows: number one, model how you want it done; number two, do it with the trainee; and number three, leave and let them do it alone. It's as simple as one, two, three. Try it!

☆ ☆ ☆

Further Study: What was the last thing you delegated? Did they qualify with the formula?

MOM

Her children arise up and call her blessed, her husband also, and he prizes her.
Proverbs 31:28

Her ability to love is exceeded only by God's love itself.
Rex Burns

All that I am or hope to be, I owe to my angel mother.
Abraham Lincoln

It's at our mother's knee that we acquire our noblest and truest and highest ideals.
Mark Twain

☆ ☆ ☆

The love of a mother is never exhausted; it never changes, and it never tires. Our society has placed a demeaning connotation on the title of housewife and mom. What people tend to forget is that it's a mother who makes a house a home. Career seems to have edged out the most important job on this earth, mothering a child. I need a little room on this page to flat out brag on my wife, who is the greatest mother to my three boys. My sons worship the precious ground she walks on. Why? Because she cares like God cares for them. No, she's not perfect by any means, but you'll have a heck of a time convincing my boys she's not. When God created the female, He personally installed in their chassis a gift for nurturing that seems to work on auto-pilot all day, every day. There is no greater responsibility or job, yesterday, today or in our hi-tech future, that equals motherhood. I try (as a father), but I can't hold a candle to my wife when it comes to raising God-fearing children. She soothes with her voice and she loves with her heart.

No matter what you might think of your mom, realize this–she's the only mom you'll ever have. Respect your mom, honor your mom, care for your mom, protect your mom, pray for your mom, encourage your mom, and lastly . . . value her.

☆ ☆ ☆

Further Study: Go right now, no matter where she is and tell your mom you love her. Write her a love note, give her a hug, serve her, make her breakfast in bed, do your chores without being told. Tonight, hit your knees and pray for your mom and the mom you want to be or marry.

CATCH THE VISION

Where there is no vision the people perish.
Proverbs 29:18

☆ ☆ ☆

Years ago before Disney grew into the number one tourist attraction in North America, Walt Disney created a vision. During the building and before the completion of Disneyland in California, he put together a huge banquet/cookout which cost three million dollars for all the workers who would be involved in building this theme park. The plumbers, concrete layers, electricians, roofers, welders, painters, bull-dozer operators, surveyors, crane operators, and so on, were all gonna' be invited to this bash. Walt Disney had the architects design a small "model" of the finished product, so that all these workers would be able to see it during the banquet. The purpose was to create a vision in the eyes of each worker so they just didn't hammer a nail, wire a building, weld some pipe, lay some concrete, survey the dirt, paint a building or bull-doze a rock. After seeing the model, the workers wouldn't just put forth their muscle and effort, but also put their hearts into their work.

We, too, need to have a vision for all that we do in this life. We need to catch a dream of not just what we're doing but who we're doing it for and its purpose. You've got to have a vision for being a follower of Jesus, or your gas tank will run dry quickly. You've got to see the reason for waiting until marriage to have sex. You must see that there is a purpose for spending time in God's Word and praying to Him. See the light at the end of the tunnel today, and your path will be a lot easier to follow because of focusing on it. Believe you me, I think Disneyland is the neatest spot on earth, but it can't hold a candle to your spot in heaven. It won't cost you a three million dollar banquet to catch this vision, just a little time spent in the Word. And who knows, maybe Mickey and Minnie will be waiting at those pearly gates greeting you on the way in.

☆ ☆ ☆

Further Study: Do you have a vision? Of what? How can a spiritual vision help you in your walk with Christ? How can it help you remain pure? Where can you catch this vision?

CONFRONTATION

NOSE TO NOSE

Faithful are the wounds of a friend, but deceitful are the kisses of an enemy.
Psalms 27:6

☆ ☆ ☆

Why doesn't everyone think like you? Why did God have to create so many, so differently? As the gray hair begins to sprout on your head like daisies in a field, you'll realize how difficult it is to get along well with people. Whether at work, on a team, in a club, or even in the midst of your own family, you'll always find conflicts in interests and beliefs. The problem rears its ugly head when we don't handle differences as God intended. Violence and anger seem to be popular means of dealing with differences. Why? Because we don't realize that difference can be the sharp tool God uses to chip away character flaws. Think about it, confrontation has a way of bringing out both the best and the worst in us.

Our society seems to have lost the meaning of friendship. We label as friends those who are really only acquaintances. A real friend is someone for whom you would lay down your life. A friend is someone who sticks closer than a blood relative through the highs and lows. A friend loves enough to point out flaws in our character in order to make us better. A friend warns us of upcoming dangers and hazards we may soon encounter. A friend loves at all times. Don't be afraid to point out, not judge, a friend's weaknesses that are inhibiting a fulfilling life with Christ. Don't nit-pick issues that don't matter, choose what mountains to climb with a friend and go for it. Deal with issues that go against scripture. To love a friend, you'll have to learn to be one first!

☆ ☆ ☆

Further Study: What is your definition of friendship? Are you a real friend? What could make you a better friend? Ask a friend what you could do to be a better friend.

SELF IMAGE

EXPRESSING INDIVIDUALITY

*I will give thanks to thee, for I am fearfully and wonderfully made;
wonderful are thy works, and my soul knows it very well.*
Psalms 139·14

✫ ✫ ✫

When in doubt, blame it on a low self-image, right? It seems like every-body who is anybody wants a scapegoat, so we have chosen the old self-worth. The problem with not only non-believers, but Christians too, is that we don't see like God sees. A friend of mine, a very talented Christian singer, Billy Sprague, sings a song with catchy lyrics that say, "I am as I am if I am all I see, but if He is all I see, then I see me as He" (confusing, isn't it?). The gist of it simply states that when we put our focus on the Creator and not the cre-ation (me), then the fog of worthlessness is lifted.

Get this . . . you need to be taking a victory lap, not singin' the blues about you as a valuable vessel. You need to be spending less time trying to revamp the system and more time sharpening up what and who you are. Listen to me for one minute, and I promise you I won't stutter and make sure your ears don't flap, but you are wonderfully made! Okay, was that loud enough for ya'? Let me clue your brain in to this wave, too . . . God doesn't make junk! Hear that too? We all, including myself, should jump out of bed like a missile off the launch pad, throw our hands up heavenward and say, "thanks a ton, God, for making me like me." What a new outlook on life, not having to be something you're not. If you're created to be a duck then don't try to be like your neigh-boring squirrels (ducks look stupid climbing trees and squirrels look even dumber swimming). Before you go to bed tonight I want you to read the verse above 10 times and try to memorize it (oh no, homework, dude!), cuz' it's worth your time.

✫ ✫ ✫

Further Study: Do you know deep in your soul that you are a wonderful cre-ation? Do you feel like a castle or a shack? According to this verse, what did God create? Do you believe it?

OUT OF BOUNDS

*Now the deeds of the flesh are evident, which are: immorality, impurity, sensuality,
idolatry, sorcery, enmities, strife, jealousy, outburst of anger, disputes, dissentions,
factions, envying, drunkenness, carousing, and things like these, of which
I forewarn you just as I have forewarned you that those who
practice such things shall not inherit the Kingdom of God.*
Galatians 5:19-21

☆ ☆ ☆

Close your eyes for a moment and imagine a football game with no
end zone, a basketball game with no hoop, a golf course with no fairway, a
tennis match with no net, and a track or swim meet with no lanes. Now, correct me if I'm wrong, but that would be the ultimate in confusion. Basketball
without sidelines, referees or a goal is rugby. If you have ever been on a canoe
or raft trip down a long river in Colorado you know the ride is defined by the
beauty of cliffs that grow out of the river banks up to the clouds. Boundaries
communicate a standard set by a scholar of the game and help produce a
sport that's fun, yet fair to all.

Whether you like them or not, agree or disagree, you live in a civilization
that has a few rules and boundaries. They are in place to help, not hurt you.
Why a speed limit? So you don't kill yourself or others. Why gun laws? So no
one shoots you. Why a judicial system? So everyone goes by the same laws.
God has set in place rules and laws that are there for your benefit. The Ten
Commandments are not a list of suggestions. Do yourself a favor and stay in
the bounds that God laid down. It makes life so much easier and less painful.
God is not some cosmic kill-joy looking to punish you for living. He desires
to provide a wonderful, fulfilling, joyful game of life . . . just stay in bounds or
you'll lose.

☆ ☆ ☆

Further Study: Why are there rules? Why do sports have boundaries—to help
the game or destroy it? Do you play in or out of bounds in God's game most
of the time? What can you do to stay in bounds more often?

BEING THANKFUL

GRATITUDE

*Let the peace of Christ rule in your hearts, to which indeed you
were called in one body, and be thankful.*
Colossians 3:15

☆ ☆ ☆

Mother Theresa, one of the most godly women to roam this planet,
told this story in an address to the National Prayer Breakfast. In a foreign
country one evening, she went out and picked up four people from off the
streets (bums). One of the four was in sad shape, so she told the other three,
"I will take care of the one in the worst condition." Mother Theresa did for
her all that her love could do. She put her in a warm bed, and there was a
smile on her face as she did so. The sick woman took her hand and said only
two words, "Thank you," and then she died. Mother Teresa addressed the
group, "I couldn't help but examine my conscience before her. I asked myself
what would I say if I were in her place? My answer was simple. I would have
said I'm hungry, dying and in pain. She gave me much more than I gave her
(a bed), she gave me her grateful love and died with a smile on her face."

Isn't it ironic that gratitude brings a smile to people and becomes such a
wonderful gift? Mother Theresa had such a neat perspective and wonderful
outlook on life. God puts you in situations daily where you can take the honors or give the glory to Him–your choice. To be grateful means to appreciate
the kindness and grace you have been given or shown. Calvary (the cross) is
a supreme (and we're not talking pizza) example of gratitude. Be thankful for
every day you live and all the many blessings which come standard with each
day.

☆ ☆ ☆

Further Study: For what or whom are you thankful? What does gratitude mean
to you? Are you one of those who takes things for granted? Why? How can
you be grateful for all you have? Will you? When? How?

COSMETIC CHAOS

*For God sees not as man sees, for man looks at the outward
appearance, but the Lord looks at the heart.*
1 Samuel 16:7

☆ ☆ ☆

Thank God we live by the laws of the Creator and not the created! It seems like we live in a world of public displays, or like fish in a fish bowl where everything and everyone is judged on appearance. This cosmetic cosmos we call earth seems to have lost its perspective on what really matters and what doesn't. I heard a story of a unique burglary which took place in the windy city of Chicago, but the robbers didn't steal anything. They broke into a department store and switched price tags to make cheap items expensive and expensive merchandise cheap. A few hours past the store's opening, one chilly Monday morning, the salespeople began to notice something was definitely amiss. It seems that Satan (the thief) has come into our store (life) and switched around our priorities. He has taken the superficial and made it more important than the inward qualities of the heart. Can you imagine marrying someone for his/her appearance only, knowing full well that everyone gets older, grayer, more wrinkled and less mobile by the day? Our hearts, however, (Jesus' temple) get better by the day and more attractive by the hour. How refreshing it would be to have someone walk up and say, "you have a beautiful heart," or "your heart gets better lookin' everyday!"

It never fails that God's way is the right way. What a difference it would make in our social system if we would see as God sees.

☆ ☆ ☆

Further Study: How do you feel today about yourself? Are you looking from God's eyes?

FRIENDSHIP

A FRIEND IN DEED

A man (or woman) *of many friends comes to ruin, but there is
a friend who sticks closer than any brother.*
Proverbs 18:24

✯ ✯ ✯

You can't live with 'em, and you can't live without 'em. If there is one area considered as important as tick spray is to a dog, it's friendships. Every person alive today (including you) desires close, intimate relationships with others outside of dating. The one thing all these high-powered psychologists and psychiatrists, both secular and Christian, agree upon is that everyone has two needs. One is the need to be loved; the second is the need to love someone else. You know our dating relationships would be a lot longer lasting and closer if they started out as a friendship first and then graduated into a dating relationship. Marriages would be easier and more fruitful if they were an extended friendship which blossomed into a lifelong commitment.

Growing up, I didn't come from a church-going, meal praying family. I attribute my spiritual guidance to my uncompromising Christian friends. The Bible says, "bad company (not the rock group either) corrupts good morals." How often we run around with whom we may call friends, but who are only mere acquaintances, in actuality. If we use God's definition of true friendship to pick our friends, I think we would not be as apt to say, "I have tons of friends." A real friend is one who is like-minded with you in beliefs, ethics, morals and standards, one who challenges you to grow closer with Christ before growing closer to him, one who will stick with you through the highs and lows, ins and outs.

God gives you the model relationship and then leaves it up to you to follow the instruction manual (Bible) and build it. Don't hang out with the pigs if you don't want to end up in the mud. If you have a friend (not acquaintance) who sticks with you like a fly to fly paper, then invest your heart in him/her. Use your tongue wisely and be as loyal as a dog is to his owner. Believe me, this will be one investment with big returns even when the market falls.

✯ ✯ ✯

Further Study: Who would you die for out of your friends today? Why or why not? Are the reasons derived from scripture?

FORGIVENESS OF SIN

BATH TIME

*If we confess our sins, He is faithful and just to forgive us our sin
and cleanse us from all unrighteousness.*
1 John 1:9

☆ ☆ ☆

There is no time more fun at my household than a home cooked supper, followed up with the priceless dessert of "bath time." The kids can hardly finish their last bite before they are dashing off up the stairs, leaving a trail of clothes, headed for that big warm bath filled with Mr. Bubble. I always thought (that is, until I had kids) that the sole goal for a bath was to get clean. The purpose, to my surprise, of baths is to experiment with toys to see which float and which don't, how long it takes little brother to start kicking after holding him under for a new record or what amount of water can be deposited on the floor before Dad gets mad. No matter how you've grown up, you'll probably always remember those tub-times, and if not, you will when the kiddos come.

So often in scripture you'll find a passage, word, or verse that you have heard so much that you become numb to it. This passage is one of those that you just glide right past as you fly through your quiet time. Do you see two mighty characteristics of God . . . faithful and just? Did you miss the part about what you have to do in order for Him to respond? How about . . . you confess your mistakes; He cleanses you. In John 13:10 Jesus explains to Peter, prior to the last supper and after He had washed Peter's feet, that there was not a need to take another bath (accept Christ as your Savior again). Just repent daily (wash your feet) to be cleansed and make things right with God. Wow, what a deal! How easy it is if we just stay soft at heart, He gives us our own "bath time" cleansing.

☆ ☆ ☆

Further Study: How often do you have a "bath time" with God? Do you need a bath today?

COMMITMENT

TURN OR BURN

Suffer hardship with me, as a good soldier of Christ Jesus.
2 Timothy 2:3

⋏ ⋏ ⋏

In July of 64 AD, a fire broke out in a ghetto area of Rome and burned down half the city. The rumor was that Nero did it to free up space for new building plans, but his scapegoat became the Christians in Rome and an active pursuit to persecute Christians began. Paul was in prison, but a guy named Demas wasn't, and he decided to run before he was persecuted and condemned as well. He decided to run to his home in Thessalonica (2 Timothy 4:10). His concern for safety in this present world caused him to lose sight of the future kingdom which Paul so eagerly awaited.

When Paul referred to being in love with this world, he was speaking of its prosperity, profit and fame. To Demas, life was too precious and short, too full of delight, to be thrown into Nero's lions' den as an amusement for thousands of bloodthirsty spectators. He recalled all the friends and fortune he left behind to become a Christian, and his excitement for missionary work with Paul faded. Demas had not heeded Paul's advice to set his "affection on things above, not on things on this earth" (Colossians 3:2), and he had slowly become more and more "conformed to the world" (Romans 12:2). As a result of this, Demas was unwilling to maintain his commitment to Paul and God during that time of intense pressure and persecution.

The true test of ourselves and our allegiance is when the heat is turned up. You really don't know what level of commitment you or the other party has in a friendship, working relationship, marriage or to God until everything ain't goin' so good and you "bail out." Are you one who jumps ship when your life begins to take on water (hard times), or are you one who sucks it up and goes down with the ship? The true test of commitment is when faith is all you have, but it's all you need. The true test of a race isn't how you start, but if you finish.

☆ ☆ ☆

Further Study: Define commitment in your terms, then in God's terms. How committed are you when the walls fall down around you and things look bleak? How can you prepare now for those tough times?

DEATH

Now You See It, Now You Don't

You do not know what tomorrow has in store . . . your life is but a vapor.
James 4:14

☆ ☆ ☆

It would have been considered a normal day at the office. At 9:03 a.m. on April 19, 1995, federal employees were doing what needed doing in downtown Oklahoma City at the Alfred P. Murrah Federal Building. At 9:04 a.m. the blast from a 24-foot rental truck filled with explosives sent a shock wave, causing total destruction at the site and severe damage to buildings blocks away. Hundreds of fatalities and injuries resulted from the blast consisting of two tons of ammonium nitrate fertilizer, doused in fuel oil, ignited by some sort of detonator. This terrorist act was the worst in U.S. history and stunned the American public. Who and why? Timothy James McVeigh, a 27 year old man portrayed by some in the media as easygoing and introspective, certainly did not seem to fit the profile of someone who could cause this terror. Since returning from the Gulf War, though, he reportedly fathered an illegitimate child, lost jobs, drank a lot, fought often, set off explosives, bought guns, occasionally attended right-wing militia group meetings, and lived like a nomad. Timothy was angry at the world (especially the government) for the way the cult compound in Waco, Texas, was handled. He harbored vengeance, fueled by an anger without regard for life, just as long as his statement was made.

Four days after this morning of terror, I was in Oklahoma City for a speaking engagement. I rented a car and was compelled to drive downtown to see the devastation. I stood by the roped off building, wept and prayed for the victims and their families. I thought about the one minute (9:03) prior to the blast and one minute after (9:05). One minute alive . . . the next dead. I recalled the verse in James that illustrated to me that our life is a mist . . . the wisp of steam that rises off an early morning cup of coffee, then vanishes. Life is short and unpredictable. My prayer was that they all (children, men, and women) went to heaven . . . Amen.

☆ ☆ ☆

Further Study: What is anger? How is it manifested? How do you control it? What happens if it's not dealt with?

GIFTS

GIFTED

I will give thanks to Thee, for I am fearfully and wonderfully made;
wonderful are Thy works, and my soul knows it well.
Psalms 139:14

✩ ✩ ✩

There is nothing quite like laying on your back, gazing up on a crystal clear night, looking at the stars. On a dark, quiet night sitting alone just looking up in the sky, at first glance, all the stars seem to be identical. But if you look through a telescope you will notice differences in size, color, intensity, shape and structure. I bet if you were to crack a few of those stars open like an egg, you'd find each one is even composed differently. You can say the same of people. How similar one seems to the other, just like stars, until you look more closely and get to know them. At that point, a special transformation of thinking and perspective occurs, and you realize we all are uniquely different. Even a person's own name is a unique characteristic. You soon realize that each person is made up of a variety of hopes, dreams, theories, perspectives, goals and cherished thoughts. It's the unique differences that allow us to exist separately and yet combine harmoniously like the multiple pieces of a jigsaw puzzle fit together to form a whole.

God has specifically made each of us different, but at the same time He gave us equal opportunity to develop our gifts and talents. Utilize your special God-given gifts as only you can and learn to accept and encourage the talents of others. Throw away petty jealousy and have the mature attitude that encourages others to be all they were meant to be in Christ. If you can't win the race yourself, make sure the guy that beats you breaks the world record. Be a Barnabus who saw his limits, but saw Paul's exceptional gifts and encouraged him to use them. Plant trees that you'll never sit under . . . that's a Christian outlook.

✩ ✩ ✩

Further Study: List what you think your talents are. Now, how do you utilize these gifts for God? Are you one of those who doesn't see his/her talents, just those of others? Take a minute to ask God to use you and your talents today.

PERSON OF CHRIST

IDENTITY CRISIS

To the degree that you share in the sufferings of Christ, keep on rejoicing.
1 Peter 4:13

☆ ☆ ☆

In the town of Stepanvan, Armenia, there lives a woman that everyone calls "Palasan's wife." She has her own name, of course, but the people of this small town call her by her husband's name to show her honor. In 1988, a devastating earthquake struck this town in the early noon hour. Mr. Palasan was at work when the quake hit, and he rushed over to the elementary school his son attended. By the time he arrived, the school was already destroyed, but he entered the building to carry children outside to safety. He saved 28 children, but when he went back inside for a final check, an aftershock hit. The school building completely collapsed, and Mr. Palasan was killed.

Being the son of a professional football player was a great honor. To be associated with him when I went to the University of Oklahoma and played basketball (even though his illustrious career there was in football) was also a great honor. Sometimes a person's greatest honor is not who they are but to whom they are related. The highest honor of any believer is to be called a disciple of Jesus Christ, who laid down His life for all people. To be called "child of God" is more of an identity and honor than any other name in the universe. The Armenian woman was honored to be called "Palasan's wife." It is much more of an honor to be called "a disciple of Christ."

☆ ☆ ☆

Further Study: Who do people say that you are? Are you associated with Christ? Do people see you in your lifestyle as a relative of the Creator? Why or why not? How can you obtain that title? Are you willing to do what it takes to get it?

THE MAJORITY

Blessed is the man who doesn't walk in the counsel of the wicked,
stand in the way of sinners or sit in the seat of mockers.
Psalm 1:1

✩ ✩ ✩

You live in a civilization where the majority has ruled throughout history. The greatest injustices of history have been unchecked "majority rule." It was the majority that crucified Christ, burned Christians at the stake, established slavery in the South, chuckled when Columbus said the world was round, cut off the ears of John Pym because he advocated the liberty of the press, put Hitler into power and overturned Roe v. Wade to legalize abortion. As you can see (and I'm sure you could add a lot more to this list), the majority is not necessarily always best for you or your country.

As a Christian you have the governing authority to choose what is right or wrong, to decide to run with the majority and to not run with the minority. People in our culture (including Christians) have a natural tendency to always choose the easy way. The problem comes when the easy way isn't the right way. You didn't see Jesus choosing the easy way, did you? You didn't hear Him saying, "Hey, these spikes in my wrists and this thorn crown on my head are a pain, so I quit." Jesus, the ultimate role model, shows and proves that most of the time the harder way (less traveled) is the best way. Every day you face the intersection of choosing to go with the flow or swim against the current (like a salmon). It's usually the majority that will be drinking, getting divorced, cheating on tests, not telling the truth or trying pre-marital sex. I'm definitely not telling you choosing the harder way will be easy, but neither did Jesus. You'll have to have the faith, which is what it takes to stand your ground and do what Jesus would do in every situation and circumstance. Most of the time it's what the few do that leave a lasting impact on the world for Christ.

✩ ✩ ✩

Further Study: Why do most vote with the majority? How tough is it for you to go against the flow? Will you do it today? Why or why not? What kind of impact will you have for standing firm in your faith?

ENCOURAGEMENT

HOPE SET HIGH

And hope does not disappoint us because God has poured out his love into our hearts by the Holy Spirit, whom he has given us.
Romans 5:5

☆ ☆ ☆

Now, here is a classic. Do you remember the childhood movie about the circus elephant with the enormous ears? How at first he was mocked and abused by some (the crows), and then, he was praised and applauded by all (the crowd)? *Dumbo* is a classic because it shows how an apparent goof can become a gift. The circus mouse plays a key role in the movie as the one who initiates the forward progress. He has a desire for Dumbo with expectations of success. He looks past the obvious to see the hope. Realize that hope will never disappoint you. How does the mouse pull this off? What else . . . the magic feather. Remember that it was Dumbo's belief in the feather which allowed him to soar through the air with the greatest of ease.

You and I have a responsibility to be like the mouse and desire others to be better than ourselves. Set goals to serve the servants; delegate yourself out of a job; be a "give fanatic" (anything to anyone). Give what you're asking . . . magic feathers, of course. That little something extra which will encourage someone else to succeed (maybe before you do). It's not the final destination that is so exciting; it's the journey. It's not the final bang but every step along the way. Give out feathers on the journey and not at the finish line. You realize that to do this you'll need the mind set of Christ (think like Him). Jesus succeeded because He had hope in heaven with His Father. When the world tells you to put all your hope in money, clothes, cars, medicine, houses, jobs, etc., you'll have to fight the thought and focus on the truth. Our hope in Christ is the promise of tomorrow. Dumbo may have started out his career as the brunt of jokes, but he ended up the talk of the town with a little help from a hope giver (the mouse) with a magic wand (the feather).

☆ ☆ ☆

Further Study: What is a magic feather to you? What magic feather can you give to someone else today?

SELF

DISCHARGED

*In this you greatly rejoice, though now for a little while you may
have had to suffer grief in all kinds of trials.*
1 Peter 1:6

☆ ☆ ☆

I'm slowly figuring out this family stuff. I'll do my best to try and share a few helpful hints so that your learning curve will be less dramatic. First and foremost, when you find out you're "expecting," purchase a video camcorder. There are about 2,000 different types of camcorders on the market, old fashioned, big ones, palm size or picture view. Costs range from hundreds to thousands, depending on your weakness for gimmicks (bells and whistles), or your preference for quality. You can buy all sorts of junk with them like bags, tripods and lenses. Whatever you buy, you'd best get several batteries and lots of video tape.

After I purchased my camcorder, I then read the instructions (which is uncommon for me) on the use of the battery. The manufacturer recommend that the battery should completely discharge before recharging it, especially the first few times. This procedure actually increases the endurance of the battery.

In a like manner, our trials in life "discharge" us, emptying our dependence on self (our own human strength) and increasing our capacity to receive God's limitless power to endure. It's not easy to totally eliminate self and allow God to intervene as our true power source. To "discharge" means to acknowledge that we are incapable, yet our Savior is very capable. Trials are in our path to teach us endurance, to mature us, and to deepen our faith and love for God. Next time you're playing with one of those one-eyed monsters and the battery runs out, recall that the same will happen to you someday. Recharge it to full power . . . Jesus will recharge you.

☆ ☆ ☆

Further Study: How do you handle the times when you are completely depleted of self? How do you recharge yourself? Is God anywhere in the picture? Why does God allow trials to discharge you?

CROSS EXAMINATION

You who are going to destroy the temple and rebuild it in three days, save Yourself!
If you are the Son of God, come down off that cross.
Matthew 27:40

✫ ✫ ✫

If you've never seen it on TV, you surely have seen this rush hour of rhetoric take place on the evening news. It's a dueling tongue tango between two attorneys (that's a tongue twister if I've ever seen one) which takes place daily across this country. The arena is a big courtroom, the referee is the judge (the dude in the black robe with a mallet), the coaches are the lawyers (dressed in starch), the player is the accused (scared spitless), and the onlookers are the jurors (the ones summoned to do this). The prosecutor and the defender are going at it, like two cats after the same mouse, politicizing to win the votes of the jurors. They call on witnesses and testimonies of folks and begin to cross-examine them to shreds. What takes place during a cross examination is that a witness is called to the stand by the opposing party for the purpose of testing the reliability of his previous testimony. Boy howdy, that's when all the prior law school know-how comes in to play and things get ugly.

Read the verse above again . . . I'll wait for ya'. Okay, did you see it or even hear it from the mouthy mockers? They were cross examining Jesus right there. Those worthless chumps were checking out the reliability of Jesus' previous statement. The problem is that they didn't or couldn't see the tree cuz' of the forest. What they should have been doing instead of a cross examination is an examination of the cross . . . get it? They didn't see what was happening right in front of their flappin' lips. They didn't realize the most important trial in history had taken place, and the jury found Jesus guilty of nothing but fulfilling prophecy. I would have to say that the scene in this courtroom was not, and never will be, re-enacted in any court of law again. Gahl-Lee, aren't you glad Jesus didn't decide to come down off that cross and commence kickin' some tail? That was what I'd have done, but then again that's exactly why I'm not the Savior and Jesus is. He can handle the toughest cross examination to this day.

✫ ✫ ✫

Further Study: Do you daily cross examine God or examine the cross? Why not? How can you begin today? Will you? Who will hold you accountable to do that?

RELATIONSHIPS

RESOLVING CONFLICT

Be angry yet do not sin; do not let the sun go down on your anger.
Ephesians 4:26

☆ ☆ ☆

You know what? The older you become, the more you're gonna' realize how different and unique people really are. If you're lucky, you'll realize just how unusual people think, act, believe, walk and talk. In your search, you may also arrive at the brilliant conclusion that along with differences, conflict also seems to arise. And where conflict lives, you'll find strife as its neighbor. Strife resides next door to disharmony and anger. Now, after that boring little speech, I'd like to walk you through a way to solve the problem of anger and bitterness with a set of guidelines. These can be called "The Twelve Ground Rules of Confrontation by Communication."

Acknowledge your contribution to the problem.
Stick to today's problem and don't use the past as ammo (no "you always" or "you never" phrases).
Identify the real issue at hand; don't deal with the layers surrounding it.
Express your feelings and emotion with statements that begin with "I" instead of "you."
Avoid analyzing the other person's character (talk or behavior).
Avoid counterattacks and accept criticism graciously as a mature person.
Avoid "mind reading" what the other person means by a comment.
Keep short accounts (don't let the sun go down on your anger).
Maintain control of your tongue and emotions.
Don't attempt to win; seek mutually satisfying solutions to your disagreements.
No hitting below the belt (no cut-downs allowed).
When any of the above rules are broken, call a foul and get back on track.

If a problem should arise between you and anyone else, you must "get it right" with them soon. Remember, you don't make things right or resolve conflicts through gossip, letters, or denial—you do it by face-to-face communication. Good luck!

☆ ☆ ☆

Further Study: Who do you have anger toward today? When are you gonna' resolve it? Today?

MARATHON RUNNERS

*Now faith is the assurance of things hoped for and
the conviction of things not yet seen.*
Hebrews 11.1

✷ ✷ ✷

Have you ever asked yourself why this race we call Christianity is a marathon and not a sprint? Boy, oh boy, would it be one heck of a lot less tiring and complicated if it was. Just think . . . if it was a sprint, it would be like a fast food drive-through where we put our order in and in just a matter of seconds could see the end product. Take a look at some people of the past whom God called to strap on the lightweight running shoes and start runnin'. Noah, for instance, was called to build a yacht in the middle of a dry spell in preparation for one whopper of a downpour that would last 40 days. One hundred and twenty years after God commanded those crazy antics it happened . . . and boy did it happen! For Noah's willingness to run, God spared his life and his family's. Look at Sarah, Abraham's wife who was unable to have kids, and then at the age of 90 became pregnant with Isaac. Imagine what the neighbors said! What about Moses who was called to lead some three million whiny babies out of slavery and pulled off a few smooth moves along the way like parting a sea, making a river turn to blood and watching his cane become an irate snake?

The reason we are called to this marathon is because we don't need faith or training to run a sprint. We can see the finish in a sprint from the start but we can't in a marathon. Anyone can run a sprint any time (it may take a calendar year) and finish, but a marathon takes extensive training and sacrifice. Admit it, we need God's help to finish this long race with the faith that He will have a final finishing place (heaven) to rest. Our reward is eternal, our endurance imperative, and our course unpredictable, yet exciting. So what are you waiting for . . . on your mark, get set, go!

✷ ✷ ✷

Further Study: What is the toughest part of your race? What causes you to want to quit? How can others before you like Noah, Sarah, and Moses inspire you today?

SHOCK ADS

*Jesus replied, "Love the Lord your God with all your heart
and with all your soul and with all your mind."*
Matthew 22.37

★ ★ ★

"Whatever it takes to get their attention," is the motto of the ad agencies. The competition is getting so fierce, so dog-eat-dog, that they will try just about any shock method to stimulate the viewer to purchase. The Independent Media Network based in London, England, was the first to set the perverted pace as they allowed new shock ads to be aired on TV. They showed horse corpses falling two stories, transvestites in cabs, topless women, bondage, mock sex, and to top it off, dismembered body parts. The point is that the folks who are supposed to be screening these ads have instead bought into the hype. Now, you might be saying, "Hey, that's in London, not Dallas," but I'm saying it's on its way to good ol' America in just a matter of time.

Our human (sinful) nature is and always will be on the fast track to hell if we let it take its natural course. The TV is gonna' get worse, the domestic violence, the chemical abuse, killing of babies, homosexual activity,   disease . . . need I go on? Jesus is the one and only answer to our problems. Whether here or abroad, via media or on the streets, in the clinics or in the hospitals. Our love (passion) must be for God Almighty and not for the newest style or latest car. Our love must first be for God, above the opposite sex, career placement or dollar bills. Come on, "Holmes," how tough is it to see that without Him we crater and with Him we climb? This devotion, I'm sure, is not a revelation in Calvinistic Theology, but it is an attempt to get you off your content behinds and on your faithful knees. Loving God is not a one time decision that lasts forever . . . it should be renewed daily.

★ ★ ★

Further Study: Do you really love God? How much? When? For how long? Daily? Weekly? Monthly? How about lifely (is that a word)?

BELIEVE YOU . . . ME

*Glory to God in the highest, and on earth, peace among men
with whom I am well pleased.*
Luke 2:14

☆ ☆ ☆

One of the greatest storylines ever placed in a film can be found in the movie *Hook*. Robin Williams played a "success-driven" father who desired to love his family, but was caught up in the corporate scene. His children ran away to the fantasy world of "Neverland" to look for happiness, but ran into "Captain Hook" (played by Dustin Hoffman) The children's father became Peter Pan in search of his kidnapped kids, along with his trusty side-kick, "Tinker Bell," played by none other than Julia Roberts. Pete and Tinker teamed up with a ruddy band of young brigades to bring down "Hook" and his not-so-merry men. In the climax, Peter Pan and Captain Hook faced each other in a final duel of swords. At one point during the fight, it looked as if Hook would be victorious. Peter seemed without hope, until . . . his grungie brigade of boys quietly began to chant, "I believe in you . . . Peter, I believe in you." This gave Peter a sudden burst of energy and new-found confidence to ultimately defeat Hook, return to reality, and become a great dad.

I enjoyed this movie most, not because of the Academy Award acting or special effects, but for the one punch line, "I believe in you." What an awesome transformation occurs when we're told that someone out there believes in us. God said of Jesus, "This is my Son with whom I am well pleased." The flip side of this statement shows how to believe in someone else (verbally). There is no mountain you can't climb or tough time you can't overcome knowing that someone believes in you. Being believed in is just one step beneath being told you're loved. In fact, they should go together like peas and carrots (a Forrest Gump line). Show your confidence, support, and trust, in someone today by telling them you believe in them . . . start with your Savior first.

☆ ☆ ☆

Further Study: Who was the last person you told, "I believe in you?" Who has said they believe in you? Does God believe in you? How do you know? Go tell someone!

SEX

SEX

SEX — MAY 31

URGED TO MERGE

This is the will of God, your sanctification; that is, that you abstain from sexual immorality.
1 Thessalonians 4:3

✶ ✶ ✶

By the time a young person finishes high school, he/she will have spent 18,000 hours in front of the boob-tube (TV) and only 12,000 hours in class. That is equal to more than two years spent staring at a hi-tech fish bowl. Daytime television contains 50 percent more sexual references than "prime time," so you can see why it's so popular. Sixty percent of graduating teenagers say they learned about the "birds and bees" not from their parents or sex education class, but via the television. Take a second and read through some facts that may just enlighten you about the urging from our society to have sex before marriage:

The average American teenager has had sex before their 16th birthday.
57% of high school and 79% of college students polled say they have lost their   virginity.
80% of all teenage intercourse is spontaneous, not planned.
Reasons for having premarital sex are 1) peer pressure, 2) everyone's doing it, 3) curiosity, 4) gratification–not for love.
39% of high school and 58% of college students use contraceptives when having sex.
More people have died of AIDS than died in Vietnam.
(Statistics accumulated from USA Today, Journal of Marriage & Family, Center for Disease Control, Planned Parenthood)

Our sick society has discovered that exploiting young people for money is big business. We use sex to sell cigarettes, cars, toys, sports and movies. You can't read, see or hear anything today without catching a sexual reference. You, yes you, must decide where you stand and what you're standing for. Sex is not some sneaky, ugly, evil, ritualistic act portrayed by Hollywood, but a function designed specifically by God. What our Creator planned, the world has perverted. Resist the urge to merge and willfully wait until marriage . . . it is well worth it.

✶ ✶ ✶

Further Study: Why wait? Give reasons to wait. Why does God want us to wait until marriage? What steps can keep you out of a bad situation? Are you willing to wait?

GOD'S WILL

Warning Labels

*By faith Noah, when being warned about things not yet seen, in holy fear
built an ark to save his family. By his faith he condemned the world
and became heir of the righteousness that comes by faith*
Hebrews 11:7

☆ ☆ ☆

You see them everywhere if you look closely. They inform, encourage
and instruct concerning possible dangers. What are they? Warning labels.
You've seen them on medicines, chemicals, sports equipment, electric devices
and on heavy machinery. Their purpose is like the ol' saying goes, "an ounce
of prevention is worth a pound of cure." If you defy them, you could be
harmed or possibly, even killed. If you play with fire, you will probably get
burned . . . if you don't heed the warning, you'll probably feel the effects. Why
is it that our old self steps in and whispers lies to us like, "Go ahead, it couldn't
be that bad," or, "Step out, take a chance, live life to its fullest."

God's word is full of thousands of warning labels to communicate the
dangers ahead and describe the hazards that could occur if overlooked. Isn't
it great that we have a Master who looks out for us more than we do? What
an awesome way of showing one's love for another! How incredible it is to
tell others of potential potholes on life's highways and byways. The real question is do you listen and obey them? Do you actually take the warnings from
your navigator (God) that bad weather could be ahead if you continue flying
as you are? Begin today to read the labels (in the Bible), heed the warnings
and obey your spiritual instinct. Who knows . . . someday they will probably
save your life.

☆ ☆ ☆

Further Study: What warning label did you read today in the scripture? How
does it apply now? With whom can you communicate what you've learned?

LISTENING

THE ART OF LISTENING

Listen to advice and accept instruction, and in the end you will be wise.
Proverbs 19:20

✩ ✩ ✩

He had run with some of the roughest, toughest outlaws to ever show up on the Wild West scene. His area of expertise was his capability to crack the toughest bank vaults without ever laying a finger on them. You didn't read about him in your history books or see his story brought to life on the silver screen. His name was Tanner Watson, and he was blind at birth. He ran with Jesse James and "Wild Bill" Hickock. Their victims were towns like Tombstone, Abilene, Dodge City and Deadwood. They had to fight off Indians led by Sitting Bull and Crazy Horse along with cattle thieves out of the Mexican badlands south of Texas. The heyday of this historical cowboy lasted from 1867 to 1887, and life wasn't as glamorous or as romantically dangerous as it has been portrayed by the movies. Tanner survived those days to become the master of safe crackers. Because of his incredible ability to "listen" to the flaws in locks, he could pick them or figure out their combination in just a few turns of the dial. He would pull up a chair in front of the vault and have one of the outlaws spin the lock's dial until told to stop and write down the specific number they stopped on. This process was done day after day, bank after bank.

This Old West character had a gift that we can utilize in a little more positive, productive and much less dangerous way. The following techniques are a few ways in which you can increase your effectiveness in the art of listening:

Maintain eye contact.
Always sit or stand facing your partner.
Concentrate on what's being said.
Avoid distractions such as constant movement.
Use facial responses (nod) to show you're listening.
Ask relevant questions.
Re-state what your partner said to assure correct interpretation.

God has given each of us the capability of listening. Listening to someone translates into "you care." Be a collector of the tools for the art of listening.

✩ ✩ ✩

Further Study: How well do you listen? What makes listening so hard? Why

TRUTH AND CONSEQUENCES

This is what the Lord said, "Behold, I will raise up
evil against thee out of your own house."
2 Samuel 12:11

☆ ☆ ☆

All we know of King David's beautiful daughter, Tamar, we learn from one chapter in 2 Samuel 13. This chapter, tough to read, is the beginning of the fulfillment of the prophet Nathan's strong words to David. David was reaping the consequences of adultery with Bathsheba and murder of her husband Uriah. David ignored warnings about marrying Maacha who bore two children, Absalom and Tamar. Amnon was the child of David and Ahinoam, and this dangerous combination is what set the explosive stage for a cover-up for rape. Amnon lusted for his half-sister Tamar. Amnon was a favorite of King David and an obvious heir to the throne. David granted an unusual request to Amnon to eat food at the hand of Tamar in his apartment. Amnon trapped her, then raped his naive half-sister and threw her out (2 Samuel 3:17) in disgrace. If he had been witnessed doing this act, he could have been tried for forcible rape and incest. With no witness, though, Amnon was free from persecution and was now trying to save face at the expense of his sister Tamar. Absalom found out about this event and, filled with hate, murdered Amnon in full view of his other brothers (2 Samuel 13:28-29), then fled to Geshur in exile for three years. Nathan's prophecy had been bitterly fulfilled: Amnon, the crown prince, was dead as a result of lack of morality; Absalom was dead as a result of rebellion and hate; Tamar was desolate in her brother's house (2 Samuel 13:20).

This sad story is a simple reminder of the true character of our Lord, which is . . . He is a God of love and mercy . . . judgment and consequences. God will bless you because you obey, or judge you with consequences because you didn't. Here, an innocent victim, Tamar, suffered disgrace and pain which were ultimately conceived by her father's (King David) disobedience. Our sins usually affect far more than just ourselves. What we do in disobedience today can and will affect our tomorrow. Trust and obey because . . . it is really the only way.

☆ ☆ ☆

Further Study: Why does our culture tend to think in semesters, thinking that what I do in this semester doesn't affect the next one? How does disobedience carry over into the future? What does a life pursuing obedience reap?

THE CHARACTER OF JESUS

THE REAL THING

Jesus Christ is the same yesterday and today, yes, forever.
Hebrews 13:8

☆ ☆ ☆

When was the last time you were at your local Quik-Trip store and asked the attendant at the register for a Coke? You were probably presented, after the strange, clueless look, with a barrage of selections like nothing you've ever seen with the naked eye. You can get a Classic Coke, New Coke, Coke in a bottle, in a can, in a plastic bottle or liter, diet, sugar free, caffeine free, diet caffeine free, cherry . . . need I go on? Why does it take an act of Congress to make a decision that used to be a no brainer? It seems we have taken everything fun out of the "real thing" and made it into a close twin of pond water.

Isn't it a relief to know that our God doesn't change to suit the demands of others? What a nightmare, to think that Jesus would not be consistent in our future. What if He, just one day, woke up on the wrong side of a cloud in a bad mood and decided you weren't welcome in His family anymore? What if He decided we were saved by our works not grace, so we had to earn our way to those pearly gates? What if He decided He didn't love us and was tired of playing with what He created and dumped us like a hot potato? There is comfort in knowing that the Original is still the Original; the Classic is still the Classic, without any of the vital ingredients removed for the sake of keeping up with the fads of society. Read the verse above again   (I'll wait) . . . Jesus is the same forever and ever. Amen. This translates into having a Savior who follows through with what He started in perfecting us daily. Now, sit back, relax and ponder this some time today, and do yourself a favor, treat yourself to the "Real Thing."

☆ ☆ ☆

Further Study: What would it be like if Jesus wasn't the same today as He was 2,000 years ago? How does consistency make you feel?

THE TREASURE

For where your treasure is, there will your heart be also.
Matthew 6:21

☆ ☆ ☆

A farmer, soon before his death, wanted to tell his sons of a secret. He gathered the boys up and said, "Boys, I am soon to die of old age. I wanted to tell you of a hidden treasure that lies in the vineyard. Dig, and you will find it." Soon after, the father did pass away, and so the sons took a couple of shovels and other gardening tools and began to dig. They turned the soil in the vineyard over and over, yet found no buried treasure. What they did find was that because of all the digging and loosening of the soil, the vines produced abundantly and yielded a record breaking crop like none had ever seen before. The moral of the story is . . . there is no treasure without toil.

We all seem to be looking for that buried treasure throughout our lives. We want to live out those fantasies we see on all those Disney pirate movies. Little do we all realize that what we really treasure is what we talk of the most. In other words, all you have to do to find out what someone really treasures is listen to them for a while. We treasure various things like people, places, things, moments, memories, feelings, etc. God wants, and is literally jealous of our hearts, and desires us to treasure our relationship with Him. Don't forget though, just like the moral to the story, there will be no treasure without the accompanying labor. You don't ever just stumble upon your treasure like the movies portray; you'll have to inject a little time and toil. You're not limited to only one treasure chest either; just make sure that the most valued one is your relationship with your Savior in shining armor. I'm sure that when you uncover the hidden treasure chest and open it up, you'll find your heart there also.

☆ ☆ ☆

Further Study: What do you treasure most in your life? What treasures have a way of coming between you and God? Why? What can you do to keep your heart in the right treasure chest? Why does work always shadow true fulfillment in our lives?

DEATH

SUDDEN DEATH

There is a way that seems right to a man, but it ends in sudden death.
Proverbs 16:25

☆ ☆ ☆

There are two arenas of conversation where you'll find the term, "sudden death." One is the sports arena, and the other is life. We love it in the first context and fear it in the other. It's not a subject fondly looked upon at a party or during dinner, yet it's destined to become reality in both circles. Death, or even the thought of it, runs a chill up one's spine. It's been said in a world of uncertainty, there are only two absolutes–death and taxes. The older you get the clearer this will become. The funny thing (sorry about my choice of words) about dying is that it really isn't the deciding time . . . it's just the final chapter. But once a person passes through those doors, we never hear from them what's on the other side. So, we must rely on the "faith factor."

My question to you is this . . . where are you going? Death is swift, sudden, sad, and very real. You will die and either spend eternity in torment and torture, or paradise and peace. The decisions and choices that you make today will affect your ultimate destiny. My suggestion to you, no matter how long you think you may live (no guarantees) or how comfortable you might become, is that you take a good hard look at yourself and see who is gonna' win in your sudden death. Side note: Don't think for a moment that you're gonna' take your worldly possessions with you to comfort you. Have you ever seen a U-Haul behind a hearse?

☆ ☆ ☆

Further Study: If you were to die a sudden death today, where would your new residence be?

SIN

It Will Find You Out

And the Lord called to the man and said to him, "Where are you?" And he (Adam) said, "I heard the sound of You in the garden and I was afraid because I was naked, so I hid." And He replied, "Who told you that you were naked?"'
Genesis 3:9-11

☆ ☆ ☆

It didn't take me long to break one of the Ten Commandments at the young age of 10, but I did it. I had just received one of those (what I thought at the time) manly items for my birthday . . . a cap gun. Listen up now because this assault weapon could make your ears ring like you'd just walked out of some rock concert. I mean, this was one of those heavy duty plastic jobs with the fake red barrel for visual effect. Only one small problem to overcome upon its arrival to me as a gift . . . no caps. That's right, my mom didn't quite get all the necessary items for me to reap havoc on my neighbors and sister (ha ha). The cost of one roll of caps was a $1.25, but I had no money in my piggy bank. The next day I accompanied my mom to Safeway (a grocery store) to pick up some milk and eggs. There I decided to permanently borrow from the toy rack a roll of caps. That's right, the old five finger discount, or you might just say stealing. I was successful in my first heist . . . until my mom asked me that fatal question. No, she didn't see me do it, or hear me shoot my gun (I may be dumb, but I'm not stupid). She simply asked me if I wanted to earn some allowance so I could buy some caps for my gun. My conscience was eating a hole in my stomach like battery acid on a T-shirt. I immediately broke down crying and confessed my offense in detail.

In the Garden of Eden, Adam and Eve knew they had done wrong and were guilty. It's the first time in the history of mankind we see that sin produces self-consciousness. God knew what they had done, but you read in Genesis 2:25 that they were naked and not ashamed until now. This is why God immediately knew they had done wrong by the simple fact they were hiding and ashamed to be naked. Sin causes us to look at ourselves and not others. It forces us (by guilt) to give ourselves away because we want to be found out to relieve the strain of guilt on our hearts. Take my word for it . . . your sin will find you out.

☆ ☆ ☆

Further Study: How do you react when you're not right with God? What makes you self-conscience?

CASH MONEY

For the love of money is the root of all kinds of sin; some have wandered
from the faith and pierced themselves with many griefs.
1 Timothy 6:10

★ ★ ★

You can't live with it, and you can't live without it. What is it? Cold,
hard, cash money. There is nothing more consistently found in society today
that causes marriages to malfunction, companies to crumble and societies to
become stale, than money. I heard recently of a friend of mine who for the
love of money lost a thriving business, his loving wife and now his blue-eyed,
blonde-haired children. I spoke with this person on the phone and asked him
a direct question, "Was it worth it?" You don't have to be a rocket scientist to
figure out his answer . . . "No, no, no!" You can look throughout history and
see that the dynamite that destroys so many circumstances is what is produced by the Department of Treasury daily. Guess what though? It's not the
money itself that is the problem . . . it's the love of it. It's kind of like that cute
toy poodle at your grandparents' house that looks harmless yet will bite the
fire out of ya' when you touch it. Money can be a good thing if it's managed
from a godly bank account. You can probably name several people (not
many) that have lots of money yet keep it all in perspective. You'll probably
also notice that those people who play with the poodle and don't get bitten
are believers and givers.

Realize this, that money is the root of all types of evil if it's loved, and
God gives and God takes away at His own free will. Don't get swindled by
the theory that waits out there for you right after college graduation that tells
you that "to have is happiness." That's one piece of advice that's not worth its
weight in gold.

★ ★ ★

Further Study: How does the love of money affect you? How can you begin to
de-program yourself of the thinking that money buys happiness?

COUNSEL

UNWISE ADVICE

Wisdom comes from the abundance of wise (godly) *counsel.*
Proverbs 12:15

☆ ☆ ☆

Nothing in our social system is given out as freely as advice. People will give it out for marriage, business deals, daily living, purchases and tastes, without even the slightest attempt at thinking ahead of their words. You will find out for the rest of your life, we live among a people who rarely seek the right kind of biblically-based counsel. There is a huge difference in advice and counsel. I'll make a gentleman's wager that at least two-thirds of the advice you receive today, and in the days to come, will have little regard for your best interest. If we made it a rule that everyone who gave advice must first give you a dollar (hit 'em where it hurts . . . in the pocketbook) every time they gave their airborne advice, things would be said less swiftly. scripture tells us to be "slow to speak and quick to listen" for a definite reason.

Look again at this nugget of scripture found in the book of Proverbs. Do you see that there are several words which are key in the context? First of all, make sure your counsel comes from more than one person, in fact several persons. Second, make sure it's wise (godly) counsel from sources who are walking with God on a daily basis. And lastly, make sure that it is not advice, but well thought out, pondered counsel which seeks to point you closer to your Savior. There are far too many of us who can find holes in the system and will seek counsel from the "rubber stamp" people. In other words, these fellows are the ones who give us the answer we want but not necessarily what is right or what we need.

Get yourself your own personal "board" of older individuals who think not as you do but are different, yet all follow the Savior sincerely. Use this group of folks to bounce off ideas, whims, thoughts or career moves. If a decision you're making affects your future, or others close to you, then give your board a call and ask them to think and pray about what the right answer is. Don't ask for a decision right then. This will take some preplanning, but give them time to seek God's counsel first and then get back to you. Remember, advice is not what you're after. God-seeking counsel is.

☆ ☆ ☆

Further Study: When was the last time you let someone else in on your decision making? What type counsel do you give?

GOALS

YOUR MISSION

As for me and my house, we will serve the Lord.
Joshua 24:15

★ ★ ★

Every effective ministry I'm aware of has a statement of purpose in their material somewhere. A mission statement is a key ingredient in getting from point "A" to point "B" in a ministry. I am amazed how the organizations that don't have a mission statement make it, even for one year. The purpose of a mission statement is:

To direct.
To maintain a distinct purpose.
To hold accountable.
To assign a calling.
To deputize a task.

As you can plainly see . . . this way of attaining a specific goal isn't limited to Christian ministries. In fact–does your family have a mission statement? Why not? The first place we need these guidelines in place is with our families. What an awesome way to show to a community of friends and associates the direction your family is headed. Mission statements are useful tools for checking out other church and para-church organizations. They provide a window to the philosophy and theology of the group.

A mission statement should be a lot like an advertising slogan. Nike's "Just Do It" was a huge hit because it says so much in so few words. In the same way, a mission statement should make a point without being wordy. My personal guide is to say what needs saying in 20 words or less–that makes you think through what you want to communicate. Use direct, targeted words, not cliché or general terms. Make your mission statement a community of goals that can be used to direct your ship.

★ ★ ★

Further Study: Write out your own personal mission statement in 20 words or less. Sit down with your family after supper and write out a family mission statement, frame it and put it in your family room. Review this statement monthly and evaluate how you're doing personally and as a family.

SPIRITUAL WARFARE

WE'RE NOT JUST PLAYIN'

For the weapons of our warfare are not of the flesh, but divinely
powerful for the destruction of fortresses.
2 Corinthians 10:4

☆ ☆ ☆

I guess you could classify me as an "outdoor fanatic," but I consider myself one who just loves to be out in the woods. One of my past motivations for getting out in the woods was hunting trips with my father, but now I find myself out there just to get out of chaos and watch animals on their turf. Living in Colorado offers ample opportunity for watching wildlife. It's just a short trip north to Estes Park where during the "mid-September Elk Bugle" a natural phenomenon takes place. The males (bulls) of the elk herds battle for dominance, going head-to-head, antler-to-antler, for breeding rights with the females (cows). The largest, heftiest, strongest antlered bull with the most endurance will win the battle of the hormones. The defeated bull leaves and the victorious bull licks its wounds and rests up for the next challenger. The lead "herd bull" will lose hundreds of pounds, tons of strength and suffer many wounds during the breeding season.

The ironic thing about this natural ritual is that the real battle is won during the summer when elk eat continually. The one that consumes the best diet for growing antlers and gaining weight will be the heavyweight champ of the fight in the fall. Those that eat inadequately sport weaker antlers that break in battle and obtain less bulk for the fall confrontations.

Satan will choose a season to attack. The question is whether we are prepared for the battle. Much depends on what we are doing now before the war begins. Enduring faith, strength and wisdom for the spiritual wars ahead are best developed before they're needed. We're not just playin' army . . . there's a war out there. Go get ready!

☆ ☆ ☆

Further Study: In this spiritual war, will you walk away victorious or will you fall to defeat? Is this a serious battle? Do you think you're playin' army, or is it a war?

ACCOUNTABILITY

IRON ON IRON

Iron sharpens iron, so one man sharpens another.
Proverbs 27:17

☆ ☆ ☆

Have you ever wondered why God didn't put each one of us on a planet of our own? I mean, hey, it's not like the universe in which we live doesn't have enough outer space places for us to live. Wouldn't it be cool to phone up a friend and tell him that your new address is 1124 East Venus, or Apartment 4 Jupiter Drive?

If you've never been to a blacksmith's metal working shop, you've missed out. The shop is full of scrap-iron piles, 75-pound anvils, coal burning furnace and lots of metal mallets. It's amazing to watch a true blacksmith mastering an old piece of black metal into a piece of art. When heated, the smith can force, bend, pound, torque and flatten any piece of iron into a useful tool. It's awesome to see that an iron hammer can contour an iron rod into a knife, a fireplace set or dinner bell. Two of the same materials can function for the same goal in the end.

No matter what you do or how you make your career, you will deal with people (iron). This world goes round because of common folks just like you and me. God placed us in the mortal madness for a distinct purpose and that is to be sharpened and shaped into a better person. Iron does sharpen iron. We, at times, would like to say, "Beam me up, Scotty" to escape this process, but we can't. You won't always see things the same way, have the same opinion, agree with a plan, like the same movies, date or marry the same type person, enjoy the same sports, read the same books, like the same foods, listen to the same music as others you come in contact with. God made each of us different and unique for a reason (praise God), and we should learn to appreciate and admonish our differences, not condemn them. So the next time you're about to blow a lid because someone doesn't see as you see, remember this, they are "no better, no worse, just different" (NBNWJD).

☆ ☆ ☆

Further Study: What type people rub you the wrong way? Why? How can you learn to appreciate them?

FALSE PROPHETS

DEADLY VENOM

And in their hearts they put God to the test
by asking according to their own desire,
Psalm 70.18

☆ ☆ ☆

On a cool, tranquil evening in the Georgia hill country, a congregation trickles into the "Church of the Lord Jesus Christ." Old parishioners chat, young couples juggle babies, and children play amid the pews. Cutting through the church-goers, three men stride quickly, carrying small wooden boxes, and place them near the pulpit. The service begins with a warning, "We have serpents up here, and there's death in their bite. If the Lord moves you to handle them, obey the Lord." The pastor pulls out a four-foot rattlesnake and a few sleek copperheads to wave around his head. The congregation screams, chants, convulses. This nonsense stems from misunderstanding the verse, "And these signs shall follow them that believe: In my name shall they cast out devils; speak with new tongues; take up serpents, and if they drink any deadly thing, it shall not hurt them" (Mark 16:17-18). The snake-handlers accept this verse out of context and believe if they have the faith, they won't get bitten. Suffering bites and deadly venom rarely discourage these people. Even though 75 to 100 people have died of bites, there are still those who follow this belief.

There are places of worship that allow a fallen person to receive clear thinking and good judgment. Gang, God will not be mocked or put to the test like a new hi-tech gadget. God is to be worshiped and left in a holy place. God is to be feared and respected as Jehovah. There were false prophets in Jesus' time and they are still around today. These false teachers use magic, illusion, lies, deceit, dictated conviction, control, physical force, and even sex to lure in their prey. James warned us not to be easily deceived. Faith in Jesus isn't avoiding a bite from a poisonous snake, it's "the assurance of things hoped for and the conviction of things not seen" (Hebrews 11:1).

☆ ☆ ☆

Further Study: How can you avoid falling victim to a false teacher? How can you avoid taking a verse out of context?

LIFE IN THE '90S

Be still and know that I am God.
Psalm 46:10

⋏ ⋏ ⋏

If you feel like you really are a person of the '90s and on the fast-track, then you probably see your life something like this:

Your life passes you by at 90 miles an hour.
You end up working 90 hours a week.
Your to-do list has 90 items on it.
You're on a 90 calorie a day diet because you're 90 pounds overweight.
You have at least 90 bills to pay each month.
Your bank account is $90 overdrawn.
The minimum payment on your credit card is $90 (and that's just interest).
You'll be paying off student loans for 90 more months.
You don't know where you'll get $90,000 (each) to send your kids to college.
Your TV has 90 cable channels, and there's nothing good to watch.
You have 90 different activities to attend each week.
Your car just rolled over 90,000 miles.
You just answered the phone for the 90th time today.
The cheapest pair of tennis shoes you can find cost $90.
Life would be just grand if you only made $90,000 more a year.

Life in the '90s is definitely not all it's cracked up to be. It seems the faster you run, the further you lag behind, the days get shorter, while the list of things to do gets longer. Our lives get tangled in a web that can soon strangle us. We get so involved with our busy agenda that we lose sight of our purpose. God is not as concerned with what we do, as who we are in Christ. Take time away from the rat-race to be still and take quiet refuge with your Creator. You'll never cope with the agenda of the '90s until you tank-up with God for your fuel each day. Take a time-out and re-group.

☆ ☆ ☆

Further Study: How busy are you? Are you too busy for God? When was the last time you were still? Do you meet with God in your stillness? When and where can you be still for 30 minutes a day to meet with your Savior in prayer and meditation?

FISHIN' HOLE

*And Jesus said to them, "Follow me, and I will make
you fishers of men"* (women too).
Mark 1:17

☆ ☆ ☆

Before we begin, let me address you, ladies, before you turn this devotion off like a bad TV show. Please, (okay, pretty please with sugar on top) listen up because this verse applies to you as much as it does the guys. Have you ever been fishin', either on a lake, river, pond or ocean before? Well, if the answer is yes, then you will relate like an ol' relative. If not, maybe this will motivate you to try it.

Realize this first, that I grew up hunting, but never fishing, so I am definitely no Jimmy Houston (a Pro fisherman). I have done little that is as much fun to do with the whole family as landing a "lunker." We live close to a great trout lake and try to go as often as we can with the kids on weekends. There is nothing more exciting for a youngster than when the end of the pole takes a dip and begins to tug. Boy howdy, the kid's eyes light up as big as a Texas sunset, and the voice volume begins to go up at the expectation of catching a "Big One." Just the thought and anticipation of going to set the line will be enough, even if nothing is caught, to make a fishing outing a success.

I love the way that we can relate today with what happened yesterday in scripture. What would this world be like if we got as excited about "fishing for friends" as we do about "landing a lunker?" Notice that you don't have to be qualified to fish. God does that for you, and He will make you an angler for people's souls. Again, what a huge deal it is when God depends on you to follow Him, and in return you will catch others before they are caught by the evil one. Another important thing is that Satan always kills his catch, but God chooses the "catch and release" program. That release is called our freedom in Christ, something not many fine-finned fish can hope for.

☆ ☆ ☆

Further Study: What pond are you fishin' in? What does your spiritual bait look like? Catchin' any?

WORLDLY WAYS

A WEAK THINK

For as he thinks within himself, so he is.
Proverbs 23:7

☆ ☆ ☆

Years ago I went along with a handful of fellow believers on a mission trip to Trinidad. Now, hear me out, I couldn't even spell it, much less feel spiritual enough to do such a trip-but I went anyway. To give you a run down of this Third World country is a sad story. Dirt poor, used and abused by the oil industry, no stable government in place, apathy running rampant, immorality evident and directions to nowhere. Our mission was to go door to door to every house on the island and personally share Jesus with a population whose religious melting pot included Hindus, Muslims and a few Rastifarians for flavor. While sharing with a gas station attendant for about 30 minutes, I looked over the register counter to see a sign that read, "The brain is only as strong as its weakest think." What a fact of scriptural truth, yet a catchy play on the original, "the chain is only as strong as its weakest link."

If you think for a moment, you'll realize all it took for adultery, murder, theft, gossip, lying, disobedience, rebellion, lust, greed, envy and a long, long list was a weak think moment. What's that? That is a time when you weren't in tune with God and you followed the old nature path. It's the second you gave up hope for harmony, purity for passion or contentment for compromise. Realize that you are gonna' have those weak moments, you will lose a few battles (you're saved, not perfect), but you don't have to lose the war. We are overcomers!

☆ ☆ ☆

Further Study: When was the last "weak think" moment you had? How can you avoid it next time? What prevents those moments in your life?

ReRuns

As far as the east is from the west, so far has God thrown away our sins from us.
Psalm 103:12

☆ ⋔ ∧

They're back! What's back? Old reruns (and they're great)! The Andy
Griffith Show, Flipper, Superman (black and white version), Bonanza, The
Adams Family, The Brady Bunch, The Partridge Family, Leave It To
Beaver . . . you betcha', and they're worth bringing back from the sitcom
cemetery to live again. Have you had the fortune, and I do mean fortune, of
tuning in your tube to one of these vintage shows? The networks have begun
to air these oldies but goodies on weekday afternoons. Some shows are in
black and white, the clothes worn are so outdated they're back in style, and
the hair-do's are real doosers. The plots are simple, the pace is slow, the sets
simple, the humor tired and the language clean. Do yourself a favor and feast
your fancy on one of these re-runs soon, soon, very soon. They're so bad,
they're good. I suppose the thinking behind the network big shots' decision is
to appeal to those older generations who grew up watching these shows. To
be honest, it's not a bad way of getting viewers to watch a little tube in their
busy daily schedules. Even though the targeted audience may be a little older
and grayer, they still have a memory that works.

I'm glad that God doesn't like to watch old re-runs of us and our mess-
ups. We have a Creator that has all the capability (like a computer) and technology (like a laboratory) and storage space to retain the films of us falling
short in our Christian walks. God could very easily air our sins back to us at
judgment day. He could keep a little list of the times we chose our way and
not His. He could point out just how big of a scab we all are and make us feel
like an old shoe. He could keep the score in this game, and I bet we'd see we
lose by a lot. Guess what? He doesn't! He says that after we confess and
repent of them, He takes all our bloopers and throws them so far that even
man can't measure the distance. Correct me if I'm wrong here, but that's one
heck of a throw, and I'm glad. heaven doesn't show re-runs! And God seems
to have a bad memory, too!

☆ ☆ ☆

Further Study: How far is east from west? When does God throw our sins
away? Do you have some you need chucked? What does this gift do for your
relationship with Him?

GOD'S WORD

FROG IN THE KETTLE

He who separates himself seeks his own desire,
he quarrels against the sound of wisdom.
Proverbs 18:1

☆ ☆ ☆

We've all heard the analogy about the frog in the kettle. The idea behind this is that when you put a frog in lukewarm water and slowly heat it up to a boil, he obviously will become frog soup. Not only that, he will never even realize the temperature is rising.

You know, the same thing can happen to us if we are not careful. That Proverb reminds us that whenever we separate ourselves from the Word of God, we argue against what we know is right from the Word of God.

Psalm 119:9 reminds us that a man keeps his way pure by keeping it according to God's Word, not worldly ways. We must remain constantly (daily) in the Word. It is the only sure thing in a changing world. The frog in the kettle analogy can happen to anyone, at any age. None of us are above being pulled away slowly by the world. Satan is very cunning in how he lures each of us in his own way. If we are not saturated in the Word, we become very easy victims of his tactics.

The Word of God is not a bunch of outdated, unrelated fiction stories about people who never were. It is exactly what it says it is . . . The Word of God.

☆ ☆ ☆

Further Study: When have you seen yourself make a bad decision because you have not spent time in the Word? Why is it so hard for us to remain consistent in God's Word? How can we become like Jesus if we don't know what He is about or what He says?

DISCERNMENT

OUR TIMES

Men who understood the times with knowledge of what they should do.
1 Chronicles 12:32

✩ ✩ ✩

What if you went into a final exam without studying or challenged a team without scouting them first? We live in an information rich country which prides itself on being there when the action happens. News stations and major networks spend millions of dollars on equipment designed to allow live broadcasts from random locations. If you want to find out what has happened in our world, country or cities in the last 10 minutes, all you need is a remote or 25 cents for a paper. We have the capability (or technology) to be on top of the trends and times in a matter of minutes. The warning is that we can be fed the wrong perspective on the wrong story. In other words, our madness of media is a melting pot for a secular humanistic view. Our liberal media can spoon feed us, from behind the desk of the nightly news, a method of thinking and viewing certain situations. We, as a nation, saw the power of the media during the presidential race between George Bush and Bill Clinton.

You have a responsibility and a duty to keep up with what's going on around you. I like to say, "keeping your finger on the pulse of the times." You can do this by watching the news, reading the papers, listening to tapes and reading books. Make sure these sources are reliable and conservative in nature. Don't just say this world is going downhill fast without making an effort to re-direct its course to the Cross. We, as Christians, are not of the world, yet we do live in the world by Divine design. Understanding the times of our world will help us direct our lives. We must view the news with a critical eye and acknowledge it's run mostly by secular people who have not the knowledge of Christ. Make sure you spend more time studying the original (Bible) and not the counterfeit. Doing this allows you to tell what is true and what is false.

✩ ✩ ✩

Further Study: How much do you understand the times in which we live? How can you prevent being fed slanted liberal news? What one area will you choose to do something about?

YOUR MIND

WHATEVER, DUDE

*Finally, brethren, whatever is true, honorable, right, pure, lovely,
of good repute, if there is any excellence and if anything
worthy of praise, let your mind dwell on these things.*
Philippians 4:8

☆ ☆ ☆

It's a pretty uncommon sight for a school, office or now even a home to
be without a computer. The Age of Aquarius has evolved into the age of technology. Schools are training our youth to use computers from kindergarten
up. The computer has brought to the table organization, memory, data processing and graphics like never before. You would think this conglomeration
of wires, plastics and micro chips had a mind of its own. Realize this, a computer is a tool, and only as smart as its programmer. *Excel, Pagemaker* and
ClarisWorks weren't programmed by a computer named Bob. Millions of dollars are being made by professional programmers coming up with developing
programs for business and personal computers. A computer takes the input,
stores it, performs calculations or processes on it, then spits it back up as output when recalled (how's that for simplicity?).

Your mind is a super computer. When used properly, it is a tremendous
tool that can recall details from years past, visualize scenes from TV shows
and old movies, trigger emotions, control every muscle movement, distinguish between two means and create new ideas. Whether you realize it or not,
whatever you see and listen to (input), goes directly into your mind for processing. Every bed scene on TV, every curse word on the silver screen, every
lyric at a concert, every word blurted out of the radio. You are being programmed by someone and its root is either in heaven or hell. Your mind is
like a sponge, your eyes like a camera, catching every move and wiping up
every worldly spill. Be careful and downright picky about what you watch, listen to and who you follow. Set your mind on things above and not below. Be
your own censor and screen the bad from your mind. Remember, what you
are is connected to what you think.

☆ ☆ ☆

Further Study: How careful are you with your mind? Do you screen what goes
in or is it an open door policy?

GOD'S WILL

FOLLOWING IN MY FATHER'S PAW PRINTS

Many are the plans (future) *in a man's heart, but the*
counsel of the Lord will stand.
Proverbs 19:21

☆ ☆ ☆

From the magnificent musical opening and breath-taking African vistas, to the rip-roaring, (pun . . . get it?), emotionally charged climax, *The Lion King* movie reigns as animation's supreme champion. Set in the majestic beauty of the Serengeti, Disney's epic tells the heart-warming story of the love between a proud lion ruler, Mufasa, and his young son, Simba–a curious cub who "just can't wait to be king." Out from the darkness crawls Simba's jealous Uncle Scar and his hyena hitmen. Their scheming for the throne leads to Mufasa's tragic death, and Simba's exile from the kingdom he should rightfully rule. Befriended by the warmhearted warthog, Pumbaa and his maniac friend, Timon, Simba forgets his responsibilities and adopts the carefree lifestyle of "Hakuna Matata" (means: don't worry). Rafiki, the wise and mysterious baboon, helps Simba reclaim his territory and eventually his position as King, just like his father.

This devotion is targeted mainly at the male species who roam this jungle of society searching for prey . . . the future. This is one devotion I feel I am qualified (somewhat) to write. I grew up with a huge desire to follow in my father's footsteps (paw prints). Males often don't realize until later on in life what an influence their fathers can have on them. God (our true Father) has a specific, hand-picked, custom designed plan for our lives and future. There is nothing wrong with wanting to do as your dad, but don't be disappointed (or surprised) if God's way points another direction. Some reading this may very well take up where their dad left off . . . but remember, no one is a failure if God leads them to a different destination. Always remember to enjoy and learn along life's journey until coming face-to-face with our Savior in eternity. Keep on prowling!

☆ ☆ ☆

Further Study: What does (did) your father do for a living? Do you see yourself following his footsteps? Why or why not? What if God's plans are different than your father's? Is that okay? Are you sure?

ACTING CHILDISH

Unless you become like little children, you won't enter the kingdom of heaven.
Matthew 18:3

☆ ★ ☆

It's amazing to me as a parent how we think we will handle our kids differently than our parents handled us. We find ourselves reminding our kids: share, play fair, don't hit, pick up after yourself, if you don't have anything nice to say—don't say anything, don't take things that aren't yours, watch for traffic, say you're sorry, stick together and hold hands. Instructions received from our parents are for our best interest. I find myself giving out orders like a general because I desire my children to steer clear of the hazards of life. I'm not a big rule person, but I have realized that the rules I initiate in my household are motivated by love for my kids, not because I dig laying down the law.

Scripture is full of boundaries and guidelines to heed for our own good. My boys must have faith that their father knows what's best for his kiddos, and desires the best for their well-being. God has the same perspective as human parents, but we need faith in Him as our Creator to understand. God warns us in His word to flee sexual immorality, love our neighbor, be thankful, never steal or lie, live an unstained life and so on. Why? Because He wants to be a Hitler god? Not! Because He loves to write rules? No way! Because He is crazy in love with us as His own children? You bet! Heed the warning of Jesus Himself. If you don't have that child-like faith (faith that will jump from anywhere, any height, into your father's arms because you know he won't drop you), you won't inherit a spot in that heavenly hotel. Grow up and be a child. What??

☆ ★ ☆

Further Study: Are you a child of God? Do you obey your Father in heaven? Did you (or do you) obey your parents' standards?

ABRASIVNESS

What is desirable in a man is his kindness.
Proverbs 19:22

✦ ✦ ✦

Gentleness is a word not often used in circles of conversation these days. I recall a story from April 19, 1992, about former U.S. Senator John Tower of Texas and 22 others. The *Chicago Tribune* headline read, "Gear Blamed in Crash That Killed Senator." A stripped gear in the propeller controls of a commuter plane caused the plane to take a nose-dive into the Georgia woods. A specific gear that adjusted the pitch of the left engine's propellers was slowly worn down by an opposing part with a harder titanium coating, the National Transportation Safety Board reported. It acted like a file and over an extended time period, wore down the teeth that controlled the propeller. Once the teeth were sheared off, the mechanism was not able to continue working.

After reading this article, the thought that we can be a hard material that wears other weaker working materials (people) out hit me like a ton of bricks. Like the titanium-coated gear wore away the softer gear engaged to it, so one abrasive, unkind friend can wear away the spirit of another. To be kind to someone else is to have the spirit of God thriving (living actively) in your life. Don't be a titanium person who goes throughout life wearing down others by abrasive words and actions. Gentleness is a great way to attract friends and bond relationships that will last a lifetime. Abrasion kills others and sends friends into a nosedive of despair.

✦ ✦ ✦

Further Study: Would anyone describe you as kind? Why not? Are you an abrasive friend that wears down others? How can you practice kindness in your relationship?

DECISIONS

A NEW WAY OF THINKING

No one puts new wine into old wineskins; otherwise, the
new wine will hurst the skins and it will be spilled out,
and the skins will ruin. But new wine must be put
into new wineskins and both are preserved.

Luke 5:37-38

✫ ✫ ✫

Have you ever run across one of those passages of scripture that seemed to have applied to you as much as fleas on a dog? That's right, it just doesn't seem to fit your life, nor does it look like it ever will. For years I seemed to have stumbled over this verse in the gospel of Luke like a big pair of shoes in a dark hallway and never quite clued in to its real meaning. What this verse is saying, simply stated in modern terminology, is to keep the standards, yet apply them and use them more creatively. This whole devotional book is meant to come alive in the present. If you're gonna' bore someone, don't bore them with the Bible. It's key that we don't water down the richness of scripture, yet learn new ways and challenge ourselves daily on how we can creatively make God's word more exciting in a stagnant society. You can do things a new, exciting, different way without compromising your commitment to Christ. How about it . . . take a moment today to sit back and let those creative juices flow. After all, didn't Jesus do this same thing when His life and teachings could not be contained within the old rigid system of the Mosaic Law? Wasn't He the one who first put the new covenant (new wine) into a new generation during His days? Come on gang, let's show this ol' world just how fashionable our faith can really be.

✫ ✫ ✫

Further Study: When was the last time you used a recent event or illustration to prove a point out of past scripture? Try it . . . it's eye opening!

ABORTION

WHO BROKE THE BABY?

You shall not murder.
Exodus 20:13

✲ ✲ ✲

Well, well, let me think a minute . . . (that's long enough). Where, oh where have we seen or heard this little four-word phrase before? I know! I know! It was when Moses scaled down that mountain called Sinai after his meeting with God-In-Person. He was carrying those tablets with the "Ten Suggestions" on them, right? Absolutely wrong, Pickle Lips! If your Bible reads the same as mine, I do believe they were called the "Ten Commandments," not suggestions. Herein lies the problem that we face today . . . folks don't respect, adhere, listen to, abide by, or follow these commandments, or worse yet, can't even identify these 10 phrases of protection! I won't bore you with mind bloating statistics on our subject of discussion today–abortion. Help me out; clue me in; beam me up; do whatever tickles your fancy, but tell me how people get off on the idea that we have a "pro-choice" to eliminate human life? How and where did we develop the standard that if life inconveniences us, we play God and choose someone else's destiny? I mean, hey, the next time someone pulls out in front of you while you're driving, just pull out your trusty six-shootin' handgun and kill 'em! (Sound absurd? It is, but so is abortion.)

Forgive me for being on my soapbox, but reader (you!), clue in and realize we are going "to hell in a hand basket" as a society. God commands us not to kill anyone, no how, no way, no one. Children are a gift from God no matter how they are conceived. I have a question. Is God all knowing? Does He know who is pregnant now (even if they don't) and who will be pregnant in their lifetime? Then why, even if someone becomes pregnant out of wedlock, do we think we, as a civilized (questionable) society, can choose someone else's destiny? Come on people, the choice is and always will be God's. Bombing clinics and killing doctors is not the solution to this problem–it's that people need a Savior, and you need to tell them about yours. The right choice is God's choice.

✲ ✲ ✲

Further Study: Can you write down all Ten Commandments? Why do we have these guidelines? Will you memorize and live by them?

LASER GUIDED PRAYER

*I urge then, first of all, that requests, prayers, intercession
and thanksgiving be made for everyone.*
1 Timothy 2:1

☆ ☆ ☆

During Operation Desert Storm, the Iraqi war machine (the tank) was overwhelmed by the Coalition Force's ability to strike strategic targets with never-before-seen accuracy. Unknown to the Iraqis, the Allied Supreme Command dropped "Special Operations Force" (SOF) units deep behind enemy lines. These men provided bombing coordinates for military targets and first-hand reports on the effectiveness of subsequent bombing missions by the U.S. Air Force. To avoid unintended targets, pinpoint bombing was often required. A soldier from an SOF unit, standing on the ground, would request an aircraft high overhead to drop a laser-guided missile. Using a hand-held laser, the soldier would point at the target. The missile would lock on the target for a direct hit.

In much the same way, the prayers of Christian focus are often general in intent. Our prayers and conversations with God should target specific needs and petitions. A good way to pray is:

1. Praise God for who He is.
2. Confess sins.
3. Petition for needs of others.
4. Thank Him for answers which come as yes, no, or wait.

Take time out of each day to commune with God. Pray specifically for things you would like to see Him take over. Pray to Him like you would reveal needs and concerns with your best friend. Prayer is what we need to do before we do anything. Prayer and God's Word are the only two offensive weapons we have as Christians. Use them wisely, and you will win this spiritual war.

☆ ☆ ☆

Further Study: Spend the next 15 minutes praying.

OBEDIENCE

SAY IT ISN'T SO

*And Simon answered and said, "Master, we worked (fished) hard all night and
caught nothing, but because you (Jesus) say so, I will let down my nets"*
Luke 5:5

* * *

This is one of those "gold nuggets" of scripture that, after you read it,
causes tons of lessons and practical applications to flood from the page. Will
you do yourself a favor and read Luke 5:1-11?

I am sitting on my front porch in Castle Rock, Colorado, after supper on
a cool August evening, watching a rainstorm roll over the Rockies, reading
the same passage of scripture you just read. If you don't mind, I'd like to share
a few thoughts, then you as a family do the same around the supper table. The
scene sets itself up perfectly as the three amigos Peter, James and John are out
all night fishing. Obviously they aren't new at this, nor is the water they are
fishing foreign uncharted waters. Jesus is overrun by a crowd, so He takes His
podium into a boat and preaches off shore. After He's done, he offers a bit of
advice to Peter, who takes it and makes the catch of all catches. Peter catches so many fish that his fishing boat begins to take on water (sink), and so
does James and John's boat.

Now, what struck me was this . . . Jesus was a carpenter, these three were
fisherman, yet they listened and didn't smart off at Jesus' request to go back
where they just came from (unsuccessfully) and try it again. None of the three
were disciples yet, but they still obeyed and were blessed. After Peter "saw,"
he was humbled at the feet of Jesus and worshiped Him along with his com-
rades. Jesus told them not to fear; from now on they wouldn't catch fish, but
men (unsaved folks). And finally, they left all they owned (boat, nets, family,
possessions, boat-load of fish, which meant cash money) and followed Him
as disciples of Christ. WOW! What a story of obedience, humility, courage,
fear, priorities, compassion and love. Now it's your turn . . . what are the
lessons you got out of it? Go ahead and say it isn't so.

* * *

Further Study: What one "nugget" did you get out of this message of scripture
you can apply today? Will you do it?

GIVING

A CHEERFUL GIVER

*Let each one do just as he has purposed in his heart, not grudgingly
or under compulsion; for God loves a cheerful giver.*
2 Corinthians 9:7

* * *

There tells a story of a wealthy man who lived in Scotland years ago.
He had outlived all of his family and was recently diagnosed with a terminal
illness that would allow him only a few months to live. He had been successful in about every business deal he had been involved with and was looked
upon by the locals in high esteem. During the final chapter of his life he wanted to know what it was like to live as a beggar on the streets, scurrying for
food like a street rat. One day he was digging through a pile of rubbish for a
morsel of food when a poor young boy came up to join in the search. After a
few minutes the boy, being a pro, found half a loaf of stale bread, and the
wealthy man found none. The boy, with excitement of the find, jumped for
joy and began to devour the bread. All of a sudden, he noticed the wealthy
man (disguised as a beggar) had no food, so he gave him the half loaf and
walked away. The man, heartfelt at what had just taken place, ran after the
boy to say thanks. He asked the boy, "Why did you give me your only meal
this week?" to which the poor boy replied, "To give is to get." The man,
amazed at the boy's answer and heart, decided to give him his entire inheritance of wealth.

We live in a "me first" world where our national motto should be "looking out for number one" (and that's self). What a joy it is to have the privilege
of giving to someone in need. In the story of the widow's mite, you see a great
example of not only giving of a mite (last penny), but also giving with a cheerful heart. Giving comes from the heart, not the pocketbook. Giving doesn't
necessarily have to be money; it could be a listening ear, service or time. God
loves a joyful giver who's not as concerned with the 10 percent tithe issue as
He is the attitude in which you give. What a testimony you will be to simply
meet someone's need by giving. Who knows, God has His ways of rewarding
you far better than you'll ever know from a savings account. Remember, to
get, you've got to give it up.

* * *

Further Study: When was the last time you gave? Who could you give to
today? What does Jesus say in His word about giving? (Look it up.)

CHURCH CHOOSING

Realize this, in the last days, difficult times will come. For men will become lovers of self, money, boastful, arrogant, disobedient to parents, ungrateful, unholy, unloving, gossips, brutal, haters of good, conceited, lovers of pleasure rather than lovers of God; holding to a form of godliness although they have denied its power; avoid such men as those.
2 Timothy 3:2-5

☆ ☆ ☆

For years I thought that this verse was aimed at communicating the details of a fallen world headed for hell in a hand basket. It seems to give the specifics of what this society will be looking like prior to the return of the Creator. Guess what? There are two ways to look at something . . . my way and the right way. It just so happens that Paul is describing what the Church is going to look like with all its splendor in the last days. Don't hang up on me yet and mishear what I'm saying. I am an avid church member and a firm believer in the body of Christ meeting weekly. I'm not big on giant steeples, ornate pews and lofty budgets being our only definition of a church, but I do believe the Church is the bride of Christ. Take a moment to read this scripture again . . . slowly.

Beware of a church and a teacher (pastor or priest) who don't preach the truth and live it out in their own lives. Heed the warnings Paul gives Timothy in these verses of validity: there will be churches that are not what God intended them to be. How do you know if a church is for real? What sort of check-list can be used to test its spiritual substance? A legitimate church 1) takes God and the Bible seriously, believes it is the inherent word, teaches about Jesus' deity, servanthood, humility, faith, purity, creation, agape love, discipleship, heaven and hell, and doesn't water down or misuse scripture, 2) looks hard at what God has wrapped up in you; has some expectations of you and how your unique contributions can be better used in the body of Christ; helps you to realize your importance in the family, 3) is an equipping church; provides its congregation with tools to live; pastoral staff sees itself as a coaching staff; equips you to do the work of the ministry. Once you've found a church that qualifies, pour not only your heart into it, but your actions too . . . it's well worth the effort.

☆ ☆ ☆

Further Study: What should a godly church look and act like? Do a checklist on your church . . . how does it come out?

GOD THE FATHER

GREATNESS

*Know therefore that the Lord your God is God; He is the faithful God, keeping
His covenant of love to a thousand generations of those
who love Him and keep His commands.*
Deuteronomy 7:9

✳ ✳ ✳

Gladys Aylward, a missionary to China more than 50 years ago, was
forced to flee when the Japanese invaded Yangcheng. She was so dedicated
to her cause she just couldn't leave her work behind. With only one assistant,
she led more than 100 orphans over the mountains toward free China. In their
book, *The Hidden Price of Greatness*, Ray Besson and Ranelda Hunsicker tell
what happened:

During Gladys's harrowing journey out of a war-torn Yangcheng . . . she
grappled with despair as never before. After passing a sleepless night, she
faced the morning with no hope of reaching safety. A 13-year old girl in the
group reminded her of their much-loved story of Moses and the Israelites
crossing the Red Sea.

"But I am not Moses," Gladys cried in desperation.

"Of course you aren't," the little girl replied, "but Jehovah is still God!"
The purpose of sharing this unique story is to illustrate a point which holds
true some 50 years later. When Gladys and the orphans made it through to
safety, they proved once again that no matter how inadequate we feel (don't
let your feelings become facts), God is still God, and we can trust in Him in
every circumstance. I recall a friend telling me early in my life, "God doesn't
call the qualified, He qualifies the called." scripture logs a multitude of stories
(true ones) that reveal just how involved God our Father is in each of our
lives. You will be confronted with odds that seem overwhelming at a glance,
but are peanuts to God. The same God of the Old Testament is still active
and working today in lives and situations to provide a way to victory if we
only trust Him. You don't have to "have it all together" or "be perfect" for
God to use you in a situation that glorifies Him. God is in the business of
pulling off miracles against all odds.

✳ ✳ ✳

Further Study: How big is God? Why is God so interested in you and your life
that He even knows the number of hairs on your head? What does God ask
from you to pull off a miracle? How deep is your faith and strong is your trust
in Him? What could you do today to strengthen them?

First Impressions

Greet one another with a holy kiss of love.
1 Peter 5:14

☆ ☆ ☆

There used to be a TV commercial where the punch line was, "You never get a second chance for a first impression." Oooh, how important that sentiment is when it comes to developing quality relationships. A good first impression can either take you a long way or put you in the ditch. Christians, without a doubt, should be the forerunners when it comes to making a good first impression on people. There has to be a balance between doing what is needed and overdoing it. Ask yourself this question . . . what do people say about you after you meet them for the first time? Do they feel encouraged and energized, or do you leave them tired?

I have a few basic suggestions that I hope you will try out when you first meet someone (if you're not doing them already). Here they are in "Cliff Note" form:

Look them in the eye.
After hearing their name, say it five times to yourself.
Stand tall and be excited about their acquaintance.
Ask questions about them.
Show interest in their answers by responding with phrases like, "That's great!," "How exciting!" or "That's neat to know!"
Don't become distracted or lose eye contact during a conversation.
End the conversation by saying their name and, "It has been a pleasure talking with you."
Always use Mr., Mrs., or Miss if the person is older than you (until they tell you to do otherwise).
Always be respectful, polite, and courteous.

I hope that you can use these tools to make a good first impression. Remember you are the salt and light to a dark world and good impressions definitely season a relationship and light the way for friendship.

☆ ☆ ☆

Further Study: Practice the above steps when you next meet someone for the first time. Practice with your parents or a friend.

PRIDE

How'd You Do That?

I am well content in my weaknesses with insult, with distress, with persecutions, with difficulties for Christ's sake, for when I am weak then I am strong.
2 Corinthians 12:10

☆ ☆ ☆

Talented people in this country are as numerous as ticks on a coon dog. We are saturated with folks who are heads above any other Western civilization. Athletically, technologically, educationally, militarily, socially and politically, we are heads above anyone in our class. With talent running as thick as motor oil, our awareness of God's ultimate control over situations has diminished. Believe it or not, God is all knowing and is the ultimate producer of everything that occurs every second of our days. You are probably blessed with talents such as athletic ability, intellect, appearance (looks) and don't know where they may take you. Let me ask you a question . . . has anyone ever said, "How'd you do that?" after an accomplishment? In reality what they were saying was that they knew the limits of your abilities and talents and could see that you didn't have the tools to pull it off. Catch my drift?

What a spiritual victory it is when you bring an upset victory to the front page of your life's daily news. Those are the times you allow God to override your inadequacies to produce a standing ovation performance. Those are the times when your world has fallen apart and the pieces are lost, yet you allow Him to pull it all together to finish the puzzle in style. In the midst of turbulence, turmoil and trials, you draw on God to help you survive the crash and land your life safely. There will be peer persecution, verbal tongue lashings, and harassment from humans, but to come through the manure piles of mankind smelling like a rose is a credit to God's loving kindness. It will be those weak times of your life that God can make you as strong as a steel beam. So, next time someone says, "How'd you do that?" simply smile and say, "I had a good coach."

☆ ☆ ☆

Further Study: When was the last time you were weak? How did you react? Did or didn't you use God? What will you do next time?

WHEN IT RAINS IT POURS

And everyone who hears these words of Mine, and doesn't act upon them, will be a foolish man, who built his house upon the sand, and the rain and floods came and the winds blew and it beat upon that house and it fell, and great was its fall.
Matthew 7:26-27

☆ ☆ ☆

If you aren't already, you will someday be involved in one of the largest investments a person will make in a lifetime . . . a house. Whether you are going to build, buy or lease, you will sink about one-third of your paycheck into this money-muncher. A home is a nest for a family and a refuge from the rat race. You put your money, mind and muscle into making it your dream home, the kind you imagined while growing up. The style may be Victorian, contemporary or rustic; it may be spread out, two-story, or split-level; the colors may be subdued or outstanding. Whatever the case, it will be yours to call "home, sweet home." Through the Sermon on the Mount, Jesus gave insights for living. Jesus warns you of what happens to a home (meaning your life) that is built on false pretenses. Jesus reminds us that tough times, like bad weather, will come. When buying or building a house, you must first check out the foundation's structure to make sure it is built on a firm footing of rock. You build your life each day either on the soft sands of society or the bedrock of Christ. What will it be, a house that stands through the storms of time or a shack that melts like cardboard at the first sign of bad weather? You're not forced, but you are warned of the consequences of a poorly built home. In today's world we have building inspectors that do the checking for us. In our spiritual life we have fellow believers that warn us of a faulty framework. Heed these warnings not only in your pursuit of the "Great American Dream," but also in your journey with Jesus.

☆ ☆ ☆

Further Study: What kind of foundation have you built your life on? Is it on sand or "the Rock?" If sand, what can you do to beef up the framework?

RESPECT

With All Due Respect

*Honor your father and mother, that your days may be prolonged
in the land which the Lord gives you.*
Exodus 20:12

☆ ☆ ☆

The United States Code says that "the flag represents a living country
and is itself considered a living thing." A set of rules accompany this code: for
example, standing at attention and facing the flag with the right hand over the
heart. The flag should never touch the ground or be used as wearing apparel.
The flag should be displayed during school days and near every polling place
on election days. When raising the flag, it should be hoisted quickly and lowered slowly.

I don't know about you, but for the majority of Americans, this stuff
seems to be a lost tradition. Most folks don't even know to take off their "lids"
(hats) when putting up or taking down the flag. Why is it that this great
nation of ours, you know, the one nation under God, has such a distorted
view of our past history? I believe I know . . . lack of respect. The closest that
some folks ever come to that word is singing Aretha Franklin's hit, R-E-S-P-
E-C-T, on an old 45 rpm record.

No matter what you might have heard on TV documentaries, we live in
a great country. We see public flag-burnings nowadays about as often as we
see car wrecks. If we knew, or had a relative who fought and died for this
great nation, I think it would be a little burr under our saddle to see Ole Glory
go up in a puff of smoke. Why are some irreverent to the flag under which we
live? Lack of respect. This same scenario holds true in our society of siblings
who disobey and run uncontrollably in our homes and on the streets because
of no respect for their parents. Respect is not some title we put on an album,
but a responsibility to our authority. God put you with the parents or authority figures in your life for a specific purpose, and you are to obey them under
the borders of the Bible. I realize you sometimes wonder if they have a clue
as to what they're doing, and the answer is, they are doing the best they can
(parenting is tough stuff). Allow them to make mistakes in the process, yet
respect and obey them, too. Being both an American citizen and an obedient
child are things to be proud of.

☆ ☆ ☆

Further Study: What does respect mean to you? How can you show your par-
ent(s) more respect?

SEX

Truth or Consequences

This is the will of God, your sanctification; that you
abstain from sexual immorality.
1 Thessalonians 4:3

☆ ☆ ☆

America has by far the highest reported rate of AIDS infected people in the industrial world, and the number of cases diagnosed continues to multiply as we speak (or read). A total of 361,164 cases were reported through 1994. Nearly two-thirds of those have died. It's estimated that approximately one million Americans are infected with AIDS; that's one out of every 250 folks. According to a *USA TODAY* report, by the year 2000 it is predicted that everyone will know someone personally who has contracted and died from this killer virus.

The "politically correct" teaching that AIDS doesn't target any particular lifestyle continues to be popular. Now for the truth . . . if AIDS had not targeted a specific political activist group, it would probably have been brought under control long ago as other epidemics have been controlled by isolation and quarantines. It is too late to start now, or even consider, as the disease is spreading like a grass plains wild fire in summer into the general population of America. Raising children in the midst of this epidemic is down-right frightening. In most cases AIDS is a consequence for an immoral, impure lifestyle which seems to continue the thinking, "If it feels good, do it." We are to pray and have sincere compassion for individuals who are sick with this virus. Love the sinner, but learn how to hate (despise) the sin (immorality). Whether you think so or not . . . this is your problem now. God has ground rules for sex, not because He is some modern day kill-joy. It's because He cares! Morality in this country is better caught than taught. We need to focus in on the root of the issue, not just deal with the leaves.

☆ ☆ ☆

Further Study: What is morality? What do you see as immoral in our society? Does it effect you directly or indirectly? What can you do about it?

OBEDIENCE

JESUS NO. 3?

But I say to you who hear, love your enemies and pray for those who persecute you.
Matthew 5:44

☆ ☆ ☆

A few years back I was waiting in a friend's living room before going out to dinner and noticed a very interesting title on the book shelf. I know curiosity killed the cat, but I ain't no cat, so I went over and picked it up. The book was *100 of the Most Influential People in the World.* As I browsed through it, I quickly noticed that Jesus was ranked number three behind Isaac Newton and Mohammed (not the fighter either). Man, was I as mad as a chained guard dog! I could not believe this flaky author had the guts or lack of brains to put Jesus behind those boneheads. What was he thinking (he must not have been)? Then at the end of the chapter on Jesus, I read where the author literally apologized for not putting Him as number one, citing several reasons. He stated Jesus could not be ranked before the others because Jesus' believers don't obey His words. Quoting Matthew 5:44, the author explained that he had seen few Christians praying for the folks who persecuted them, or loving their enemies. He stated that the followers of Mohammed did as they were commanded and, therefore, deserved recognition. Wow, what a blow! Here we are again–Christians with egg on our faces!

Gang, we as followers, ambassadors, disciples or believers have to be obedient to our Master's ways. Yes, the author probably wasn't a believer, but he called it like he saw it, which is his and every other non-Christian's right. You see, we live our lives under a microscope, like it or not. No, we are not perfect, just forgiven, and we have to change our ways if we actually want to be a light and make a difference. Begin today to give it all you can to obey and trust in the final outcome. The results could be, who knows . . . maybe a number one ranking in that guy's book for Jesus someday. Miracles can happen.

☆ ☆ ☆

Further Study: Do you obey God's word? What percentage of the time? Why do you sometimes not? Do you think Jesus should have been number one? What can you do to get Him there in this world's eyes?

THE CROSS

A REAL RESCUE RANGER

*He who has found his life shall lose it, but he who has
lost his life for my sake shall find it.*
Matthew 10.39

☆ ☆ ☆

If you've ever been snow skiing, you're gonna' appreciate and relate to this story. A group of college folks went on a ski trip to Colorado during Christmas break and were greeted with record setting snowfall. The ski conditions had been ideal: tons of snow, blue skies and warm temperatures. The last day of skiing they all decided to catch the last lift of the day up to the top of the mountain and have a race down to the warming hut. They sat at the top until most skiers were out of sight so they would have the mountain to themselves and be clear for take-off. There were no rules on how, just be the first down and you win. Off they went in a downhill tuck position, any run they wanted, but fast. One of the guys was a real tree basher, so he decided to go the shorter way down through an avalanche roped-off area. Later on, all the group met at the hut only to notice that one guy hadn't made it down, and it was nearly dark. They quickly warned ski patrol of the M.I.A.S. (missing-in-action skier) and set out to find him. The patrol returned late, unsuccessful and decided to send out a trained rescue dog to find him. The young man had gotten lost and when night fell had decided to build a lean-to and sleep. The dog found the young man who had experienced hypothermia and was slipping into a deadly state of sleep with no awakening. The dog was trained to find the victim, lay on top of him to warm him and stay there until help arrived. The dog's warm temperature brought the young man out of his frozen sleep to awake with some furry creature on him. He panicked and stabbed the dog to death with a nearby ski pole.

Did you realize that Jesus found you in a state of death and covered you with His blood He shed on the Cross in order to revive you back to a living state called eternity with God? Jesus' sole purpose was to save the unsaved, love the unlovable and rescue the lost. He did it all for you, then He died. It's a hard thing to think, but yes, you had to kill Him so He could save you. What a hero!

☆ ☆ ☆

Further Study: Have you ever been lost with no hope? Did you realize that Jesus is the ultimate rescue team?

TRIALS

HE WILL PUMP YOU UP

*But in everything commending ourselves as servants of God, in much
endurance, in afflictions, in hardships and in distresses.*
2 Corinthians 6.4

★ ★ ★

Now, this devotional is gonna' seem like one of those macho-nacho,
he-man devotions, but it's not . . . so hang with me, and I think you'll catch
the lesson as I develop the point. An activity that I have loved for years and
still do is weight-lifting. Now, I realize that if you saw me, you'd question if
I've ever seen a weight room . . . with the spaghetti noodles hanging out of
my sleeves. My health club has a weight room with wall-to-wall machines,
equipment and dumbbells for every muscle in your body. Not to mention that
a few guys in the gym look like clusters of grapes on steroids. If you can get
past the neon spandex, this sport is a great way to work off a little stress.

The thought hit me as I was pumping iron that the strain, sweat, fatigue,
soreness and red faces are all necessary for physical growth; you can't build
muscle without the strain. Did you catch that? Let me say it in life application
terms . . . you can't prepare yourself for the tough times without the daily battles. Life is full of more downs than ups, yet those seeming problems become
challenges with the right perspective. I work out four times a week doing stationary bikes, stair masters, aerobics, pumping dumbbells, doing curls for the
girls, leg squats . . . Why? So that my body can take the punishment I put it
through skiing, rock climbing, hiking a fourteener or playing tackle football
with my kids. God sets up little pop quizzes every day to get us ready for the
mid-term and final. It's all "mind over matter;" if you don't mind, then it won't
matter. The strains in life, of just getting by at times and barely making it,
serve as strength training for our spiritual workouts. Just as physical training
is necessary for the body–maintain a healthy diet, rest, keep a balance
between work and play, so spiritual training is necessary for the soul- time in
scripture study and fellowship with other believers in church. Both will make
you look and feel better. Pump it up!

★ ★ ★

Further Study: What troubles do you encounter that cause you to strain? Why
does God cause us to go through tough times? Are you doing your spiritual
workouts with time in Bible reading, prayer time and fellowship?

PRAYER

PLANTING PRAYERS

And this I pray, that your love may abound still more and more . . .
Philippians 1:9

☆ ☆ ☆

Elzeard Bouffier was one of those people I wish lived in our day in time. He was a shepherd in the French Alps at a time when people were cutting down trees left and right in the mountains around Provence, France. After supper each night, the shepherd sorted through a pile of acorns, throwing away those that were small or cracked. For over three years, while herding and watching his sheep on the barren mountainsides, he planted these acorns and eventually planted around 100,000, of which 20,000 sprouted. He expected half to be eaten by animals or die due to the elements, but the rest to live. After World War I, the mountainside blossomed with acorn trees. In an ecology sheltered by a leafy roof and bonded to the earth by a mat of roots, willow rushes, meadows, gardens and flowers were birthed. The shepherd, ignoring the war of 1939 just as he had ignored the war in 1914, continued his planting on other barren mountains. The streams, fed by the rains and snows that the forest conserves, are flowing healthier today than ever before, due to one man's quest.

People who are prayer warriors are like spiritual reforesters, digging holes in a barren land and planting the seeds of life. Through these seeds the dry spiritual wastelands are transformed into harvestable fields, and life-giving water is brought to parched and barren souls of the lost. You have a responsibility as a Christian, as did the shepherd, to replant your prayers in this barren, ugly world. God has given each of us an incredible opportunity to commune (talk and listen) with the Creator and petition needs (not wants) for yourself and others. Take the time out of each busy day to plant a prayer, then sit back and watch it grow into a miraculous answer.

☆ ☆ ☆

Further Study: How often do you pray? How can you become a more diligent prayer warrior? Take a minute right now to pray for your needs and others' souls.

SATAN

ALERTNESS

Don't be easily deceived, brother.
James 1:16

★ ★ ★

The January 1992 issue of *Fortune* magazine featured a piece on "the biggest goofs of 1991." In an act of corporate cooperation, AT&T reached an agreement with the power company of New York City. The contract stated that whenever power demands exceeded the utility's grid, AT&T would lessen their demands by throwing a switch, unplugging some of its facilities and drawing power from internal generators at its 33 Thomas Street station in lower Manhattan. On September 17th, AT&T acted in accordance with the agreement, but when their own generators kicked in, the power surge knocked out some vital rectifiers, which handled 4.5 million interstate calls, 470,000 international calls, 1,174 flights carrying 85,000 passengers, and total communications systems linking air traffic controllers at LaGuardia, Kennedy and Newark airports. Alarm bells at the 33 Thomas Street station rang wildly for six hours. AT&T personnel in charge of the rectifiers were away attending a one-day seminar on how to handle emergencies.

What a hilarious story about how we can appear to be prepared on the outside, but remain wide open for an attack. You must be wise to the ways of the wicked or you could be caught in a trap that won't let go without first inflicting much pain to your body and soul. Now, I'm definitely not suggesting that you study up on all that satanic stuff, but I am telling you to know he does lurk in the darkness, and he will bite you when you least expect it. Prepare yourself for the worst attacks. Be informed what scripture says about Satan so that when an emergency hits, you'll react in the right manner.

★ ★ ★

Further Study: How alert are you to Satan's ways? Are you alert to his deceitful schemes? What can you do to be more watchful?

REWARDS

TROPHIES

When the Chief Shepherd appears, you will receive the unfaded crown of glory.
1 Peter 5:4

☆ ☆ ☆

You probably have a wall decorated with ribbons, trophies, medals, plaques, letters of recommendations and awards for a job well done and a goal accomplished. I grew up with a father who was the quarterback of the football team with the longest winning streak (Oklahoma University 1954-58) in the history of the NCAA . . . 47 wins and only one loss. Can you imagine playing four full seasons at anything and only losing one time? Wow, now that is something to pooch your chest and strut around town about. That is an accomplishment that few will ever know and deserves the right to brag. You know what? You can go up in my dad's attic, under piles of junk and dust and find all his championship trophies, national championship rings and plaques. He never displayed them, flaunted or boasted about them; he just didn't see the purpose. His humility and perspective was something you won't see much anymore. A lot of times our self images are all we're wrapped up in.

God calls you to arenas to participate in other events while you're here on earth. This game lasts a lot longer and requires stricter training in order to win His trophies . . . crowns. The difference between earthly and heavenly rewards is that one fades and is forgotten, the other sparkles and survives. The rewards given by God to you for enduring hardship, surviving servanthood and conquering compromise is far greater than any medal, trophy or plaque. No, those rewards aren't wrong or bad, but they are second place in this category. If you're gonna' boast or show off a reward . . . try a crown from the Creator.

☆ ☆ ☆

Further Study: What honor have you been most proud of that you received? Have you ever been rewarded by God? How? How do they compare eternally?

BEING ALERT

LIVING LARGE

The naïve believe everything, but the prudent man considers his steps.
Proverbs 14:15

✩ ✩ ✩

If you've ever stood close to one, you don't easily forget this magnificent beast of overwhelming size; some bison (buffalo) measure 12 feet long, 6 feet high and weigh as much as two horses (3,000 pounds). They are the largest of the North American land animals and have few enemies. In the early 1800s, their peaceful coexistence with the Indians began to change as they became a threat to this "king of the plains." The Indian's hunting equipment like the bow, arrow and lance were no match for these swift, massive animals, so they found creative ways to kill them. The Indians used to their advantage the creature's poor vision along with strategically located hunters to eliminate herds of 15-20 in one swift fall. Knowing bison were nervous and short-tempered, the Indians crept up close to the herd, using crawl tactics and the wind direction, and scared the herd's lead bull. What happened after that was amazing; the startled animals would follow the leader in a chaotic stampede across the plains right over an unseen, unsuspecting cliff and all fall to their death. As quickly as it began . . . the hunt ended.

Our social circles are populated with folks who walk through life about as alert as a basset hound. Faithful followers of Christ can get led into cults that end in death, like those in Waco and San Diego. How can people be so blind? Are they stupid? Are they careless? No . . .. Their vision has been impaired, and the enemy (Satan) has startled them into making poor decisions. Our God is an awesome God, and He reigns over careless decisions here on earth. Your responsibility is to stay in the Word, stay in fellowship and stay on your knees. God can and does protect us from fatal stampedes into uncertainty if we hang close with Him consistently. The key is to recognize opportunities and dangers which others overlook. Remain humble as a sheep because the minute you feel large (like a buffalo) the bigger you are . . . the harder you fall.

✩ ✩ ✩

Further Study: Look back on a big mistake you've made in your life and see what lessons you learned in order to not make that same mistake again. How can you avoid making fatal mistakes today?

GOD'S SOVEREIGNTY

THE GOOD GUY WINS

Assuredly, the evil man will not go unpunished.
Proverbs 11:21

☆ ☆ ☆

Don't you just love it when the good guys win: Aladdin, John Wayne, Pongo and Purdy, Luke Skywalker, King David. I have that Pollyanna Syndrome . . . you know . . . everybody needs to be happy all of the time. I can't stand to go to a movie with a sad ending. I want them to say . . . "And they all lived happily ever after" (I know, cheesy).

One of my all time favorites is in a book of the Bible called Esther. Here's the Cliff Note version of her story. Esther is a young girl (about 15, 16 or 17), and she is chosen to be queen (because the previous one got booted). King Ahasuerus (we will call him "King A") doesn't know her Jewish nationality. The king's right hand man, Haman, is in a very powerful position, and the king's servants bow and give homage to him. However, Esther's uncle, Mordecai, (who had saved the king's life in an earlier situation) is at the gate praying to God for Esther's well being. Mordicai neither bows nor pays homage to Haman. Haman is filled with rage, but he waits to kill Mordecai because he wants to kill all of Mordecai and Esther's people.

Soon after (the saga continues), "King A" can't sleep one night, and he orders that the book of records be read to him. During that reading he finds out about Mordecai saving his life. (OK . . . hang in there, this is where it gets good.) "King A" calls Haman in and asks him, "What should be done for the man whom the king desires to honor?" (Haman thinks "King A" is referring to him!) So Haman begins to describe this elaborate procession through the city. After all of this, the king says, "Go get Mordecai and you, Haman, do all you described for Mordecai." Well, to make a long story short, the king has Haman hung on the very gallows that Haman made for Mordecai. The Jews were saved.

So, what does all of this tell about our God? He is awesome, and He sees all the details! Just remember, when it looks like the bad guys are going to win . . . our mighty God will have the final say.

☆ ☆ ☆

Further Study: What do you do about your enemies or people you don't like? What would Jesus do? If we know in our minds that God will take care of us, why is it so hard to trust God?

CHILDREN OF A LESSER GOD

No one can serve two masters, either he will hate the one and love the other.
Matthew 6:24

⋏ ⋏ ⋆

It was a spot specifically designated for voicing opinions on any subject matter. Hundreds of people gathered at "Speaker's Corner" in Hyde Park, London, England on a sunny Sunday morning. Talk about a melting pot of humanity! I'm not sure everyone was there for the same reason. Some just happened to drop by, seeing the crowd gathered, but others came to seek out answers to life's questions. Whatever the reason, the intent was obviously to persuade the audience from theory to fact. I was surprised that the subject all (not just some) the participants chose to speak on was religion. I mean, come on, freedom of speech to the maximum, and all these milk-crate lecturers chose religion as the topic. The speakers might have selected politics, feminine rights, minority rights, abortion, the death penalty or any other sizzling topic, but they chose religion . . . why?

While I was there, five different speakers discussed the New Age, Muslim, Hindu, Mormon, and Christian religions. I am proud to report the Christian was right-on and the others were one sandwich short of a full picnic. The crowd gravitated to the speaker teaching the truth (which is all bogus and relative without Christ). You see, the "truth" is a person (the truth shall set you free), not just something you say to stay out of trouble. Everyday we pass those who worship a dead, dull, deceiving god that will get them nowhere. Lesser gods are those gods society follows that offer a false sense of security and happiness. Jesus is, and always will be, the only God that will be standing when all else falls. Don't be easily deceived, brothers and sisters; don't bite a hook that will get you nowhere but in the frying pan. It is ultimately your choice . . . just make sure it's the right choice, okay?

☆ ☆ ☆

Further Study: What sets Christianity apart from other religions? Why do people historically choose to stay on a religious topic? Are you sure who you worship and believe?

TEMPTATION

SETTING YOURSELF UP

Each one is tempted when he is carried away and enticed by his own lust.
James 1:14

☆ ☆ ☆

It has become a tradition in the Dodd household. We load up the tent, grill, sleeping bags, waders, sunscreen and BB guns, along with the Dodd boys and old Pops. We head down to Ponca, Arkansas, on the banks of the Buffalo River for our annual father and son canoe trip. Along with about 15 other fathers and sons, we canoe through the Ozark mountains in a line strung out for miles. The river in the late spring can get kinda' hairy in spots. I have learned, as a kayaker, that the key to not swamping (turning over) a canoe is how you set it up for rough waters. Good canoers always align the canoe in a proper position to avoid getting caught in a situation of helplessness.

On my latest trip, I realized how we, as Christians, can get into a ton of trouble by setting ourselves up for a spill. I've counseled hundreds of folks who have put themselves into a situation that guarantees failure, a place where no follower of Christ should be. The verse above gives us incredible insight that often we put ourselves in predicaments that breed (guarantee) sin. The old saying, "an ounce of prevention is worth a pound of cure," is corny, but true. Don't set a trap, then walk into it and wonder what happened. Sin is deceitful, but not undetectable with the spirit of Christ as a helper. Set yourself up for victory, not a major spill that will leave your life in one uncomfortable state . . . take it from an experienced river rat.

☆ ☆ ☆

Further Study: Do you ever set yourself up for failure? How? What preventative measures can you take?

SALVATION

RESCUE 911

That if you confess with your mouth, "Jesus is Lord," and believe in your heart that God raised him from the dead, you will be saved.
Romans 10·9

* * *

The *Reader's Digest* reported the incredible story of Walter Wyatt's flight from Nassau to Miami (normally a one hour flight) on a stormy night in December of 1986. Thieves had broken into his private twin-engine plane to steal valuable navigational instruments. With only a compass and a hand-held radio, Walter flew into skies blackened by storms. When his compass gyrated, he knew he was going the wrong direction. He put out a "May Day" for the Coast Guard Falcon search plane. But at 8 p.m., he ran out of fuel and could do nothing but crash-land in open water. Walter survived the crash, but the plane sank quickly, leaving him floating alone in the rough waters. With blood on his forehead, he floated on his back until he felt a hard bump on his back—a shark. He floated 10 hours until morning when he saw the dorsal fin of another shark headed for him. Twisting, he felt the hide of a shark brush against him. In a moment, he was surrounded by dozens of sharks. He kicked them off, and they veered away, but he was nearing exhaustion. Suddenly, he heard the hum of a distant aircraft. He waved his orange life vest, and the helicopter crew lowered down a rope ladder to haul him to safety. Walter had been saved from the jaws of death.

We are like Walter Wyatt in that God comes along at the opportune time to snatch us from the jaws of eternal death. We float in despair, fighting off the enemy and out of nowhere comes our rescue vessel (God) to save the day and our lives. What an awesome thing it is to be saved. What an incredible moment when we give it all up to a Savior who cares that we live with Him in eternity where there will be no despair. All we have to do is call out, "May Day!" and He'll be there in a flash! Go God!

* * *

Further Study: Have you ever felt like it was all over, and God saved the day? Has your navigational equipment ever failed you? Take a moment to thank God for saving you from the jaws of eternal death.

SIN

A REAL SHRINK

Therefore confess your sins to one another, pray for one another, that you may be healed. The effective prayer of righteous man accomplishes much.
James 5:16

☆ ☆ ☆

Ask yourself this question real quick . . . what would it be like if I was alive when Jesus was? Can you even imagine? You wouldn't have to worry about hairstyles (they had no salons), the car you drove (no gas stations), what you wore (fluorescent was out), or career opportunities (not a lot offered). In that day life was so much simpler (I think) and less stressed-out than today. Folks 2,000 years ago seemed to take life one step at a time, day-by-day, minute-by-minute. The current didn't seem to flow as fast, yet it still did flow. Folks still incurred problems and difficulties, whether it was sickness, survival, or what would be for supper. The way people of that culture dealt with tricks, impurity and a hurting conscience was by confession, not necessarily to a priest or mediator, but to each other.

Do you realize that if our society today would listen and act upon this scripture, we would virtually put every psychologist and psychiatrist out of business? If we could learn to confess to God and others in our troubled times when we have fallen short, we would have no need for a shrink. Depression would be only a word we used to describe America in the '30s. After you heard a confession, then you would take some serious action and begin to pray for them and their needs so the healing process could begin. I realize this formula seems to be too simple to do any good, but take it from "The Man" and His counseling skills; it works wonders!

☆ ☆ ☆

Further Study: When was the last time you confessed a sin to a reliable friend? How did it feel? Why do you think counseling clinics are packed with clients today? What would this formula for freedom do for you in your relationship with Christ? Will you do it? Why not?

GOD'S PROMISES

A PROMISE TO RESTORE

Then I will make up to you for the years that the swarming locusts have eaten.
Joel 2:25

☆ ☆ ☆

The prophet Joel is writing this truth to the southern kingdom of Judah. He reminds them of the historical judgment of the Lord and warns of future judgment. He exhorts them to "rend your heart and not your garments." Judah had experienced a terrible plague of locusts which destroyed the vegetation of their land. This land was desolate.

My heart can feel that same desolation emotionally if I focus on my years of not knowing Jesus, living contrary to God's commandments and doing nothing with eternal significance. Because of the choices I made in my early 20s, I can easily jump into the sin of self-protection of my heart.

I claim and cling to this promise from my God to me. He promises to restore to me all of those lost fruits of wasted years of living in disobedience. As I increasingly become aware of the reality of His forgiveness and the way He presently views me, I do walk in that restoration. I do begin to feel again, to want to love again. Joel 2:26 says, "And you shall have plenty to eat and be satisfied; and praise the name of the Lord your God, who has dealt wondrously with you, Then my people will never be put to shame." My heart is overwhelmingly grateful to Jesus for making it possible for me to walk in satisfaction and without shame about who I am. All of this only because of the blood of Jesus.

This promise reminds me that God is not concerned with who I was in the past, but who I am becoming right now. It reminds me of God's grace and desire for me to have an abundant life now! Every day He does move me closer to a point of being able to love people with a reckless abandonment and truly receive and experience love in return.

☆ ☆ ☆

Further Study: Do you feel at times robbed of a future? What is the difference in the old law and new one in Christ? What made it possible to restore our hope? How can you really believe?

YOU BET YOUR LIFE

Now to Him who is able to do exceedingly abundantly beyond all that we ask or think, according to His power that works within us
Ephesians 3.20

☆ ☆ ☆

Like it or not, the amount of money changing hands from bettors to bookies every day is astronomical. Individuals bet on golf matches, sports events, horse and dog races, lottery tickets, poker games, slot machines and the roll of dice. If you've ever been to Las Vegas, you've witnessed first hand enough money being lost to pull this country out of its national debt. I once heard a professional gambler say, "I never meet anyone ever satisfied . . . they've either not won enough or lost all they had." The world in which you exist is continually trying to persuade you to bet your life on sex, looks, possessions, money or chemical highs. Some do win the "jackpot" but most come up empty handed and defeated in more areas than the pocketbook. This roulette wheel we spin each day called life is more than winning or losing money; it's your life.

Let's bring this illustration home by asking a very important question. What are you betting your life on? What machine, table, arena or race do you set high stakes on? We are all looking to find the pot of gold that sits at the end of every rainbow, right? We all search high and low for that one jackpot that will supposedly bring us joy and happiness, but what's our guarantee that we'll win? Jesus takes the guessing out of the game by making our stakes attainable by a simple commitment, not a wad of money or a handful of chips. He eliminates the anxiety by taking upon Himself the stress of the wager (life). Jesus comes to give us an abundance of life, which means by dictionary terms "more than enough." Isn't it a dream come true, pot of gold, and jackpot to know that He is our provider for a life in paradise after this life? Go ahead, place your bet, roll the dice, spin the wheel, but make sure it's on Christ for the sure win.

☆ ☆ ☆

Further Study: What are you betting your life on? What makes your face smile most in life? Can God provide you with the ultimate jackpot in the long run? How?

COMMITMENT

THERMOSTAT OR THERMOMETER

This world has blinded the minds of the unbelieving, that they might not see the light of the gospel of the glory of Christ, who is the image of God.
2 Corinthians 4:4

✦ ✦ ✦

Nationwide, one of the biggest battles that goes on day after day, season after season, is over the thermostat. It seems to me, men are more thick skinned and women more thin skinned. Therefore, they can't agree on a common temperature setting. I know that the gender issue is not true of everyone because some folks are just hot natured and others cold natured, "N.B.N.W.J.D." (which means after interpretation "no better, no worse, just different"). As a child my little sister, (she is now a genius), used to tell me, "Stop changing the thermometer, the house is freezing." I would reply, "Hey goofy, it's a thermostat." You see, the difference is that one tells the temperature, yet the other dictates it. The common thread is that they both deal with temperature.

Here's a crazy analogy for ya'. Whether you're a follower of Christ or not, you were born into this world (this is the given, the temperature). Some people let the world dictate their thoughts, actions, decisions and attitudes; they are the thermometers. Now, on the other hand, there are those who dictate the temperature around them through setting the pace by example for the thoughts, actions, decisions and attitudes of folks they come in contact with (the thermostat). Here is an interesting thought to bubble your brain cells over. Just what can you control in your life? Answer . . . only yourself. Another bubbler–can you control others? Answer . . . no. Dictators have tried but wound up with revolutions on their hands.

It's a goofy illustration, I know, but I think the point is proven. Yes, you have the daily ability to not be influenced by this wicked world but to help in the prevention of decay by simply deciding. You are what you are because Jesus made you what you are . . . don't forget it!

✦ ✦ ✦

Further Study: What are you, a thermostat or thermometer? What do you want to be? How can you do that?

PENNY POWER

The root of all kinds of evil is the love of money.
1 Timothy 6:10

☆ ☆ ☆

All right, let's test our trivia knowledge. You have thirty minutes to complete this test. Please use a number two pencil and remember, no cheating. Begin now:

Questions concerning American money:
   What is a torn bill worth?
   Who is the only woman to be on a bill? When?
   Who's picture is on the $1, $2, $5, $10, $20 and $50 bill?
   How long is a bill used before it is recalled by the U.S. Treasury for wear and tear?
   What do the words "E Pluribus Unum" mean? What language is that?
   Whose job is it to find counterfeiters?
   In what cities are coins minted?
   On what kind of paper are bills printed?

Okay, pencils down. How do you think you did? This devotion relates to us all because we all deal with its subject daily. Street names are cabbage, cash, green, bucks, change, two-bits, moolah, lucre, gelt, mazuma, red cents or boodle. No matter what you call it, it's the good old dollar. You can't live with it, and you can't live without it. It buys, separates, orchestrates and devastates. It changes from one pocket to the next every second of our lives. Money though, is not the problem; the love of money is. It can make us happy as a lark one minute and send us into depression the next. Gang, money, if handled wrong or idolized, will destroy your life. Money is useful and can be a good thing if you don't fall in love with it. Steer clear of this monster of humanity or your life will end in one heck of a wreck. You'll always find those who have just as much chance roping the wind as finding fulfillment and satisfaction in money.

Answers:
3/5 or more = full amount; 3/5 or less = 1/2 value
Martha Washington in 1886
$1-Washington; $2-Jefferson; $5-Lincoln; $10-Hamilton; $20-Jackson; $50-Grant
18 months
"One from many" in Latin
Secret Service (and you thought they only guarded the President)
Denver; Philadelphia; San Francisco; West Point (gold only)
Paper with no pulp (regular paper has pulp in it)

☆ ☆ ☆

Further Study: How do you handle your money?

Mr. Nice God

*"I am the Alpha and the Omega," says the Lord God, "who is
and who was and is to come, the Almighty."*
Revelations 1:8

☆ ☆ ☆

A French philosopher once wrote, "God made man in His own image,
and man returned the favor." Ever since sin entered the garden and ruined
that perfect image, we (Christian society) have been trying to recreate God.
We want a god we can comprehend in neat, finite, human terms. We want a
deity we can understand, predict and figure out. In The Temple of the
Thousand Buddhas, a place of worship in Japan, the followers design their
own god. This temple is filled with a thousand likenesses of Buddha, each different from the next. Worshipers pick and choose which likeness of god they
prefer. Isn't this a bit like some Christians today whose search for the "quick
fix" leads to a religious compromise? We have given God a "modern day
make-over" at the expense of reverence for His sovereignty. We have made
Him a "user friendly" pal–a God who makes allowances for our sin and excuses for our unholy behavior, a non-judgmental God who will fit right in to our
lifestyle and give us "brownie points" for doing a good job.

Martin Lloyd-Jones said, "People who teach that God is love without
teaching that He hates sin are presenting another god–essentially Satan with
a mask on." The hottest selling books in Christian bookstores are the touchy-
feely type that focus on self-esteem, self-fulfillment and self-analysis. Books
that encourage self-sacrifice are the ones gathering dust or out of print, yet are
what we need to be reading (along with the Bible). A 1994 *U.S. News and
World Report* cover story on spirituality states, "American religion has taken
on the aura of pop psychology. Many congregations have multiplied their
membership by going light on theology and offering worshipers a steady diet
of sermons and support groups that emphasize personal fulfillment." Folks are
giving the Bible a make-over and revising the Lord's Prayer to say, "Our
Father and Mother who art in heaven . . .." Give me a break! God is God!
Don't forget . . . it's Christ who changes us–not the other way around.

☆ ☆ ☆

Further Study: Who is God to you? Do you try to change Him? Don't!

WORLDLY WAYS

SLIPPERY WHEN WET

For I was envious of the arrogant, as I saw the prosperity of the wicked.
Psalm 73:3

☆ ☆ ☆

Take a moment, open your Bible to Psalm 73:1-19 and read those few verses (read slowly and I'll be here when you're done). Wow! What a nugget of wisdom spoken by Asaph (no, that's not a brand of running shoe). Do you see what is going on here? Asaph is stricken with the thought that he perceives how the wrong people seem to be the ones who always get promoted. Isn't that true today? Think about it . . . when was the last time someone came up to you and asked for your autograph for following Christ daily? Now, I'm not saying that Christians are the scapegoat of society by any means, but I am saying that we live in a world that promotes worldly ways, not God's guidelines. It's the bad guys in the movies who are the ones riding off into the sunset on their horses. Asaph is so honest with God (I love it) and bares his soul and emotions in a Psalm. At times, you and I can become disheartened by the thought or questions of "is it worth it?"

It is so ordinary for the dishonest, arrogant, unfaithful and unholy to seem like their paths are always paved with success. Don't be fooled into thinking that an ungodly lifestyle will not eventually destroy you (read verse 19). The benefits of being a Christian are numerous. Let's take a quick peek at just what those perks are in Psalms chapter 73:

> He'll always be there (verse 23).
> He'll hold your hand along the way (verse 23).
> He'll always guide you (verse 24).
> He'll give you a future in heaven (verse 24).
> He'll meet all your needs (verse 25).
> He'll give you a testimony to see (verse 28).

Now, I'm not bright, but I can see that this is a life worth leading.

☆ ☆ ☆

Further Study: What frustrates you most about this world? How does God's way look to you? How can you encourage yourself when you get to wondering if it's worth it?

THE CROSS

CARRY ON LUGGAGE

*Jesus said "Anyone who does not carry his own cross and
follow me cannot be my disciple."*
Luke 14:27

☆ ☆ ☆

The young man was frankly at the end of his rope. Seeing no way out, he dropped to his knees in prayer saying, "Lord, I just can't go on." He continued saying, "I have too heavy a cross to bear." The Lord replied, "My son, if you cannot bear its weight, just place your cross inside this room, then open that other door and pick out any cross you wish." The young man, filled with relief said, "Thank you a ton, God," then sighed and did as he was told. Upon entering the other door he saw many crosses, some so big that the tops weren't visible. All of a sudden he spotted a small cross leaning against the far wall. "I'd like that small one, Lord." The Lord replied, "My son, that's the cross you just brought in."

Trials are kinda' like a giant 14,000-foot mountain that looks small from an airplane . . . until you land and try to hike up that puppy. The cross that God our Father has asked us to carry is gonna' feel heavy and burdensome at times. The stress of carrying it will sometimes drop you to your knees (it did Jesus, too). Take courage and tap into God's power and might to continue on. If you want to be a true modern day disciple of Christ, you're gonna' get sore muscles, weak knees and be humbled daily. That's okay though, because your labor is not in vain, nor is your pain. A quick thought about this cross carrying stuff . . . where are you carrying it to? The answer is, the same place Jesus did . . . to your death; and realize it's a one way trip to Calvary. The next time you feel too faint to go on, look around you and see others struggling with their own crosses, bigger and smaller. Jesus just tells us to press on!

☆ ☆ ☆

Further Study: When was it toughest for you to carry your cross? Have you ever wished you could chuck your cross? What stopped you? How can we learn that we all have a cross to bear and none is easy or light?

RUNNING THE RACE

DON'T GIVE UP

Do you not know that those who run the race all run, but only the one receives the prize? Run in such a way that you may win.
1 Corinthians 9:24

☆ ☆ ☆

Mamo Wolde of Ethiopia finished first in the 26-mile marathon at the Mexico City Olympic Stadium on October 29, 1968. An hour and a half later, the last of the marathon runners were carried off to the first-aid station, exhausted. As the remaining spectators prepared to exit the stadium, those near the gates heard the sound of sirens and police whistles. Everyone turned to look as a lone figure, wearing the colors of Tanzania, entered the darkened stadium. His name was John Stephen Akhwari, and he was the last participant to finish the race. He entered the stadium on legs all bloody and bandaged, severely injured in a fall, and he grimaced with each step. The remaining spectators rose and applauded him as if he were the winner. After crossing the finish line, Akhwari slowly walked off the field without turning to the cheering crowd. Seeing how he was injured and had no chance at all of winning the race, a reporter asked this young man why he didn't just quit and get medical attention immediately. The runner replied, "My country didn't send me seven thousand miles to start the race; they sent me seven thousand miles to finish it."

You just don't find many folks these days with a focused, die-hard attitude in whatever they do, whether it's sticking with a job, playing sports, remaining married, staying consistent in their walk with Christ, or whatever. I call those who stick with it "people with a purpose." Our society is training up and cheering on a quitter's mentality of "when the going gets tough, quit," instead of "when the going gets tough, the tough get going." Realize that every time you start something and don't see it to completion, you're developing a life-long pattern. Start now to live by the motto "Quitters never win and winners never quit."

☆ ☆ ☆

Further Study: Why is it so hard to stick with it? Have you ever started something and not finished it? Why? How can you develop a die-hard attitude?

LOYALTY

WAFFLING

*The two officials who guarded the door became angry and sought to kill King
Ahasuerus. The plot became known by Mordecai, and he told Queen
Esther and she informed the King in Mordecai's name. After an
investigation, they both were hanged on gallows.*
Esther 2:21-23

☆ ☆ ☆

Being an avid bird hunter, I have spent many a day down near El
Campo, Texas, on a duck and goose lease, living out my passion. It has
amazed me throughout the years how Greater Canadian Geese demonstrate
loyalty to a wounded mate. If a goose is shot down during the fall migration
flight, its mate has been known to circle back, risking death itself, in order to
help its partner. It will remain there until the wounded bird is able to fly again.
If the partner can't be found, the other will stay behind to look for it, enduring the hardship of winter in that area in order to continue its search.

Why is it that nature "gets it" and humans don't? I'm talking about good
old fashioned loyalty and stick-to-it attitudes. People leave jobs, marriages and
friendships like a burning house. I guess this isn't any new news, considering
that Peter, Judas and other disciples of Jesus couldn't stand the heat so they
got out of the kitchen. Even these two personally appointed guards to the
bedroom of King Ahasuerus named Bigthana and Teresh (two eunuchs) were
turning their backs. These boneheads were supposed to be the Marines or
Secret Service of their day, yet even they couldn't be trusted. It took a lower
court official, Mordecai, to step up to the plate and exemplify love and loyalty. Mordecai had a good reason to despise the King because his family had
been brought there as exiles from another land. For his loyalty, he not only
was a great example to Esther, but he was raised by the king to a new level
of honor.

The greatest test of true loyalty is when things aren't going as planned
and you pass the test and show the power of God through your example to
a give-up world. Will you remain loyal or quit? It's your choice; make the right
one.

☆ ☆ ☆

Further Study: Who are you loyal to? Why? Why is our society so fickle when
it comes to being loyal? How loyal are you to God? What would happen if
you were persecuted for your faith? Would you still be loyal?

THE BELL CURVE

Let us keep living by the same standard to which we have attained.
Philippians 3:16

☆ ☆ ☆

The bell curve has been as much a part of the American education system as recess and sack lunches. Teachers use this curve as a scale for fairness in the grading system. It was adopted by our school systems to allow pupils to be graded with fairness and equality. The curve is a measuring tool for the teacher to judge whether a test was too difficult (or easy) and prohibits the entire class from receiving a failing grade. For instance, if one out of 25 students scores 100% then the teacher has a problem setting the curve. The teacher has to make a decision whether to fail the low scores and allow the one student to pass or question the superior student.

Jesus' classroom was the corrupt world in which He traveled. The test was righteousness verses worldliness. The consequence was death. You see, the high score only makes the low scores look even worse and messes up the grading system. I'd say that Christ did a good job of messing up the world standards of good and evil. He made the Pharisees seem not quite as good as they appeared to be on paper. He brought to light a new definition of real love. He broke the mold. The test results? Failure of a superior Savior by the world teachers, put to death as a thief, but exaltation to the throne of God the Father. Make straight A's in God's classroom and guess what . . . it's okay to flunk this world's tests. God's class is one you can't take again in the next semester (life) . . . so be on the "honor roll."

☆ ☆ ☆

Further Study: Do you set the example at home, at school, with your team, or with your peers? Why is it so important to be an example, not a follower, of this world?

WORLDLINESS

THRILLS YET SPILLS

*Do not love the world nor the things in the world; if anyone
loves the world, the love of the father is not in him.*
1 John 2:16

☆ ☆ ☆

For years Disney theme parks have beguiled nearly three hundred and fifty million visitors (including Presidents, Hollywood stars and foreign royalty) with their charismatic assortment of entertainment, spectacle, magic and fantasy. The emphasis on adventure and thrills is unprecedented. For years these parks in southern California and Florida have been global leaders in adventure rides for all ages. The Matterhorn, Thunder Mountain, Star Wars and the Jungle Cruise are big names in theme park rides. Each year, to stay on the cutting edge of technology, these parks open up a new ride or attraction to cast their nets for the American public's vacation dollar. Disney executives, "imagineers," builders, and technology experts mesh their talents with great minds like George Lucas (creator of Indiana Jones and Star Wars movies), and high-profile celebrities like Michael Jackson and Jim Henson (deceased mastermind of The Muppets).

Don't try to read between the lines here and conclude I'm down on Disney. I'm not. There is no greater place on this planet to spend a family vacation and your hard-earned dollar than one of these spectacular theme parks. My point is that the world is a lot like a theme park trying to lure you into a thrilling ride that can end up being a spectacular spill. This world has a lot to offer that may rob you of the riches of being a committed follower of Christ. The flash will soon fade and the sizzle go silent if you choose to indulge in its ways. Don't be fooled or taken in by the attractions of this world which will get you nowhere. These joy-rides don't let you off at the same place you entered in your life. They'll set you back, rough you up, bounce you around, then spit you out. Jesus' plans, on the other hand, are designed to be fun, yet safe as you commit to a ride which will take you into eternity. Now that's one ride that won't get old.

☆ ☆ ☆

Further Study: What does the world offer you that steals from you? Why is it so dangerous to ride the world's joy-rides? Has Jesus ever offered you or asked you to do anything that might harm you?

GOD'S POWER

GOD'S POWER PLANT

I will instruct you in the power of God.
Job 27:11

✶ ✶ ✶

The process is amazing when you see it all at work. Huge shovels dig house-size scoops of lignite coal. Pulverized and loaded onto railroad boxcars, the coal travels to a generating plant in east Texas where it is further crushed into powder. Super-heated, this powder ignites like gasoline when blown into huge furnaces that crank three turbines. Whirring at 3,600 rpm, these turbines are housed in concrete and steel casings 100 feet long, 10 feet tall, and 10 feet across. They generate enough electricity for thousands of people. A visitor to this plant once asked the chief engineer where the electricity was stored. The answer was, "We don't store it, we just make it." When a light switch is flipped 100 miles away, it places a demand on the system and prompts greater output.

Not that you are interested in power plants or their usage, but I think it makes a great point of how God's power cannot be stored up either. Though inexhaustible, it comes in the measure required at the moment needed. God's power has a way of not overloading our circuits and causing a thermal melt-down, but being just enough. God's almighty power is not to be concealed or unused. It is to be a source of stabilization and divine energy that comes to us at the flip of a spiritual switch. God intended us to access this source through His Spirit. There are no forms to fill out, no waiting list and no bill at the end of the month . . . just flip it on and use it up, for His Glory and Praise, Amen!

✶ ✶ ✶

Further Study: How powerful is God's grace? When are we to use it? How does He supply us that power we need at an exact moment? Do you tap into it often? Why or why not?

YOUR TONGUE

SNAIL OR CROCODILE

Avoid worthless and empty chatter because it leads others to
ungodliness, and their talk will spread like gangrene.
2 Timothy 2:16-17

⋆ ⋆ ⋆

Growing up, I bet you had some pets around your house. I would wager to say that one pet you never had was a snail. Now I'm not referring to a slug because there is a major difference (and not that one melts with salt and the other one doesn't). Believe it or not, the little crawling creature has teeth on its tongue. That's right. Scientists have examined the tongue of a snail (they must have been bored) and found that the microscope revealed as many as 30,000 little teeth. It keeps its tongue coiled up in its mouth like a roll of toilet paper until it's needed. Then it shoots that dude out, using it like a chainsaw on leaves and stems. Wow! You've learned some trivia about the snail, so don't hesitate to enlighten others during a dinner conversation, okay?

You're gonna' say this is one lame similarity, but we, too, use our tongue like the snail. We walk around with this muscle next to our molars and lash out for the purpose (at times) of sawing down people or reputations. We talk about things that are empty and basically useless to even bring up, and we tear down more than we build up. What I call "tainted talk" eventually ends up producing a gangrene that will only be cured by amputation. We would do better to pattern our life after a crocodile. Why? Because a croc' has powerful jaws, large sharp teeth and lips, but no tongue. Be careful what and who you talk about, and shall we say, "Tis better to be a crocodile than a snail."

⋆ ⋆ ⋆

Further Study: What sort of things do you talk about with your friends? Are you more like a snail or crocodile? Do you see how empty chatter leads others into sin? How can you avoid that?

COMFORT ZONE

This is my comfort in my affliction, that thy word has revived me.
Psalm 119:50

☆ ☆ ☆

Those wonder years in junior high are stepping stones for some, but potholes for most. Between the ages of 12 and 15 seems to be a sort of testing ground for finding one's self. By that I mean that most young teenagers are kinda' learning the ropes of this world. During those molding years we first realize the importance of being accepted by our peers, styles of clothes, girls instead of G.I. Joe or guys instead of Barbie, and the latest in cool lingo. We're kinda' setting down those roots that will either make or break us when we start off, head first, into high school. It's funny, but in a way it's not, to see how we all react in those situations we get ourselves into and squirm our way out of. Those are the times that seem to come our way far too often when we are out of our so-called "comfort zones." These zones are like climate changes that make it difficult to adapt quickly. They're those times when we try to be casual in a certain situation, but find we fit about as well as a square block in a round hole.

We all, admit it or not, have a zone or shield around us that is booby trapped with alarms, flashing lights and sirens. Inside this zone we begin to use body language and double talk (babble) to protect us from the intruder. All of us desire to be accepted, not rejected, by society and friends, but at times we feel very uncomfortable. Comfort itself is a kind of utopia that we can relax in and feel like we have what it takes to be "with it" in a certain situation. God definitely has a sense of humor, judging by the way He puts us in circumstances to kinda' humble us and allow us to realize we need Him to be "hip." God's Word is a tremendous kick-stand to fall back on every day when we do (and we will) get into those certain situations where we feel we will "lose face." When they come, He will be there. Your comfort should always lie in God, and if you look at His word, there are no rejection zones to deal with. Yippee!

☆ ☆ ☆

Further Study: What sort of circumstances make you feel most uncomfortable? What type of alarm system do you have that is set off by discomfort? How can God's Word aid in this struggle? What visual ways do you show you're not feeling like you fit in?

SECURITY

SOLID AS THE ROCK

Be to me a rock of habitation to which I may continually go; Thou hast given com-
mandment to save me for You are my rock and my fortress.
Psalm 71:3

☆ ☆ ☆

A sailor in a violent shipwreck was thrown overboard and onto a rock in the sea where he clung for his life throughout the dark, stormy night alone. Later on, while being rescued by the Coast Guard, a crew member asked, "Didn't you shake and tremble with fear for your life when you were clinging to that rock?" The sailor replied, "Yes, I did . . . but the rock didn't."

Today, hearing the word "rock" may bring thoughts of dancing, a particular band, style of music, a boulder or cliff or the motion of an unstable object. We may think of a rugged, unfeeling type of a person. The "rock" I'm referring to is the "Rock of Ages, cleft for me, let me hide myself in thee." This is The Rock who doesn't roll and who doesn't even budge with a blast. The old hymn, which is the third most widely known and sung hymn in our Christian heritage, seems to sum up what Jesus is to us. When we are cast into the turbulent water of time, He is all we can hold on to.

We seem to be living in an exercise oriented society which has begun to love to explore its limits with climbing and rappelling rocks. Why so? For the feeling of accomplishment and challenge? For the extremes of the elements? For the rush of a 300-foot rappel or a 1,000-foot north face climb? I believe we, as a people, are fascinated with rocks because of their unique beauty and strength. Whether you're a geologist, climber, bulldozer operator, dynamite specialist or collector, rocks are interesting. Our God is an awesome God, and He alone is the rock of our salvation and the foundation on which we build our lives. He is the fortress that we hide behind and the matter in which we cling in stormy seas. Whichever picture shows up in your head when you think of a rock, there are none so big, sturdy, awesome and available as God our Father. Study Him, collect His thoughts, cleave to His commandments and hold to His holiness because this Rock don't roll.

☆ ☆ ☆

Further Study: What is the rock you cling to? Why are we told to grow and build our lives on Him? What security do you have hugging this rock in turbulent times?

CONTENTMENT

I Wish

*Not that I speak from want, for I have learned to be content
in whatever circumstances I am.*
Philippians 1.11

★ ★ ★

Wow . . . that is a hard verse to swallow, isn't it? I wonder how many hours a week we spend wishing we had someone else's house, car, body, money, personality, job, etc. Think about it.

Have you ever been to a big amusement park and just sat down and watched the people? What goes through your mind . . . "she's pretty," "oops, God goofed on that one," "he looks wealthy," "bad shoes," "who's her hairdresser?" . . . you know, all that kind of good and bad stuff! What are we doing when we dwell on others? We begin to compare. And when we compare, two things usually happen. One, we place ourselves higher than that person, or two, we place ourselves lower than that person. And you know what? Neither is good, and neither is worse than the other. They both make you wish you were different and hence you become discontent.

Let's be reminded of that verse in Philippians again . . . I don't think we can even imagine what kind of experiences Paul went through. If you have ever read Paul's books he wrote in the scriptures, it is very obvious that he suffered many things and went without many earthly pleasures. But you know what? His heart was content. We need to pray for this same contentment. We must get into God's Word and remember what God is about. He is not about STUFF and giving you someone else's body, money or possessions. He's about being a God who doesn't make junk! He's about being a God who created every living thing to His satisfaction. He is a God who is about knowing when the tide comes in and out. Don't argue with Him . . . He knows what's best for you and your future . . . .. He cares.

So when you begin the "I wish I hads," quickly get back to God and be reminded of all that He is and what He can do with you if you rely on Him.

★ ★ ★

Further Study: How often do you think about another person's possessions? What should you do when you get the "I wish I hads" or "if onlys?" Why is it so hard to be content?

OLD MACDONALD HAD A . . . WAY?

Now to Him (Jesus) who is able to do immeasurably more than all we ask or imagine, according to His power that is at work within us.
Ephesians 3:20

☆ ☆ ☆

As a parent, you will know that there is only one place to pull over on a cross country trip for lunch and that's . . . the "Golden Arches." Yep, you guessed it–Mickey D's; Mac attacks; two all beef patties; hamburger heaven, and I'm sure you have more to add. I cannot believe how this burger joint attracts youth worldwide with the power of a magnet. You can't drive more than 10 miles before seeing "the sign" and the kids in your car go ballistic for a Big Mac or a Happy Meal. Kids of all ages seem to see right past other burger barns (you know how they all seem to clump together like a covey of quail) to see McDonald's. What kind of marketing monster do they have to create this mystique? Why do kids stampede over one another to get chicken nuggets and the toy at the bottom of the Happy Meal box?

Can you imagine what our local newspapers and TV news stations would be saying if we, as Christians, were as excited about the Bible as kids are about a Big Mac!? What if the kids were crawling over the seats as fast for church as for chicken nuggets?! What if we didn't need a Happy Meal to make us happy?! Guess what? We don't! We have Jesus! That's right, we can actually get excited about a Savior who does more for us mentally, physically and spiritually daily than any McLean could think about. Come on, let's start showing this dark world we live in what Christians on fire for their God look like. But, as you know, excitement burns calories, so you may want to take a detour to you-know-where, for some fuel for your fire.

☆ ☆ ☆

Further Study: What would it take for you to really get excited about what Jesus is doing for you right now and share it with someone? Just do it!

STRETCHING EXERSIZES

Jesus answered, "You know not what you ask. Are you able to drink
of the cup that I shall drink and be baptized with the baptism
that I am baptized with?" They said to him, "We are able."
Matthew 20:22

☆ ☆ ☆

I have participated in sports all my life and by doing so have found one practice necessary prior to any event–stretching. Come on now, we've all tried this ancient ritual to loosen up hamstrings as tight as guitar strings Remember trying to touch your feet with a straight leg and feeling as if your arms had shortened or your legs had grown? I am still amazed at those flexible folks who can do the splits (ouch!) or even plant their face on the ground between their outstretched legs. These maneuvers are all designed to allow the person performing them an edge against injury and the opponent.

Throughout years of conducting job interviews, I've heard over and over again the same answer to this question. "Why do you want this job?" "I really want to be stretched." Now, that answer may be well and good to land a job, but most folks don't know everything that it entails. Yes, we all want God to stretch us, but I've found we usually want it done our way and on our time schedule. In other words, we want perseverance without pain. We want growth without groans. We want maturity without madness. Realize that God sees areas in our lives that we hide even from ourselves, and He performs surgery. Now, correct me if I'm wrong, but when a doc' goes to cuttin', a patient has to have anesthesia to deaden the pain, otherwise it's gonna' hurt like a big dog. Yes, God will stretch your spiritual muscles to prepare you for the game of godliness. Okay? Now, count to 10 and hold it!

☆ ☆ ☆

Further Study: Why do we need to be stretched? What causes us to pull spiritual muscles? Are you being stretched today? How?

CASTING

Casting all your anxiety upon Him, because He cares for you.
1 Peter 5:7

☆ ☆ ☆

There is nothing quite like being the father of three boys and taking them on a little father-sons fishing outing. We went to a private area (not open to the general public) called Dogwood Canyon, located in the Ozark Mountains of Missouri. I'd heard the spring fed stream was loaded with trophy size rainbow and brown trout, and they weren't kidding! I named the first fish my oldest boy caught Moby Dick. Get the picture? We had the time of our lives casting our lures into the stream and on every cast, within a matter of seconds, catching Jaws II on our hooks. Even though we did the "catch and release" thing, we made a memory on the trip of a lifetime.

I learned a spiritual lesson that day about casting and catching. I learned how much fun the art of casting is and what rewards come from such an elementary effort. God calls us to cast our hooks of life (anxiety in tough times) into the calm waters of our Creator and catch that peace that surpasses all understanding. God wants your problems because He knows you can't control them and He can. God is on the diet of eating problems for breakfast and you starve Him by not letting Him eat yours. To cast means to take your bag full of stress to the foot of the cross through prayer, lay them down and walk away. That's right . . . walk away and don't look back. Casting your cares will free you up to . . . who knows . . . maybe go fishin'?

☆ ☆ ☆

Further Study: How do you handle your problems? Who fixes your life for you? How often do you cast your cares on Him because He cares for you?

HAPPINESS

HAPPY MEAL

Happy are the people whose God is the Lord.
Psalms 144:15

✯ ✯ ✯

I can't help but think about "Mickey D's" when I talk about my kids. The "golden arches" hypnotize the kid population of America to believe the only place to eat is McDonald's. I think my kids learned to say "Happy Meal" before "Mommy" or "Da-da." For years I've tried to understand the lure (magnetism) of those golden arches to the 12 and under population. Marketing strategy is directed at kids, not parents. If I'd bought stock in this billion dollar company years ago, I'd be a rich man about now, due in part to all the money I've spent myself buying Happy Meals. Now, catch this thought with me . . . what about these Happy Meals? Why do kids desire them so? Is it the food? Is it the free dinky ice cream cone or the toy surprise? I don't have the answer, but I know that they do what they intend to do–make kids (mine, especially) happy!

Adults have a similar diversion, but they call it "happy hour." The purpose is to provide beverage and atmosphere to take the edge off a work day. My question is: Why do we need a specific meal or hour to be happy? Does it mean that for the other 23 hours we should be sad? We (Christians) are a chosen people of royal lineage whose sheer existence as children of God should mean happiness. We have a reason, through God's grace, to be joyful and bubble over with excitement at the kingdom that awaits us. Happiness is a frame of mind, an attitude, an awareness, an understanding, a gift. You don't need a meal, hour, material gift, cause, promotion, award, mortal relationship, deed or anything else to be happy. Like the song says, "Don't worry . . . be happy!" And watch out for Ronald's house . . . it will steer your car right in.

✯ ✯ ✯

Further Study: Are you considered happy by your peers? What makes you happy? Does knowing you're a child of God make you happy? Why or Why not? Do you like Big Mac's?

TOUGH TIMES

WE ARE OVERCOMERS

He who overcomes, I will grant to him to sit down with Me on My throne,
as I also overcame and sat down with My Father on His Throne.
Revelation 3:21

* * *

The popular soul Christian group called The Winans had a song titled *We are Overcomers* in the early '90s. Listening to the words of that song (along with a great tune) made me realize just how blessed we are in life. To be a conqueror, one must first realize it's not an overnight ordeal, it's a process (t-i-m-e). Reflect back for a minute on all the great people of this world, and I'll bet you a nickel they just didn't wake up one morning and arrive. Training is as important to our spiritual beings as it is to the sports stars. Isn't preparation a key to survival? We are done a great dysfunction, in one sense, through being programmed by society into thinking if it doesn't come quick then it's not worth waiting for. I call this the McDonald's Mentality. You know, when it takes the drive-through attendant longer than three minutes to get your order, you go ballistic and speed off.

I see a whole lot more preparation and persevering going on in scripture than I do quick fixes. Noah waited 120 years; Sarah was 90 when she gave birth; Moses waited patiently for his people's freedom; Paul walked miles on missionary journeys; Jonah lived in a whale belly; and Job went from something to nothing and back to something. Isn't it wonderful how we have a hero like Jesus who asked us to follow Him and do as He did? Look at that again, He wants you to overcome tough times. Why? Because He did first. Hey, I love playing follow the leader when my leader is worth following. God may call you to overcome sickness, a broken heart, the loss of a loved one, surviving with less "things," a personal setback in your career, or whatever. His promise is that when, not if, you overcome these challenges, you may sit with Him at the head of the table (the Throne). That's right . . . sit beside the One who holds every star in place. Now that promise from God is what I'd say is worth persevering for.

* * *

Further Study: What trials have you overcome lately? How did God help you through? How can you prepare now?

DIVORCE

IN-N-OUT

Are you married? Do not seek a divorce.
1 Corinthians 7:27

☆ ☆ ☆

The West Coast state of California is known for a lot of things. I'm not talking about surfing, The Beach Boys, wine vineyards, L.A., the 49ers, or Lakers. You can find one legendary location if you will drive north out of San Francisco on Interstate 80 about 20 minutes just off to the right in Vallejo. They're only in California and they've only been around since the '50s and they're packed around lunch time. What is this place? In-N-Out Burgers. They're as popular as swimmin' pools in the summer or Tiger Woods at a golf tournament. The menu is as simple as first grade spelling, and the french fries are as addictive and tasty as chocolate syrup. Folks from all over the country will travel all the way to the West Coast just to order a "double-double" or real "potato fries" and a thick shake. You can't go there without snagging a famous In-N-Out '50s theme T-shirt to prove you were there and cause those who haven't been there to gloat with jealousy. It's exactly what the name reflects . . . you can be "in" and "out" with no inconvenience to your daily schedule.

In 1955 there were 385,000 recorded divorces in the United States. In 1993 there were 1,315,580 divorces. Today, four out of ten marriages end up in divorce court and five out of ten children will grow up in a single parent home. One of those was my home life growing up. I'm not writing this to bring up a sore subject or point a finger, just to cry with my heart for the pain one goes through as a victim. If we'd stop watching the soap operas and quit reading the love novels that paint the picture that marriage is easy and intimacy (not godly love) will carry you through the hard times, we'd be better off. Divorce courts and attorney offices may as well be an In-N-Out fast food joint . . . as fast as they come in joined, they go out separated. Couples today will marry "for better or worse" but not "for good." If you're married, stay married and prove the power of God can do all things (Philippians 4:13). If you're not, realize the purpose and reality of the institute of marriage. A godly marriage is far better and much more satisfying than a bucket of In-N-Out fries.

☆ ☆ ☆

Further Study: Why does God "hate" the act of divorce? How can you begin to prepare yourself today for a godly marriage? What does the scripture say about marriage and divorce?

MATURITY

You're Acting Childish

When I was a child, I used to speak as a child, think as a child, reason as a child; but when I became a man (mature), *I did away with childish things.*
1 Corinthians 13:11

* * *

Have you ever sat back and taken a gander (look) at how our society is set up? Kids are doing those kid things, adolescents are doing the teenage things and adults are doing those adult things. Kids are walking in diapers, riding bikes, building forts, playing with dolls, jumping rope and picking their noses. Teenagers are checking out the opposite sex, hot-rodding the cars, manicuring the nails, deciding on colleges, cramming for tests, playing the sports and still (more discretely) picking their noses. Lastly the adults are going to work, raising the kids, meeting deadlines, taking vacations, playing more golf, setting up wills, managing the assets, caravaning to the games, cleaning the house, mowing the lawn and getting more gray hair. This civilization, whether you realize it or not, grows you up naturally. We all graduate from diapers to dialect, project to progress, hand-me-downs to honeymoons without ever giving it a second glance.

The natural system grows people up, but the spiritual curriculum takes studying and effort on our own part. We have in our Christian circles today adult babies. Now, I don't mean that in a demeaning way, just factual. We grow up in every way but in our faith. What would it look like if a 40-year-old person went back to a third grade classroom to learn to read and write . . . silly. You will look pretty silly, too, if you have been a "true Christian" for 20 years but still walk and talk like you're a babe. Maturing and growing up in our faith means doing things as Christ would, not as our old nature does. It means taking on the divinely injected characteristics of our Creator which makes us salt and light. It means seeing situations, circling circumstances, loving the unlovable, taming the tongue, terminating the thoughts and walking the way we should. We need to grow up in Christ just like we grow up in life. We need to mature in wisdom like we mature in years. Come on, grow away from those childish conducts and ripen in righteousness.

* * *

Further Study: Have you done away with childish ways? Why or why not? How can you practically do this?

PEACE OF GOD

RANKED NO. 1

Love your Lord God with all your heart, soul, and might.
Deuteronomy 6:5

☆ ☆ ☆

You don't have to look too far to see the ol' pointer finger raised high parading the symbol for being number one. Each week, college and high school polls rank teams according to their previous records and recent performances. Tennis players, cheerleading squads, debate teams, all jockey for that prestigious spot of the top gun. To be number one in anything, whether it's sports, academia or mutual funds, is to let the facts speak loudly for themselves. The strange thing about being a lonesome dove at the top of the perch is that it's easier to get there than it is to stay up there. To hold that spot for very long takes a lot of dedication and determination on the team or individual's part.

Ted Koppel, while speaking at commencement at Duke University a few years ago, referencing the Ten Commandments, was quoted, "Moses didn't come down from Mt. Sinai with the Ten Suggestions." After Moses had a one-on-one meeting with the Father of Light and returned aglow, he had with him the "Top Ten" in working order. In other words, the first command handed down from divine to domestic was to love God with all that you are. Let's take a second to look at the three areas God asked us to give Him as a deposit down on eternity. Number one is your heart, your pumper, your livelihood, your existence. Number two would be your soul which is made up of three areas, mind, will and emotions. Number three concludes with might which is your energy, strength and every muscle fiber you own in your earth suit. Listen, the number one ranking commandment is there for a reason, a good one too, because God knows if you love Him with all you can be, that you'll go places for Him. Love God first and all the other nine commandments will come easy. Remember too that these are commands, and not mere suggestions. God loves to stay atop the polls.

☆ ☆ ☆

Further Study: What do you love God with? How do you practically love God with all you have? How hard is it for you to love God first in your life and rank Him number one on your poll?

GOALS

YOUR PASSION

*And also that every man should eat and drink, and enjoy
the good of all his labor, it is the gift of God.*
Ecclesiastes 3:13

★ ★ ★

Take a moment, rock back in your chair and ponder (ponder, not take a snooze). Now, ask yourself a few direct questions about what you love to do. What do you talk about most? If money was no object, what would you be doing today? What do you do best? After answering those, realize that the joy of your life is determined by doing what you have a piercing passion for doing. Look at the life of Jesus and see His passion every day He roamed the earth. He loved to tango with the tax collectors, fellowship with the fishermen, dialog with the doctors, philosophize with the Pharisees and commune with the common folk. I dare to doubt that everyday He woke up before His alarm went off, excited about another day of focusing in on His goal and purpose in life. He knew what His mission was and that it seemed impossible to a faithless world. He held true to His commitment to a lost people because He knew that failed focus is a reason why so many men fail. There are folks who have taken a job because it's convenient or close to home, yet they are miserable. A friend of mine who is a pastor in Chicago told me one time, "There is nothing more dangerous than being comfortable out of God's will." How true that is with so many folks who have fallen into that hopeless hole. What you love to do is a clue to your calling in life. Jesus knew this and was determined to set the stage for a spectacular climax to 33 years of being obedient to His calling. Do what makes you happy as long as it is within the parameters of scripture. Live out your dreams with Christ close beside you; after all, dreams are what make this world go around.

★ ★ ★

Further Study: What makes you tick loudest? How are you preparing yourself today for what God has in store for you tomorrow?

EVOLUTION

FACT OR THEORY

For by Him all things were created, both in the heavens and on earth, visible and invisible, whether thrones or dominions or rulers or authorities–all things have been created by Him and for Him.
Colossians 1:16

★ ★ ★

Let's see how well you listened in your history class. I'll give you some clues and you give it a guess. He (obviously not a female) was born in 1809 and died at the age of 73 in 1882. At the age of 22 he was about to pursue a career working in the church, but decided at the last minute to take an offer as a naturalist (whatever that is) on a survey ship called the H.M.S. Beagle in 1831. He traveled abroad collecting organisms from all the major continents and returned to England to sort through his findings in 1836. For 20 years at his home in Kent, he dissected his thoughts, theories and material, finally publishing a book in 1859 entitled *Origin of the Species* which supported his theory of evolution. Who was this man? (Give up yet?)

He was Charles Darwin, a man who impacted and influenced history as much as any one man ever has. His theory, which I'm not sure was ever meant to be considered factual, was and is a major influence in the debate of where we come from . . . God or monkeys. Now, you might be wondering why I'm making such a big tiff about this man. Why . . . ? Because if his theory is true, then you and I have no higher authority, no Savior and surely no hope but to evolve into bones in the dirt. All who have grown up in a public school have been pounded with this theory. If you are told something enough, you may eventually believe it as truth. I'll tell you what this theory is in four words: a big fat lie. You, me, and whoever will be are created by the Creator (Abba Father) and our family tree doesn't have apes hanging on it. Evolution is a joke and creation is the fact . . . learn it, live it, and believe it.

★ ★ ★

Further Study: How come Darwin's theory is a theory, not a proven fact? If it is only a theory, then why do we believe it and teach it as fact? What can you do to transform your thinking?

STATUS QUO

*I am confident of this very thing, that He who began a good work
in you will perfect it until the day of Christ Jesus.*
Philippians 1:6

☆ ☆ ☆

Talk about a buzz word for the '90s. You'll hear the word "status quo" used more in describing a person, place or thing, and as often as you hear the words "politically correct." I'm about as bright as a two-watt lightbulb, so I had to look up what this "hip" word meant. It means a condition or state in which a person or thing is or has been stuck in. A few years back we used an uncool word to describe a similar expression: stereotype. This good old country of ours seems to "tag" people or classify them in a category, and it's heck to get out from under that label. If you personally haven't been labeled, I'm sure you have seen it performed. You know, someone is overweight, so they're a slob; skinny, so they're a wimp; big, then they're dumb as a rock; don't make A's, so they're retarded; don't drive a Lexus, so they're poor; have a nice house, then they're a rich snob; don't have a pretty face or perfect teeth, so they're ugly; and so on.

Why do we do this to others or allow it to be done to us? There is a huge, loving, caring God who desires to inject His working Spirit in us to help make us better and transform us to be more like His Son. People fear God because they are afraid of Him judging them harshly. The funny (really sad though) thing is that we judge ourselves and others more harshly than He does. We pass personal judgment then condemn to the seller of self-image. Status quo is a phase we pass through on life's journey, yet we don't have to reside in it. We don't need to park there; we can put our lives in drive with God at the wheel and watch Him pull off miracles in areas we fail in. A good friend of mine always says, "It is no secret what God can do, but it's sure fun to watch Him pull it off." Go ahead . . . punt the "status quo" and let God pull off some miracles in your life. Don't settle for second best.

☆ ☆ ☆

Further Study: In what areas of your life do you feel you're stuck in the status quo? What practical ways can you and God improve through them? What does stereotyping do to a person's self-image?

A Giant Success

What will be done for the man who kills this Philistine and
takes away the reproach from Israel? Who is this that he should
taunt the armies of the living God?
1 Samuel 17.26

☆ ☆ ☆

You have probably read this or had it read to you at bedtime or maybe even in Sunday school class. Remember it? It's the one about an overlooked young man named David and a giant named Goliath, who had a little disagreement on issues, so they went head to head. David had an ancient slingshot and rocks as his artillery, and Goliath, a big sword that could have been used as a double for an airplane wing. David was on paper, outsized, out-muscled, out-equipped, and should be considered out-to-lunch for even taking on this dude. Well, enough, you know how this story goes. David smacks this giant in the coconut with a rock and hence becomes the King of Israel (Cliff Notes version). What David gave us in this bit of scripture is more than a fun bedtime story. It's the secret to success when facing overwhelming odds in our lives. Check out these six secrets to success: 1) David sized himself up before he sized up the obstacle. Note: Ignorance about yourself is a self-imposed obstacle. 2) Don't let the failure of others stop you. Note: Most failures are followed by successes. 3) Former victories will guide future successes. Note: Nothing breeds success like success. 4) Don't be handcuffed by traditional thinking. Note: Be aware of statements like "we've always done it that way before." What works for others may not work for you. 5) You will have to find courage to stand alone at times. Note: God will never leave or forsake you. 6) Never forget who gives you success. Note: God alone gives success.

Look around you and see all the folks who strive a lifetime to gain success. Success itself is not wrong, as long as one is striving for the right reasons. The process too, is part of the beauty that God allows you to enjoy during your journey. Go ahead . . . take on the Goliath in your life with the weapon God provides, His Word and your knees.

☆ ☆ ☆

Further Study: What is a major challenge (Giant) you face today? Are you equipped for the battle? Is God behind you?

YOUR BODY

SHOWROOM TO JUNKYARD

Glorify God with your body.
1 Corinthians 6:20

✩ ✩ ✩

I know the answer to this question before I even ask it, but let me give it a try. Have you ever taken a tour of an automobile junkyard? If yes, you're weird; if no, you've missed out. I'll betcha' that Henry Ford, after he first invented the motorized buggy, never dreamed his little idea would take off like it has. Basically, the whole city of Detroit exists because of the mass production of automobiles, hence it's name, "Motor City, USA." We have junkyards nowadays about every 20 miles, and in some cases they really trash up the landscape. Junkyards, as the slang term goes, are full of frames, lights, tailgates, transmissions, seats, tires and wheels, gear shifters, engine blocks, and much more. Vehicles wind up in a junkyard because they were either totaled in a wreck or just sold as scrap metal from a poorly taken care of auto. No matter what the reason, it's definitely not what a car has in mind when it thinks of "shining on the showroom floor."

Ripley's Believe It or Not, I am going to make a simile (show comparison) from this word picture and our world. I got to thinking how folks start off with no miles, dents, or oil usage, just like a new car. Let me explain . . . we all are born new and ready to run, but as time goes on we do things to our bodies (and engines) that tend to wear down their longevity and nullify the warranty. Whether it's stress relating to working too hard, drugs, alcohol, smoking, eating poorly, playing a sport that we shouldn't play, or whatever, it still adds up to the depreciation of our bodies. Of course, we don't call them junkyards, we call them hospitals and rest homes, but they both serve the same purpose. Don't do me the favor, do it for you and God. Think about what you're doing to your body before you do it. "Just do it" can do more harm than good at times, and you only have one body here on earth,so treat it like a temple, not a piece of junk. There's nothing quite like a fine runnin' car but better yet even is a well-maintained earth suit.

✩ ✩ ✩

Further Study: Do you take good care of your body? In what areas could you improve? How can you improve your temple of God? Make a list of goals that will help you to keep focused and disciplined.

A PERSONAL PUMP

*I am the way, the truth, and the life. No one comes to
the Father except through me.*
John 14:6

✬ ✬ ✬

One of the many hobbies I enjoy, along with thousands of others, is biking. There are few better methods known to mankind for seeing the scenery and getting the old heart rate up than jumping on a bike and pounding the pedals. Not long ago I went on a Saturday afternoon ride of about 20 miles with some buddies of mine. I was well equipped with my "skid lid" (my helmet) in place and a few tools accompanied by a spare tube. About 10 miles down the road I noticed my ride getting tougher and a slight wobble in my rear (tire, that is). I glanced down to find I had a flat. I pulled off the road (that's best for your safety) before I became a road rash and began to fix my tire. I opened my tool pouch and went to work like a pit crew on an Indy car. After the tube was in place, I began to pump up the tire to get me back in working order. I pumped and pumped but with little success in filling the tire. Finally, I noticed that the tube valve had to be unscrewed before the air could flow into the tube.

How many popped pedestrians, who fail to open their heart valve to a good pumping up of the knowledge of Christ, do we see all around us? God could have designed us (remember, He's God) with no valve (our will) at all, but He didn't. He didn't make us robots but gave us the option of opening our lives to Him in response to his invitation. God doesn't force His ways or His lifestyle on us. He lets us find our own way (remember, He knocks at our door but doesn't kick it down). Open up your heart and mind to the truths of our Creator who cares if we ride again. Don't allow the debris of this world to let the air out of your life without having a spare ready to replace and fill with God's breath of life. Go ahead, ride on!

✬ ✬ ✬

Further Study: Why did God allow us to keep our "wills?" How do you submit to God? Why is our God a jealous one? How can you pump someone up today? Will you?

TONGUE TIED

He who guards his mouth and his tongue keeps himself from calamity.
Proverbs 21:23

☆ ☆ ☆

I love the Christmas season and all that goes with it. There is nothing quite like all the festive rituals, gifts and TV specials which all tend to set us in a festive mood. *A Christmas Story*, the classic movie, is a nostalgic look at a boy growing up in the midwestern town of Gary, Indiana. In one memorable scene we find Ralphy (the boy) at a recess in school in the middle of winter. Two boys, surrounded by their classmates, argue whether a person's tongue will stick to a metal pole in below-freezing weather. Eventually, one of the boys folds under peer pressure and a "triple-dog dare," and sticks his tongue on the frigid metal flagpole. Sure enough, it gets stuck, and the bell rings to begin class again. Everyone, including the boy who made the dare, runs into the school building, leaving one sucker stuck to the pole. The teacher asks where the absent student is, and then looks out the school window to see the boy in pain with his tongue frozen to the pole.

Now, I realize this is a little extreme, but I want to make a valid point. Though few of us are brainless enough to get into this kind of predicament, we do let our tongues get us in trouble. When we (you) suffer the pain that eventually recoils on everyone who speaks boastful words, lies, bitter or cruel words, hypocritical or doubting words, we learn the truth of the proverb at the top of this page. Guard–literally guard–your tongue like a wild prisoner and don't allow it to escape and cause trouble in someone's life. Sticks and stones will break your bones, but words can do much worse. Tie up your tongue, except to encourage or speak God's truth.

☆ ☆ ☆

Further Study: What is gossip? Is it of Satan or God? How much trouble does a loose tongue cause? Do you use your tongue as a weapon? Why? How can you realistically guard your tongue so it won't hurt someone? Make today a day in which your tongue does nothing but encourage others.

SEA OF CROWNS

*And before the throne there was a sea of glass like crystal
and in the center and around the throne.*
Revelation 4:6

☆ ☆ ☆

This is one of those verses that has intrigued folks for many moons. Most would pass this right by without catching a glimpse of the true meaning and visualize just what's going on here. Throughout your journey on this Christian road, you, by your efforts in obedience, will be rewarded by our Lord with various crowns. Through your perseverance and endurance in this race you might receive the crown of exultation (1 Thessalonians 2:19), the crown of righteousness (2 Timothy 4:8), the crown of life (James 1:12) or the crown of glory (1 Peter 5:4). All these crowns come after persevering through trials, being approved, for those who wait for His appearing and all are promised by God to those who truly love Him. In the book of The Revelation, you find contained in John's dream and vision, a sea of believers wearing their crowns, gathered at one place, the foot of the throne, doing one thing. Don't miss this now . . . they will all be throwing their crowns at the feet of the Savior, praising Him for who He is and what He has done. Wow! A multitude of common folks who have been tested and tried by this wacko world and been found worthy to receive a medal of honor (a crown) to be given back ultimately to the giver.

You, yes you, whether you realize it or not, are accumulating crowns, invisible to ordinary individuals, but seen by the Savior. One day, when we all meet in that place as one body, crowns glistening like a sea of crystals, we will remove them and throw them like Frisbees at the Throne of God. Come on now, partner . . . if that doesn't jump-start your heart, nothing will. Get excited about an opportunity to be able to give back a small portion to our Lord. Practice up your Frisbee arm because some day it will come into good use.

☆ ☆ ☆

Further Study: Why does God reward us with crowns? What do you think these crowns looks like? Are you prepared to give them back to the Creator?

THE ANT AND THE GRASSHOPPER

That we may live a tranquil and quiet life in all godliness and dignity.
1 Timothy 2:2

✴ ✴ ✴

In the famous *Aesop Fables*, a story is told of an ant and a grasshopper. As winter is approaching, the hungry grasshopper, his fiddle under his arm, comes up to the ant and humbly begs for a bite to eat. The ant does not respond very kindly. He asks, "Haven't you stored anything away for the winter? What were you doing all summer?" The grasshopper whines that he was too busy making music to have time to store food. To which the ant replies, "Making music? Well then, dance!" and he walks away!

What is the moral to this far-fetched fable? Well, I find this to be so very true of many Christians today (me included at times). Our calendars are filled with such wonderful activities from dawn to dusk, and then it is time for us to lay our head down at night. As we reflect on our day . . . meeting at church, Bible study, lunch with someone needy, exercise, etc . . . has there been any time for the Creator of our souls? Most of the time, the day is done, and we are beat and toss up one last prayer, "God, I'm sorry that I didn't have any time. Please forgive me; I'll do better next time." But . . . the next day, same old routine.

How do we get off of this crazy ride? Well, someone or something has to go . . . and it better not be Jesus! He is the sustainer of souls. Without Him we are nothing. We cannot expect Him to work despite us for very long. He does not need us, but He desires us to know Him above everything! Experiences, adventures and relationships are very important, but they should confirm and bring personal meaning to the truth of Him and His written Word. We, too, need to strive for the simple and quiet life which ends up with God as our foundation every day.

✴ ✴ ✴

Further Study: What does your calendar look like? What do you need to cut out in order to make time for God and His Word? Find someone to hold you accountable to spending time in the Bible.

BEING CHILDISH

*Truly I say to you, unless you have child-like faith, it is
impossible to inherit the kingdom of heaven.*
Matthew 18:3

* * *

Few times, to none, has a perfect stranger pranced up to me, whipped out a pencil and paper, and asked me for my autograph. Now, on the other hand, it's part of daily rituals for the likes of Michael Jordan, Jackie Joyner Kersee, Cindy Crawford, Emmitt Smith, Bonnie Blair, the President of the United States, Michael Jackson, and the list goes on. Let me tell you about my biggest fan of all time . . . my son. To him I am someone famous who can do no wrong. I don't break world records, model for *Vogue*, have my picture in *Sports Illustrated*, or run a nation. I do far more important stuff like fix training wheels, unscrew jars with crayons in them, catch crickets and snakes with my bare hands, mow the yard and do cheerleading stunts with his mom in the living room. To my kids I can do it all. Little do they understand that most of what I do, anyone with two legs could do. They say, "Wow, Daddy, you're so strong," when I'm not, or "My Dad is faster than a plane," when if I went any slower, I'd be in reverse. Are you catching my point here? My children think I'm "great" because they depend on me for all the small things of a functioning little person's life. With dependence comes faith in what or who is being depended on.

How much do you depend on your Father (God) for the small things in life, daily? Gang, when you revert back to depending on God for your smallest needs (i.e. tests in class, friendships, dates), then you will see God as He desires to be seen. Watching the faith of children is an incredible sight to see. At the age of four, my son jumped off a roof top to me and would do the same again today. Why? Because I have never dropped him. So, why shouldn't he trust me. He has no reason to believe otherwise. Your Father in heaven wants you to jump to Him because He never has and never will drop you. Dependability is a dying quality in society today, and believe-you-me, it's great to depend on Someone who is bigger and stronger than we are, to seek refuge in His big open, loving, caring, tender arms daily . . . for the small things, too. So come on, and be a kid again! Just see again how great your Savior really is.

* * *

Further Study: How dependent are you on God? Today what do you have going that you could give to Him to handle?

SWORD OF MERCY

For the word of God is quick, and powerful, and sharper than any two-edged sword, piercing even to divide the soul and spirit, and of the joints and marrow, and is a discerner of the thoughts and intents of the heart.
Hebrews 4:12

☆ ☆ ☆

On February 24, 1995, my family and I found ourselves in London, England, for my brother-in-law's wedding. Needless to say, this old Texan felt a little out of place! If you were to ask me (doesn't matter–I'll give my opinion if you ask or not), I'd just as soon keep my big old size 13 feet on good old American soil, but the in-law factor has a certain persuasiveness. Well, to make a long story longer, I figured if we had to be there, we should make the best of it and take a tour of the city. Believe-you-me, we saw it all, plus some. One of my favorite stops was the Tower of London. We got to see where some old king got tired of his wife and had her beheaded (obviously not while we were there). Besides heads rolling, we also saw the crown jewels of Queen Elizabeth and other British royalty.

One item that caught my eye was a sword called the "Sword of Mercy." It looked like all the other swords except that it had no pointed tip. Made total sense after I thought about it! A sword that showed mercy to its victims because without a point it couldn't kill them.

How Christians can learn from this! Are there times that we use God's word as a weapon, not to teach, but to destroy? Yes, the Bible is powerful, but do we use it to hurt instead of heal? Is our intent to tear down or rebuild? God has given us a weapon of truth to be used to fight the sin (Satan), not the sinner (person). Next time you pull out your sword to do battle, pull out the sword of mercy–Jesus did.

☆ ☆ ☆

Further Study: Why did God give us His word? How do you use it? Is your intent to help or hurt someone?

HELP!

But the Helper, the Holy Spirit, whom the Father will send in My name, He will teach you all things, and bring to your remembrance all that I said to you.
John 14:26

✫ ✫ ✫

Help! How many times have you gotten yourself into a predicament and needed a little help? You searched like a stray dog for a bone of relief, aid, improvement, assistance and a remedy to your distress. There's nothing like being stranded on the road of life and finally flagging down the assistance that leads you out of a bad circumstance. In Genesis 2:18, God said, "It is not good for man to be alone, I will make him a helper suitable for him." From the beginning of time, God knew that we would need all the help we could get to make it through life on earth.

In the Old Testament, Christians had prophets like Isaiah, Jeremiah, Ezekiel, Daniel, Hosea and Joel to help them out in times of chaos. In the New Testament, they had Jesus. But now, what do we have? The Holy Spirit. The Greek word "paraclete" is an ancient warrior term. Greek soldiers went into battle in pairs so that when the enemy attacked, they could draw together, back-to-back, covering each other's blind side. The battle partner was a "paraclete." God does not send us into a spiritual battle alone (He even sent His disciples out to the mission fields by twos). The Holy Spirit (Helper) is the battle partner who covers our blind side and fights for our well-being in time of war. Today, you have a Helper to come along side in time of distress, to work with you, like a team works, for one purpose–victory, and to bring it home for the "God Squad." What assurance and peace we have in knowing we can call on God, any time, any place. What a team!

✫ ✫ ✫

Further Study: What does the word "Helper" mean to you? Do you allow the Holy Spirit to come back-to-back with you to do battle against the dark side? How can you utilize the Helper more in your daily trials?

YES I AM

And Jesus answered them and said, "I Am He."
They drew back and fell to the ground.
John 18:6

☆ ☆ ☆

Unfortunately, some of the funniest commercials on the tube today are beer commercials. *Bud Light* aired an ad with a guy coming off a plane, walking up to three limo drivers holding signs with names, asking which one of the drivers had *Bud Light* in his limo. When one fessed up to having the requested item, the guy quickly looked at the sign and said, "then I'm Doctor Gal-o-week-its." The limo driver abruptly asked this guy, "You're Doctor Galakowetz?" to which the impersonator answers very clearly, "Yes, I am."

You know, when I first heard this commercial during a televised football game I recalled another person in the history of time answering the question with a similar, "Yes, I am He," but under different circumstances. Let's look back at the time that Jesus and Peter were confronted by an army of soldiers searching for Jesus to take Him to trial before the people and Pilate. I guess the commander came up to Jesus, asked if He was Jesus the Nazarene, and Jesus replied, "I Am He," and the entire army fell flat. God told Moses in Exodus 3:14, "I Am who I Am." In other words, there is only one "I Am" and that is God, the creator of everything. There is so much power in those simple words, yet in this day and time so little respect for our Lord. We, too, should fall on our faces daily to praise and worship and give honor to the God who cared enough to incarnate in a flesh suit to save us. We shouldn't be messin' with the CEO of our world, God. Hey, one more thing . . . if you're gonna' be a light, don't be a *Bud Light*. That type of light flutters to a mere flicker quickly!

☆ ☆ ☆

Further Study: Why is the title "The Great I Am" so powerful? What does "I Am" do for you? How can we be more reverent to our Lord and Creator?

A RUBBER BAND

*For the Lord your God is testing (stretching) you to find out if you love
Him with all your heart and with all your soul.*
Deuteronomy 13.3

☆ ☆ ☆

Now, you talk about a wacko thought fixin' to fly out of nowhere.
Recently, I was performing my morning ritual, which includes reading the
morning newspaper at the breakfast table. When I rolled off the rubber band
that holds the paper together, it flew up and smacked me in the bottom lip.
After my blood pressure subsided, a thought hit me as well. Are you ready for
this one? A rubber band is only useful if the object it surrounds is bigger than
it is. Let me rephrase that . . . a rubber band is worthless if you put it around
anything that doesn't stretch it. Catch my drift?

I'm sure that if rubber bands had feelings and could talk, they would tell
you they don't much appreciate being stretched, pulled and twisted to serve
someone else's purpose. As Christians, we don't take kindly to being stretched
by God in our lives either. You hear all the time how people really want to be
stretched and grow in life. Yeah, right. We say that, but in our minds, we want
to be stretched our way, on our timetable, and painlessly to boot. God doesn't
work that way. He has to catch us off guard and do it His way or we really
don't get the full perspective or learn the lesson. You see, when we are
stretched, we have no one else to lean on except God (and He likes it that
way . . . no other providers). Death, rejection, failure, humiliation, despair, broken hearts and separation are some means God may use to draw us to Him.
I saw a billboard by a church once that read, "Anything that causes you to
pray is a good thing." How true that is!

☆ ☆ ☆

Further Study: When does God stretch you? How often? Do you ever feel like
you're gonna' break? Why does God use the stretching method to teach and
mature us as followers? How do you handle being stretched? Can you see the
value in it?

ALCOHOL

IT JUST DOESN'T LOOK RIGHT

It would be better for him to tie a millstone around their neck and be thrown into the sea than to cause the least of the little ones to stumble.
Luke 17:2

☆ ☆ ☆

Let the facts speak for themselves:

Eight million teens use alcohol regularly.
Alcohol related incidents kill ten thousand ages 16 to 24 each year.
The number one killer of teens today is alcohol.
Forty-one percent of all college students consume five alcoholic drinks in a row each week.
Sixty-four percent of all violent crimes on college campuses are alcohol related.
Alcohol abuse kills brain cells.
Thirty-five percent of all academic problems relate to alcohol.
USA Today News

You sure don't have to be a rocket scientist to see that alcohol in America has become a huge problem. In 1990, a survey of college presidents by the Carnegie Foundation found that alcohol was "the most serious problem we face on our campus today." There are 637 references to drink and drinking in the Bible. In those, there are 13 different words (translations) for wine. We all can read that it's wrong to drink "strong drink" or to be "drunk," but what about casual drinking? We need to see that in the Bible the translations for wine are yayin, shekar and tirosh, and in the New Testament they are sikera and gleukos. All words for wine are equivalent to our modern day meaning for grape juice. The water to wine made biblical wine about two-percent alcohol (our wine today has eleven to twenty percent alcohol) and during biblical times was considered nothing more than purified water. By comparison, modern brandy is 20-percent alcohol, and other hard liquor is 40–50-percent alcohol.

You can state all the facts you want, but the best reason to abstain from alcohol is . . . it just doesn't look right. To compromise a lifestyle for a quick fix or social image is a gamble you can't afford to lose. Step back, count the cost, weigh the pluses and minuses, and take a radical stand for the cause of Christ. If you're gonna' be a light, don't be a *Bud Light!*

☆ ☆ ☆

Further Study: Why should you not drink alcohol? What does it do for your image? Why do you feel most people drink?

Hilarious Medicine

A joyful heart is good medicine, but a broken spirit dries up the bones.
Proverbs 17:22

☆ ☆ ☆

The Executive Digest printed an interesting article on the results of a scientific study of the effect of laughter on humans. The study showed that laughter had a profound effect on virtually every important organ in our bodies. The study showed that laughter reduced tension and relaxed the tissues as well as exercising them. It said that even when laughter was forced it resulted in beneficial effects, both mentally and physically. So, the next time you feel nervous or stressed out, or have the jitters, indulge in a good gut laugh and see what happens.

Laughter, when untainted, can be one of the most productive resources known to mankind. It is amazing how in the midst of this rough and tumble world, when laughter makes an appearance, it soothes our souls. Laughter was invented by God and was intended to be used for a kind of spiritual medicine. Have you ever noticed that laughter produces smiles, and smiles seem to be contagious? Joy seems to be born from the capability to laugh in the midst of trials (pain). Learning to laugh at yourself and not take yourself too seriously is a benefit in itself. Warning: don't be of the type that chimes in with the distasteful or discolored (ungodly) humor that you find around a lot. When you're having a gut buster of a chuckle, make sure its stimulus is pure and holy in the sight of the Savior. Once again, Satan has taken a God-made product and distorted its true purpose. Go ahead, laugh at something goofy you or a friend did (be careful not to demean), laugh at a "foot in mouth" incident or a hilarious situation. You'll be amazed at just how healing this medicine can be, and you don't need a doctor's prescription to use it.

☆ ☆ ☆

Further Study: What are the benefits that you see in laughter? When did you last have a gut wrenching laugh? How did it make you feel? What makes you laugh? Would Jesus laugh with you?

A CHRISTIAN'S EMANCIPATION

What shall we say then? Are we to continue to be a slave to sin that grace may increase? May it never be! How shall we who died to sin still be a slave to it?
Romans 6:1-2

✳ ✳ ✳

Back in the days of Abraham Lincoln and slavery, we as a nation experienced tremendous tension. Slaves were bought and sold faster than used cars, and they had little hope for freedom. That was until Honest Abe came around and released the pressure by signing the Emancipation Proclamation–the slaves' ticket to freedom. His desire was no more chains and poor living conditions, no more beatings and small food portions, no more high fences or free labor, no more long hours and back pain, no more, no more, no more. A weird thing occurred though, when the slaves were told they were free, some stayed with their masters. That's right, some slaves chose to pass on freedom and continue the lifestyle they had known, probably all their long lives.

The apostle Paul writes in the sixth chapter of Romans the Emancipation Proclamation for Christians who are slaves to the meanest master of all, sin. You as a new creature in Christ were a slave bound hopelessly to sin, but through Christ's crucifixion, are now given the bill of rights for freedom. This freedom allows you to look sin in the slithery eyes and say, "get behind me," and walk away from a potential trap. You now have the capability to live, not a perfect life, but a life unshackled by the chains of sin. Jesus sees daily the same problem Lincoln experience–freed slaves returning to their deceitful masters. Choosing to stay under the rule of sin is a choice that could kill. Read through your "Bill of Freedom" in Romans chapter six until God enlightens you to His truth. Refuse to be contained by a way of life that will take you nowhere but hell. Why? Because, where there is freedom and hope you'll find happiness and heaven. Go on . . . cut those chains of bondage and walk in the love of the Savior to freedom.

✳ ✳ ✳

Further Study: What are you a slave to today? Do you believe you once were captured by sin but now you're free in Christ? Why or why not? How do you cut those chains? Why do some stay slaves even though freedom has been issued?

WISHES DO COME TRUE

*And God made man in His own image, in the image of God He
created him, male and female He created them.*
Genesis 1:27

☆ ☆ ☆

The scene opens in a mythical, magical city called Agrabah; the story opens with a peasant boy named Aladdin and his side-kick monkey Abu. Aladdin falls head over heels in love with princess Jasmine, but they are limited by law that she can only marry a royal suitor. Aladdin's life takes a turn when he finds a magic lamp that contains a fun-loving, wish-giving genie who turns this peasant into a prince. Something begins to smell up the room when an evil sorcerer named Jafar and his mouth-all-mighty parrot, Lago, want this lamp for their own devices. If Aladdin is to have victory in this battle and win the lovely lady's heart, he must learn to be himself . . . one wish the Genie cannot grant.

People every day of their lives get up, look in a mirror and see the reflection of someone they don't feel will be accepted in society. They desire to soar on a magic carpet ride of fantasy into being someone they are not. How frustrating it is to have to decide daily who and what a person wants to be in view of an audience of critics. You might recall that the lovely princess ends up loving Aladdin for being himself, not the painted up phony prince. You, too, can be accepted by just being you. As they say, "U.B.U." and that is enough for anyone to step back and admire like a Picasso painting. Don't forget that your mold was broken upon your delivery and that you will be the best "you" that will ever be. Get this, you won't have to act a different way because now you're acting naturally . . . the way God intended. Yes, the reality is that some will find fault in you no matter what, but you can enjoy the phenomenal fun of being whom God intended you to be since the beginning of time . . . anytime you wish! (Get it?)

☆ ☆ ☆

Further Study: Do you try to act like someone you're not? Whom, if you could, would you like to be like? Why? How valuable are you to God? Why? What comfort is there knowing you are unique in this world?

TIGHT LIPPED

*What I tell you in the darkness, speak in the light; and what you
hear whispered in your ear, proclaim upon housetops.*
Matthew 10:27

✯ ✯ ✯

I'll never forget that first step. It was a dooser of a drop-off, too, but well worth the effort. It was my junior year of college and my year to have a shot at being one of five starters for the upcoming season. Our team had just come off a championship season, making it to the Top 10 in the nation. I had worked at a Christian sports camp called Kanakuk in the Ozark mountains in southwest Missouri that summer. It had been a great summer of off-season training along with the benefits of being around other Division I athletes who had a tough time, too, of making this Christian stuff work in the "big time" on and off the court. I had been really challenged to take a stand for Christ (which I knew meant a fall), but it would mean standing alone cuz' I was the only Christian on the team of 15, coaches included. I'll never forget the day we all reported to training on August 20, 1980, when my roomate asked me how my summer was and where I'd been. I knew this was my first test, but I was scared spit-less to share about Jesus to a guy I had been pretty wild with for two years. I knew he'd think I "got religious or something" if I shared, but I had to, so I did it. I was right . . . he asked me what I'd been smokin' and why I'd even waste a summer at a camp full of do-gooder Bible beaters!

That was the beginning, but I can tell you that seeing me take a stand and change my past lifestyle so radically was testimony enough for three players and my head coach to become Christians. I know I was only a part of the process, not the reason, but what an awesome reward from God for a job well done in faith. Just like this verse says, whatever lessons you learn, convictions you acquire, habits you break or faith you attain, shout it loud from a point where all can hear. Trust me again, the view from the top with God is majestic.

✯ ✯ ✯

Further Study: Does witnessing to others about what Jesus Christ has done for you, scare you? Why do you think that is? What can you do today to begin to be comfortable about sharing your faith? Have you earned the right to be heard by being a good friend? Have you asked the Lord for help in being a faithful witness for Him?

No Butts About It

I buffet my body and make it my slave, lest possibly, after I have
preached to others, I myself should be disqualified.
1 Corinthians 9:27

☆ ☆ ☆

I can't quite figure it out. Call me Boy Clueless, but is our society trying to snub out smoking or cater to the coughing? Everywhere you look (and smell), cigarette smoking still catches the eye of fashion and the look of the luxurious. Now, maybe to some this devotion is gonna' be as helpful as tennis shoes on ice, but maybe it could help just one of those who are hooked on this habit and need the incentive to quit. Well, honey, are you talkin' to the right guy! Let me impart to you just a few raving reasons why it's never too late to stop smoking.

After one day of not smoking:
Blood pressure levels will near normal
Blood oxygen will near normal
Carbon monoxide in blood will decrease drastically
Heart attack risk will decrease
After 48 hours:
Nerve endings begin to regrow
Sense of smell and taste improve
After two weeks to three months:
Circulation improves
Exercise becomes easier
Lung function increases 30-percent
After one year:
Risk of heart attack falls by 50-percent
After five years:
Stroke risk reduced
Reduced risk of several types of cancer
After 10 years:
Pre-cancerous cells will have been replaced by the body
After 15 years:
Risk of coronary disease same as non-smoker

God didn't intend for us to smoke these cancer sticks. If you don't smoke, don't start. If you do, stop! This world has enough natural hazards to survive, let alone creating our own.

☆ ☆ ☆

Further Study: Why do you think our bodies are a temple of God? Do you do anything that harms your body?

HEAVEN

WELCOME HOME

Our citizenship is in heaven.
Philippians 3:20

☆ ☆ ☆

*I*n childhood's day, our thoughts of heaven,
Are pearly gates and streets of gold,
And all so very far away;
A place where portals may unfold,
Some far off distant day.
But in the gathering of the years,
When life is in the fading leaf,
With eyes perchance bedimmed with tears,
And hearts oft' overwhelmed with grief,
We look beyond the pearly gates,
Beyond the clouds of grief's dark night,
And see a place where loved ones walk,
Where all is gladness and light.
And overall we see the face
Of Him who will bring us to our own,
Not too far off distant place,
For heaven is, after all, just HOME!
Sue Milan

Just like the song says, "heaven is a wonderful place, filled with glory and grace." Are you convinced there really is a distant destination of deity? How often does your mind drift away to dream of that refuge from pain? Can you imagine what this heaven is gonna' be like? Our residence is earth, but we all carry a foreign travel visa that states as a Christian, our citizenship is in heaven. Yes, the task on earth is difficult, so don't relax; opportunities are brief, so don't delay; the path is narrow, so don't wander and the prize is glorious, so don't faint. Trust me, the ride is gonna' be far more impressive than anything Disney World has to offer. The place is gonna' be far more beautiful than St. Paul's Cathedral. The future is gonna' last far longer than life here on earth . . . they call it eternity!

☆ ☆ ☆

Further Study: What do you think heaven will look like? Be like? Do you think of eternity on a timeline or never ending? Do you think of your citizenship as being on earth or in heaven?

GOD'S WILL

WHAT'S UP WITH THIS?

*For it is better, if God will it so, that you suffer for doing what
is right rather than for doing what is wrong.*
1 Peter 3:17

☆ ☆ ☆

You talk about a situation or circumstance that is best described as "stinky." Have you (and I'm sure you have) ever had the finger pointed at you for doing something you didn't do? It was probably one of those backward judicial systems that says you're guilty until proven innocent. Granted, in my own personal life, I would be considered your basic, strong-willed, free spirited, trouble maker by society (and my parents), so this situation didn't happen to me much. If you came into a crowed room of people looking for the guilty party it wouldn't have been a bad pick if you singled me out. There are those angels of our society (like you, I'm sure) that seem to always be innocent because it's someone else's fault.

You know, ol' Peter had an interesting perspective on this finger pointing stuff and the scapegoats of society that would be totally opposite of what one might expect. He states that if God puts (or allows) you in a situation where you are pronounced guilty of a crime (or act) that you never committed, it's good (a blessing). Get that? Good . . . I mean read it with your own eyeballs and see for yourself. It is looked at as a blessing to suffer the consequences that someone else should be taking. God views it as better for this sort of thing to happen to you than the other. Now, if I read this right, it's gonna' take a strong faith (and cool temper) to survive this crash with cruelty. So the next time you're strolling down life's merry highway and get broadsided, jump out and praise God for another opportunity to show you are different as a believer. What an incredible witness this will be and only a real Christian can pull it off.

☆ ☆ ☆

Further Study: When was the last time you were accused of doing wrong when in fact you hadn't? How did you react? Was it God's way or the natural way? Why would it be a blessing by God to be blamed when you're not guilty?

EXCEL STILL MORE

I have fought the good fight, I have finished the course, I have kept the faith.
2 Timothy 4:7

꙼ ꙼ ꙼

During the Summer Olympics, watching Ben Johnson and Carl Lewis, two world class sprinters going head to head in the 100-meter sprint, I remember the TV commentator just ranting and raving about the start of this run and its importance. Johnson was known for his explosive start to the point that both feet were literally off the ground at once when he blasted off the blocks toward the finish line. Lewis, on the other hand, was a slow starter (almost last out), yet his strength of speed was in the last 30 meters of the race. What a run of two fleet of feet it was!

In life, so many people make such a big deal about the beginning and not the ending. Focus seems to have finished on the start and not the tape at the end of the race. Isn't it ironic that the winner is not determined by the first out of the starting blocks but down the track at the timer table? Consistency and perseverance seem to have lost their way in our list of needed character qualities in today's trends. Isn't it more important anymore to celebrate a 50 year wedding anniversary, or 20 years on a job, or receiving a diploma? Yes, the starting blocks and the beginning are important, but not as important as the finishing. God calls us to a trip that is going to take time and endurance to complete. This scripture stresses the importance of fighting the fight, finishing the race, and keeping the faith throughout. You are a runner; you are a participant; you are a starter, and you are able to finish with Christ as your strength (in your heart and legs). Go ahead, take off the warm-up, stretch out, crawl into the blocks, and focus on the finish.

★ ★ ★

Further Study: What enables us to finish the race strong? How can you train to endure?

WORLDLINESS

ODE TO SELF

Instructing us to deny ungodliness and worldly desires and to live sensibly, right-eously and godly in the present age.
Titus 2:12

☆ ☆ ☆

When I was growing up, we played a lot of board games, and my family continues that tradition today. One of the legends in that industry was produced by Parker Brothers in "Monopoly." Each participant starts the game with the same amount of play cash. By a combination of calculation, chance and costly misfortune, depending on the luck of the roll and capability to purchase properties, the game moves to a conclusion with a dethronable winner. This game really is a realistic metaphor (picture) of our culture today. Here in this game are all the elements of modern life: ruthlessness and unpredictability with only one survivor. Players often try to get away with what they can; there is no place for virtues, mercy or compassion. In fact, with this game, as in life, there is no place for anyone but oneself. Even the evolution of magazine popularity in our society has moved from *Time* to *Life* to *People* to *US* to *Self.* In our society, we as individuals sell our personalities as commodities in the workplace because there is a bull market for image and personality. Therefore, we have self-promoting tactics we teach to supposedly "make it." Heroes used to be people others emulated (copied), yet now heroes have been replaced by celebrities. A hero created himself; a celebrity is created by the media. The hero was a big man; the celebrity is a big name. The moral culture elevated a hero; the commercial culture produced the celebrity. Boiling it down . . . the celebrity replaced the hero, image replaced character and commercialism replaced morality. Wow!

Our God is bigger than any board game mock-up or an eroding culture. We can still be salt and light (Matthew 5:13-16) in a tasteless, dark society. Virtues and character can be more valued than signing your own autograph and stomping out the little guys. There still are a few endangered heroes and mentors around, but not many. How are you setting yourself up in this world governed by Monopoly laws to be different for the cause of Christ? Are you buying into the world's ways or creating for yourself through scripture a new set of standards that include character and integrity? Why? Because this game of life is one game you can't afford to lose.

☆ ☆ ☆

Further Study: How does your moral character compare today? Are you doing anything to offset worldliness? What? By whose set of rules are you playing?

LOVING OTHERS

OPEN YOUR MOUTH

Better is an open rebuke than love that is concealed.
Proverbs 27:5

※ ※ ※

Let me start this off by presenting you with a situation and see how you would respond. Let's say you were a real outdoor personality (tree bark eater), and you had lots of years experience hiking and camping in the southwest range of the Colorado Rockies (not the baseball team either). On this day you have invited a close friend to go and enjoy the clean air, vast beauty and sore muscles of a weekend backpacking experience. While walking on a two-foot wide path on the northern face of a mountain some 11,000 feet up, you encounter a shale slide area. Now, the pathway sits about three feet from (this sounds like a riddle) the edge of a 1,000-foot cliff on which many have slipped and plunged to death in prior expeditions. You saw your friend walking haphazardly (not paying much attention), about to come upon this risky, dangerous portion of the pathway. Would you warn your friend of the upcoming danger, or just hope he/she would make it on their own? I know this is a stupid question, but think about your answer.

Now, to tie this goofy illustration into a thought provoking point. You rub shoulders every day with friends, some acquaintances and others who are about to take a dangerous plunge in their lives. This plunge could be in a relationship, bad judgment or whatever. You, yes you, have the chance to warn (rebuke) this friend with and out of love before he/she slips off his mortal mountain to a decision of death. Self-destruction is as prevalent in our world as flies in a cow barn. Don't be afraid to step out of your comfort zone and confront someone who needs some tender love on their decision making process. Care enough to risk the relationship for the rewards of agape love. Don't conceal your love; let it be active and useful in your relationships. Who knows, they may thank you later for saving their lives.

★ ★ ★

Further Study: How much do you care for your friend(s)? Do you warn them of upcoming dangers? Why or why not?

GOD'S WILL

A PROCESS

*This is the will of God that by doing right you may silence
the ignorance of foolish men.*
1 Peter 2:15

★ ★ ★

I had a friend once who said, "There is nothing more dangerous than becoming comfortable out of God's will." Wow! Now, that's a truth you can hang your hat on. This devotion is a custom-designed formula to help determine God's will for you in the big decisions for your life. This formula is practical and simple. Before beginning you must let go of (ditch it!) your own will and sincerely desire God's will for your life. Otherwise, this process is about as helpful as a screen door on a submarine. Each step will build on itself, and you may find the answer is obvious before you get to the end. If it doesn't make itself clear, keep moving through the steps until it does.

Step 1. Write down the decision you're trying to make. Nothing clarifies thinking more quickly than paper and pencil because half the decision is knowing the problem. What are the choices?

Step 2. Write out a statement of purpose that explains why you are considering this decision. Why do you need to decide? What is the content (meat) of this decision? Are you unhappy? Is this a need or a want?

Step 3. Submit your statement of purpose to a series of questions. What are you trying to accomplish and why? What are your expectations? What would Jesus do? Is it a sense of calling or duty?

Step 4. If your answer isn't obvious, list all your options on a separate sheet—left side, pros (good), right side, cons (bad).

Step 5. If the answer still isn't clear, then . . . wait! Never push God. He is in a different time frame. He may use the time to work something into or out of your character. Note: God is not the author of confusion, Satan is! Peace is the umpire in this game.

Hey, this is one of many ways to search out God's clear pathway in the midst of a fog. Ask Him to open your spiritual eyes and show you the way . . . trust me, it's the only way!

★ ★ ★

Further Study: Do you have a major decision on the horizon? What are you doing about it now? Is it important to you to be in God's will?

POWER SOURCE

Hear my prayer, O Lord, listen to my cry for help; be not deaf to my weeping, for I dwell with you as an alien, a stranger, as all my fathers were.
Psalms 39:12

☆ ☆ ☆

They all huddled in their yellow slickers while a deafening roar shook the ground like a herd of wild mustangs on a stampede. Six million gallons of water a minute burst over the falls in haphazard style. Onlookers were stricken with awe in the presence of such raw liquid power. For decades Niagara's "Maid of the Mist" has shuttled tourists safely to the brink of disaster for the sheer terror of being close to the source of power. No one who has ventured to this site will ever forget the experience.

Prayer should be like that. Drawing near to the source of life is indescribable. It's kinda' feeling safe and awestruck at the same time. Prayer, to this day, remains a ritual many speak about but few encounter personally. *U.S. News and World Report* polled Americans about their spiritual lives, asking: "What best describes your beliefs about God?" 66% said God is a Father that can be reached by prayer, 11% said God is an idea, not a being, and 8% said God is an impersonal creator. Clearly, according to the results of this poll, Americans believe in prayer, yet the average believer spends less than two minutes a day doing it.

What prayer is not:
An occasional tourist excursion to the source of power.
A New Age feeling of oneness with Mother Earth.
A grocery list of "gimmies."
An alternative action.

What prayer is:
Abiding (resting) in God's presence.
Intimacy with the Father.
A personal relationship.
A warm embrace with God.
Attainable by all who believe.
Quote: "Anything that causes you to pray is a good thing."

☆ ☆ ☆

Further Study: What is the average amount of time per week you spend praying? What do you pray for? Why do you pray? What could help you to become a prayer warrior?

THE GOLDEN YEARS

Grandchildren are the crown of old men, and the glory of sons is their fathers.
Proverbs 17:6

☆ ☆ ☆

It's a shame what our society is doing to and with our elderly. The system throws off to the side, like an old pair of shoes, some of the wisest people on the planet. Yes, they may drive a bit slower than most or need additional volume when being addressed, but they are precious to our livelihood. We all, in due time and if we're lucky, will grow to be a ripe old age and be a grandparent someday. Sit down, if your grandparents are still alive, and take a few moments to just tap into their past experiences and keen knowledge of this life we all seek to live abundantly. Do you realize how valuable you are or were to your grandparents? Read that scripture again, and this time, mix in a little perspective and heartfelt compassion. Do you see how it's worded? Do you catch the true intent of the real message? You are (or were) the crown of Grandma and Pa. God uses crowns to reward His children for a job well done. Grandparents view their children's children as a reward from the Lord which they desire to show off.

Let me ask you a straight-forward question; do (or did) you respect, love and honor your grandparents? Do you value time with them like they value and cherish the time with you? I realize that time and geography hinder us at times on the visits, but hey, we do have the technology of the telephone and postcards. Just a simple note (not a novel) will do as an expression of your love and commitment. When people receive a note, they see one thing, that you, wherever you are, took the time out of your rat race schedule to think of them and write something on a card, lick and stick a stamp and mail it. Don't ever forget . . . life is just full of a lot of little things stacked up. Make today a day when you can honor your grandparents and show them that they, too, are a crown of honor.

☆ ☆ ☆

Further Study: When was the last time you told your grandparents you love them? Why or why not? How can you better cultivate that relationship today? Will you? (You better!)

DEEDS

ACTIONS SPEAK

*Deeds that are good are quite evident, and those which
are otherwise cannot be concealed.*
1 Timothy 5.25

* * *

Major Osipovich, an air force pilot for the former USSR, planned to give a talk on peace at his children's school. He would need time off, so he volunteered for make-up night duty. That is how he found himself patrolling the skies over eastern regions of Russia on September 1, 1983—the very night a Korean airlines flight accidentally strayed off course into Soviet air space. Osipovich was caught in a series of blunders and miscommunication that night. When all was said and done, he followed his orders from control central in Moscow and shot down an unidentified aircraft. The actions of an air force pilot preparing to talk to a bunch of kids about peace, not only caused 240 innocent passengers to die, but sparked an international incident that pushed world powers to a military stand-off.

Even though this mishap was unintentional, it exemplifies that even though talk is important, actions carry far more weight. We can learn a valuable lesson. Our deeds are powerful. Innocent spectators watch for the truth of scripture in us. We can totally blow our witness and damage our testimony with one single deed. Now, I'm not saying we must be perfect little angels with spotless lives. I am saying we should walk carefully and realize how our actions speak louder than words. Learn to walk your talk. Every time we exemplify sin in our flesh, we not only set ourselves back, but a whole lot of other believers trying to make a significant impact for Christ. What we do, much more than what we say, makes a real impact.

* * *

Further Study: How do people view your deeds and actions as a Christian? What is more important to Christ, what we say or who we are? How can you avoid fatal deeds?

RACISM

COLORING FRIENDSHIPS

If someone says, "I love God," and hates his brother, he is a liar; for the one who does not love his brother whom he has seen, cannot love God whom he has not seen.
1 John 4:20

☆ ☆ ☆

I realize that this is the second devotional I've included on this topic. I don't mean to beat a dead horse (figure of speech), but this is a sensitive, highly volatile subject. You can interchange words easily—prejudice, discrimination, hostility, bias, partiality, racism, bigotry or whatever. Webster's (you know, that thick book you'd just as soon not use) defines racism as the belief that race is the primary determinant of human traits and capacities and that racial differences produce an inherent superiority of a particular race. We operate under the false pretense that our race, whether it be African American, Anglo-Saxon, Asian, Hispanic, or another tribe, people, or nation, is better or more elite than another. Now, I realize writing a devotional on this touchy subject is not gonna' solve the racial tension we have in this world, but conviction through impacted scripture can change hearts. A good friend of mine saw a picture of two young boys returning from a fishing trip, walking down a dusty country road, arms around each other . . . one black, one white. The caption under the picture was, "The more color, the more better."

This world has always had folks who are prejudiced, but you and I don't have to join in on stupidity and ignorant thinking. Your brother is anyone you come in contact with (it doesn't mean literal kin), and you are to love them for being created by God, loved by God, directed by God, as a child of God. There is no racial superiority on this earth because we all are sinners (losers) who need a Savior. Cultivate new friendships outside your race; find value in not going with the flow. Prove the love of Christ in your heart, and love your brother no matter what color his skin is.

☆ ☆ ☆

Further Study: How do you feel about other races? Do you have friends of other races? Do you laugh at racial jokes or use racial slamming, stereotypical words? Do you love your brother no matter what his color?

BIG HE, LITTLE ME

*This is the word of the Lord "not by might nor by power but
by My spirit" says the Lord.*
Zechariah 4.6

✫ ✫ ✫

You've probably seen the T-shirts that say "big team little me" or "I is in the middle of sin." They are usually advertised by different teams to express their motto for the upcoming season. We, the people of America, are rich in talent and twist. Look around you, and you'll see a wealth of resources, technology, military capabilities, leadership qualities, agricultural production, economic stamina and creativity. The people of this great nation do a heck of a lot just on sheer raw talent and gifts. I dare say that the great things accomplished have been empowered by God but credit goes to self. If you listen real closely to conversation going on around you, you'll hear the word "I" used more often than "us" or "we." We produce faster than Detroit does cars, an environment that structurally seems to cultivate an independent mentality and way of thinking.

You will never understand the true meaning of teamwork until you join forces with the Creator of Accomplishments. Come on, I mean, how many individuals do you know who went into their office, workshop or meeting rooms and came out with an entire universe stacked with creatures. God knows you have talents and what they are because He gave them to you. You did nothing to earn them, and He sure didn't owe you them. True joy in an accomplishment is giving the credit to what and to whom the credit is due. If you think you pulled your own self up by the boot straps, I got news for ya'. God put those boots on you to begin with. He is the Master Mechanic that fine tunes us daily to be the fuel efficient, motorized mortal we were meant to be. Before you start out after a goal like a bluetick hound chasing a coon, stop and ask God to guide and direct your every move and step along the way, so that you'll begin to be a winner by His Spirit, not your flesh.

✫ ✫ ✫

Further Study: Ask a friend how often you use the word I. How much do you do without God? How can you start doing things with God?

POWER OVER THE PAST

Purify yourselves for tomorrow the Lord will do wonders among you.
Joshua 3:5

☆ ☆ ☆

The word purity seems to be used in the modern day language about as much as dinosaurs are used in a circus (let me give you a hint . . . never)! The thickest book in your library defines the word to mean "quality or state of being pure in thought and act." A pastor by the name of H.D. McCartney said it best, "The only power we have over our past is purity in the present."

Everywhere you look you see a corrupt world telling you purity is a thing of the past and your actions today will not affect you in the future. When you read the headlines, watch the tube, drive by the billboards, feast on the lyrics and glance at the magazine covers, you will see a one-sided report. Isn't it funny that God invented sex to "be fruitful and multiply" before He allowed sin to exist? Isn't it ironic how we have taken a thing (sex) of beauty, designed to stay within the context of marriage and allowed this deceiving world to turn the tables of creation? Your body is a beautiful temple designed to be a dwelling place of your Savior. Your desires, spun for a specific time, place and function, are not evil, if handled by the hands of the Master Potter.

As you sit here and chew on this nugget of scripture, allow commitment to enter through the doors of your heart. Make a deal with God on your knees that you will guard your heart, mind and body and wait 'til that special day when you will be the one at the altar looking into the loving eyes of the spouse you will share your life with 'til death do you part. It doesn't matter what you've done in the past; purity beginning today will do wonders for you.

☆ ☆ ☆

Further Study: What kind of commitment can you make today concerning your purity? Will you?

GROANING FOR GOD

Consecrate a fast, proclaim a solemn assembly; gather the elders and all the inhabitants of the land to the house of the Lord your God and cry out to the Lord.
Joel 1:14

☆ ☆ ☆

Have you ever dared to pray the prayer, "God, let me feel as you feel?" I was recently at a prayer and fasting conference in Los Angeles and, boy, was that an eye-opening experience. Most conferences I've been to over my lifetime have had the motto "eat out and sleep in." Needless to say, any conference that Dr. Bill Bright and Campus Crusade for Christ put on is going to be all business, with purpose. This particular conference was held in a huge room (airplane hanger) in the L.A. convention center, close to where the riots took place. When you walked in the room, the seating arrangement was some 10,000 chairs, separated in groups of 10 to a circle. The walls were lined with purified water dispensers with a huge stage bookend with two 40-foot viewing screens. Now . . . get this, for three solid days from 8:00 a.m. until 10:00 p.m. we circled up the troops and prayed on our knees. Yep, 14 hours straight, cuz you shore didn't need a break for meals; this was a four-day fast. We heard speakers communicate needs of specific areas of this world for about 10 minutes, then we'd pray corporately and individually for that need for the next 30 minutes.

I recall Kay Arthur of Precept Ministries coming on stage in black sackcloth, reading a scripture and asking us the question, "What in our sinful society makes you cry out in sorrow?" Then she began discussing abortion, immorality, drug abuse, divorce, abuse of people, persecuted Christians overseas, gang violence in our inner cities, etc. The Spirit of God really took my heart and began to squeeze it hard and guess what . . . the juice began to come out of my eyes as I cried and felt as God feels about disobedience and unholiness in our world. I believe that if we "feel" the hurt and sorrow that our Creator feels when we (you) are disobedient, sinful, unrighteous and ungodly, it will cause us to stop, think and, hopefully, repent and turn from our wicked ways. Why? Because God's way is the best way.

☆ ☆ ☆

Further Study: Read 2 Chronicles 7:14. Does your sin hurt you as much as it does God? How do you get to the spiritual point of feeling the hurt and sorrow in our land to begin to do something about it?

Tᴀɢᴇᴅʏ

*So Delilah said to Samson, "Tell me the secret of your great
strength and how you can be subdued,"*
Judges 16:6

✶ ✶ ✶

A Greek philosopher named Aristotle would have loved the story of
Samson and Delilah. The reason is because it would fit his definition of
tragedy; to see a strong human be destroyed by a single character flaw. He
also claimed that to see this happen should deeply affect those watching. He
said that tragedy would lead to a "catharsis" (cleansing) in those who truly
understood what went on. In this gold nugget of scripture one can see that
Samson takes a fall. Delilah's Philistine friends have a plot and offer her big
bucks to try and chain down the guy who was a symbol of strength to the
Israelites. If she could get him to tell the source of his strength, she would be
well rewarded. Samson may have had bulging muscles but not the brains of
his father. Four times Delilah tried (nagged) to subdue Samson before she
finally succeeded (you'd think he'd have clued in). Man, oh man, if I was
Samson, I'd have chucked this chick out on her head, but he didn't. Why?
Pride!

Aristotle states that one flaw which gets more folks in trouble is pride.
Samson's tragic fall led to the end of his freedom. He became a prisoner and
was used as entertainment for the crowds like the headliner in a freak show.

After reading (seeing) a story such as this, we should all learn from someone else's mistake and cleanse ourselves of any pride we might have. We
should see ourselves as Samson, committing a grave mistake and falling. This
is the scripture we should recall when we catch ourselves walking around all
"puffed up" with pride over some accomplishment, taking credit for it instead
of giving the glory to God. Pride is definitely a character flaw which seems to
entangle each one of us daily. Say no to the Delilahs of your life who try to
get you to sign your autograph or read your own press clippings. Remember,
pride goes before a fall.

✶ ✶ ✶

Further Study: What are you most proud about? Who gets the credit when
you are successful? How can we be less prideful and more humble?

FRIENDSHIP

Don't Rock With Bad Company

Do not be unequally yoked to non-believers; for what
partnership have righteousness and lawlessness or
what fellowship have light and darkness?
2 Corinthians 6:14

✦ ✦ ✦

You know something? Being a Christian and a friend can at times drive you crazy. We, as followers of Jesus, are called to live in this stinky world but not be of it. We are called to share our biggest joy with non-followers yet not get sucked into the cave of compromise. A friend of mine told me that who and what I hang out with is probably what I will become. Let me put that in English for you. If you hang around the pigs long enough, you'll probably get pretty fond of the mud. The Bible tells us (warns us really) to beware of what type of people we 'yoke' ourselves to. A yoke can best be described as a large wooden harness which goes over the necks of a team of oxen to provide steering and stability to the plow. When the yoke is not fitted properly or if two oxen of different sizes or types are put together, they go at a different speed and plow a crooked row. The result is frustration on the farmer's part and extended work hours to redo mistakes. But put a team of oxen of identical size and type together and the outcome is a nicely plowed field in which to plant a crop.

You see, the apostle Paul knew that if we, as Christians, were to yoke ourselves to a non-Christian as a companion, our lives would be pretty tough to steer. The result is a difference in beliefs, philosophies, actions, morals, ethics and destinations for eternity. No, I'm not saying not to associate yourself with non-Christians each day, just don't yoke yourself to them. Be a light and witness to them but not a foxhole mate. Trust me, your life won't be such an up and down roller-coaster ride if you follow Paul's advice . . . if anyone knew, he surely did.

✦ ✦ ✦

Further Study: Do you yoke yourself to non-Christians? Why? Why should we not? What benefits are there in yoking to a fellow follower?

ARMCHAIR QUARTERBACK

As you judge others, so you will yourselves be judged.
Matthew 7:1

☆ ☆ ☆

They always know the way to go . . . and never go themselves.
It is easy to make decisions . . . when the responsibility is not yours!
It's easy to know what to do . . . when you don't have to do it!
They always know what to do . . . and never have to do it.

Some of the most peculiar creatures that roam our streets are those who are free from responsibility, yet tell those responsible what to do. The slang for these aggravating, vocal critics who always seem to have the answer is "armchair quarterbacks." There is a huge chasm between the spectator in the bleachers and the participant on the field. Now, don't limit your thinking to the sphere of sports . . . let's use everyday life. There are experts who pontificate on every conceivable issue in life. These "armchair quarterbacks" never seem to make any mistakes. This doesn't mean that advice and opinions are wrong . . . that's what democracy is made of. The problem lies in the spirit (motivation) of the critic.

This spirit should always be sensitive to the burden of decision(s) borne by the one being criticized. Always place yourself in the other's shoes before you "give them a piece of your mind." More often than not, the critic doesn't know all there is to know about a certain situation or the decision-making process. Armchair play-calling doesn't hold water when the consequences don't ultimately rely on self. So, if you're one of those folks who always tend to call the plays (answers) from the sidelines, then take a chill pill. Extend grace and understanding to those who are on the frontlines of the decision-making process.

☆ ☆ ☆

Further Study: Do you see yourself as a critic or an encourager? Why? Do you like to point the finger at poor play-calling? Why?

TRIALS

WARTS

To keep me from exalting myself, there was given me a thorn in the flesh, a messenger of Satan to buffet me–to keep me from exalting myself!
2 Corinthians 12:7

☆ ☆ ☆

Today we are going to talk about "warts." A wart is something in your life that you wish you didn't have–hair, weight, voice, height, toes, birth defect, mole, physical handicap. If you have ever said, "If I could only get this or get rid of that, it would make my life a lot more enjoyable," then that's a wart. A wart could be petty or small, then again, it could be serious and overwhelming. Take a moment (put this devotion on pause) and think about your own warts. A lot of times we try to plead our case with God and explain to Him that if only this wart in our life was gone then everything would be real peachy. Warts make us feel inadequate in life, so we do our best to have them removed or "fixed." Catch this . . . God's grace is what is adequate, not our abilities. scripture tells us that when we are weak (wart infested), then we are strong in the Lord. In other words, God shines brightest when we (self) are out of the picture. The apostle Paul had a major wart given to him. He didn't do anything to get it (warts are funny that way). The wart definitely kept him from exalting himself; he pleaded with God three times to take it from him. Some folks out there are saying that if you really love God, He will take away all the pain (warts) you have in your life, then everything will be okay. Wrong, amigo. I don't know what Bible they're reading, but it's not like mine. Life is going to be tough, and you will have warts. Why? To get rid of self. Warts don't make you ugly like a wicked old witch on Halloween . . . they make you a dependent child of God.

☆ ☆ ☆

Further Study: What warts do you have that hinder you? Would these warts cause you to depend on self or God? What are your warts?

STAYING POWER

Those who regard vain idols forsake their faithfulness.
Jonah 2:8

☆ ☆ ☆

Correct me if I'm wrong, but things just ain't the same as they used to be. Now, I'm not saying that we've reversed in the productivity department, but I am saying we do live in the "drive thru" mentality. If it's not done quickly (less than five minutes), then we don't have time to wait on it. Go to your grandparents' home sometime and talk to them about the way things used to be made . . . to last. Durability, withstanding and just down right tough were key marketing buzz words in the sales departments. You didn't have to, nor need to, buy a car every three years because at that point you were just getting it broken in real good like a worn pair of jeans. To stick with something like the same job for 30 years and get a gold watch upon retirement is unheard of today. To view a marriage not lasting for a lifetime was frowned upon by the public eye. Not to be loyal to your friend(s) to the core of your heart and not gossip about them behind their backs was as normal as breathing. What has happened to staying power?

Look at the life of our friend in the Bible, Job. Boy, would his life make a great silver screen movie in our time. Riches to rags, plush to poverty, fearless to frailty, happiness to homelessness. Say what you want, but you can't deny the one thing Job did and did well . . . he stayed. He stuck with it through the thick and thin of it. Our world is full of single parent families, prisons full of quitters and job switching yearly. Understand, as Job did, that staying power means sacrifice and giving up self for others. Jesus exemplified this on the Cross at Calvary to us all. The mentors who roam are loyal, humble, visionary and not divorced. You, yes, you, have plenty of opportunity to turn back the tables of time to the old ways of thinking and suck it up and stick it out. So do it!

☆ ☆ ☆

Further Study: Do you have a habit of quitting when times get tough? Do you think a pattern of quitting starts small and grows with age? How can you train yourself in staying power?

TONGUE

MOUTH TRAP

Keep your tongue from evil and your lips from speaking deceit.
Psalms 34:13

☆ ☆ ☆

"Sticks and stones may break my bones, but words will never hurt me." NOT! Whoever wrote that perverted poem must not be living in the same world I am. They (words) are one of the few things that can both build up and tear down. They consist of nouns, verbs, adverbs, prepositions, conjunctions, pronouns, adjectives, compounds, prefixes and suffixes. You can express, utter, promise, articulate, corrupt, inform, negotiate and interject with them. The mouth is the starting line and the ear is the finishing line of our words. The tongue is a muscle, the strongest muscle in our body (due to intense workout) and our ears are wimpy (from lack of exercise). Why is it so easy to talk and so hard to listen?

Our government is constantly trying to fight the uphill battle of domestic violence in our society, yet one weapon we seem to overlook is the tongue . . . it's lethal. Very few times have I seen someone get praised or asked for an autograph for being a good listener. I love the saying "It's better to remain silent and be thought of as a fool, than to open your mouth and remove all doubt." Now, don't hear me wrong, there is a time to speak, but not all the time. Communication is a two way street . . . talking and listening. Go through a day listening more than talking and see what you learn. Don't trap yourself with your mouth (open mouth, insert foot). Believe you me, you'll stay out of a lot of trouble by keeping that dude shut more than open, and less people get hurt that way, too.

☆ ☆ ☆

Further Study: Are you a good listener? When you're nervous, what do you do–talk or listen? Why do we learn more when we listen? What can you do today to make yourself a better listener?

BETRAYED

The Son of Man is to go, just as it is written of Him; but woe to that man by whom the Son of Man is betrayed! It would have been good for that man if he had not been born.

Matthew 26:24

☆ ☆ ☆

Talk about a subject that can bring your blood to a rapid boil. There is not one poor soul who reads this that has not been betrayed in some form or fashion (guess what . . . more to come). Jesus had a front row seat when it came to betrayal. Judas, the betrayer, was not only trusted and respected in his community of converts, but was a doggone disciple. Better yet, Judas sold out for a measly 52 bucks (thirty pieces of silver), betraying his so-called mentor, Jesus. How do you handle it when you are betrayed by a good friend? What is your first reaction? Is it Christ-like?

It is still true today that people sell their souls for the love of money. Money can make a woman a whore and a man a pimp. It can turn a shepherd into a skunk, make business go belly-up (broke) and turn an athlete into a liability. Now that we have identified the problem, what is the solution when you've been dealt a bad hand from a friend? What I'm about to say goes totally against the norm, and only you and God could pull it off. Ready? (Is the anticipation killing you?) Do two things when you have been betrayed. These are not secrets; Jesus did them with Judas. First, pray for their (the persons who betrayed you) conviction of the wrong doing. (Note: don't pray for their punishment . . . that's the world's way.) Second, pray for their forgiveness through you . . . the victim. (Note: extend grace to them, not judgment.)

Okay, has it sunk in enough for the steam to rise from the top of your head? These two simple steps will clear you of any bitterness and anger that ultimately will eat at you like cancer. Plus, it will be an example of what real Christ-like living is all about.

☆ ☆ ☆

Further Study: Have you ever been betrayed by a friend? How did you react? Was it like Jesus did, offering Judas the first morsel of food as the honored guest?

THE RACE

I have fought the good fight, finished the race, and I have kept the faith.
2 Timothy 4:7

⋀ ⋀ ⋀

It took place at the NCAA Cross-country Championship held in Riverside, California, when 123 out of the 128 runners took the same wrong turn. One competitor, Mike Delcavo, stayed on course and tried waving for fellow runners to follow him. He was only able to convince four runners to stay on the right course with him–everyone else followed the crowd. Asked what his competitors thought of his mid-race decision to use his own judgment instead of following the crowd, Delcavo responded, "They thought it was funny that I went the right way."

In the same way, our goal as Christians is to run correctly and finish the race that has been marked out for us. We can celebrate with those few runners in this Christian race who have enough courage to ignore the laughter and tongue-lashings of the watching world, stay on track and finish. This race we (you) are called to run is not a 100-yard dash . . . it's the marathon of life. You see, we don't need much training to finish a sprint, but to finish a race where we can't see the finish line from the start (like a marathon) we need a Savior. I have personally run only a half marathon (13 miles) and thought it was gonna' kill me. I can only imagine running two or three hours (for me it would take two or three days) for 26 miles. I get tired just driving that far, much less using my legs to get me there. The race God has called us to run takes:

Daily training in the Word of God
Faith in our Lord
Discipline to follow the course, not the crowd
Stamina to persevere in tough times
Love as our carbo-load fuel

Finish well!

☆ ☆ ☆

Further Study: Are you swayed by others to take a course in life other than the one laid out by Christ? Is it important to finish our Christian race? Why? Who ultimately gets all the glory?

GOOSE OR BUFFALOS

Let him who is greatest among you become as the youngest,
and the leader a servant.
Luke 22:26

☆ ☆ ☆

I heard some interesting stuff the other day concerning animals. Do you know the difference between a herd of buffalo and a flock of geese? Okay, besides the fact that one flies and one walks, one has feathers and one fur, one is on an old nickel and one honks like a horn. In the days of the Old West, when Indians hunted buffalo for meat, they shot the lead buffalo of a stampeding herd and the rest would stop and freeze like statues at a museum. As for geese, when the lead goose flying in a "V" formation is shot, a replacement moves up from the flock and assumes the leader's position (taught you something didn't I . . . admit it). Now, it's interesting to me that in one case, leadership doesn't continue, but does in another. You tell me, which scenario appears to be the smarter of the two?

My definition of correct leadership tends to lean toward the style of the goose rather than the buffalo. Effective leadership is working your way out of the job by training, teaching and placing others in positions to lead. The big, successful companies of today are run by a multitude of qualified, capable people who have been given specific functions in the company and fulfill those roles. No ministry, team, company or organization should exist solely because of one person, or their future will be short-lived. If someone was to leave or something was to happen to an organization you're a part of, is a person in place to keep it going or would it fold up like a wilted flower? Check it out, Jesus left, and His 12 kept it going. Now, that's effective leadership!

☆ ☆ ☆

Further Study: Which team would you choose to be on . . . the buffalo or the geese? Why? Do you agree or disagree with this form of leadership?

THE TRUEST THING ABOUT GOD

My purpose will be established, and I will accomplish all My good pleasure.
Isaiah 46:10

☆ ☆ ☆

Whatdo we know about God? We have His Word at our fingertips, but what do we really know about His character? We have heard things from our parents, teachers, friends, preachers, youth leaders and the world, but what is the most accurate?

Many times we want to place our own ideas on God. We think God would be a certain way or react in a particular manner. This verse reminds us that He is God, and He will do what He wants when He wants. After all, the truest thing about God is what He says about Himself! And that is that! It's not what you think about God or what anyone else thinks about God . . . it's what God says about Himself.

A lot of people have so many misconceptions of God. Many times we pick and choose the parts of God we want to see. Of course most of us would choose the characteristics of love and mercy as our favorites. However, God is a perfect God, a God of many qualities. He is a just God, an honest God, a sovereign God, a providing God, a gracious God, a fair God and many other character qualities.

So when in doubt about what would Jesus do . . . ask Him and search His Word for truth in each and every situation. You might be surprised what Jesus would do.

Remember, the greatest thing about Him is what He says! He knows all, and His purpose will be established. It will be for His good pleasure and with our (your) very best in mind. Trust the Almighty.

☆ ☆ ☆

Further Study: Where has God surprised you? What characteristics do you rely on more than others? What ones do you fear and forget?

MY RIGHTS

RIGHTS?

*If thou wilt take the left hand, then I will go to the right; or if thou
depart to the right hand, then I will go to the left.*
Genesis 13:9

☆ ☆ ☆

Our society is big on rights as a nation. We hear it on the radio and
TV talk shows, read it in the papers, listen to it in conversation–but what does
it mean? We have the constitutional rights granted all United States citizens–
free speech, a fair trial, freedom to worship whatever or whoever we wish, the
right to bear arms (guns). My question is, do we have rights as followers of
Jesus Christ? The answer is NO! As Christians (derived from scripture, not the
world), we are now slaves, branches, sheep, children, ambassadors and fishermen, all with a purpose. Our rights now become an extension of grace to live
a life of love, joy, peace, abundance, fulfillment and kindness, all with a final
destination of eternity with God. They could be thought of more as privileges
than rights.

As soon as you start to live a life of faith in God, a fascinating concept
opens up before you and the blessings are yours. You exercise the privilege to
waive your rights and let God choose for you. God sometimes lets you get to
a place of testing, a place where your own welfare would be the thing to consider if you weren't living a life of faith. When you are living by faith, you will
joyfully waive your right to choose and leave it to God to decide what's best
for you. Whenever your rights are made the guiding light in life, your spiritual vision is dimmed. You see, the great enemy of living life by faith in God is
not sin, but the good which is not good enough. Good is always the enemy
of the best. Waive your rights . . . all right?

☆ ☆ ☆

Further Study: What rights do you have as a follower of Christ? What rights
do you have as a person apart from Christ? Do you exercise your rights or let
God choose for you? Why or why not?

PRACTICING "SAFE" SEX

Let marriage be held in honor among all, and let the marriage bed be undefiled; for fornicators and adulterers God will judge.
Hebrews 13:4

* * *

Talk about a catchy ad. This one showed up in the University of Missouri school paper on February 14, 1995. The caption was, "Practice Safe Sex," and the picture, which spoke loudly, was a married couple walking down the aisle in the tux and wedding dress. Waiting until one is married to have sexual relations (they're kidding, right?) is a message that can't be stressed enough in our generation. Whether we like it or not, sex is more than just a handshake. It is more physiologically, psychologically, emotionally and spiritually than we make it out to be. Sexuality is a gift from God that is ours to share with someone in our future married life. Sex is not dirty, evil or wrong. To the contrary, it is wonderful and miraculous. Sex is the most intimate, deepest part of ourselves, but our sexuality can become unsatisfying and unfulfilling if we use it inappropriately.

It is important to understand that sex will always seem appropriate and necessarily good because it is a desire we possess so deeply as human and spiritual beings. We all desire to commune with one another, yet we go about it wrong. Although the present can be passionately deceiving, it is always the case that sex outside a lifelong, monogamous, committed relationship (marriage) is ultimately unfulfilling beyond physical arousal and release. Many, unfortunately, have learned this lesson the hard way. Those who lost their virginity prior to marriage often look back in wonder at something meaningless and empty that seemed "right" at the time. It's always worth the wait. Sex within the parameters mentioned above will be exponentially and unequivocally more wonderful and secure than one could ever dream. Practice "safe sex" and wait until you're married.

* * *

Further Study: Why is it so hard to wait? Why don't so many wait? Are you willing to see beyond the passion and wait until you're married? Why is virginity the best wedding gift you could ever give your mate?

Authenticity

*For I have no one like him of kindred spirit who will be
genuinely concerned for your welfare*
Philippians 2:20

* * *

Every so often, you run across a person you immediately "mesh" with. So authentic, real, sincere, open, vulnerable and positive is this person, that you walk away wishing you could have had a little more time with 'em. Somehow you click, a mix of personality and chemistry of thoughts and ideas. How does this happen? Is it mutual interests, common backgrounds, similar personalities or what? I believe it's more than coincidence. Some people seem to be born with an almost magical, magnetic ability to draw others close to them. What is it? I believe it's open-heartedness, sincere transparency and unblemished authenticity. Whatever you label it–it involves an ability to accept one's self, accept other people and humbly open your heart. Somehow, when you meet such a rare breed, you're left with the undeniable impression that "what you saw was what you got." There was no front, camouflage or deceptive label. There was no, "Nice to know ya'," while eyes scanned the room for someone more important than you. I think it was this kind of transparency that made *Forrest Gump* such a successful film. His genuine nature enlisted strangers on benches, befriended fearful soldiers, won over a hard-nosed officer, attracted a blue-eyed blonde, appealed to presidents and impacted an entire community. Certainly no "normal" person could be so open, simple-hearted, accepting, lacking prejudice or pretense . . . or could they? Without authenticity, a friendship goes nowhere. It's right at the core of what bonds a friendship. Forrest was real and you should be, too.

* * *

Further Study: Are you "real" when you first meet someone? Would anyone describe you as authentic? Do you carry hidden motives and agendas into a conversation? How can you be more "real?"

A REAL PEDICURE

If then, the Lord and the Teacher, washed your feet,
you also ought to wash one another's feet.
John 13:14

* * *

It should have been His time to recline, kick up His feet and say, "Serve Me." He was the one who was fixin' to hang on a cross upon the city dump pile and die for a cause, not them. The disciples should have been looking for every opportunity to show their appreciation and love to Him. It was His last supper, not theirs. It was His hour to wave the banner and sign the autographs, not theirs. But as usual, God's way is not our way. Even in ancient times, the teacher with the higher rank was to sit at the head of the table and the rookie was to do the dirty grunt labor. It is always amazing to see just what servanthood, true serving, looks like in full swing. Jesus, looking for every opportunity to use a teachable moment with His running buddies (disciples), seized the moment and grabbed the towel and wash bowl first. I'm sure there wasn't exactly a rush, nor did any disciple pull a hamstring to get to do this lovely job of washing all those nasty feet. This janitorial job was one for the low ranking, not the top brass.

One of the key ingredients to the special recipe of Christianity is serving. To be a Christ-like servant you must first be humble in spirit. Second, you must be willing (we're all able), and third, you must have a watchful eye for opportunity. You wanna' make a grand appearance or leave your mark on this world? Do you want to go out in a blaze of glory? Then serve someone else. Washing feet was for the maid of the house, not the owner of the world. Today you have, and will have, a chance to humble yourself and serve someone if you only look for the chance (they come often). If you're feeling sorry for yourself, down or depressed, don't take an aspirin, just serve someone else. Serving has a way of taking your eyes off self and putting them on someone else.

* * *

Further Study: When was the last time you served someone? Have you ever washed someone else's feet (literally) like your parents, friend, etc.? Who can you serve today? Are you following our Lord Jesus' example in serving?

WHAT IF?

Now to the King eternal, immortal, invisible, the only God,
be honor and glory forever.
1 Timothy 1:17

☆ ☆ ☆

Let's play the "what if" game for a minute. What if you could make yourself invisible for one day? What sort of things would you do, and where would you want to go? Okay, since you didn't answer quick enough, I will. If I were invisible for just one day of my life, I'd do things like:

Hang out at the water fountain and turn it up full blast when someone leaned over to drink.

Go to a library and play tricks on the librarian.

Pull up to a McDonald's drive-through window in a car (with no driver) and order fries.

Push the ball off the tee during kickoff at a televised football game.

Go to the zoo and mess with the gorillas in the cages.

Change the channel on the TV when my dad was watching golf.

Scream in church (I'm warped).

Trip a thief making his getaway.

Help a kid learning to ride a bike by holding him up to keep from crashing.

Clean up litter without anyone knowing.

Believe it or not, we worship a living God who is omnipresent (everywhere at once). Did you know that one of many differences in Satan and God is that God can be everywhere at the same time, but Satan can only be in one place at a time (demons make up for his shortcomings)? It is so reassuring to know that when I drive, fly, walk or run that I can talk to the Creator local, not long distance. With this invisible quality we have a guarantee He's there. How? Just like the wind you can't see, but can feel and know its power. The sheer fact that Jesus is so nearby gives me the luxury of calling upon Him at a moments notice and not having to wait for a response time. Next time you're in your car, jogging, playing sports, walking to class, working and trying to talk (praying) to Him with your eyes open in your heart, trust me, God will still hear you even if you're not on your knees, eyes closed. We are able to pray unceasingly (1 Thessalonians 5:17). Now, what would you do if you were invisible for a day? Have fun dreamin'.

☆ ☆ ☆

Further Study: Why do you think God chose to be invisible? What security do you have knowing He's always there?

FREE FOR ALL

It was for freedom that Christ set us free, therefore keep standing firm and do not be subject again to the yoke of slavery.
Galatians 5:1

☆ ☆ ☆

The big city can be one of the most happenin' places on the planet. In my years of travel, I have had a blast mixing with millions and loving the lights. Those cosmos of confusion can get on your nerves after a while though. Recently, on a trip to London I realized that in a city of eight million people, cabbies, discos, theater districts, subway rides, concrete buildings and nerve racking noise levels, I needed some relief. My relief came not from an aspirin, but from a jog in beautiful Hyde Park. The feeling of satisfaction was not necessarily from the jog (I run like a pregnant elephant), but from the sheer fact that in the midst of metroplex madness, I found freedom in the wide open spaces of a luxurious landscape. There were all shapes, colors and sizes of pedestrians roller-blading, feeding the ducks, flying kites, baggin' rays, pushing strollers, swinging, throwing Frisbees and just plain chillin' out with a friend on the lush green grass. It was a real free-for-all for anyone who wished to partake (free of charge, too!). It was like one minute I was in the city, the next minute in the country, and the line that separated the two was a single street.

What a neat lesson! I learned that in the midst of madness (this busy world) I can still find a refuge in the park (God's presence) and the price and reward for both are the same . . . freedom. We all need to take a daily break from our treadmill lives and find time to sit down with God in a park (or any quiet spot), early in the morning or late at night. You may not think it's important, but it's essential for your sanity and spiritual survival. Being a growing, thriving, excited follower of Christ can be as easy as a walk in the park . . . it's freeing for all who take it.

☆ ☆ ☆

Further Study: Are you entangled in your daily routine? How do you cope with it? Where does God fit into your schedule each week? How can you fit Him in more often? Then do it!

CLEANSING

COMMUNION

Do this in remembrance of me.
Luke 22:19

☆ ☆ ☆

When was the last time you took communion? Do you know what this ritual of righteousness (and just plain getting right) with God means? What does it mean to drink and eat of the body of Christ? What does the wine (juice) and bread symbolize?

These are all great questions with valid answers. Communion should be a regular occurrence in our lives as followers of Christ. I'm going to share an illustration I heard once that explains what communion is all about. A few years ago the father of a family died from a sudden heart attack. The mother decided not to take their two young children to the funeral. She thought it would be too hard for the children to see their father being put in the ground. For the next several years, the cemetery remained a fearful place for them. Then, six years after the funeral, a friend of the family invited them all to go see the grave and read what was inscribed on the tombstone. It read, "Here lies a kind and gentle man." The friend brought along a basket of food in hopes they could have a picnic near the grave. At first it seemed a strange idea to the family, but they consented. After the event, the kids lost their fear of the cemetery forever.

Isn't this similar to what Jesus told His disciples to do when He asked them to share bread and wine in memory of Him? Wasn't the tomb that Jesus was buried in empty now? Isn't remembering His death and resurrection more of a celebration than a time of sorrow? Communion is a celebration of remembrance. It's a time of renewal and redemption that cleanses our mistakes and draws us from the death of sin to victory in Christ. Next time you take communion, enter into the holiness of God and ask for pardon. Prepare for victory as you eat and drink of Christ's cup.

☆ ☆ ☆

Further Study: When did you last take communion? How often do you take it? Is it just a rehearsed ritual or an awesome attitude?

OBEDIENCE

NOT ME!

*Before I formed you in the womb I knew you, before you were born
I set you apart; I appointed you as a prophet to the nations.*
Jeremiah 1:5

✷ ✷ ✷

I've always admired the prophet Jeremiah and his willingness to be used as a tool in the Master's hand, a prophet to Judah. When God called him to his occupation in life, he was more than happy to fill the orders as a soldier in God's army. Like so many God calls to serve, Jeremiah immediately began making excuses why he didn't qualify. A prophet has to speak, so Jeremiah explained, "I don't know how to speak, and I'm only a mere child (verse 16)." God patiently (as always) assured Jeremiah that he didn't need to be fearful of this position or any other. God communicates, "I will be with you and rescue you." I'm sure the word rescue raised some suspicion in Jeremiah as to what he was in for. Then an interesting thing happened—God touched Jeremiah's mouth and put His words there.

Why is it that God, with all of His might, continues to put up with us? We doubt, dodge, deliberate, defy and deny Him, yet He still has the patience to "hang with us" through it all. You, as Jeremiah, were created for a specific purpose and have a reason for being here. The problem comes when we doubt the deity of His selection process. No one knows for what purpose or achievement he/she was created, but each of us are capable because He qualified us with honors. Don't doubt God's intent or plan, just obey it. Don't question His judgment, just submit to it. Don't hide from His calling, just do it . . . sound like a catchy shoe slogan?

✷ ✷ ✷

Further Study: Why were you born? For what purpose do you see yourself existing? Are you listening to God's direction? Why or why not?

MUSIC

THE BEAT OF A DIFFERENT DRUMMER

Whatever is true, honorable, right, pure, lovely, of good repute, if there is any excellence and if anything worthy of praise, let your mind dwell on these things.
Philippians 4:8

* * *

You hear it in restaurants, airports, cars, elevators, hospitals, dental clinics and office lobbies. It might be ragtime, jazz, rock, polka, waltz, rumba, cha-cha (what?), soul, swing, country, pop, bolero or blue grass. Its sound may be vocal, instrumental, lullaby, big band, symphonic or easy listening. Tired of this yet? It's written with keys, bars, clef, signature, notes, slurs, pitches, chords and flows from arrangements, compositions, melodies, performances, concerts and orchestras. Come on, take a wild guess what's being described here. Hint: it starts with an m, ends with a c, and it ain't microscopic. It's music!

Music runs in and out of our ears and minds daily, depositing unscreened thoughts. It strikes me ironic that God created us with one mouth and two ears. One can be open and shut at will, the others stay open all the time, like an all-night truck stop. We must be cautious what we let into our minds through those two doors called ears. Why? Because what gets funneled through the ears may eventually end up etched on the stone tablets of the heart. Variety and taste is the name of the game when it comes to music selection. We all have different likes and dislikes, but one thing is true for   all . . . music conveys a strong message. The problem is not the music itself, but the words that escort those tiny tunes. Guard your heart. Be picky about who and what you let preach to you through songs. Your mind (thoughts) will eventually dictate the feelings of your heart. If your heart (your livelihood) becomes hardened from false counsel, then you're in deep trouble. Don't be deceived. Listen to the beat of a different drummer.

* * *

Further Study: What kind of music do you listen to? Do you think Jesus would listen to it too? Why or why not? Why is Christian music a healthy alternative?

PLEASE

And without faith it is impossible to please Him, for he who comes to God must believe that He is, and that He is a rewarder of those who seek Him.
Hebrews 11:6

☆ ☆ ☆

I believe that teaching kiddos to say the word "please" is as difficult as teaching them to sing Jesus Loves Me in Hebrew. No matter how young the teaching starts, it always seems like there is an echo in the house trying to train a five-year-old to say "please" when he demands something. I do believe that 65-percent of my conversations with my kids somehow incorporate the word please.

Faith is such a tough concept to understand, especially when we live in such an intellectual world of "for sures." People for generations have tried to figure out what it means to have faith in something. It seems easier to have faith in a bungee cord, friends, car tires driving 65 miles an hour, bridges, airplanes and skyscrapers than it does to have faith in God. Little do we realize that our foundation for future, our anchor of acceptance, our rock of righteousness all settle on faith . . . faith that Jesus is alive, He did die for my sins, He does love me unconditionally, He is returning, there is a life here-after, the earth was created by Him and so on.

We need to realize we cannot please Him without faith, and we need it to live. Many examples throughout the Bible model for us how this is done and what it takes to do it. Don't go to sleep tonight without hitting your knees and pleading with God to deepen and strengthen your faith in Him.

☆ ☆ ☆

Further Study: How deep is your faith today? What pleases God more, your works or faith in Him?

The Trap

> *But each one* (you) *is tempted* (trapped) *when he is*
> *carried away and enticed by his own lust.*
> James 1:14

☆ ☆ ☆

I'm gonna' tell you a real life happening which is tough to swallow but really brings this verse home, so bear with me. The sport of trapping animals, fish, etc., has been in existence for centuries. There are different reasons for this sport (if you want to call it that), and sometimes it's done humanely for a good reason. All too often it's done for no positive reason. In this scenario we're talking of how raccoons are trapped. If you've ever seen one of these creatures in the wild, you notice several character qualities. First, they are clean animals who are required to wash all their food because they have no saliva glands to assist in the swallowing process. Second, they are very curious, and are always into things and situations they shouldn't be. Third, coons use trees as hiding places, so they're great tree climbers with powerful hind legs. One way a trapper, trapping coons for their fur, would use these qualities against the coon itself is by covering a small six-inch steel trap with leaves and placing it under a three-foot branch, hanging from it a piece of shiny metal or foil. Following this set-up, the coon, with its curious nature, would see the shining object, stand up to touch it with its front paws and walk right into the trap. The trap would engage and with severe force speed-cut the hind legs off the animal and leave it unable to seek shelter in a tree (no back legs). The coon would lie there and bleed to death.

This world, in which you live, is full of soul trappers looking to destroy you with the glamour and glitter of what the world has to offer. You are a curious creature who could be enticed (fishing terminology for lure) to play with what looks good (sex, money, etc.) and end up snared by the trap of Satan. If you think the story which was told is mean, you have a similar scenario going on around you every second you live. Folks who play get badly burned and some are never able to recover. Don't be easily deceived, and know that the world will offer you something which appears good to rob you of something great (God's gift). You see, Satan knows our weaknesses and uses them to destroy us.

☆ ☆ ☆

Further Study: What does the world offer you that glitters? How can you steer clear of the trap?

MONEY

UP IN SMOKE

Lift up your eyes to the sky, then look to the earth beneath, for the sky will vanish and all will go up in smoke, and the earth will wear out like a garment and its inhabitants will die in like manner, but my salvation shall be forever
Isaiah 51:6

☆ ☆ ☆

We had pinched our pennies, collected our cash, and socked away savings for years to build our dream. The sacrifices had been many and the spending sprees few, but what we had done it for was worth the wait . . . a home. To map out the details, draw out the blueprints, decide on the tile, pick the paint, plot the location was all a part of the journey. To build your home is to be a part of the American dream. To cut out pictures from *Better Homes and Gardens* and tour other newly built homes gathering ideas was a total blast. I never in my wildest dreams could believe we were actually going to meet with a home builder (contractor) to fulfill these dreams. It took a lot of wood, cement and nails, but four months later we went from soil to structure.

We had lived in our home about 18 months when one September afternoon I received a phone call from my panicked wife that our home was on fire. That's right, up in smoke with no hope to put out the blaze before total destruction. We lost everything in a matter of moments . . . all we owned were the clothes on our backs and an alive family. A few months before the fire, a friend had told me, "Hold everything you have with open hands." God does give and take away, and all you have for the rest of your life is strictly on a rental basis. "Why did this happen to me?" I'd ask myself. To teach me that our job on this planet is to have joy when we get and keep and when it is taken from us, like Job. Take some simple advice from me, what you have and will have is okay, but it's a gift from God, and really all that matters is your relationship with Him.

☆ ☆ ☆

Further Study: How tightly do you hold what is yours? Do you see it as yours or God's? What helps you hold material items with a loose grip?

MR. FIX IT

Peter took Him (Jesus) aside and began to rebuke Him saying, "God forbid it, Lord! This shall never happen to You." He (Jesus) turned and said to Peter, "Get behind Me, Satan! You are a stumbling block to Me; for you are not setting your mind on God's interests, but man's."
Matthew 16:22-23

☆ ☆ ☆

We are all in old "Peppermint Socks" shoes whenever we open our mouths and insert our pedal extremities (feet). Peter was no different than any one of us today. His sole desire in life was to be a friend and help out. The Savior first called Peter a rock, then four verses later tagged him as a stumbling block. Peter the rock turned into a rolling stone, tripping up those following the path of righteousness. Jesus described to His disciples the course necessary to fulfill His tour of duty on earth. The process included suffering, death and the resurrection, but it just didn't compute for old Pete. He only heard (selective listening) the first two segments and never got to the part of the story where Jesus would ride off into the sunset of eternity with the Father of the heavens.

I'll bet my bottom dollar that most of us have tried at one time or another to be a Mr. Fix-It and jump into what seemed like a broken area of a friend's life where God had initiated a remodeling project on some character flaws. The Creator is in the business of rebuilding broken homes and hearts. Suffering and rebuilding are part of the process, so you and I need only to encourage and pray for those who are being rebuilt. Jesus' response to Peter was harsh because He knew His Father's will for His life. Any barriers to that were considered evil.

So, the next time you see a friend or relative going through a tough time, determine if it's God doing some interior designing or the world doing some destroying. If it is of God, let it be. If it is of the world, jump in and help. The finished product will be in the next heavenly issue of *Better Homes.*

☆ ☆ ☆

Further Study: Why does God rebuild our lives? How can we know if we need to stay out of the way or help? What will your next response to another person's trouble be?

In The Rough

Suffer hardship with me, as a good soldier of Christ Jesus.
2 Timothy 2:3

★ ★ ★

I took up this sport at the tender age of 10, yet 25 years later I'm not much better. It's a goofy activity that uses lingo like "birdie, grain of grass, chip shot, lay-up and in-the-rough." This game of madness is called golf. If you've tried your luck (I emphasize the word luck) at this sport, you know just how frustrating hitting a little white ball with a metal club toward a waving flag can be. In Texas we call it cow pasture pool—a more appropriate name for the way I play. You can watch the pros hack at it every Sunday afternoon on the PGA Tour at posh courses like Augusta, Sawgrass and Pebble Beach. You can watch clubbers like me on public courses, trying their hand at hittin' it long and straight down the fairway. It takes me a little longer, but the object is to keep the ball out of the rough and on the nicely groomed fairways. Guess what though? Even the pros sometimes end up smackin' a few trees and landing in the rough, a long way from the hole.

Here is a lame yet profound thought—no matter how hard we try in our Christian lives, we will all end up in the "rough" sometimes. You tend to bear down more, concentrate and often perform better when your ball lies in a tougher, rougher area. So it is in our lives. In rough times we tend to have deeper faith and bear down in our dependence on God. You see, the pros separate themselves from the amateurs, not by how well they perform on the easy fairways, but how they overcome rough shots. Make it a point in your life not to give up and head to the clubhouse of self-pity when you're in rough times, but bow up, dig in and give it all you have. See if your life doesn't end up on the green, on track, ready for the next challenge. Catch this . . . you will (not optional) end up in the rough at times throughout your life because that's not only how you become a better golfer, but a faithful follower. Tee it up!

★ ★ ★

Further Study: Where does your ball (life) lie right now? Fairway or rough? Where do you learn the most? How can you best get out of the rough and back in the fertile fairways of life?

GOD'S LOVE

ACCEPTANCE

For God so loved the world. . .
John 3:16

☆ ☆ ☆

In a heart warming story, Mary Bird writes in her book, *The Whisper Test:*

I grew up knowing I was different and hated it. I was born with a cleft palate (deformed mouth), and when I started school, my classmates made it clear to me how I looked to others: a little girl with a misshapen lip, crooked nose, lopsided teeth and garbled speech. When schoolmates asked what happened to my lip, I'd tell them I'd fallen and cut my lip on a piece of glass. Somehow it seemed more acceptable to have suffered on accident than to have been born different. I was convinced that no one outside my family could love me. There was, however, a teacher in the second grade whom we all adored–Mrs. Leonard. She was short, round, happy and a sparkling lady. Annually we had a hearing test that Mrs. Leonard gave to all the students, and finally, it was my turn. I knew from past years that as we stood against the door in the back of the room and covered one ear, the teacher would whisper something like "the sky is blue" or "do you have new shoes?" and we would have to repeat it back. I waited there for those words that God must have put into her mouth, those seven words that changed my life. Mrs. Leonard said in her whisper, "I wish you were my little girl."

Wow! God says to every person that is deformed by sin or poor self-image, "I wish you were my child." We can't even comprehend with our feeble minds the love that Christ has for us . . . for you! He loved you so much that He was willing to risk it all for a chance to have a relationship with you. God is not as concerned with what we do as who we are. I'm telling you that you may feel like a total failure, an outcast, a misfit, a geek, but God doesn't see it that way. God created you from the beginning of time, and He doesn't make junk.

☆ ☆ ☆

Further Study: How do you feel today about yourself? Can you relate with this story? Are you happy with the way you look? Does God love you?

INTEGRITY

HONEST ABE

My honesty will answer me later.
Genesis 30:33

* * *

For Coach Stroud of the Rockdale County High School Bulldogs in Conyers, Georgia, it was meant to be a championship basketball season. With 21 wins and only five losses they were on the way to the Georgia boys' basketball state tournament. The final game was best of all, with a remarkable come-from-behind victory in the closing moments. The Bulldogs proudly displayed their state championship trophy in the case outside the gym. Then tragedy struck. The Bulldogs were stripped of their title after school officials learned that a player on the team, who played only 45 seconds in the first of the school's five post-season games, was found scholastically ineligible. They received this information directly from Coach Stroud. The ineligible team member played only a few seconds all season, but still Coach Stroud confessed. Others told him to just keep quiet and the incident would pass unnoticed, but not in the conscience of a man of honesty and integrity. Coach gathered his team together in the locker room and told them, "People forget scores of games; they don't forget what you're made of."

Integrity and honesty are hard to come by in this world of unfaithfulness and deception. You have to look hard and long to scare up rare men and women of their word. What an awesome (I like that word, if you can't tell by now) example Coach Stroud is to us. There is more to life than winning and losing.

* * *

Further Study: Are you a person of honesty? How would you define integrity? What circumstances come up in your life that cause you to be dishonest? How can you overcome that temptation?

WASH UP

Wash me, and I shall be whiter than snow.
Psalms 51:7

☆ ☆ ☆

In 1818, Ignaz Phillip Semmelweis was born into a world where women died right and left. Even the finest hospitals lost one out of six young mothers to "childbed fever." In those days, a doctor's daily routine began in the autopsy room, dissecting bodies. From there he made his way to the hospital to examine expectant mothers without a thought to washing his hands first. Dr. Semmelweis was the first man in history to associate such examinations with resultant infection and death. His own practice was to wash with a chlorine solution, and after 11 years and the delivery of over 8,500 babies, he only lost 184 mothers (one in 50). He spent the prime of his life lecturing and debating with his colleagues over this subject. He argued that "Puerperal Fever" was caused by decomposed material transferred to an open wound. None of his fellow doctors believed this theory and instead followed the thinking of doctors and mid-wives who had delivered babies for hundreds of years without washing their hands. No outspoken Hungarian was going to change them now! Dr. Semmelweis died insane at the young age of 47, his wash basins thrown away, his colleagues laughing in his face and the death rattle of thousands of women ringing in his ears.

If you recall, the anguished prayer of King David after falling to sexual sin was, "Wash me!" "Wash" was the outspoken message to a lost world of pagan peasants. "Unless I wash you, you have no part of me," was spoken by the towel-draped Jesus to an energetic Peter. Without being washed clean by the Savior's blood, we all will die from the contamination of sin. For God's sake, wash!

☆ ☆ ☆

Further Study: Do you know someone who has not been washed of their sins? Is washing a physical or spiritual ritual? What's the difference? Are you clean? What can you do to get clean?

EGALITARIANISM

The Lord God said, "It is not good for the man to be alone.
I will make a helper suitable for him."
Genesis 2:18

☆ ☆ ☆

There is an issue that has slowly crept into our Western culture, churches, homes and ultimately into the marriage arena. What is it? Egalitarian (equality) thinking. I believe one of the reasons for the highest divorce rate in the history of our society (among believers, too) is an improper view of our roles as men and women. This devotional is not a bashing of men or women, just a scriptural dissecting of meanings and divine positioning. I have never been afraid to jump smack-dab in the middle of a heated controversy, and I realize this is one of many perspectives, yet I want you (the reader) to know without a doubt my stand on this explosive issue. I believe that in God's eyes men and women are equal when it comes to essence (Romans 2:10 and 1 Corinthians 11:11) and worth, but I don't believe they are the same when it comes to "functionality" (women were made to be a helper, suitable to man).

When God created woman out of man, He "fashioned" her to serve as a completer and helper to the male, not as a clone. If God had created them the same, both in essence and function, one wouldn't be needed because it would be a duplicated creation. Just because women are not the same in function as men doesn't mean they are less of a person of value; women are no better or worse, just plain different. This is why marriage (in a Divine context) makes the partners complete and more of a "team" to work together to build God's Kingdom. In 1 Peter 3:7, Peter addresses this same issue in his culture. Proverbs 31 addresses the wife of noble character and worth.

I realize that this subject is far more extensive than the length of this devotional, yet it's important to discuss. Why? If we truly realize the unique positions God created men and women to fill, couples would not only be marrying for better or worse, but for good! Men are to be the head of the household like Christ is of the church, which means to spiritually lead, physically provide and emotionally encourage (love) his wife and   children . . . not dominate or control (Ephesians 5:23). Let's begin today to start rockin' with the roles God intended.

☆ ☆ ☆

Further Study: So . . . what is your take on this issue according to what the scriptures say? Read: Genesis 1:26-27; Proverbs 27:17; Genesis 2:21-24.

Do the Right Thing

Hate what is evil. . . cling to what's good.
Romans 12:9

☆ ☆ ☆

Don't pass by this nugget of scripture like a pair of cheap sunglasses, look again. Do you see contradictory words in the same verse? Call it what you want, detest, despise, abhor, loathe, abominate, but it means what it says. You are to hate what is evil in this world and cling to what is good and right like a life buoy. Notice that it says "what is" and not "who is." We are to hate the sin but not the sinner.

We are to hate the evil and violence aired nightly on prime-time TV. We are to loathe what ungodly shows are shown on the big screens across this country of ours in the theaters every Friday night. We should detest the gang murders we read about on our local front-page newspapers. We are to abhor what goes on behind the walls of abortion clinics every second of the day. What can little old you do though? Love what is good, take a stand for what is right, pray for those who persecute you, be a light in a dark world for the cause of Christ, and your voice will be heard and your life will be seen.

☆ ☆ ☆

Further Study: What kinds of things do you hate? What sort of things do you love? How can you apply this scripture in a non-violent, tasteful way today? Will it matter? (hint: yes!)

LEADERSHIP

MENTORS

A pupil will eventually be like his teacher.
Luke 6:40

✫ ✫ ✫

A trusting mentor has a wide range of options for relating. He or she may counsel, teach, equip, guide, sponsor or even coach. A good, effective mentor first has a servant's attitude and only offers wise counsel that chimes with scripture. The perception is that we had strong leaders in a past generation, but we have weak leaders today. Why? Where have all the leaders (mentors) gone? We can turn to Deuteronomy 31 and 34 to see how Moses passed the baton to Joshua, or to John 13 to see how Jesus Himself was a mentor to His disciples by modeling servant leadership. Barnabas was a tremendous example of a person who lived for the next generation and not himself. We see how he spoke up for Saul who was the converted persecutor of Christians in Acts 9:26-31. Barnabus traveled to Tarsus to recruit Saul for a teaching role to the church in Antioch because he saw great potential. To be an effective mentor you must:

Believe in who you're discipling.
Serve as a team with them.
Part company and let them try on their own.
There are two rocks to avoid on your journey:
have all plans and no flexibility or
have all flexibility and no plans.

Effective leading contains as its key ingredients directing, coaching, supporting and delegating. You as the mentor need to be goal oriented. When the apostle Paul was a mentor to a younger Timothy, he did it through life-on-life, not via correspondence. Being a mentor is a hands-on process, not a step-back position. A mentor always provides an environment through encouragement and example that leads the follower to a deepened walk with the Savior. Hear this . . . being a mentor is not for cowards, but what is that's worth doing? The result of the effective mentor is that his disciple will continue the process with someone else after he's long gone.

✫ ✫ ✫

Further Study: Who is your mentor? Are you considered a mentor to anyone? Why or why not? Do you possess the tools it takes to be a hero to someone who needs one?

GOALS

SAIL ON SAILOR

I press on toward the goal for the prize of the upward call of God in Christ Jesus.
Philippians 3:14

☆ ☆ ☆

Okay, repeat this catchy rhythmic saying with me . . . "In fourteen hundred and ninety-two, Columbus sailed the ocean blue." A national holiday and two centuries of school books have taught us that Christopher Columbus, the great sailor and man of God (his name means Christ-bearer) reached America first, thus disproving the notion the world was flat. Americans celebrate this day of discovery on Columbus Day to stress the importance of the voyage and the incredible heroism and tenacity of character his quest must have demanded. Even the astronauts who flew to the moon had a pretty good idea of what to expect. Columbus was sailing, as Star Trek would put it, "where no man has gone before." After trying to sell his plan to the kings of Portugal, England and France, he returned again to Isabella and Ferdinand of Spain for one last shot. Columbus showed them that the risks were small and the potential return great, and reminded them of the chance to stumble onto gold. The Spanish monarchs agreed to his consent. Columbus set sail on August 3, 1492, from Palos, Spain with three ships . . . Nina, Pinta, and the Santa Maria. On October 12 at 2:00 a.m. right before his crew of sailors were about to mutiny and force a return to Spain, a look-out named Rodrigo, aboard the Pinta, sighted 'land' by the light of the moon.

This is an incredible story of history in which a man of God had a goal and barred nothing to achieve it. To have the "stick-with-it" mentality and a heart that never says die are two incredible qualities to bear. We can learn much from our past history and those who shaped and molded it. To have lived in 1492 without all the navigational devices or know-how of computers to guide you across seas is remarkable. All they had were God-given smarts and a passionate desire to discover all that the Creator had to offer. How good are you at taking a vision or idea and following through with it to its completion? Determine what your goals in life are and get after it with God. Don't forget the old saying, "If you don't know what target you're shooting at, you'll probably hit it."

☆ ☆ ☆

Further Study: What is your goal today? How do goals help you get things accomplished in life and for God?

INTEGRITY

LOST INGREDIENT

Is not the fear of God your confidence, and the integrity of your ways your hope?
Job 4:6

★ ★ ★

If there is one key ingredient missing today in the Christian's secret recipe, it would be integrity. You might be asking yourself, "Self, just what does this word mean?" Let me, if you will, define this word in a language you can understand. Integrity is when you are the same person on the inside as you are on the outside. You're the same in a hotel room a thousand miles away from home as you are when you're sitting in church. Integrity is being a person of commitment and being bound by your word. You could say that you walk your talk around your peers and in the private places of your life. Your tongue will not be flapping like a flag in the wind with gossip as your venom. Integrity says that when you say, "I do," that means until death.

Isn't it a relief that when Moses came down from Mt. Sinai, he didn't come down with the Ten Suggestions? Our Christian belief is filled with absolutes with little room for finding loopholes. Isn't it nice to know that our God doesn't have a bad day and decide to send another flood to destroy every morsel of mankind without warning, even though He promised He wouldn't? My Father and your Father in heaven is bent on maintaining a model of integrity for you and I to follow. You might be asking yourself, since we live in a society where integrity is scarcely found, "How could little ol' me make a difference and begin to change the trend of the '90s?" Does your vote really matter? Yes! With God as your guide, it does matter. One vote put Hitler in a position, one vote brought Texas into the Union . . . so I guess you do matter after all.

★ ★ ★

Further Study: What will integrity do for your example? How can you show integrity today to others?

THROW UP!

This book of the law shall not depart from your mouth, but you shall meditate on it day and night, so that you may be careful to do according to all that is written in it, for then you will make your way prosperous and then you will have success.
Joshua 1:8

✯ ✯ ✯

Being a father, I have heard some of the most creative one-liners imaginable. Each night when we go to bed with the kids, we talk a lot, memorize some and pray a little. At times we read out of the children's Bible which I love because it's so simple and has bunches of pictures to boot. I recall a picture-moment comment when we were talking about Moses throwing down the scepter which turned into a snake. Daniel (my oldest) looked at me with those big brown eyes and said, "Come on Dad, you're kidding." You can imagine at the age of four how hard it would be to fathom a stick (which he plays with often) turning into a snake.

We, as adults, occasionally have a hard time, even after we read it, accepting that God really expects us to believe Him. Come on God, that's not in there, is it? Sex before marriage, gluttony, lustful thoughts, gossip, causing someone to stumble, mediocrity, are all sin. God has to mean those things are just bad, not a sin. We are called to do all (and live by) that which is documented in scripture, and we are to meditate on it 24 hours a day. Meditate means to "throw up" throughout the day, in our lives and hearts. It's similar to a cow throwing up what she had eaten previously (her cud) and chewing on it again to retrieve more nutrition from it. When you read a verse or passage, do you recall it (throw it up) later to gain more wisdom to live like Christ? Why not? We should because then we will be prosperous and successful in God's eyes whatever we have on our agenda during the day. Take a big chomp of scripture and try to meditate on it all day . . . you'll have a great day!

✯ ✯ ✯

Further Study: What did you read today out of the Word? How can you practically remember it throughout the day? What will remind you to do this?

WORKING TOGETHER

A TEAM PLAYER

*Make my joy complete by being of the same mind, maintaining the
same love, united in spirit, intent on one purpose.*
Philippians 2:2

☆ ☆ ☆

The guru who brought Chrysler Motors out of financial mire was Lee
Iacocca. He was a miracle worker; he took control of the automobile producer and brought it out of the woods and into the light, as he did for other
powerhouse companies like Ford and General Motors. A man in constant
pursuit of perfection, he once asked the legendary football coach Vince
Lombardi what it took to make a winning team. In Iacocca's book he writes
the coach's response to his question:

"There are a lot of coaches with good ball clubs who know the funda-
mentals and have plenty of talent and discipline, but still don't win the game.
Then you come to the third ingredient: if you're going to play together as a
team, you've got to care for one another. You've got to love each other. Each
player has to be thinking about the next guy and saying to himself, 'If I don't
block that man, Paul is going to get his leg broken. I have to do my job well
in order that he can do his.' The difference between mediocrity and greatness
is the feeling that these guys have for each other."

Whether it's on a team, in a church, running a business, or in a family,
healthy survival depends on how much you care for each other and work
together toward a common goal. Books dealing with self, individuality and
success sell like hotcakes, but they seldom promote caring for teammates. If
God intended us to be "loners" He wouldn't have put us all on the same planet. Two strands are always stronger than one, and so is a team that cares for
each individual. You'll never see the letter "I" in the word team. A team player cares more about team success than his own glory. Be a team player. When
you win, you all win. When you lose as an individual, you lose alone.

☆ ☆ ☆

Further Study: How well do you work with others? Are you an individual or
team player? Do you care for those you're working with whether it be on a
team, at work, at church or in your own family? What do you need to do to
become more team-oriented? Are you willing to sacrifice?

GOD'S LOVE

Getting To Know You

But the very hairs of your head are all numbered.
Matthew 10:30

☼ ☆ ☆

Talk about being really bored, listen to this. Years ago, a German scientist did a study and counted random people's hair content. The study showed that the number of hairs on a human head is linked to the color of the hair. There are more hairs on a black-haired person's head than a red-haired person's; more on a brown-haired person than black-haired; and more on a blonde-haired person than brown-haired. A black-haired female has about 110,000 hairs and a blonde about 140,000 hairs on her head. The average female will lose up to 100 hairs a day. A man daily shaves off about one sixty-fourth of an inch, and over a period of 40 years will cut off 25 feet of beard. Wow, interesting stuff, huh?

Now, if you think that is a brain teaser, try this one. God knows exactly how many hairs every person living on this earth has on his head. What that translates to is not that He has a hang-up about hair, but He does make a career of caring. How awesome to think that God, the Creator of all this, is so flipped out about you that He even wants to know the details about you. I'll bet you a Yankee dime you don't know of one person (family, friend, or spouse) who knows that number. And guess what? No one is even gonna' waste his time to find it out either. I really feel that the reason this verse is even in the Bible is not to show you how smart God is, but to prove to you (which He doesn't have to do) that even the smallest, seemingly meaningless details about you, He cares about. Now, that is what I would call true love in its purest form.

☆ ☆ ☆

Further Study: How many hairs do you have on your head? Do you care? Then why do you think God does?

GROW WHERE YOU'RE PLANTED

Faith is the assurance of things hoped for, the conviction of things not seen.
Hebrews 11:1

⚜ ⚜ ⚜

Talk about a racket! It wasn't like I had a whole lot of choice in the matter—either Ryder or U-Haul. We were moving from the world's largest parking lot, Branson, Missouri, to the Mile High City of Denver, Colorado. It was 826 miles cross-country to the Rockies, and we had to cross Kansas (boring). We (mostly my wife) packed boxes for about six weeks and still it seemed we had a ton to do. Our local Bible study group was a huge help, and without them we still wouldn't be moved. The night before the drive, my exhausted wife and I sat amid our crashed-out kids, staring at the shell of a home. We were really gonna' miss our friends, yet the excitement and anticipation was fun.

There's something unnerving about packing up and moving to an unfamiliar destination. It reminds me of packing up for the first year of college and moving into the athletic dorm at Oklahoma University. All so different, uncertain what to expect around the next corner—new home, new friends, new schools, new church, new roads, new scenery. Like the *Mayflower's* maiden voyage into uncharted seas, faith is all about the unseen and uncertain. God asks us every day to set sail into waters never crossed before . . . do something that we've never done, speak when we've never spoken, share when we don't know how. Jesus didn't let the grass grow under His or His disciples' feet. So, next time God transplants you in some unfamiliar place, realize that you'll grow where you're planted because He goes, too. Bon voyage!

☆ ☆ ☆

Further Study: Why is it so hard to accept change? Do you see how change draws you close to God and increases your faith in Him?

TIME, TIMES AND HALF A TIME

And he will speak out against the Most High and wear down the saints of the Highest One, and he will intend to make alterations in times and in law, and they will be given into his hand for a time, times, and half a time
Daniel 7.25

☆ ☆ ☆

Growing up, I wasn't sure if the bike ride home from school was just bad navigation or a second tour in Vietnam. As the crow flies, from my house to the bike rack on the south lot at McCullough Middle school was only about two miles from home. The trip on my bike should have only taken me 10 or maybe 15 minutes max, yet in reality it took me 30. Why? You just sit tight and I'll tell you why . . . obstacles. What kinda obstacles you ask . . .? Big dogs, pot holes and road construction; no matter which street, route, short or long cut I took, it seemed I ran into something that paused my pedal power. Trust me, I got real good at spotting those labs, retrievers, dobermans and even a few poodles on steroids (big ones) behind hedges, trees, cars and front-yard toys before they launched their attack at me. What did I ever do to them? They acted like they paid taxes and owned their neighborhood homes.

Life is kinda (a lot) like that, too, isn't it? No matter where you go or hide, boring or creative, energetic or tired . . . you run into obstacles (tough times) that slow you down and change your agenda. They are real inconvenient and their timing is pitiful, but guess what . . . you can't get around them. In the passage above, Daniel has a vision from God that upholds this concept as he sees a future where believers (saints) will be "worn down." Obstacles, trials, tragedy, people, mishaps, bad luck etc. . . . are there to grow you up. The farther this world gets from godliness, the closer believers better get to their Creator. Don't try to pray your way out of them or steer your way around them . . . pray your way through them!! The trail is tough but the scenery is beautiful . . . enjoy the journey. How long? Time, times and half a time.

☆ ☆ ☆

Further Study: How do you view life's unseen mishaps? Why does God want His children (you) to go through rough times and rocky roads? Why does our nature tell us to avoid them? How should we (you) view trials?

THE MEASURE OF A MAN

Consider it pure joy when you encounter various trials, knowing that the testing of your faith produces endurance.
James 1:2 3

✻ ✻ ✻

I read a quote once that said "a tree is best measured when it's down." All of my life, one of the things I looked forward to the most was cutting down big, tall, dead trees for firewood. Nothing makes you feel more manly than getting out the ol' chainsaw and going to town on a tree that would make Paul Bunyan proud. Years ago, I was with a friend who was new (to say the least) to the sport of wood cutting. We had an okay from the Forestry Service to cut down and clear an area of National Forest, so we loaded up the trucks with chainsaws and gas, and headed out for a hard day's work droppin' trees. My friend picked a tree far too big for a beginner to start on, which would prove to him that cutting down a tree is an art, not a game. He proceeded to cut around the trunk of this tree for the next hour to have it fall right on him and his saw, hard enough for him to see stars on a cloudy day. He later stated his surprise that the test for his tree cutting 'class' had been such a difficult trial.

God's word tells you that as a Christian your tests will come in all shapes and forms. We are told by Jesus' half-brother, that the trials and tough times of our lives are for the good of our faith, and the end product is the endurance to make it through more to come. You see, trials are a part of the curriculum of God's classroom, and you are to be joyful in knowing they are good for you and needed for strength. Just as my friend (who was fine after the stars faded out) learned that you can't really measure how you're doing until you're on the ground (in the midst of tough times), you too can see how deep your faith is, not when all is well, but when all seems to be wrong.

✻ ✻ ✻

Further Study: What trial faces you today? How can you handle it and be joyful?

ENCOURAGEMENT

SPUR 'EM ON

And let us consider how to spur one another on to love and good deeds.
Hebrews 10:24

☆ ☆ ☆

Hey buckaroo, when was the last time you went to, or saw on the tube, a real live rootin'-tootin' western rodeo? (Well, that's too long.) A friend of mine is a real life rodeo cowboy who lives on a ranch in a Little House on the Prairie look-a-like log cabin with walls lined in trophy saddles and bookshelves displaying gold buckles of past arena victories. It is amazing that some folks view mounting up on a 1,200 pound bull with sharp horns, or a crazy bucking horse, as a sport, but hey . . . some folks' pain tolerance is higher than other's, right? One time I asked him why, when riding a bucking bronc, he continued to run his spurs in the neck of this beast that was already mad enough to send a cowboy ballistic. He tilted his hat back, leaned against the bucking shoot, and proceeded to explain that one can make a pretty mellow horse into a champion bucker by spurring him on to a peak performance.

We live in a world which seems to always view things negatively. The art of stimulating or spurring on folks around us with a smile, brief note or a soft, sincere word of encouragement seems to be classified as an "endangered species." As a disciple and ambassador (representative) of Jesus, you and I are to live a life different than that of the world. We (as a minority) are called to love our enemies and encourage others in a time when the majority says discourage and hate. What a different view would be seen of Christians if their army was one that didn't shoot the wounded, but helped them.

Today, you can either view a half cup of water as half-full, or half-empty. You see, it's all in the eyes of the viewer, not in the circumstance. Be a person who sees the good in others, and make it your goal to bring out the best in them. Go get 'em cowboy (or cowgirl), and let's make it a ride!

☆ ☆ ☆

Further Study: How can I spur someone on today? What specific ways can I do this?

THAT LINE IS BUSY . . . WANNA' HOLD?

I love the Lord because He hears my voice (prayers) *and my supplications.*
Psalm 116:1

★ ★ ★

In this age of communication headaches and technological takeovers, you almost don't know which lie to believe. AT&T is slamming MCI, MCI is mocking US Sprint and US Sprint is manipulating AT&T . . . when will this cycle stop? No matter how advanced our phone lines become, we will always be one step behind the population growth of this country. In other words, by the time you expand and get up to date you are already one step behind. We have fancy little gadgets and gimmicks like call waiting, party-lines, conference lines, voice mail and call forwarding, but no solutions to the age old problem of busy signals. Where I work, the phone seems to ring off the hook all day long, but I've realized I can only talk on one line at a time. Therefore, someone is always on hold, waiting. Isn't it a bummer when you call someone long distance or from a pay phone and you're put on hold for an hour or cut off for some unknown reason? How do you feel when you're put through to the wrong extension and you talk 10 minutes to the wrong person before you realize he is not who you thought he was? Oops!

Here are some words of hope for your listening ears . . . God puts no one on hold. AT&T should have God as a consultant to their technology department because He is always one step ahead of the game. What if . . . when you had an important or maybe life threatening request for the Creator and all you got was an angelic operator message singing, "that line is   busy . . . would you like to call back?" Or how about, if in a moment of sorrow or pain, you cry out to the Lord and all of a sudden you heard a dial tone because you got cut off? Gnarly, dude! You can take this and deposit in a   bank . . . God cares for you and values His time to communicate with you through the phone lines of prayer. So, while the "Big Three" are battling out who is the cheapest long distance carrier . . . remember, Jesus paid your phone bill on the cross, so talk all you want.

★ ★ ★

Further Study: What do you feel like when you're put on hold? What about hung up on? How does it make you feel to know that God puts no one on hold? Call Him today!

TRAIL BLAZER OR BLAZE TRAILER

*Enlarge the place of your tent, stretch out the curtains of your dwellings,
spare not, lengthen your cords and strengthen your pegs.*
Isaiah 54:2

* * *

My philosophy on life is this: There dwells among us two types of folks, those who read stories and those who make stories. I love those people who are spunky and spontaneous enough to step out and do something totally opposite to their personalities. For those who like living life by a thread and on the edge, that steppin' out may mean sitting down to read and pray for a whole afternoon in the country. For those more conservative, it may mean getting out, letting their hair down, and going hiking, bungee jumping (not!) or whatever. What I'm trying to say is the same thing that the prophet Isaiah is saying . . . branch out! The life we live in this earth suit is too short to not step out of our comfort zones and try something a little different. Obviously, this wild hair needs to be done in the framework of God's word, but once you've been okayed for take-off, then fire up those after-burners and take air.

You will notice that branching out will cause a spiritual turn of your faith. When we step out, we are going beyond our limits, out-punting our coverage, or competing out of our league. God loves those times when we come to the end of self and to the beginning of Savior. Go ahead with it then, broaden the borders of your tent (life) and experience those uncharted regions. Make a story today for God and this world to read from your life . . . it will be on the best-seller list, I bet.

* * *

Further Study: What legal thing have you always wanted to do but never did? What are those regions of life which make you feel uncomfortable? How deep is your faith? Can it be deeper? What can you do differently this week to deepen your faith?

WHO AM I IN CHRIST

THE MASK

For I am confident in this very thing, that He who began a good
work in you will perfect it until the day of Christ.
Philippians 1:6

✳ ✳ ✳

"SSSmokin'!" . . .. "Somebody stop me!" . . .. In the blockbuster movie, *The Mask,* when Stanley (actor Jim Carey) finds an ancient mask under a bridge, he believes his luck is finally going to change. By putting on the mask he is transformed into an indestructible, wise-cracking, smart-talking hero who fights the mob to save his girl. This comedy is full of one-liners, animation and plenty of gut-bustin' laughs. The story line, in a nutshell, is that when the mask is worn, the innermost desires come to the surface. In other words, if the wearer is a good person, the mask enhances those qualities, but also does the same for a bad person.

How many folks do you know who wake up with one mask, but wear another when they leave the house? How about you? We live in a self-fulfilling, self-satisfying, self-fish (get it?) world of people-pleasers. We are constantly trying to be accepted, not rejected, fit in, not fade out, set the pace, not fall from grace. It seems like all that junior high peer pressure would wear out by the time we get to college. Let me clue you in . . . it doesn't get easier as it goes. The one and only reason folks masquerade in a custom-fitted mask is the "fear" (broad term) of rejection from peers (fancy, over-used word for friends). In our ruthless social circles we defriend, defile, and deface those who defy the rules and stand confident of who they are. The common thread that runs through all those who are socially secure, is Christ. We won't be satisfied, stable, unselfish or secure unless divine intervention occurs. The ending to the movie is a great shot of Stanley throwing his mask off a bridge and being accepted for who he really is . . . fearfully and wonderfully made. Clothes, diets, sports, cars, jobs, dates or hair-do's don't make a person—only Jesus does that, and He did it in His biography called The Bible. Read it sometime. It receives rave reviews.

✳ ✳ ✳

Further Study: Why do people wear masks? Do you wear one? If you do, why? If you don't why don't you? If you are wearing one now, how can you get rid of it?

GOD'S LOVE

THE TRANSFUSION

*Walk in love, just as Christ also loved you, and gave Himself up for us,
an offering and a sacrifice to God as a fragrant aroma.*
Ephesians 5:2

☆ ☆ ☆

In old westerns, the town "Doc" carried his little black bag from home to home via horse and buggy, making house-calls to all the area residents. This is the true story of Dr. Cain, a small town doctor from the midwest in 1910. Dr. Cain received word that a six-year-old girl had suffered a severed artery and was bleeding to death. He raced to the scene, as does a modern day paramedic (except he was on horseback). After applying direct pressure and stitches, he had the bleeding controlled, but the girl had lost too much blood and would soon die. Dr. Cain knew her only hope was a transfusion, yet in that day and time, this practice was just that . . . a practice. The little girl's 10-year-old brother overheard the conversation between the doctor and his parents and quickly volunteered his services as a donor. After a successful transfusion, the boy lay shaking on the table next to his sister. The doctor asked, "Son, why are you shaking?" The boy replied, "Doctor, when am I gonna' die?"

What an awesome visual picture of what Jesus did for you and me. The little boy thought he had given all his blood so that his sister might live. Jesus did die for you and me. Sacrificial love is something we don't often find. It seems that most people are out to see how much they can get, not give. The premier example of sacrifice took place on Calvary 2,000 years ago as our Creator in the punished flesh, hung to die between two criminals. Be a follower who is ready to volunteer his life for the cause of Christ.

☆ ☆ ☆

Further Study: When you hear the word sacrifice what do you think about? Is it worldly or divine? Are you really willing to lay down your life for Jesus daily? What's stopping you?

CONTENTMENT

BEING CONTENT

*Not that I speak from want; for I have learned to be
content in whatever circumstance I am in.*
Philippians 4.11

* * *

I once rented a movie I thought would be a total flop. I was wrong. *Cool Runnings* was about a Jamaican bobsled team training for the Olympics (like they've got snow in Jamaica). John Candy, now deceased, played a former American gold medalist who coached this joke of a team. The team members grew to like their coach and called him the "sled-god." Later in the movie, the coach's dark history came out. In the Olympics, following his gold-medal performance, he broke the rules by weighting the U.S. sled, bringing disgrace on himself, the team and America. One of the Jamaican bobsledders couldn't quite understand why anyone who had already won a gold medal would cheat. The coach replied, "I had to win. I learned something though. If you aren't happy without a gold medal, you won't be happy with one either."

To be satisfied by who we are and what we have is a rare thing. Most of us want a bigger house, nicer car, fatter bank account, better weather, younger look, smoother talk, more satisfying relationship and more comfortable life. We get frustrated when our path is blocked by a trial or unusual circumstance that causes us to step back and see what is really important in life. You, yes you, will learn which mountains in life you must climb. You can't climb them all, so you have to prioritize. The older and grayer you get, the more you find out that what's important isn't places, circumstances or things, but faith, family and friends.

* * *

Further Study: What satisfies you best? Are you a content person? Why not? What would make you content? Is contentment a place you arrive, or an attitude between your ears?

BURNOUT

You saw with your own eyes the great trials, the miraculous signs and wonders, the mighty hand and outstretched arm, with which the Lord your God brought you out. The Lord your God will do the same to all the peoples you now fear.
Deuteronomy 7:19

☆ ☆ ☆

Watch the weather channel from around the first of July until mid-October, and you'll most likely hear about forest fires in the western United States. In 1994 dozens of fires were set by both careless campers and natural causes, scorching millions of acres and destroying forest land in approximately half of Yellowstone Park. Most folks across the nation saw this as a total disaster. However, former Yellowstone Park Superintendent, Thomas O. Hobbs, said good things come out of seemingly bad situations. He went on to explain that major fires actually benefit the park in the long run. "Burnouts" rejuvenate park land by cleansing it of insect and plant disease before the natural growth cycle starts again.

Let me draw a parallel from this disaster to the devastation in human lives. Trials and tough times come in so many different ways like: death, financial failure, disappointment and unintended heartache. As we go through trials, we may feel as if we've been dealt a bad hand. We can't imagine a loving God allowing these disasters to happen to us in light of our walk with Christ. The point we miss is that down the road of time, we will see new growth and rejuvenation. In the end, we are strengthened with a newfound faith and dependence on God. Remember that God sees not as man sees and that He is in total control of every situation, no matter how out-of-control it may seem to us. Try not to start your own fires, but when God starts one, let it do what it's intended to do . . . clean out the old and bring in the new.

☆ ☆ ☆

Further Study: Why is it so important to allow God to clean up our lives with trials? Is this process fun? How should we respond to His fires in life? How can we prepare for a burnout?

LOVING OTHERS

YOUR NEIGHBOR

Love your neighbor as yourself.
Matthew 22:39

☆ ☆ ☆

I've always wondered just exactly who my neighbor is. Does this command really mean the family that lives to my right or left? Do you find it as hard as I do to love some folks at all? They delight and distract, they demand patience, they are people of confidence and conflict, they love us then leave us, they understand then judge us. We start talking to God and pointing out to Him things like, "But God, have you ever met my neighbor?" or "Hey God, I'll tithe my 10 percent, but witness too?" Remember the old song, "They will know we are Christians by our love, by our love; yes, they'll know we are Christians by our love?" To obey this command we must look at two things. First, what does love mean, and second, who is our neighbor? I heard a quote that states "love is like a ghost few have seen but a lot talk about." Another one is "love is like a creeping vine; it withers if it has nothing to cling to."

The love God is talking about and models best is agape. In other words, a love with no strings attached, not based on conditions of performance. Secondly, our "neighbor" could be defined as the people God puts in our lives every day of our lives. Folks like gas station attendants, garbage men, short tempered drivers, teachers who fail you, police who give out speeding tickets, a locker mate, politicians, folks we just plain don't like. You must possess sensitivity and sacrifice of self to attain this command. We all know we love ourselves (a lot) and that if we actually loved others as much as we adore our own selves it would be quite the sight. Try it today and see if you don't end up feeling better about yourself and your example to an afflicted world who hates more than it loves. What an awesome impact it will be if we actually take this command and live it out in our daily lives. Go on . . . try it; you'll like it. Who knows . . . you may need to start with the person next door.

☆ ☆ ☆

Further Study: Who are your neighbors in your life? How can you actually love unconditionally? Did Jesus model this lifestyle? How? Can you? When? Today? Go for it!

ATTITUDE

ATTITUDE EQUALS ALTITUDE

Have this attitude in yourself which is also in Christ Jesus.
Philippians 2:5

☆ ☆ ☆

They say there are two types of people in our world—those who read stories and those who make stories. I happen to have the temperament of the latter, in case you haven't noticed. Well, one of my new found hobbies is riding a Harley-Davidson "soft-tail" motorcycle around the beautiful Colorado Rocky Mountains on a warm, sunny day. There is nothing quite like rounding up a bunch of riding buddies, dropping any agenda and heading for the mountains. I think one of the reasons I enjoy this new adventure is that when I'm on the back of a Harley Hog, I've got an attitude. That's right, you have never seen the likes of the "too cool for school" looks I can give passing motorists when I'm ridin' with the pack.

You hear about folks with attitudes a lot these days. Just what does it mean? Where does an attitude take you? An attitude is a position, stand, belief or state of mind. Get this one—we as Christians are to have an attitude. Frankly, this attitude should be quite different from the worldly attitude seen more often, since it is a Christ-like one. An attitude will give you altitude if it's the right kind and dig you a grave if it's the wrong kind. An attitude reflects who you are and what you believe. Ask yourself what kind of attitude you suggest to the folks you come in contact with. What influences your attitudes? Is it emotion or false feelings? Is it your environment? Do you act differently according to who you are with or are you consistent in your actions?

☆ ☆ ☆

Further Study: Get an attitude! (The Christ-like type.)

BECOMING A CHRISTIAN

A FACADE

Even so consider yourselves to be dead to sin, but alive to God in Christ Jesus.
Romans 6:11

☆ ☆ ☆

The *Washington Post* reported a story on October 27, 1993, concerning an elderly woman named Adele Gaboury. When Adele turned up missing, concerned neighbors in Worchester, Massachusetts, informed the police. A brother told the police that Adele had left to live in a nearby nursing home. Satisfied with the information, the neighbors began keeping an eye on the house and watching out for her property. Michael Crowley noticed the mail piling up in the mailbox and decided to deliver it just inside the front door of her home. Adele's next door neighbor began paying $10 a week for her grandson to mow and manage the lawn. At one point the grandson believed the pipes had burst in the house because water was flooding out under the front door. He called the utility company to come shut off the water and repair the leak. What no one knew until then was that Adele was inside the house, dead in her bed. Investigation revealed she had died from natural causes four years prior.

You see, the respectable appearance of Mrs. Gaboury's house hid the harsh reality inside. Something similar can happen to people we rub shoulders with regularly. They may appear to have it "all together" on the exterior, but their interior is dead. All kinds of religious activities may be happening on the outside while the real problem is missed. They can say all the right things, do all the right deeds, and even put up a front of being "all together," yet no Savior lives inside their heart. Investigate yourself and see where you fall into this story . . . check out your friends and see if they are dead or alive in Christ. We need life (Christ), not a tidy facade!

☆ ☆ ☆

Further Study: Where are you today? Are you alive in Jesus or dead to the world? Do you put on a facade for others just to play the Christian game or has true transformation come through a personal relationship with Christ? How about your friends?

SAVED BY GRACE

GUILTY OR NOT GUILTY

*But because of his great love for us, God, who is rich in mercy, made us
alive with Christ even when we were dead in transgressions—it
is by Christ you have been saved.*
Ephesians 2:4-5

✩ ✩ ✩

Seen by millions as a media obsession, it was impossible to flip through
the channels without finding an update of the most recent events. Society was
addicted to the case; conversations filled with speculation. Coverage of the
O.J. Simpson trial dominated nightly news and check-out line tabloids. This
case became the cultural phenomenon of the century. I got caught up in the
intensity of the interrogations as attorneys Marsha Clark and Johnny Cochran
went head-to-head, combating with literary clichés and courtroom jargon.
We all knew O.J.'s past college football stardom at USC and celebrated professional career. Who could ever convince a jury to believe that such terrible
charges could be justified against one so widely admired? In every sense of the
phrase, "the jury was still out," until the verdict was released.

The great theologian, John Calvin, wrote brilliantly about the "total
depravity of man," charging that within us all resides the capability or propen-
sity (what a big word) to commit horrible acts. Until we realize our need for
a Savior, it is difficult to get very excited about the work that Jesus accomplished on Calvary's cross 2,000 years ago. It is against the ugly, black and
despairing backdrop of our own capacity for evil that the offer of God's mar-
velous grace shines like the crown jewels. In some sense, the O.J. Simpson trial
forced us to ask deeper questions about ourselves and our own condition.
Could O.J. have done it? Maybe we asked the wrong question . . . think about
it. Without Christ anyone has the capability.

✩ ✩ ✩

Further Study: How is it that evil prevails? Who invented evil? Are you personally capable of committing evil? How do you prevent it? Is it important to
you to spend daily time with Jesus? Do you? Why or why not?

GOOD & EVIL

GOOD OR EVIL

For God knows that in the day you eat from it (wrong tree) *your eyes will be opened, and you will be like God* (bad theology), *knowing good and evil.*
Genesis 3.5

* * *

In our yuppyfied culture, you don't have to watch TV much or walk by too many newsstands to see that a spirit of lawlessness among advertisers is treading on a well-worn path of using immoral methods to sell products. In 1995, Calvin Klein tested the public to see just what they would accept through airing some advertisements that showed adolescents in sexually provocative poses. This kind of stuff is the spirit that says there should be no limits to the expression of our instinctual urge, do whatever you want with no moral absolutes or constraints. The pioneers of catchy hip phrases came up with Nike's "Just Do It," Burger King's "Sometimes you just gotta break the rules," Bacardi Black Rum's "Some people embrace the night because the rules of the day don't apply," Easy Spirit shoe's "Conforms to your foot so you don't have to conform to anything," Ralph Lauren's Safari "Living without boundaries," and Neiman Marcus' "No rules here." The moral space between law and freedom shrinks daily and what can't be enforced, it is now assumed, shouldn't be a matter of obedience or standards. This is a recipe for social disorder, because we have lost our ability in this culture to differ between the absolutes of good and evil.

It all started with a simple slither of the slimy serpent's tongue as he said to Eve, "You surely shall not die" when he talked to her about eating of the fruit from the wrong tree. The serpent's (Satan's) tactics haven't changed much and deceit and self-fulfillment still are two bullets in his gun. He deceives us into thinking we can actually be the god of our own destiny. And once we eat of deceit and lies, we pass it onto someone else like Eve did to Adam. God gave Adam and Eve instructions in verse 3:3 and He continues to do so through His Word and Spirit; all we need to do is heed the warning not to proceed with our own plans. In our fast paced society where buzz phrases and individuality supersede obedience and wisdom, you best be on your toes to not make a mistake that costs you a legacy of heartache.

* * *

Further Study: On a scale of 1 to 10, how obedient are you? How does Satan deceive you into thinking you know it all? What can you do to remain strong? Are you willing to die to self?

BEING LOST

For the Son of Man (Jesus) *has come to seek and save that which is lost.*
Luke 19:10

☆ ☆ ☆

Have you ever been lost as a little kid in a mall, grocery store or stadium, isolated from friends or family? What a terrible, traumatic experience this can be at a young age. I personally thought after the age of sixteen (the age of freedom to drive), that this fear would be forgotten . . . until Idaho.

At the age of 35 I was invited by a close friend to go on a hunting trip in Idaho on the middle fork of the Salmon River in a five million acre wilderness. The only way in and out was by horseback, and we were forever away from the nearest paved road or town with any sort of population. Animals of all shapes and sizes, some had never seen a human, existed in large numbers. There in the mountains, I somehow lost my bearings and got separated from my party with no food, water or matches to survive. I can't explain adequately with words the fear that overtook me, as I searched frantically for anyone who walked on two feet. My emotions could have been measured like the magnitude of a California earthquake. After about two hours of walking up, down and all around, I sat down and began to make some deals with God. I have never, to this day, experienced anything quite like the fear as a grown man lost and never choose to experience it again.

Do you realize how many people you pass every minute of your life who are lost in the wilderness of eternity? How hopeless one begins to feel while contemplating never being found and dying just a memory. We have been, one might say, chosen by God to be His Rescue Team for the lost souls of this world. Finding a lost, unsaved being and leading him home (salvation) is one of the most precious experiences you will ever know. Sharing the Savior of your soul to a wanderer in the wilderness is better than any rush this world could ever deliver. Do your part and find someone. Take it from me, it's great to be found.

☆ ☆ ☆

Further Study: When was the last time you shared Jesus with someone lost? Why not today?

CEREMONY OR VOWS

Therefore what God has joined together let no man separate.
Matthew 19:6

✯ ✯ ✯

We're in the age of technology and descriptive words, so we have changed a bit. Years ago if your parents got a divorce it was called "growing up in a broken home," but now in the more hip lingo we call it "coming from a dysfunctional family." Call it what you want, but six out of every 10 people who read this devotion come from a "whatever" family such as mine. I remember 20 years ago being looked at by others as some sort of pitiful freak of hard luck. Divorce today is not as harshly looked upon and, in fact, is becoming more common than weddings. I could rattle out a list of statistics that would raise the hair on your back, but I think you're all too aware of the dangers. Most of you reading this book have dreams of getting married, buying a home surrounded by a white picket fence, on a one-acre lot with a stream running through it, having a mess of children playing games on the green front lawn while you and your spouse grin from ear to ear on the front porch swing. If it only was as easy as it appears.

The minor prophet Malachi gives God's verdict on divorce . . . "I hate it" (Malachi 2:16). Many folks today think this is too rigid or harsh, but the covenant made between a man and woman must be taken with seriousness. Jesus talks of divorce in the Sermon on the Mount and echoes this opinion. Not everyone is going to be called into the bond of marriage, but if you are, realize that a marriage for life is not built on the wedding ceremony, but the vows. I personally feel there is too much emphasis placed on all the hoopla of the building, tuxedo and dress styles, catering, special singers, and get-away car, than listening to the vows repeated. Don't get me wrong now, the ceremonies aren't bad as long as they are the start of a life-long covenant to Christ and each other. Coming from a person who saw and went through the divorce of parents, do yourself and God a big favor by marrying for life or don't marry at all.

✯ ✯ ✯

Further Study: Why are we called to marry for life? What kind of witness is it to be faithful to God and your spouse? Are you willing to be different?

It's Your Duty

*Preach the word, be ready in and out of season, reprove, rebuke,
exhort with great patience and instruction.*
2 Timothy 4:2

☆ ☆ ☆

In 1992, a Los Angeles county parking control officer came upon an El Dorado Cadillac illegally parked next to the curb on street-sweeping day. The officer wrote out a ticket, ignoring the man in the driver's seat, reached inside the open window and placed the $30 citation on the dashboard. The driver made no excuse for his poor parking, no argument ensued–and with good reason. He was dead. The driver had been shot in the back of the head 12 hours before, but was sitting up, stiff as a board with blood running down his back. The officer was so preoccupied with his duties that he was unaware of anything out of the ordinary. He got back in his patrol car and drove away.

What an incredible example and lesson to us all to slow down from our fast-paced lives and take the time to share Christ with those who are dead in their sins. What should catch our attention most is their need, not their offenses. We, as Christians, get so caught up in judging others' offenses that we lose our focus and purpose. They don't need a citation, they need a Savior. Your goal as a Christian is that when you die, you take along as many souls with you as possible. Sharing Christ with someone is not an A+B=C formula . . . it's original and fueled by the Holy Spirit. An effective evangelist is sincere, obedient to the Spirit, a good listener, a question-asker and tender in approach. Granted, some are better than others, but we can all get out there and practice.

☆ ☆ ☆

Further Study: Are you so busy with your Christian duty that you lose sight of your purpose? When was the last time you shared Christ with a (spiritually) dead person? Are you scared to? Why? Go with a pastor or any older Christian one night this month and share Christ with someone.

DIE HARD

But thanks be to God that, though you used to be slaves to sin, you wholeheartedly obeyed the form of teaching to which you were entrusted.
Romans 6.17

★ ★ ★

In a small, hole-in-the-wall doughnut shop in Grand Saline, Texas, one cool, damp morning a young couple was sitting in the booth next to the cashier. Judging by his attire of Red Wing boots and Carhart overalls, the young man might have been in farming, and she was wearing a gingham dress. After finishing the glazed doughnuts, he got up to pay the bill, while she was noticed not getting up to follow him. He soon returned and stood in front of her as if reporting for duty. She reached up to put her arms around his neck as he lifted her from the booth, revealing her full-body brace. As he proudly (not shamefully) carried her through the double doors and situated her comfortably in the pick-up truck, everyone in the shop watched, mouths wide open. No one said a word until a waitress remarked, almost reverently, "He took his vows seriously."

Jumpin' Jack Flash! Now, if that story doesn't well up your tear ducts I don't know what will. You seldom see folks that committed to anything anymore. Our world breeds a species trained to bail out when the heat is turned up. There are so few committed to their jobs, faith, marriages, friendships, causes or daily disciplines. Why? Have we forgotten the meaning of commitment? To be committed is to be like a car battery that can "withstand the extremes" and still serve its purpose. Life is just not fair, and tough times will be waiting for you no matter where you live or how far you run. Inject a "stick-to-it" attitude in your life now, at a young age. You will always play in the game of life like you practice when no one is looking. Make a decision (commitment) and don't waver from it no matter how tough it gets . . . good thing Jesus did!

★ ★ ★

Further Study: Are you considered by others as being a committed person? Why or why not? What could help you to become more committed in your faith, family, friends, etc. in the future? Do it!

COMPARING YOURSELF

THERE'S NO COMPARISON

But let each one of us examine his own work, and then he will have reason for boasting in regard to himself alone, and not in regard to one another.
Galatians 6:4

✩ ✩ ✩

Consistently throughout my growing up days and even at times now, I struggle with comparing myself to others. I would compare myself athletically, anatomically, monetarily, intellectually, behaviorally and structurally. The results of this continual contrast of myself to another world were inward stress, dishonesty, discontentment, hopelessness and an overall crudy self image. I'm happy to say I'm not alone in this tornado of try-to-be's. We have a culture full of murderers, folks committing suicide, stealing and using drugs and alcohol to ease the pain of not quite ever matching up.

When I was a kid, I recall my dad telling me one very important inside secret to learning to ride a bike . . .. "Don't look to the right or left, just keep looking straight ahead." God tells Joshua the same bit of advice when he is wondering how in the heck he's gonna' lead three million people into the promised land. The apostle Paul tells us to "fix our eyes on Jesus," but not on ourselves or others.

In Antarctica the people deal with not only the harsh elements, but also wild animals. The wolf is at times a terrible problem and threat to their safety. The way they killed these animals was not to hunt and shoot them but to dip a large sharp knife in blood, stick it handle first in the snow and let the blood freeze on the sharp blade. The wolves smelled the blood, began to work themselves into a frenzy, licking the knife, therefore, cutting their own tongues to pieces while bleeding to death.

Now, I know that story is a little tough to stomach, but so are people who compare themselves into a frantic state and begin to lick on the edge of worldliness. Don't compare yourself to anyone but the Savior. Don't live a life of matching up. Don't lick yourself to death . . . it's just not worth it.

✩ ✩ ✩

Further Study: In what ways do you compare yourself? Do you ever match up? What happens when you compare to the standard of Christ?

MEN'S MARGINS

And He (Jesus) *will restore the hearts of fathers to their children, and the hearts of their children to their fathers lest I come and smite the land with a curse.*
Malachi 4:6

☆ ☆ ☆

This devotion is directed mainly towards you men and your "margins" in life, to check and see if your behavior matches your focus. Leadership is all about focus because your mind will begin to believe your behavior. In history, a king would send his people out to war to die for him. Only one king (Jesus) died for his people, and we as men are to emulate that example. Our E.G.O. (Edging God Out) tends to be a stumbling block to leading our families; temptations arise and instant gratification, recognition and power tend to trap us. We can mismanage our energy and time, which takes away from our families and gives them the leftovers of our day. Rising conflicts, stacked-up home improvement lists and feeling emotionally spent, along with a spouse and kids who seem to be withdrawing more and more, are all signals pointing to the fact that you have become a workaholic. We as leaders of the household need to realize we can't say "yes" unless we first learn to say "no" to some things. The maintenance of good "margins" can be found in that domain located between load and limits.

What is a leader anyway? A good leader of a home gets his family from "A" to "B" as a team. Leadership is influence, not a title or position. A good leader equips family members around him. Leaders who maintain a good attitude know that it leads to success. You're gonna' fail and mess up, but good leaders fail forward, not backwards. Leaders are dreamers who give vision to their families of where they're headed. They dream God-size dreams and look for ways to make them a reality. Leaders excel until the end; they do the job of raising a family until the end, and then some. Leaders maximize effort for a maximum return. Lastly, the leader of a home is a reproducer. What you are is what you'll deliver in the end; we don't attract what we aren't. You can't grow up a family beyond how well you can lead it. It's the toughest job on the planet. It is a job for those humbly willing to step out on blind faith and not fear; it is a job for those willing to fail trying. This country needs men who are willing to choose to step outside the comfort levels and model headship to a world lacking spiritual leaders of families. Step it out!

☆ ☆ ☆

Further Study: Read: Exodus 18:21, Proverbs 24:3-4, Ephesians 6:4, Deuteronomy 6:6-9, Proverbs 4:1-2. Are you, as the father/husband, capable (through Divine Help) of leading your household? Are you willing to try? Why or why not? Why did God appoint the man to be the head of the home?

ONE MINUTE PLEASE!

*I am an ambassador in chains, that in proclaiming it I
may speak boldly, as I ought to speak.*
Ephesians 6:20

☆ ☆ ☆

This Sunday was like any other Sunday afternoon for the Smith family. Everyone came through the door after church shedding their church clothes like a St. Bernard sheds hair. Dad immediately went to the EZ-Boy recliner to snatch up the newspaper and remote control and kick back to watch NFL football while Mom was putting on her apron to fix a good old fashioned home cooked lunch for the family. Big Brother went outside to try out the new jump he had made for his skateboard, and Little Sis was left with no attention at all. Mom said she didn't need any help in the kitchen, so Sis went to chat with ol' Dad during the commercials and between articles. The little girl tugged on Dad's shirt sleeve to be granted some attention and asked, "Daddy, do you think you could live like Jesus for one year?" The father folded up the paper and answered in his mega-voice, "No, honey, that is impossible to do." The little girl waited patiently until a timeout in the game, then interrupted her dad, asking, "Well then Dad, do you think you could live like Jesus for one month?" The father, a bit frustrated with the interruptions, answered in a harsh voice, "No! Now honey, you know Jesus was perfect and that we aren't. Run along and help Mom fix lunch." Upset but not defeated, the little girl walked a few feet, then abruptly turned and asked, "Okay then, do you think you could live just one minute like Jesus?" With smoke bellowing from his ears, Dad answered, "Okay, okay, okay! I guess we could live a whole minute just like Christ." To which the child replied, "Daddy, then why don't we live like Jesus one minute at a time?"

☆ ☆ ☆

Further Study: Why don't we try to live like Christ just one minute at a time? Why does our nature tell us to broadjump instead of walk? How can we seriously live like Jesus each minute, each day? How can you live today like Him? Will you give it a go?

MORTAL MADNESS

*For kings and all who are in authority, in order that we may lead
a quiet and tranquil life in all godliness and dignity.*
1 Timothy 2:2

☆ ☆ ☆

If you want to take a trip you could classify as educational, you might try "The Big Apple." You know, home of the Mets, Broadway shows, population seven million, Wall Street, subways, Statue of Liberty, 30 dollar taxi rides, Central Park, Madison Square Garden, Time Square, LaGuardia Airport, World Trade Center, Queens, Macy's, Trump Towers, Plaza Hotel (where *Home Alone* was filmed), and on and on. Never in my life have I been in a place where I felt like I had been "beamed up" on the Starship Enterprise and relocated to another planet. It's a concrete jungle of huge skyscrapers, and conversation is muffled by tourists and taxis.

A stunning thought to realize is that even in Christ's day among the multitudes, Jesus saw the benefits of mellow times in the mountains. The forethought and wisdom that flows from scripture is refreshing to apply in our modern daily lives. How important is it to you to grab moments of peacefulness and tranquillity? I'm not saying that you can't live in a big city, and that if you do, you need to pack it up and move to a farm in Iowa. My point is that the food for our soul is found in a consistent place of escape from the rush hour traffic and daily to-do lists. I chill out with our friend, Jesus. We've only got a mist of a time table to enjoy on earth, so we should do just that. Detour your daytimers to a place of stillness above all the hype and slow the aging process down. Believe you me, New York is a fun place to visit, but residing with my Creator is a spiritual homestead.

☆ ☆ ☆

Further Study: When was the last time you led a quiet life? What does it take to do this? How married to your daily schedule are you? Do you find time for God?

THE FAMILY SHRINE

Your eyes will see strange things, and your mind will utter perverse things.
Proverbs 23:33

✞ ✞ ✞

Before you read this devotional, I have a field trip I want you to take. You don't have to drive, in fact, all you need to do is walk a few feet. Take a stroll into your family room (that's the one with the TV in it) and take a look around. Okay, do you see the sofa, game table, E-Z Boy recliner, a few left-over papers and the family shrine? What's the shrine? It's the TV set–the focal point of the family room. Americans have made it a tradition to put the television smack-dab in the middle of the action. It's like TV has become some sort of god in our homes. We should bronze those things and put them in a museum of technical history for future generations to gawk over.

It scares me to think how valuable we make a box of fuses, bulbs and wires. We have cable, pay-per-view, satellite dishes and video technology as our main source of communication, education and malfunction. Whatever happened to family game nights, playing catch in the yard, going on evening walks or just talking to one another? Why have we replaced family fun with the remote control? Television is one thing that can barge into our homes and say what it wants to say without being invited or even knocking before entering. Our minds are being filled with false philosophies and twisted theology, and we sit and think, "It's not hurting me." Our lives are being molded by a foreign source, instead of God's scripture. See if there is any way you can re-arrange your furniture to make the TV as much of a centerpiece as a bath-room. Make it a household rule that if anyone or thing doesn't speak truth you set it in a corner. The TV will be the first to be punished for a foul mouth. The average person in America today spends 14 and a half years watching the tube from age five to 65. Don't waste one sixth of your life "vegging out." Make that move!

✞ ✞ ✞

Further Study: Where is the TV in your house? It is a shrine you glare at daily? What productive things could you be doing instead? Try a week without TV and see if your life isn't more productive and less ritualistic.

ANGER

DANGEROUSLY CONTAGIOUS

Do not make friends with a hot-tempered man or you may learn his ways.
Proverbs 22:24-25

� ✶ ✶

There is a story told about ex-manager of the New York Yankees, Billy Martin, and baseball legend Mickey Mantle going on a hunting trip to Texas. Mickey had a friend who allowed them to hunt on his place, but asked them to check with the foreman of the ranch first. Upon their arrival Billy waited in the truck while Mickey checked in and told the foreman they had arrived. The foreman quickly gave permission, but asked for a small favor. The foreman had a pet plow mule that was going blind, but he didn't have the heart to put it out of misery, so he asked Mickey if he would mind shooting it. When Mickey was walking back to the truck, he decided to play a joke on Billy. He acted angry with the foreman and told Billy the foreman said they couldn't hunt and to get off of the property immediately. Mickey told Billy, "I'm gonna' show him. I'll just go and shoot one of the old man's mules." Billy said, "You're kidding! You can't do that." Mickey loaded his rifle, aimed at the blind mule standing in a nearby corral and pulled the trigger. Boom! Down went the mule, dead as a door nail. Before he had a chance to look up to see Billy's reaction, he heard two more loud booms (shots fired). Billy yelled out, "We'll show that son of a gun! I just killed two of his cows . . . let's go!"

Anger can be dangerously contagious. It infects those around us whether they know the source or reason(s) for our anger. The difference in our anger and Christ's anger is that they are at opposite ends of the spectrum. Christ's anger was aimed at those who were disobedient to God's Word. Our anger usually is that of selfish desires and misconceptions. Be careful not to infect others with the virus of worldly anger. The consequences are more deadly than random gun-fire.

✶ ✶ ✶

Further Study: What ticks you off? Why is anger so destructive to relationships? How can you better take control of your anger in tense situations? How can we bridle our anger and use that energy in a more uplifting, constructive way?

A HEART FELT MESSAGE

The Spirit himself testifies with our spirit that we are God's children.
Romans 8:16

☆ ☆ ☆

In September 1993, near the close of Major League baseball season, the first-place Philadelphia Phillies were visiting the second-place Montreal Expos. In the first game of the series, the home team Expos came to bat one inning, trailing by a score of 7-4. Their first two batters reached base. The manager sent in a pinch hitter to the plate, rookie Curtis Pride, who had never gotten a hit in the major leagues. Pride warmed up, stepped up to the plate and on the very first pitch laced a double, scoring the two runners on base. The stadium thundered as 45,757 fans screamed and cheered. The Expos third base coach called time out, walked over to Pride and told him to take off his helmet. "What's wrong with my helmet?" wondered the rookie. Suddenly understanding, he tipped his cap to the fans. After the game, someone asked Pride if he could hear the cheers of the crowd. This person asking the question wasn't giving him a hard time . . . Curtis is 95% deaf. "Here," Pride said, pointing to his heart, "I could hear it here!"

Sometimes we hear things from God most strongly in our hearts. Just like Curtis Pride heard the approval of the fans, not with his ears, but down deep in his heart. It's in our own hearts that the Creator of the Universe wants us to know His approval of our faith in Christ. To walk in the spirit of Christ means to be so "in tune" with Him that we sense His urgings in our hearts. Think about it . . . our source of life is not in our minds, or ears, but in our blood-pumping hearts. The ears of our heart become deaf when sin is allowed to deafen them. Sin is a hardening agent that turns our soft, pliable, moldable hearts into granite. Realize that God is the fan who jumps, screams, yells, applauds, and whistles every time we step up to bat against this world and score a victory for His Kingdom.

☆ ☆ ☆

Further Study: Where does God speak to you? How soft is your heart? What deafens the ears to your heart? What does it mean to you to hear God's voice?

JUST BE

Be still and know that I am God.
Psalms 46:10

✶ ✶ ✶

Before refrigerators and ice boxes, people used to use windowless ice houses with thick walls and a tightly fitted door to store food. In the winter, when streams and lakes were frozen solid, large blocks of ice were cut and hauled back to the ice houses, stacked, and covered with sawdust. Most of the time the ice lasted well into summer. Once, a man lost a valuable watch while working in an icehouse. He searched for days, but to no avail. His fellow workers and neighbors looked for the watch, but came up short. A young boy heard the rumor of the lost watch and slipped into the ice house unnoticed one day and walked out an hour later with the valuable watch in his hand. Amazed by the boy's find, the others asked how he did it. He replied, "I walked in, laid down in the sawdust and listened for the ticking of the watch."

"Being still" is definitely not a common practice in society today. Appointments, meetings, deadlines and day-timers seem to crowd out any hope of finding peace in our daily routine. Often, the question is not if God is speaking to us (in our hearts, not verbally), but whether we are ever still enough to hear Him. No one gets a lot of praise or pats on the back for being still. We are a nation of doers, not sitters, but when we try to seek counsel and guidance from God in the midst of our daily rush, the world's noise overcomes His urgings. Find time each day to sneak off in a quiet corner of your house, office, school or whatever, to be with and in the presence of God. The reward will be far more valuable than any lost watch; I can guarantee that.

✶ ✶ ✶

Further Study: When was the last time you were "still" with God? Did you know communication consists of both talking and listening? What gets in the way of finding quiet time? Where could you go to be still?

COMMITMENT

STAND FOR SOMETHING

For now we really live if we stand firm in the Lord.
1 Thessalonians 3:8

☆ ☆ ☆

This is a story about a home church in the Soviet Union that received one copy of the Gospel of Luke, the only scripture most of these Christians had ever seen. They tore it into small sections and gave out the pieces to the body of believers. The plan was to memorize the portion, then on the next Lord's Day, meet and redistribute the scriptural sections. On Sunday the church-goers arrived at the house church inconspicuously, in small groups throughout the day, so as not to arouse the suspicion of KGB informers. By dusk they were all safely inside and began singing hymns quietly, but with sincere worship. Suddenly, the door flew open and in walked two soldiers with loaded guns. One soldier shouted, "All right, everybody line up against the wall. If you wish to renounce your commitment to Jesus Christ, leave now!" Two or three quickly left, then another. "This is your last chance to either stay and die or leave safely." A few more slipped out into the darkness while parents and children trembled in fear. After a few moments of silence, the other soldier closed the door, looked back at those who remained, and said, "Keep your hands up, but this time in praise to our Lord Jesus Christ, brothers and sisters. We, too, are Christians. We were sent to another house church several weeks ago to arrest a group of believers, but instead we were converted. We have learned, however, that unless people are willing to die for their faith, they cannot be trusted."

Our commitment to Christ affects every other relationship we have. The deeper our devotion and commitment to Christ, the more faithful we are to our spouse, family, church, job, friends, and people we come in contact with. Stand firm in your faith to Christ!

☆ ☆ ☆

Further Study: How important is your faith to you? Are you committed? What could cause you to flee?

DREAMS

REVELATION TO REALITY

Older men will dream dreams, and your young men will see visions.
Joel 2:28

☆ ☆ ☆

Auguste Bartholdi traveled from France to Egypt in 1856. There, the grandeur of the pyramids, the Nile and the beauty of the stately desert Sphinx aroused his artistic mind. In Egypt, he met Ferdinand de Lesseps, who was there to sell the idea of digging a canal from the Red Sea to the Mediterranean, so merchant ships would no longer have to travel around the tip of Africa. Ferdinand's concept inspired the artist Auguste to design a lighthouse for the entrance of the canal. This lighthouse wouldn't be an ordinary one; it would symbolize the light of western civilization flowing to the East. It took over 10 years to build the Suez Canal, so Auguste had time to design and build many clay models. He scrapped plan after plan until he found the right figure, the perfect design. Only one problem remained . . . who would pay for it? He searched everywhere, but no one was interested in his idea. The Suez Canal opened, but without a lighthouse. Defeated and discouraged, Auguste returned to France, 10 years of work wasted. His lighthouse would have been a colossal robed lady standing taller than a pyramid. She would hold the book of justice in one hand and in the other, a torch that would guide merchant ships to the canal. Back in France, the French Government sought a gift for America. They chose Auguste's lighthouse, which today stands in the New York harbor and is called the Statue of Liberty.

This is a wonderful account of how great dreams eventually find the right door. Who knows, maybe one of your dreams could become a reality if you just stick with it. It amazes me how God can use the ideas of His people and orchestrate a reality. You have all the ability and talent to pull off such a stunt, if you give your ideas and dreams to Him in prayers of petition.

☆ ☆ ☆

Further Study: Do you have a dream that few know? What are you doing to help those ideas become real? Have you told God through prayer about those dreams? Why not? Go do it!

Hard Work

God saw all that He had made, and it was very good.
Genesis 1:31

☆ ☆ ☆

Growing up in Dallas and working on my father's ranch in Decatur (one hour north of Dallas) presented quite a problem for maintaining sanity at both locations. Consequently, my summers were consumed with building pole barns, welding pipe fence, bucking hay bales, shoeing horses and brush-hogging three hundred acres of dry Texas coastal grass. Those events translated into what's commonly called "hard manual labor." I couldn't believe that my father would ask a budding 16-year old to sacrifice his summers at pool side for a 10 hour day in sweltering 100-degree heat. Didn't he clue in, or was he born in the dinosaur era, that my main responsibilities were to sleep until noon, eat a tropical lunch by the pool, wax my cool car, and then go to my friend's house to meet new "chicks" until curfew. Not to say that doing any of that was wrong, lazy or irresponsible; it just didn't seem to be an option with my dad.

You know, I look back now and seriously do appreciate a huge trait that was passed down to me from my father . . . a work ethic. Don't let me fool you for a minute. I still have a huge lazy streak in me, and I did spend a ton of time just chilling out and cooling out. No matter where you're from, how you've grown up, what your stature is, what your future holds in store for you or whether you're male or female, hard work is valuable and ordained by our God from the beginning of time. Yes, a key word we can't forget is balance, and few people have found it in our social system. Some are either sluggards, or they are workaholics with no balance whatsoever. The fact is that your work is valued by God and as the Word says is "very good." Work hard when it's time to work, and rest peacefully when it's time to rest. Do me a favor and don't forget to "do all your work heartily for the Lord, not for man" (Colossians 3:23). It makes all your labor not in vain.

☆ ☆ ☆

Further Study: Why is hard work so satisfying? When was the last time you slept soundly because of a hard days work? How can you work hard today?

SIN NATURE

NATURE OF THE BEAST

*Just as sin entered the world through one man and death through sin,
and in this way death came to all men because all sinned.*
ROMANS 5.12

✶ ✶ ✶

The famous cuckoo bird never builds its own nest. It searches for an unattended nest with eggs in it, lays its eggs there, then flies off. The thrush (the mother bird), whose nest has secretly been invaded, comes back, not noticing the new egg (lack of mathematical skills). What happens? Four thrushes hatch along with one large cuckoo chick, three times their size. When Mrs. Thrush brings home one large juicy worm for supper the cuckoo chick, being much larger and stronger, eats the entire meal with no leftovers for the smaller thrush chicks. The cuckoo bird gets bigger and bigger and the four thrushes get smaller and smaller. It's possible to walk along a hedgerow and find the dead thrushes a cuckoo bird has thrown out of the nest.

The apostle Paul teaches us that spiritually speaking, we've got two natures in one nest. The nature that we feed the most will grow the most and the nature we don't feed will end up starving to death. The nature that starves will diminish while the other takes charge of the nest (life). The way we feed our nature is through what we listen to, what we read and how we ultimately think. Our theology and philosophy on practical living are directly related to who we are, our character. Maturity is the consistency between who we are when we are around others and when we are not. Our constant effort to renew our minds and mold our character are tied in with divine intervention. God is, and always will be, the only source of change from a state of destruction to a place of hope. Be careful what you feed in your life and make sure it's what you want to rule your roost (life).

✶ ✶ ✶

Further Study: What nature do you feed each day? How do you feed it? Is the wrong nature growing up in your life? What practical ways can you change this feeding pattern?

In Due Time

*And let us not lose heart in doing good, for in due time we
shall reap if we do not grow weary.*
Galatians 6:9

* * *

One of many joys of being the father of three sons is coaching them on a smorgasbord of sports through the years. One of my favorites is Little League baseball in the summer time. Hundreds of games and maybe three decent umps, hot doubleheaders, finding lost balls in the creek, picking up catcher's equipment and bats are all a part of it. The stories I could tell you that would make you laugh so hard your cheeks cramp . . . once we were locked in the Dairy Queen bathroom after a post game celebration; another time I handed a protective cup to my oldest son, and he thought it was an oxygen mask; one time our third baseman fielded a grounder, picked it up and tossed it to his dad sitting in the stands . . . are they cramping yet? You get the picture by now. Being a dad and involved in the details of your kid's life is one of life's major perks.

You remember the long time cliche: "It's not quantity that counts . . . it's quality." I'll guarantee that whoever came up with that fine piece of literature has an IQ that begins with a decimal. My kids, wife and friends know I care for them because I give them a precious commodity . . . T-I-M-E. Time and land are valuable because no one is making any more of it. My kids think wrestling on the trampoline in our living room is the next best thing to a chocolate glazed donut. You can give your kids, spouse, friends, fellow workers or church money and gifts, but that doesn't cost you nor prove your commitment nearly as much as your time. Jesus gave His disciples and followers His undivided time, and that's a model for all of us to try to live up to. Invest in the Three F's: Faith, Family and Friends. Take the time out of your busy daytimers to build into others; it is your choice, and you have to make the right choice. Quality is spelled T-I-M-E!

* * *

Further Study: Look at your week's agenda and see how much time you've set aside for those who matter most in your life. How could your family spend more time together over the next month? What sort of time stealers are robbing you of your time with your family?

GOD'S WORD

KEEPING IT CLEAN

Thy word have I treasured in my heart (and mind)
that I may not sin against Thee.
Psalms 119.11

✩ ✩ ✩

A story is told of a family who lived in the deserts of Egypt. As the story begins, the family doesn't have all the modern conveniences, which we take for granted today, to make life easier. One day the father gave his young son a tightly knit reed basket and told him to go to the artesian well, about a mile away, fill up the basket with water and return home. The boy obeyed his father's request and set off across the hot desert sand in search of water. When he later returned home, to his surprise, all the water had leaked through the reeds, and all he had to show his father was an empty basket. To the son's confusion, the father instructed the boy to do the same the next day. After three trips across the hot tundra, the boy expressed frustration with his failure to deliver to his father. The father replied, "My son, the purpose was not to fetch water, but to clean the basket."

When Jesus was being tested in the wilderness by Satan himself, He used the tool of memorized scripture to fight His battles for Him. The armor of a Christian consists of only one weapon–the Word of God. The purpose of scripture memory is to purify (renew) our minds, but not necessarily to retain it. If you're like me, you may not be the most intelligent memorizer in the world. You've tried your hand at scripture memory, but two weeks later you've forgotten it completely. Yes, it is true, you won't keep what you don't use. But your labor is not in vain because as you sit down and meditate on scripture, the Word is cleaning your mind of worldly impurities. In the rough, crowded world in which we live, we must do something other than sit in a recliner with a remote control. Memorizing the Word of God is tough, but worth every second of time you invest. Start tonight with a small bite (one verse) and quote it all day to yourself, and remember the journey is as fun as the final destination.

✩ ✩ ✩

Further Study: When was the last time you memorized a verse? What is the verse you're memorizing today?

TEMPTATION

SNAKE BITE KIT

Keep watching and praying that you may not enter into temptation;
the spirit is willing but the flesh is weak.
Matthew 26:41

✷ ✷ ✷

It's not like the subject we're gonna' talk about today is new to the scene. You'll find it from the beginning in the garden of Eden to our modern world today. We didn't just recently invent this hazardous material. Archeologists didn't just dig it up. It's temptation. Have you ever noticed that we didn't have to be taught to do evil . . . it comes quite naturally? If you don't believe me, just go hang out at a kindergarten class for an hour or so and watch how little kids (even infants) will very often choose the wrong way. Things don't change too much when it comes to disobedience; they just get a little more sophisticated as we get older. Did you know the Greek meaning of the word obedient is "to listen?" Basically, we are born with a rebellious spirit sin nature, and we seem to like its style at times.

Temptation is a very serious thing, even more so than health insurance and environmental issues. scripture throughout warns us of temptation's evil venom and painfully far reaching striking distance. The big problem comes when we get into a habit of "giving in" to its lures of luxury (we think). Temptation is a bridge we cross each day of our lives when we decide between our way or God's. Temptation takes no prisoners and plays no favorites. Temptation scars our hearts, minds and hardens our conscience. In fact, we could compare this beast to a tactical unit in the military whose sole purpose is to find the weakness in the enemy's army and destroy them. Satan knows what our likes and dislikes are, and therefore, will attack us at our weak points and moments. This verse gives us ways to overcome these potholes in our path through life. First, remain alert to the enemies sly strategies; second, develop callused knees by praying often; and third, realize that if we rely on our own strength, we'll end up snake-bit in the end. Watch out . . . temptation hides in odd places and strikes at unknown times.

✷ ✷ ✷

Further Study: What temptation are you most likely to give in to? What ways do you fight the beast of temptation? If you were Satan, how would you destroy you? What does the venom of sin carry with it?

GOD'S WILL

AN END TO A MEANS

Thy will be done on Earth as it is in heaven.
Matthew 6:10

✣ ✣ ✣

How many major decisions did you make last year? Better yet, how many decisions do you make each minute of your life? Perching on the fence of decision, are issues like career moves, where to live, who to marry, what church to attend or where to go to college. We can make hasty, emotional decisions or we can let someone else make the call for us. Some demand a miraculous sign from heaven to confirm a decision, others postpone decisions indefinitely. Most decisions, I feel safe in saying, are not dictated by scripture, but brought on by pressure. Beware of making decisions based on restlessness or a desire to change. Carefully evaluate a decision that could cost you more in the long run than you can afford. Lastly, most decisions become obvious given enough time and information.

God has given us a means of guidance to help make decisions both big and small. Let's explore seven different means the Creator has supplied to help us discern His will:

The Bible (Folks read it for comfort but use *Forbes* magazine for direction.)
Prayer (It's the currency of our personal relationship with Christ.)
The Holy Spirit (He will never lead us in opposition to the Word of God.)
Our Conscience (It will be a more effective red light than a green one.)
Circumstances (Learn from them, don't analyze them.)
Counsel ("Plans fail for lack of counsel, but with many advisors they succeed." Proverbs 15:22)
Fasting (Do this occasionally, and it will amount to nothing more than priming a rusty pump; do it regularly, and it will be a gush of God's will.)

Knowing and finding the will of God for your daily life and future is not a Captain Hook buried treasure hunt. Hear this—God has a will for your life and He wants you to find it!

★ ★ ★

Further Study: Do you have a clue what God's will is for your life? How do you seek His will? How can you use this as a tool to help you in the future?

WORKING TOGETHER

HARMONIZING

The whole body, being fitted and held together by that which every joint supplies, according to the proper working of each individual part, causes growth of the body for building up of itself in love.
Ephesians 4:16

* * *

Margaret and Ruth were an elderly pair living in a convalescent center (old folks' home). They were there due to similar illnesses . . . they'd both had a stroke. The ironic thing about these two is that Ruth's stroke left the entire right side of her body paralyzed, while Margaret's stroke left the entire left side restricted. Another similarity was that both of these lovely ladies were accomplished pianists in their day. Since the strokes, they had given up hope of ever playing again. One day the director of the center encouraged Ruth and Margaret to sit down at the piano together and play separate solo pieces, each with her good hand. Not only did they develop a beautiful friendship, but they produced wonderful music. This dynamic team began performing concerts for the center and other rest homes in the community.

What a great picture of how the body of Christ is supposed to work in harmony. We have a tendency in our Christian culture to become so "individualized" that we lose vision of how Christ wants the church and parachurch organizations to work with one another. A new youth ministry comes into a community, and a lot of times the established ministries don't greet the new kid on the block with open arms and acceptance. A lot of churches compete in the numbers game and compare people not as creations of God, but as a barometer for success. Believe you me . . . real Christians sitting down, planning, talking, setting goals and performing together make wonderful music for an audience of disbelievers to see. What one member or organization cannot do alone, perhaps two or more could do together–in harmony.

* * *

Further Study: Do you ever see your church or youth group working in harmony with other churches and youth groups? Do you personally "team up" with other believers to accomplish a goal? What can you do personally to show how followers of Jesus should work together?

BEWARE OF THE BEETLE

The sting of sin is death.
1 Corinthians 15:56

▲ ▲ ▲

One of my favorite childhood memories was spending time with my dad on our ranch in Decatur, Texas. He trained horses for racing, so as you might imagine, the work was hard, and the days were long. My recreation was hunting bullfrogs on a tank (in Texas that's what we call a pond) with a 22 caliber rifle. One day I was walking along the shore looking for those beady eyes and saw a small, green, tree frog halfway in the water's edge. He didn't jump as I got closer, and I noticed how dumbstruck and dull his eyes were. As I watched, he slowly began to deflate and sag. His skin emptied and drooped, and even his little skull began to collapse like a falling tent. The frog sank as an oily fluid circled his body. I remembered reading about a water bug, an enormous brown beetle that eats tadpoles, insects and frogs. Its legs grip and hook inward as it seizes its victim and paralyzes it with enzymes. It only takes one bite to release a poison that literally dissolves the prey's muscles, bones and organs (all but the skin). It sucks out the victim's body, reducing it to a juice (gross, isn't it?).

Sin is like this giant water bug, in that hidden sin paralyzes our inner spirit and constricts our heart. It can suck the joy right out of us and leave us dead in the water. Sin is weird that way; it shows no favorites and attacks without mercy. Only God can rescue us from sin's deadly grip through confession and sincere repentance. Even though this story puts an unsettling pit in the stomach, it is not nearly as repulsive as a believer shrinking down to nothing. Don't swim in waters (circumstances) that tend to nurture giant water beetles (deceptive sin) as permanent inhabitants. Be aware!

☆ ☆ ☆

Further Study: Has sin ever gotten a grip on you? Did it begin to suck the life and hope right out of you? What do you do about such a vicious killer? How can you avoid getting caught in its grip?

GOALS

Don't Look Now

Be strong and very courageous. Be careful to obey all the laws my servant Moses gave you; don't look to the right or left so you may be successful in all you do.
Joshua 1:7

☆ ☆ ☆

If you would like to know a highlight of my life, it was teaching and watching my son learn to ride a bike for the first time. You remember . . . Don't look down, sit up tall, pedal fast, lean into turns, watch for trees and don't scream when you fall. Most parents hold the back of the seat when they are teaching (I held the back of my son's neck) the balance process. I must have run 10 miles chasing behind the little man, in fear of the first wipe-out. I remembered one thing my dad told me that helped, and I echoed it to my boy, "Don't look to the right or left, keep your eyes forward at all times." The purpose of those words of wisdom was to prevent a face plant in the pavement.

After Moses' death at the banks of the flooded River Jordan where a pupil named Joshua was to take over leading about three million whiny Israelites to freedom, you'll find a gold nugget that applies today. Joshua receives a formula from God Himself, the Father of Freedom. God tells Josh (we'll call him that for short . . . best friends we are) to be strong and courageous, knowing he had it in him, and not to be scared. Why not? Josh wasn't exactly an expert in piloting people to the land God had promised was theirs to take. He tells Josh to be obedient to the instructions (which happen to be the Ten Commandments), and then comes the one-two punch . . . don't look to the right or left so you will be successful wherever you go and whatever you do. I wonder if that advice came from my dad? (Kidding!) To put it in our loose-lipped lingo, God is telling him to focus on the goal and go for it. Be like a sprinter who stares at the finish tape, not the boy in the grandstands selling popcorn. Who knows, this advice could come in handy for you someday.

☆ ☆ ☆

Further Study: How important is it that you focus in on your goal? What distracts you to your right or left? How can you prevent it?

SHARING CHRIST

A KNOCK-OUT!

When the kindness of God our Savior and His love for mankind appeared, he saved us, not because of righteous things we had done, but because of his mercy.
Titus 3:4-5

☆ ☆ ☆

It was one of those days when the fast lane got even faster. I drove up and parked in the lot of T.J. Rusk Inner-City Middle School in Dallas, Texas, waiting on my mom, who teaches there. Obviously, school had just ended because the yellow limos (school buses) were parading past to deliver kids to their homes. I was pondering what life in middle school was like when I noticed two boys about 13-years-old just being boys, kinda' mock (slap) fighting. You know what I'm talking about . . . releasing that excess educational energy that builds up throughout a day sitting behind a desk. It seemed to be two friends sparring until the jabs became punches, and the punches became down-right slugs, and I realized (I'm slow) I had a brawl on my hands. I jumped out of the car and ran to stop this main event. No one else seemed to care, but I for one, was not gonna' be an idle spectator to this foolishness. After a few close calls from stray punches, I settled the two boys down and began to sort through this madness.

After the blank stares, swollen knuckles and winded breathing calmed, we got down to the source of the swings–nothing! That's right ladies and gentlemen, absolutely no reason for the fight except a big, fat . . . "because." They were best friends, neighbors and get this–relatives. Why? (Let me ask one more time.) Why? What is happening to our world? This incident, in a few years, could end up in a stabbing or shooting. I'll tell you my thinking . . . we are a society on the edge of insanity, missing the key ingredient of godly love–love for your neighbor, brother, sister, parents, friends. We as Christians have no choice but to show (notice I didn't say tell) this fallen world about Christ's love. Just continue to keep this little secret to ourselves (believers) and see how insane this planet will become . . . unbearable. Jump into the ring, throw a few love punches yourself and knock 'em out in an early round for Jesus . . . ding! ding!

☆ ☆ ☆

Further Study: How do you tell others of Jesus' love? Do you at all? Why or why not? How can you train yourself to do this? Will you?

THINKING FEAST

Let the peace of Christ rule in your hearts, to which you were
called in one body and be thankful.
Colossians 3:15

☆ ☆ ☆

One of the least used phrases in the English language is "thank you." As the father of three bone-headed boys, I can personally testify that they would much rather say things like "no" and "mine."

The Masai tribe in West Africa has a very unusual way of saying thank you. Translators tell us that when the Masai express thanks, they bow, put their forehead on the ground, and essentially say, "My head is in the dirt." When members of another African tribe want to express their gratitude and appreciation, they sit for a long time in front of the hut of the person who did them a favor and literally say, "I sit on the ground before you."

These Africans demonstrate well the meaning of true thanksgiving. At the core is a sincere act of humility and grace. Even Jesus must have been disappointed when He healed the 10 lepers of their skin disease and only one returned to say thank you. Why is it so difficult to utter those two simple words to our parents, friends, God and anyone who deserves them? Being gracious and courteous requires maturity and wisdom. Why do we need a holiday each year to remind us to be thankful? Humble yourself today, go to those who have sacrificed for you and give them the greatest gift . . . a thank you. Look them in the eye, give them a sincere hug (no handshakes) and humbly say thank you for all they've done for you. Be like the one leper who treasured his gift and returned his appreciation.

☆ ☆ ☆

Further Study: When was the last time you said thank you? Why is it so hard? Do you have an attitude of humility when you say thank you? Make it a point today to say thank you at least 20 times to your teachers, parents, coaches, friends and gas station attendants. When you pray tonight thank God.

MATURITY

THE MILKY WAY

I gave you milk to drink, not solid food, for you were not yet able to receive it.
1 Corinthians 3:2

⋆ ⋆ ⋆

It won't be until the day you have your first child that you will truly understand. You'll find out, in the world of resources, that there is still a lot you'll learn through experience about having a baby. Never did or could I imagine what a joyful "job" it is to maintain a kid. I mean these bubbly bouncing balls of baby blubber are an adventure to experience. Basically, all they do in their first six months of existence is eat, sleep, poo-poo and cry all the time. Every now and then you can uncross their baby blue eyes and get a goo-goo-ga-ga accompanied with a cock-eyed grin, but life stays pretty routine for the most part. The only food they consume in their early months is milk. You know, the stuff like the Wonder Bread commercial says "builds strong bodies 12 ways." No vegetables (yuk), no chocolate sundaes, no T-bone steaks, no double cheeseburgers with fries, not even a pepperoni pizza (what a drag) . . . just milk!

In this excerpt of scripture the apostle Paul is speaking after his visit and through his first letter to the church in Corinth. What he is saying, in layman's terms, is that there are folks who are baby believers who are not yet ready for tougher scripture steaks. There is nothing wrong with that–just as it would be foolish to try to force feed meat to a little newborn right out of the incubator. Some people who are new to the faith and family of God should be allowed the right of "growing up in Christ" just as they grew up into an adult. Don't choke new Christians on information or doctrine that they just can't digest yet. Don't force them to deal at the same level as someone who has been a believer for five years. Give them, (they deserve it), the right to mature at God's pace, not your pace. Believe you me, feeding too much is as bad as not feeding enough, and who knows . . . you'll probably end up getting it burped back at you. Remember, also, that babies grow at different rates.

⋆ ⋆ ⋆

Further Study: What sort of spiritual supplements should you feed a new Christian? How important is it that you allow them to grow up at God's pace? Do you feed the wrong food to baby believers? What happened?

WORRY WARTS

Be anxious (worry) *for nothing, but in everything by prayer and supplication with thanksgiving let your requests be made known to God.*
Philippians 4:6

☆ ☆ ☆

What do people worry most about?

> People (family and friends)
> Things (material goods)
> Future (job, relationships, spouse)
> Appearance (physical looks)
> Image (view others have of you)
> Death (life after)
> Pain (physical or emotional)

Boy, if there is one area we all deal with on a daily basis, it's worry. It seems as though this creature rears its ugly head at every opportunity. We all desire a life of comfort and security (just look at how well insurance companies do), yet we live in a world of people and change. The older we get the deeper and taller the problems seem to get. How in the world are we to fight this monster and win a few battles? Once again the Bible seems to come up with yet another simple solution.

The apostle Paul, a man who had a lot to worry about, tells us that the key to this buried treasure lies in prayer. We are not to worry about "anything" (yes, it means what it says), but our thoughts are to be thankful that we have a God above who cares about us down to the smallest details of daily life (Matthew 6:25-27).

Let's face it, if our lives were all comfortable and unchanging, we would not only be bored stiff, but we wouldn't have any use for a Savior. When you face the monster of worry, punch him with prayer.

☆ ☆ ☆

Further Study: What really worries you today? How are you going to deal with it?

COMMITMENT

SOLD OUT

And as they were going along the road, someone said to Him,
"I will follow you wherever you go."
Luke 9:57

✫ ✫ ✫

What an awesome, bowed-up statement this is. Very few people would take a mouthful of commitment like that and say it. The multitudes today would at best only follow at a distance and when the heat was turned up, run for the hills. To Jesus, being committed means a 100 percent sold out, lock and load, willing to die definition. Our society will jump on the bandwagon for a cause like animal rights, gay rights, historical rights, minority rights, but not for Jesus' rights. Webster defines commitment as a pledge or promise to do something for some person, place or thing. Other religions like Jehovah's Witness, Mormon, Buddhism, Islam, and New Age are, for the most part, more committed to their cause than we are our own. You know, when you get right down to the brass tacks of it, to be committed you have to believe whole heartedly first.

What are Christians honestly to be committed to? Five things:

1. Committed to the word of God (2 Timothy 3:16-17)
2. Committed to God's will, not ours (Ephesians 2:8-10)
3. Committed to be obedient to the demand of Christian life
   (2 Timothy 2:4-8)
4. Committed to the total cost (2 Timothy 1:8)
5. Committed to making disciples (2 Timothy 2:2)

You won't be an effective follower of Jesus if you become disobedient and take your eyes off Him. The developing stages toward obedience are: don't care, me first then you, Jesus first then He will surely give back to me, and lastly, true obedience is give no matter what is in store for me. Satisfaction like you've never experienced before will surface after you commit your life totally to your Savior. All these movements we stand for in our culture are great, but they can't hold a candle to the cause of Christ. Make a movement for the Master today!

✫ ✫ ✫

Further Study: Define what commitment means to you. What are you most committed to today? What hinders you to becoming totally committed to Christ?

YOUR BODY

EARTH SUITS

Do you not know that your body is a temple of the Holy Spirit who is in you,
whom you have from God, and that you are not your own?
1 Corinthians 6:19

✳ ✳ ✳

Today's devotion is a subject that we all live with and yet can't seem to ever be satisfied with. What subject might that be? Your ol' bod. Only today, we will classify and rename this concentrated mass of skin and bones as an Earth Suit. Do you realize the amount of money spent on marketing and advertising products designed with the sole purpose to better that bag of bones? Hours sweated upon hours are spent daily, running, walking, lifting, playing, biking, rowing, skiing, swimming, climbing and dying in our society each day. Don't read me wrong and think for a minute that I don't condone these frolicking physical activities, because I do. What happens in our society is a philosophy of thinking that if "something is worth doing, it's worth over-doing." The challenge is to stay trim and fit for the righteous reasons, and not the worldly whims. The issue is not one of priorities, but one of perspective. In a social atmosphere which puts emphasis on the outward lookers, over the inward beauties, we need to beware. Our value order needs to first be to develop those God fashioned, inward character qualities and then begin to focus on the outward temple.

Years ago I asked a 72-year-old man, who exercised religiously five days a week his entire life and looked to be the picture of a physical specimen, how he could stay so consistent in his training. His answer was simple, yet truthful, "I don't want Jesus to live in a run down house." Wow! How true that we are where Jesus resides and calls home. How those simple words can give us a proper perspective and purpose for keeping fit and trim, rather than our motive being to look like a model on the cover of a magazine, or to have muscles to bulge out at the ladies. If you're already working out, stay with it. If not, get after it . . . but do it for the right reasons. Now go on, lift those weights, climb those stairs, swim those laps, run those miles, bike those trails, play those sports and Just Do It for Jesus.

✳ ✳ ✳

Further Study: Do you see your body as a dwelling place of your Savior? How can you maintain a balanced life? Why should you start today to remodel your home (body)?

DISCIPLESHIP

GUILT BY ASSOCIATION

Now Peter was standing and warming himself. They said to him, "You are not also one of His (Jesus) *disciples, are you?" and he denied it and said, "I am not."*
John 18:25

☆ ☆ ☆

Good old Peter is back in the headlines for this devotion. I think I enjoy learning more about the apostle Peter than any one of the other disciples because he reminds me of me. You could call him, "Mr. Peppermint Socks" because he always has his foot in his mouth. At the time of this event, Judas betrayed Jesus for 50 bucks, and Jesus was brought before Annas, the priest of that year. Jesus was questioned by the high priest, and an officer gave him a shot in the ribs (sucker punch) for His supposedly poor presentation. A slave girl saw Peter standing around the fire with some guards at the temple and asked him if he wasn't one of those associated with this Jesus. Peter, wanting to protect himself, quickly shunned the comment. When the cock crowed after his third denial, Peter recalled Jesus' prophecy (prediction). Jesus went before Pilate, ultimately to the crucifixion.

I don't imagine Peter (a loyal follower) planned to deny ever knowing Jesus. I think Peter had a great heart of courage, but at that moment things were getting heated. Guilt by association still happens today if our lifestyle reflects a relationship with Christ. An association is a group of people with a common goal, purpose or belief. In our world we have all sorts of associations barking out their beliefs and surrendering to the group cause. What an honor it is to be found guilty of following Christ. If you're ever gonna' be found guilty of anything, make sure it's of following Jesus too closely.

☆ ☆ ☆

Further Study: With what would your friends consider you to be associated? Have you ever been associated and found guilty of being a Christian? Why or why not?

SIN

SIN'S DEADLY GRIP

Each one is tempted when he is carried away and enticed by his own lust.
James 1:14

☆ ☆ ☆

There's a story about Niagara Falls on a spring day a few years back. Ice from the hard winter months was breaking up and rushing down the river and over the falls in huge chunks. A closer look revealed carcasses of dead fish embedded in the frozen chunks of ice. Hoards of gulls rode on these blocks, pecking away to get to the frozen entree (fish). Just about the time the block of ice (and the gull) were about to take a tumble, the bird would fly away and escape death. On one occasion, a particular gull was engrossed in eating the carcass of a fish, enjoying every bite. When the brink of the falls appeared, out went the wings. The bird flapped and struggled and even lifted the ice block out of the water, but it was too late . . . its claws had frozen into the ice. The size and weight of the ice was too great, and as the block went over the falls, so did the bird, plunging to its death.

The finest attractions of the world become deadly when we are overly attached to them. They may take us to our destruction if we can't give them up. Oh, the danger of delay! Our society has a way of offering something attractive in order to misdirect us in our relationship with Christ. Time is definitely of the essence here, and we don't know what fall awaits us around the next corner. Whether it's social status, position, appearance, money, power or relationships, if it takes your focus and energy off the pursuit of holiness, then it's wrong. No matter how well you think you can ride the illusion . . . you're not strong enough to escape the weight of worldliness.

☆ ☆ ☆

Further Study: What does this world offer you that you'd like to sink your claws in? Are you aware of the dangers that lurk ahead?

A FIRM FOUNDATION

*And everyone who hears these words of mine, and doesn't act on them, will be
like a foolish man, who built his house on sand, and the rains came
and so did the floods and the winds blew and burst against
that house and it fell and great was its fall.*
Matthew 7:26-27

✩ ✩ ✩

It's amazing what realtors in our country will try to use as a selling point
for a house. They parade around and point out all the features of a home, but
seldom include the basement or structure of the foundation. Drive around any
big city and you'll see gorgeous homes with beautiful yards, three-car garages,
hi-tech appliances and all the bells and whistles. If the most awesome looking
home in the country has a cracked foundation, it will be a heap of rubble in
the long haul. Important questions the buyer needs to ask have nothing to do
with colors, square footage or floor plans. Pertinent questions need to deal
first with the thickness of the foundation walls or slab, if re-bar was used and
what the foundation sits on (sand or base rock).

We as Christians build our foundation (lives) on one of these two sub-
stances . . . sand or rock. The strong rains of trials and gusty winds of uncertainty will come, and if your life isn't firmly founded on God's truth (the rock),
you will collapse. Church pews are filled, youth rallies are packed, families are
functioning with folks who seem on the outside to have it "all together," yet
when the tough times hit, they fall with a bang. Don't be one who builds his
life on shifting sand that can't hold its ground through the thunderstorms of
life. Trials will be a part of your life whether you're ready or not . . . here they
come. Here is a little side note too . . . you can't lay a foundation (pour concrete) when it's raining–it's too late.

✩ ✩ ✩

Further Study: What is your foundation (life) built on? What will happen when
the rains and wind beat you down? Will you fall or stand firm? How can you
strengthen your foundation today? Get to work!

TICKLISH EARS

For the time will come when they will not endure sound doctrine, but wanting to have their ears tickled, they will accumulate for themselves teachers in accordance to their own desires.
2 Timothy 1:3

✫ ✫ ✫

It was a Saturday night, and like most Americans who have a VCR, I decided to rent a movie and settle in by the fire for an entertaining evening at home. Our favorite movies are the clean but funny type, which are rare releases in the video stores today. This picture met all expectations and even ended with a good ethical ending. One line in the movie from the lead actor really started my wheels in motion. Even though it wasn't intended to be a biblical truth, it sure came off as such. He was telling a beautiful young actress a truth that is a sad reality. It went like this; " . . . tell anyone what they want to hear and you can sell them anything." Wow! Was that a one, two punch off the silver screen script, or what? Read it again because it's worth its weight in gold. How true it is on this earth that people can be easily deceived when they are told exactly what they want to hear, not what they need to hear.

Hanging around our population of pedestrians, one continually sees the dangerous effects of having our ears "tickled" with the untruths of worldliness. These lies are found in locker rooms, corporate headquarters, classrooms, in the papers, amidst the media and even in some so-called churches. Isn't it funny (really sad though) that the apostle Paul warns a young man whom he tabs as one with a kindred spirit, that days will come of such nonsense? Just read the Bible at face value, and you'll notice that God doesn't mince words or pull punches. When He taught, He spoke the truth amongst those who had been told a lie. Realize those two funnels of flesh (ears) that hang on the sides of your head can't be opened and closed at will. You have to dictate by your location what goes in and out. You have to clue in that those ears are a direct line to your mind, which is the feeder to your livelihood, your heart. Be careful who and what you listen to. Don't be sold a lie in exchange for your soul.

✫ ✫ ✫

Further Study: What tickles your ears? How can you regulate what goes in your mind? What has the world lied about to you today?

SELF IMAGE

SCAR FACE

There is therefore no condemnation for those who are in Christ Jesus.
Romans 8:1

✩ ✩ ✩

If you've ever seen the move *Man Without A Face* staring Mel Gibson, you know you left with an empty pit in your stomach at its conclusion. The setting of this movie takes place on the upper northeast coast with a dys-functional family on summer vacation. The son (about 12 years old) has a desire to go to a military boarding school, but has been programmed by his family that he's not smart enough to pass the test to get in. The boy stumbles across a man (Mel Gibson) who has been burned badly over half his body who the locals call "hamburger face." This man, come to find out by the boy, is a previous teacher (now an artist) who ends up tutoring the boy for the entrance test. The small community isn't aware the boy has become such a loyal friend and is seeing the "man without a face" regularly. Well, to make a long story longer, one evening after going on a hike, while driving back the boy looks over at the man's badly scared face and says, "You know, I can't even see your scars anymore."

Isn't it great that we (scar faces all) have a friend in Jesus who looks past all our faults to love us unconditionally? Isn't it reassuring to know that we live with a Creator who continues to tutor us and care for our daily needs? You see, God is not real hung up on all this cosmetic community we dwell in as much as seeing our hearts with a need to know Jesus. You are so lucky (me too!) to be accompanied every second of our lives by a Spirit who will never leave or ditch us for something or someone better. Next time you feel sorry for someone for the way he/she was born or looks like (deformities and all), realize this, we all are like that, yet through grace we were made special and unique. Next time you feel like "Ol' Hamburger Face" realize God is in the business of making outcasts into works of art.

✩ ✩ ✩

Further Study: How often do you judge people pass or fail? Does God treat you like you treat others? How can you change your ways today?

SAME OL' SAME OL'

Jesus Christ is the same yesterday and today and forever.
Hebrews 13:8

☆ ☆ ☆

Have you ever woke with what I call "the same ol' blues?" You know what I'm talking about . . . when you wake up to that same ol' alarm clock, walk into the same ol' bathroom, look into that same ol' mirror, see that same ol' rack-head, use that same ol' toothbrush, look into that same ol' closet at those same ol' tired, out of style clothes, crack your shins on that same ol' table on your way to that same ol' kitchen to eat that same ol' cereal in that same ol' bowl and head off to that same ol' school to do that same ol' study stuff, come home to do that same ol' homework, go to sleep in that same ol' bed just to wake up and do that same ol' thing again the next day! (Okay, it's over.)

We are geared in this age to want change, the newest, coolest ways and things. I mean, come on, you buy a new outfit, pair of Nikes, computer or car, and in a matter of days it's outdated and obsolete. It's tough to keep up the ol' image and even tougher on the pocketbook to keep up with styles. There is a boat we are missing on this trip of life called traditions, anchors, dependability and assurance. What if God decided to change His ways midstream? What if the Ten Commandments changed as often as shoe styles? What if Jesus decided to return to earth in a flash telling us the "heaven deal" is off? We have a great deal of hope knowing (not wondering) that Jesus and His standards never have, nor ever will change. Jesus Christ is exactly the same today as 2,000 years ago, and will be the same in another 2,000 years (if we last that long). Take refuge in this incredibly stable thought in the midst of very turbulent worldly waves. Sometimes the same ol' same ol' ain't half bad.

☆ ☆ ☆

Further Study: How would you feel if Jesus changed His ways weekly? Isn't it comforting to know beyond a shadow of a doubt that your Savior is a tradition? Are you happy now? Why?

GOD'S LOVE

OUR GOD IS AN AWESOME GOD

*Then he said, "I am the God of your father, the God of Abraham, the God
of Isaac, and the God of Jacob." At this, Moses hid his face,
because he was afraid to look at God*
Exodus 3:6

* * *

You know the true spiritual giants who exist today are those few who
at some time become realistically conscious of the real presence of God and
maintain that consciousness throughout their daily lives. A sincere Christian
experience must always include a genuine encounter with the Creator.
Without this, a personal relationship is a mere reflection of reality and a cheap
copy of the original. This is when the "visible image of the invisible God"
(Colossians 1:15) appears to be a religious ritual instead of an intimate relationship.

Your encounter could be that of terror like Abraham's "thick and dreadful darkness" (Genesis 15:12), or as when Moses had to hide his face because
he was afraid. Usually this fear will turn to awe and level off at a reverent sense
of closeness. We know those saints of past weren't perfect, but they walked in
conscious communion with the real presence of God. When they prayed,
they did so as if they were speaking to someone who actually existed. The
essential point is, these were men who experienced God.

I know you're probably wondering if I am a few bricks shy of a full load.
When I refer to an "experience with God," I am referring to those times when
it's just you and God working through a situation. It's like those times when
you've obtained a real peace surpassing all worldly understanding, which tells
you to go on a mission trip for spring break instead of hanging with your
friends in Florida. Catch my drift? To actually walk into the omnipresent, holy
quarters of God is an awesome experience. To drop to your knees at bedtime
and pray for a miracle or wisdom is awesome. To step out on faith in an area
like finances, marriage or career, and lean totally on divine intervention is
awesome. Face it . . . God is awesome in the truest sense of the word.

* * *

Further Study: When was the last time you experienced God? In what ways
have you ever experienced the presence of God? Were you afraid?

POVERTY STRICKEN

He raises the poor from the dust and lifts the needy from the ash heap; he seats them with princes and has them inherit a throne of honor.
2 Samuel 2:8

☆ ☆ ☆

It was definitely a sight like I had never seen before. "Box City" is a whole community of poverty stricken people living in cardboard boxes for shelter beneath the mix master of overpasses and interchanges just east of downtown Dallas. We're talking hundreds of families (moms, dads, kids, grandpas, etc.), assembled in rows like a trailer park, just trying to make it until the next day. Their occupations are beggars, trash diggers, can collectors, robbers and thieves. Upon my visit, I was welcomed with open arms like a king at a banquet. This was definitely one scene in reality I won't soon forget.

Realize it or not, we are all poor in one way or another. Those who think that money is the measure of success suffer from a poverty of imagination and intellect. Some suffer a poverty of love, security, emotional stability, self-image and self-value.

The Bible makes very clear the fact that the most alarming sort of poverty is spiritual. This type of poverty affects every race, class, nationality, age and sex. The remedy for this sickness is offered by God through His Son Jesus on the Cross. Each of us show what we sincerely love by happily devoting our attention to it. Go ahead, take a look around you and see if you don't see poverty in plenty. Don't look just at those in rags living in cardboard boxes. Look also at those in fancy cars, sporting fashionable clothes and talking on cellular phones. Poverty comes in all shapes and sizes and sometimes dresses in "camo" in order to not draw attention to itself (but in reality, those who are stricken are in big time need).

☆ ☆ ☆

Further Study: When you think of poverty what do you imagine? Do you see poverty in your school, home or community? How do we help those who can't help themselves?

WHOLE LOT OF SHAKIN' GOIN' ON

*You are the salt of the earth; but if the salt has become tasteless, how will it
be made salty again? It's good for nothing except to be thrown
out and trampled under foot by men*
Matthew 5:13

✳ ✳ ✳

You may have been called a lot of things before (some too afflicted to
mention) but how about this one . . . salt? Jesus is telling you that you alone
are the salt of the earth. Have you ever thought about what salt is used for?
Besides seasoning, two other uses come to mind: First as a preservative, and
second, to create thirst. Now, those are the most obvious reasons, but what's
this about becoming tasteless? Have you ever tasted tasteless salt before? To
have tasteless salt, you must first remove the key ingredient which is sodium
(for all you inquiring minds that want to know). In ancient times the people
would mix salt and a bitter substance called gypsum to create a putty type
material which was used for patching roofs and walls in Middle East homes.
Whether you've been there or just seen in on the nightly news, you've noticed
the homes in the Far East all have flat roofs. These homes were designed that
way to double as a roof and as a patio for entertaining guests at parties. When
a hole was punched through on the roof (floor), it would be patched with the
salt/gypsum putty and hence "trampled under the foot of men." The salt lost
its taste because it was mixed with bitterness and lost its original purpose, so
it couldn't be made salty again.

You live as salt, someone who prevents the decay of society and creates
a thirst for Christ, and if you mix with the bitter ritual and lifestyles of our civilization, you will become tasteless. You alone can help prohibit the decay in
our families, schools, and among friends by shakin' a little salt on 'em. You can
lead someone to Jesus by stimulating a thirst derived from the different
lifestyle you lead. Don't forget that salt isn't worth much unless it's out of its
shaker. Your church, youth group or clique of Christian friends isn't as valuable unless you go into our lost world and let them taste. As the saying goes,
"you can lead a horse (a non-Christian) to water, but you can't make him
drink (from the living water of Christ)," but you can if you put salt in his oats.

✳ ✳ ✳

Further Study: Who do you salt daily? Do you take the initiative? How can you
prevent decay in our world today?

OLD SELF

Knowing this fact, that our old self was crucified with Christ so that our body of sin might be done away with and that we should no longer be slaves to sin.
Romans 6:6

✫ ✫ ✫

A few years ago a precious godly lady came up to me one hot summer day and gave me a gold nugget of wisdom. We had been talking of our mutual struggles to keep ourselves above reproach, yet how tough it was to not slip back in our old ways. I was sharing how even though I had been crucified with Christ, I was amazed that the reappearing of my old self was far too frequent. She reminded me that we as Christians were crucified, along with our old nature with Christ, but that in the days of the Roman deaths that the crucifixion that Jesus went through was the slowest form of death a person could go through. Death on the cross was not meant to be quick and simple. It was intended to be long-lasting and grueling.

Just as the apostle Paul writes, the old self has been put to death on the cross of Calvary with Christ, but it's also a daily ordeal, too. Yes, we as followers do only accept Christ in our hearts sincerely one time, yet we have to continually remember where we came from (sin nature). Our old, sinful, selfish self needs a good kick in the pants everyday in which we breath. We're always gonna' make mistakes, which is why we are saved by grace, not works. Our goal is not to be perfect, just pressin' on everyday of our lives to try to think, walk, talk and act like our role model Jesus. Don't try to work on your weak areas from the outside in, but the inside (heart) out. Transformation is not a snap of the finger, wiggle of the nose, wave of the magic wand occurrence . . . it's a process. Realize that daily God gives you pop quizzes in your faith to let you see what areas you need to work on in His class. Set your sights high and make your expectations attainable, and you will be on your way to a fulfilled life. Go for it!

✫ ✫ ✫

Further Study: What areas of your life do you see your old nature rear its evil head? How do you handle it? How can you handle it better next time?

MATURITY

GROWING UP

*Speaking the truth in love, we are to grow up in all aspects
into Him, who is the head, even Christ.*
Ephesians 4:15

✩ ✩ ✩

In his book, *First Things First,* author Roger Merrill tells of a business consultant who decided to landscape the grounds around his home. He hired an extremely knowledgeable woman with a doctorate in horticulture. Because he was very busy and traveled a lot, the business consultant emphasized again and again the need to create a garden that would require little or no maintenance on his part. He insisted on automatic sprinklers and other labor-saving devices. Finally, the horticulturist stopped him and said, "There's one thing you need to deal with before you go any further. If there's no gardener, there's no garden!"

Gang, there are no labor-saving devices for growing a garden of spiritual virtue. Becoming a person who produces spiritual fruit requires time, attention, and daily care. I am amazed at the number of long-standing Christians still nursing on the spiritual bottle, instead of maturing on spiritual meat. This immaturity is directly related to the lack of time invested in growth habits such as daily time in scripture study, prayer, and learning to share faith through discipleship or evangelism. Great athletes don't just wake up one day as superstars . . . it takes years of consistent practice. The old saying that "practice makes perfect" is incomplete . . . perfect practice makes perfect. Practice for spiritual growth in the game of life just as diligently as you would for an athletic or scholastic competition. You will not become mature until you see the value and importance of consistent practice and nurturing of your faith. Tend to your garden of faith every day, planting, weeding, watering and harvesting. Otherwise don't be puzzled when you look up in a few years to see a withered, wilted, worthless harvest of spiritual fruit in your life.

✩ ✩ ✩

Further Study: How mature are you in your relationship with Christ? Do you tend to your spiritual garden daily or do you lean toward labor-saving devices to do it for you? What steps can you take to cultivate your maturity? List them out as goals and give them to a friend to hold you accountable.

THAT'S UNREAL

For I am mindful of the sincere faith within you.
2 Timothy 1:5

☆ ☆ ☆

"Unreal!" This exclamation is sometimes used to punctuate a certain event in history, a sports spectacle or even a monumental task. When something is described as unreal, it may then be compared to something that is real. Reality is a term used widely today to describe a fact, a definite situation, the here and now. To be unreal, the situation is, therefore, placed out-of-reach, as in a mirage or an illusion. What am I blabbering about? Take this thought and put it in the bank. There are far too many supposed followers of Christ who aren't concentrating on the marching orders foretold in the Bible. Our lost culture needs to see a "realness" in our faith and a touchable God. A relationship with Christ is not a group commitment . . . it's personal. Not so personal that we keep it to ourselves and never share it with anyone else, but real. I believe that by our own lifestyle we paint the picture of one of two things . . . either a God who created all that exists, or an "unreal" untouchable God who only shows up in pictures on the Sunday school bulletin boards. Abba Father must be real in our lives and a reality in our hearts. God is not some fairy tale fable that only existed in the long-ago. Yes, God is hard to imagine when it comes to things like creating an entire universe or making the dead live again. He did come in a real earthsuit to live, breath, sweat, cry, bleed, laugh, avoid temptation, suffer pain and die like a criminal. But, but, but . . . He rose in 72 hours to become reality in our hearts and save us from eternal torment in hell—if we choose to believe. God only becomes "unreal" when we don't get real with Him.

☆ ☆ ☆

Further Study: How real is God to you? When does He seem to be unreal? If your friends were to determine if God is real or unreal in your life, what would they say?

THE CHARACTER OF JESUS

A POINT OF REFERENCE

Fixing our eyes on Jesus the author and perfector of our faith.
Hebrews 12:2

✯ ✯ ✯

Several years ago when the University of Colorado began its reign as a football dynasty, an interesting ritual involving the quarterback began. The starting quarterback this particular season had been a back-up for the previous few seasons to an all-conference quarterback. The relationship of the two was competitive, yet friendly. The graduating senior had done a great job of modeling just what a winning quarterback looked like and how one played. What the young quarterback didn't know was that his hero had cancer and would be watching the games from the pressbox this season. As the younger quarterback excelled along with the team during the season, he began a tradition. Every time he scored a touchdown he would abruptly look up at the pressbox and point his finger, as if to say, "that one was for you, bro." What an awesome sight to see a guy dedicate his entire season and what ended up being an illustrious career to his teammate/coach.

Whether we like football or not, we all go through life making victories. Some folks seem to be a human highlight film of successes. We all, whether we admit it or not, have a hero or mentor to whom we dedicate not our season, but our lives. The question I have for you is, who do you point at? When you score, make a grade, get an honor, land a great job, find the mate of your dreams, get promoted, or whatever, who do you give the credit to? Who do you try to impress or live up to daily? We all have a reason to point at something. We all have a "thing" we point at up on a pedestal. We all want to do something for someone. Who is it in your life? Put God up in the pressbox of your playing fields. Make Jesus your hero and your teammate/coach because He is. Allow your glory moments to matter for God and not for someone who you may never live up to. Hey, and after you get in the habit of scoring big for God and giving Him the ol' point . . . turn around and spike it for the Savior. Yeah!

✯ ✯ ✯

Further Study: Who do you point at after you score in life? Who gets all your glory moments? How can Jesus be seen in the pressbox of your life? Will you allow Him to receive it?

BUILDING TO SPECS

*For I know the plans I have for you, declares the Lord. Plans for welfare
and not for calamity, to give you a future and a hope.*
Jeremiah 29:11

☆ ☆ ☆

One of the craziest things a person can be involved in is the designing
and building of his/her dream home. It doesn't matter how big it is or how
many bedrooms and baths it has; what matters is that it's the nest to which
he/she flies home. I've built two homes in my life, been a part of designing a
custom (never built before) home, and have actually chosen a contractor to
carry out the plans put to a drafting table to produce a set of blueprints. I have
helped from the beginning of the bulldozer knocking down trees, to the foundation of concrete load, to the framing, electrical, plumbing, drywalling, roof-
ing, all the way to the carpet laying. The number of details and hours of labor
are incredible. Looking back when vision is 20-20, I realize that the contractor plays a pivotal role in the final product . . . a house. It is so key that the
builder knows how to read the plans and follows them to the detail of details.

Plans are funny things we attempt to live by daily. We make lots of them
but seldom follow through with them. We schedule ourselves to death but
rarely get the chance to fulfill our plans because of variables. It's nice to know
that God, our Contractor, follows through with the plans He laid out on His
drafting table at the beginning of time. What would it be like to have a God
who just made up our blueprints along the way with no grasp of the future
structure? Plans on paper are to give vision for the future product. What if we
had a God who let menial things and variables disturb His building in our
lives? Our ways of building aren't necessarily His ways, nor our plans, His
plans.

Take it from experience, when the final feature is presented, it's worth all
the work and wait. Give God your plans (your heart and future) then just
stand back and watch the Creator build you into the person He originally
designed you to be. One last thing, you must have faith that He knows what
He's doing. Remember, He's an expert in His field.

☆ ☆ ☆

Further Study: In what ways do you feel nervous about your future? How
strong is your faith in your Builder?

THE CHARACTER OF JESUS

What Would Jesus Do?

Whatever is true, honorable, right, pure, lovely, is of good repute, if there is any excellence and if anything is worthy of praise, let your mind dwell on these things.
Proverbs 4:8

☆ ☆ ☆

Do you remember the children's song . . . "Be careful little eyes what you see, be careful little ears what you hear, be careful little legs where you go . . . for the Father up above is looking down in love, so be careful little eyes, or ears, or legs . . . " Is it possible that we could ever be too old for this song? Well, we may not sing it on a regular basis; however, the truths are still true.

It is sad how we have become slowly desensitized to what our eyes and ears have seen and heard. Someone once said that the Christian's standards are just five years behind the rest of the world . . . so eventually we will have the world's same standards. That is so scary!

What can we do to be in this world but not of this world? That is a question we need to ask the Lord every day in each and every circumstance and with every person. We need to put on God's eyes, ears, mouth and legs at all times. There is, and will be, a battle as we begin this journey to be like Jesus. Although we know it is impossible to be just like Jesus on earth, it is certainly worth our every effort.

So even if this song is a children's song, we may need to have a child's heart and remind our eyes, ears and mind to "dwell on the things that are honorable." This may mean making a Jesus decision and walking out of a movie, not going with a particular friend, or not talking about someone. One very valuable way to be in the world and not of the world is to always ask yourself . . . "What would Jesus do?"

☆ ☆ ☆

Further Study: What have your eyes and ears seen and/or heard? How do you think you have been desensitized to the world? Does God have particular standards He wants us to follow regarding movies, friends, etc.?

SPIRITUAL GROWTH

BUD BUSTER

And he will be like a tree firmly planted by streams of water, which yields its fruit in its season and its leaf does not wither, and whatever he does, he prospers.
Psalms 1:3

✵ ✵ ✵

Don't get the idea that I'm some kind of botanist (dude who studies plants). In fact, I made a whopping "D" in that class in college. I would like to share with you a little mind tickler on plant growth. Let's say that Joe Citrus Farmer wants to increase the productivity of certain fruit-bearing plants, so he does just the opposite of what you'd expect. During the season as the plant begins to bud, Joe C. cuts off each and every bud (the bud is the area of the plant that produces fruit) from every limb. Now, as brainless as that may sound, it allows the plant to take all the energy and nutrients needed to produce good fruit, and send them to the root system to strengthen and provide growth to that vital area. We all know that for any tree, plant or shrub, the most important area is the root system (kinda' like the heart of a human body).

Now, watch me pull a rabbit out of the hat and try to tie this example into a life-practical analogy. Visualize God, our Father, as the farmer on a large fruit-producing plantation, with you and me as the citrus crop. He has to do some bud snipping in order for us (His children) to become fruit bearers to this unfruitful world. Yes, the snipping process hurts like heck, but it's all for a specific purpose. Our foundation (roots) will be deepened and strengthened to survive the long, hard, cold winter months (our life on earth), so that in our time to produce, the crop will be plentiful. Get it? God wants us to show off our juicy fruit to a world of sour grapes. Snip, snip!

✵ ✵ ✵

Further Study: Why is it so important for us to produce healthy fruit for God? What slows down your growth? What is fruit used for today? Are you producing fat or anemic fruit? Are you willing to be snipped so you can grow deeper roots?

COMMITMENT

NEVER SAY DIE

*Let us not become weary in doing good, for at the proper time
we will reap a harvest if we don't give up.*
Galatians 6:9

☆ ☆ ☆

It was tagged as being one of the most powerful messages ever spoken to an audience and yet only took two seconds to deliver and consisted of only four words. Winston Churchill was the giver during the war, and Great Britain was the receiver. It went something like this, "Never, never, never quit." The End. Wow . . . what a masterpiece, right? I mean, come on, how long did it take him to memorize this? I wonder who wrote his speeches, a second grader? It may have been simple, but like my old coach use to say, "K.I.S.S. Keep It Simple, Stupid." The message might have been short, but it communicated a much needed point. Locker rooms nationwide are full of one-liner quotes like "to quit is to lose" or "quitters never win and winners never quit."

You know people are so conditioned to "get out" if the heat (pressure) gets too tough that we bale out of marriages, relationships, jobs, school, practice and projects. It is consoling to know that Jesus didn't take on a quitter's mentality and give up on the cross. Tons of reading are available on the start of a process, but not on the middle or finish of one. To maintain a steady pace throughout the course is a tough row to hoe. You've got to have a Jesus mind set and God's heart to successfully complete the project. What we need in our communities, families and occupations today are those few and far between breeds of believers who dare the odds to win at all cost. Be one of those endangered species and see what a difference you'll make for the furthering of the Kingdom. Quitting is like a comfortable bed . . . easy to get into and hard to get out of.

☆ ☆ ☆

Further Study: What situations arise in your life that cause you to want to give up? Are you developing a bad habit of quitting? How can you not become a consistent quitter?

MOTIVATION

MIXED MOTIVES

Is your eye evil because I am generous? The first shall be last and last shall be first.
Matthew 20: 15-16

✩ ✩ ✩

The parable of the laborers was a response to Peter's question, "Behold, we have forsaken all and followed Thee. What shall we have therefore?" (Matthew 19:27) What Peter said in modern lingo was, "What's in this thing for me?" Jesus answered him in this parable, with a more than kind rebuke, that he had his focus wrong. Only the very first bunch of workers in the parable had a set contract. They all got just what they had bargained for, yet they were the ones also still unsatisfied. The other workers not under contract were grateful with the foreman's generosity. Jesus wanted followers who asked for no reward and whose concern and motive were not for their own personal gain. In other words, the greater rewards are for those who ask for only the opportunity to work in His vineyard. The parable really teaches that service to Christ will be faithfully rewarded and that faithfulness to one's opportunities will be rewarded. The amount will depend more on motive and availability than ambition and activity.

This familiar scene of a vineyard was used by Jesus to teach His disciples an important spiritual principle. We can apply this in our lives today as we examine those "hidden" motives as we do God's work. You can create a mega ministry, start a church, lead a Bible study, pray and fast all day, yet the question God seeks to be answered is . . . "Are your motives pure?" Why do you do what you do, when you do it? Is it for unselfish reasons, or are there strings of personal gain attached? The foreman in this parable accused the men of having an "evil eye," a Jewish expression for a greedy and covetous spirit (Deuteronomy 15:9/Proverbs 28:22). You can't just purify your thoughts and motives once a year and think one blanket prayer will take care of it. You must daily check and recheck your motives to weed out any hidden agendas for why you do what you do under the Christian banner. Don't stop doing . . . just do through the Spirit of Christ.

✩ ✩ ✩

Further Study: Why did Jesus address impure motives of the heart in this parable? What is a hidden agenda or wrong motive? How can we make sure what we do is done in a pure spirit without an "evil eye?"

PEER PRESSURE

CROWD BARRIERS

He was trying to see who Jesus was, and he was unable because of the crowd, for he was small in stature. He climbed up in a sycamore tree in order to see Him.
Luke 19:4-5

✳ ✳ ✳

This is a great story and a window for learning more about what's needed to follow Christ. This particular story is about a rich, little tax-gatherer who one day woke up to the sounds of multitudes and went to see what all the commotion was about. Zaccheus had evidently heard of Jesus, yet hearing wasn't necessarily believing. Old Zack (we'll call him that for short because I get tired of writing out his whole name) was no different from the "groupies" that migrate from town to city following rock bands, superstar athletes, or Hollywood heroes. Zack wanted to catch a glimpse of this man who some claimed to be God and others claimed to be a pest. No matter what the papers and tabloids were saying, he just had to get a "look-see" for himself. The only problem with the pursuit of his dream was that there were too many people in his way. Now, I don't know if he was a bonafide pigmy, or just shorter than average, but a ground-floor view just wasn't cuttin' it. So, creative genius that he was, he reverted back to his childhood days and scaled the nearest sycamore tree for a bird's-eye view of the man from Nazareth.

The lesson today, students, deals with barriers. That's right . . . those walls of worldliness that seem to park it right in front of our view of the Savior. It seems to my recollection that often the barrier comes in the form of people. People, secular and Christian, can step right in your way to block your path for following Jesus. People of any shape, form, height or religion can blockade you from a relationship with Christ. Do whatever it takes to see Jesus daily (climb a tree) and continue your growth process. I'd imagine from Zack's perspective, it's a view worth fighting for.

✳ ✳ ✳

Further Study: What barriers come between you and Christ? How do you get around, over or under them? How much sacrifice do you go through to see the Savior? Are you willing to be different and climb a few trees?

REPRODUCTION

*Go therefore and make disciples of all nations, baptizing them in the
name of the Father, Son and the Holy Spirit.*
Matthew 28:19

☆ ☆ ☆

If you've been so fortunate to have taken this class, you're educated, and
if not, you will be. It teaches you about "the birds and bees," you know . . .
those special features males and females have in order to reproduce another
person. You blush, squirm, duck your head, bug your eyes and feel more than
a bit uncomfortable, but you learn. You learn the miracle of life that takes
place when a female and male have a physical relationship and presto, a bam-
bino. It is amazing how the child grows up and genetically and habitually take
on the appearance and mannerisms of their parents . . . a "clone," you might
say.

As Christians we are told (not asked) to reproduce (spiritually, not physically) our own type–that type looks like Christ, not us–and make disciples.
First, you must be a follower before you can reproduce, an important process
we must continue or our species will become extinct. Here are seven things
that it takes to reproduce a disciple:

Able to walk your talk (model it).
Able to teach the basic truths of the Bible.
Able to communicate basic skills of life.
Able to teach basic ministry skills.
Able to confront in love when needed.
Able to impart the vision to your disciple to go and disciple
someone else (reproduce).
Able to stick with it despite disappointment and slow learning.

You see, the authority on electricity is not an electrician, but an eel. Why?
Because an electrician studies and learns about electricity, but never touches
it. An eel is made of it, so it's his source of being. As Christians, we need to
not only study about Christ, but allow Him to become the source of energy
that enables us to function every day. Find someone to disciple (pour your life
into) so that they in turn can do the same for another to reproduce our type
in a lost world.

☆ ☆ ☆

Further Study: Are you a disciple? Explain. Are you teaching discipleship to
someone else? Why not? Who can you disciple?

PRIDE

BEFORE THE FALL

Pride goes before destruction and a haughty spirit before stumbling.
Proverbs 16:18

✶ ✶ ✶

Jose Cubero, one of Spain's most brilliant matadors said, "Pali, this bull has killed me," before he lost consciousness and died. This spectacular matador was only 21 years old and was enjoying an illustrious career as one of Spain's all-time greatests. It was in a 1985 bullfight, in a sold-out arena, that Jose made a tragic mistake. He thrust his sword a final time into an exhausted, delirious bull, which then collapsed to the applause of the crowd. Thinking the struggle was over, Jose turned to the crowd to acknowledge the applause. The bull, however, was not dead, and rose to its feet and lunged a final time at the unsuspecting matador. The bull's horn pierced the matador in the back, puncturing his heart. The final scene, much to the crowd's disbelief, was a bull and bullfighter lying dead on the arena floor.

Pride entered the scene long ago in the Garden of Eden. Pride is when we choose to play god and determine our own selfish ways. Pride in any form is a disease that kills humility. As Christians, we are called to live a quiet, humble, prideless life. We are shown throughout the life of Christ and His three years of ministry, that pride has no place in the Kingdom. Pride does precede a fall for one striving to live in holiness. Pride consists of arrogance, boastfulness, cockiness, flattery, show and down-right selfishness. Don't let pride jump up out of it's deceit, and take you down to defeat. Pride can kill a friendship, family, and your faith if you don't kill it first. Finish it off in your life once and for all, but never turn your back on it. Olé!

★ ★ ★

Further Study: What is your definition of pride? Is your definition of humility the opposite? Are you a possessor of pride in your life?

UPHILL BATTLES

Anxiety in the heart of a man weighs it down, but a good word makes it glad.
Proverbs 12:25

☆ ☆ ☆

On my way to a speaking engagement in Grand Junction, Colorado, I was driving uphill (or upmountain) along Interstate 70 through the heart of the Rocky Mountains. I came upon a long freight train headed the same direction, but at a slower speed. I noticed the train was being pushed uphill by two giant diesel locomotives that sounded like they were straining at full power. Now, I'm from the great country (I mean state) of Texas, so as a flatlander I wondered if this was how trains and cargo were moved through the mountains. After a few more miles I caught up to the front of the train and there I found five more diesel locomotives pulling the train as well–seven engines in all. Where I come from there's never more than three or four engines on any one train.

That incident was a great visual lesson for me. I'd had several rough months and was under a lot of strain. I was feeling tired and about ready to give it all up to go make "hacky-sacks" in the West Andes Mountains or some weird thing like that. I wondered if I could persevere under all this pressure without blowing a fuse along my journey. Then, a divine thought hit me (like a train). When I am pushing a large load of problems and difficulties uphill with all the strength and stamina I can muster, God is in the lead, pulling with power far greater than mine. Now, if that thought doesn't get your motors going at full steam ahead and give you hope to overcome difficulties, then I don't know what will.

☆ ☆ ☆

Further Study: How do you handle uphill battles? How do you deal with the times you feel like giving up? How can this illustration relate to you in your life?

BUILDING CODES

Persecuted, but not forsaken, struck down, but not destroyed.
2 Corinthians 4:9

✰ ✰ ✰

A TV camera crew for the local news was assigned to report on the widespread destruction of Hurricane Andrew in southern Florida. In one scene, amid devastation and debris, only one house stood on its foundation. The owner of the house was cleaning up the yard when a reporter approached. "Sir, why is your house the only one still standing? How did you manage to escape the severe damage of the hurricane?" asked the reporter. "I built this house myself," the man replied. "I also built it according to the Florida state code. When the code called for two-by-six roof trusses, I used two-by-six roof trusses. I was told if the house was built according to code it could withstand a hurricane. I did, and it did. I suppose no one else around here followed the code."

You know, when the sun is shining and the skies are blue, building our lives on something other than the guidelines in God's Word can be a temptation. What we must remember in light of pleasant circumstances is that there is a hurricane coming–for everyone. The hurricane will strike suddenly and without warning. It may come in the form of death, persecution, suffering or trial. The funny thing about hurricanes is that they show absolutely no favorites. Trials are a lot like that, you know–no favoritism. Build your life on God's precepts and instruction. God laid out a building code back when codes weren't in style. When a hurricane is about to hit, there is a lot of comfort (not panic) in knowing that your life is built on the truth of God

✰ ✰ ✰

Further Study: Name three building codes God spells out in His word for you. When did the last hurricane (trial) hit your home (life)? Were you left standing or devastated? How often do you study God's codes? Daily?

INTENSIVE CARE

A fiend loves at all times.
Proverbs 17:17

✧ ✧ ✧

If you've ever been in a hospital to see someone in an intensive care unit, you'll appreciate this thought. The ICU waiting room is different from any place on our planet. The people who are waiting are different, too. They can't do enough as they care for one another as servants. No one is selfish, rude, loud or presumptuous. The distinction of race or social standards melt away like Popscicles on hot pavement. Everyone seems to pull for everyone else despite their differences. Vanity and pretense vanish. Minds and ears are focused on the doctor's next report. Everyone in the waiting room knows that loving someone else is what life and dreams are made of. Long before we are in an intensive care waiting room, we should learn to love each other like our lives depend on it.

Why does it take a death or an extreme situation in our lives to make us show (and maybe even tell) some loved one that we really care about them? Life is too short and definitely too unpredictable to be walking around with the false belief that we have a lifetime to build on a valuable relationship. Jesus had three short years to mentor, love, disciple and challenge His chosen 12. He took His relationships seriously as He worked hard at developing their spiritual lives on a minute-by-minute scale. People, not programs, are what make this world of chaos we live in go 'round. Begin to practice your intensive care for those few you call friends or loved ones. Only one minute separates time from eternity . . . don't be late.

✧ ✧ ✧

Further Study: How are you on building relationships? Do you work on them or let them work on you? Who do you know today that could use a little intensive care? Give them a visit or call!

CHRISTMAS

REAL MEANING OF CHRISTMAS

Where is He who has been born King of the Jews? For we saw His
star in the east, and have come to worship Him.
Matthew 2:2

✫ ✫ ✫

Only in California would you find this. San Jose's city fathers ordered the traditional crèche (nativity scene) removed from the annual Christmas display in the park, citing "sensitivity to the city's non-Christian population." Just a few weeks before this decision, though, they approved spending $500,000 for a huge concrete statue honoring Quetzalcoatl–the ancient Aztec snake god. Now, help me out here . . . is that art? Anyway, the city elders finally woke up and clued in, partly due to 200,000 protesters who flooded city hall and allowed the nativity to be re-instated temporarily, but the snake god is there to stay . . . a tribute to mankind's afflicted ways of handling conflict, and a triumph of multi-culturalism. Interestingly enough, the federal district court ruled that the snake god was permissible because nobody worships it anymore. A figure of the baby Jesus in the nativity scene was removed because He is still worshiped.

It happened 2,000 years ago, continues today, and will forgo tomorrow, when folks try to rid Jesus from the meaning of Christmas. We do it today when our holiday traditions consist only of gift buying, opening and exchanging. Remove Jesus from the nativity scene and you have a gathering of bigwigs in a stable starring at an empty feed trough, without hope. Jesus brings to the scene joy, hope and a future that's better than the present. Next time you celebrate Christmas, have a total blast tearing into the presents, hanging lights, decorating the tree, singing carols, visiting with relatives and stuffing your face, but don't forget the "reason for the season." I'll give you a clue . . . it ain't an Aztec snake god!

✫ ✫ ✫

Further Study: What does Christmas mean to you? What do you look forward to during this festive season? Is Jesus a part of your traditions? What can you do to make Him a centerpiece in your nativity (life)?

CHRISTIAN RACE

Participant Or Spectator

Do you not know that those who run in a race all run, but only one
receives the prize? Run in such a way that you might win.
1 Corinthians 9:24

☆ ☆ ☆

Several years ago, I decided (I must have fallen on my head) that I would begin to train for a 10K road race. Boy, did I get sick of pounding the pavement like a parade of polar bears day in and day out. I trained about three months, running my longest times on the weekends to prepare for this event. I made a phone call to a buddy in Dallas and asked him to sign me up in one of those races I'd seen on ESPN with the live band at the finish line, free T-shirts, food and lots of enthusiastic bystanders to cheer me on. Little did I know, until I arrived at the race site early one Saturday morning, that I had enlisted in a Pro-Am cross-country championship being held in the area. Six point two miles up and down, over and through obstacles, against a stacked field of 50 of the top runners in the world (some four-minute milers). Now, it didn't take me long (my wife helped clue me in) to see that this would be a rough first outing. When I finally finished, the awards ceremony was over, the band didn't exist, and I had come in 52nd place (a dog beat me, too).

I learned a valuable lesson that I won't soon forget. First of all, never trust a friend to sign you up in a road race, and second, no matter where you race or how tough it is, the finish line is still worth going for. As believers in Christ, we all need to be focused on the hope of heaven at the end of this Christian race. Many are entering the race, but not enough are participating and running to their fullest potential. By the time the race has started, the participants have changed clothes and are now spectators. Be a righteous runner for God, having faith that there is a finish line in heaven.

Everyone can run a 100-yard dash with no training whatsoever (it may take a calendar year), yet we are called to run a marathon which requires daily training in the Word. Don't be afraid to enter. God takes care of the details; all He calls you to do is run. On your mark, get set . . . go!

☆ ☆ ☆

Further Study: Are you a spectator or a participant? What motivates you to run?

DISTRACTIONS

No soldier in active service entangles himself in the affairs of everyday life.
2 Timothy 2:4

☆ ☆ ☆

The popular story of Robin Hood is the basis for several recent feature films. In one scene in *Robin Hood, Prince of Thieves*, Robin challenged a young man taking aim at an archery target, "Can you shoot amid distractions?" Just before the boy released the arrow, Robin poked his ear with the sharp bristled feathers on the end of an arrow. The act startled the boy, and his shot went high by several feet. After the laughter died down, Maid Marion (a beautiful lady) asked Robin, "Can you?" Robin Hood raised his bow and took aim, his eyes focused intently on the bull's eye. Just as he released the arrow, Maid Marion leaned over and blew into his ear. The arrow missed the target, bounced off the tree behind it and almost hit an innocent bystander.

Distractions come in all types, but whether painful or pleasant, the result is always the same: We miss God's mark. As devout followers of Christ we must be so deliberate and intense in our focus that neither big nor small distractions detour our purpose. The apostle Paul conveys a military message to his good buddy Timothy about not using the affairs of daily life as a focal point. He tells him that a real member of the "God Squad" will stick with his marching orders. Missing the mark due to a distraction is embarrassing for you and others who are watching . . . just ask the man of Sherwood Forest.

☆ ☆ ☆

Further Study: What is your biggest distraction in following God? When does it usually happen? Is there a pattern you can steer clear of? How can you keep focused on God better?

BRAIN BRANDER

We are taking every thought captive to the obedience of Christ.
2 Corinthians 10:5

☆ ☆ ☆

On top of growing up in Texas, I grew up on a ranch, so I thought I'd seen just about everything. It was the spring of 1971 on Callaway's 2,000-acre working cattle ranch. If my memory serves me correctly (which is questionable), I recall about 30 pick-ups, the same number of horse-trailers and 40 some-odd cowboys all geared up, ready to rope them doggies. The cattle herd numbered around 2,500, and our job was to sort 'em, cut 'em, rope 'em and brand 'em. I did all right, holding my own at the age of twelve, until I smelled the rankest smell I'd ever sniffed . . . skin burning. Now, I'm no genius, but I knew it wasn't some truck seat on fire. My dad tried to explain to me that branding cattle was essential to identify each cow by owner. I'll bet my boots that red-hot metal branding iron with "C Bar W" on it hurt like a big dog. Now, for all you compassionate people, we had a vet on site who administered an ointment that helped cut the pain.

Now that I am an adult (another questionable comment), I look back on this episode in my life, and the thought hits me that we as Christians should be branded (marked). Now hear me—not physically, but mentally. Brand your brain by taking all your thoughts captive (like ropin' a cow to brand it) in obedience to Christ. Every time we crack the "Good Book," we should walk away with a lasting mental brand. Let God put His mark that identifies you to a specific owner (Christ) on you (remember . . . He bought you with a price on the cross). Round up your thoughts daily, rope them down and put your mark of righteousness on them. Go on cowpokes and rope them doggies.

☆ ☆ ☆

Further Study: How do you take a thought captive? Why is it important for thoughts to be filtered by God's Word? What thought do you have that needs to be branded?

DEATH

STING OF DEATH

Knowing that Christ, having been raised from the dead, is never to die again; death no longer is master over Him.
Romans 6:9

* * *

If you've heard this story before, forgive me for stuttering . . . if you haven't, yippee! This is a neat story about a father and son driving down a country road on their way to the county fair. It was a spring afternoon, so the windows were down and the '50s music rockin'. All of a sudden, a bumblebee flew into the car window. The little boy, who was allergic to bee stings, was scared to death. His father quickly reached out, grabbed the bee, squeezed it in his hand and then released it. The boy grew frantic as the bee buzzed about him. The father once again reached out his hand, but this time he pointed to his palm. There, stuck in his skin, was the stinger of the bee. "Do you see this? You don't need to be afraid anymore, I've taken the sting for you."

Who knows if this is a true story or not; that's beside the point. The point is this: We needn't fear anymore if Jesus lives inside our hearts. Christ died and rose again to take the sting of death for us. We, as Christians, don't have to be afraid of what we learn from the newspaper or the 10 o'clock news. We shouldn't fear the staggering stats on automobile accident fatalities, AIDS or drive-by shootings because we shall experience no sting of death. Why? Because God loves us and will always be with us. The sting has been covered by the sympathy of the Savior.

* * *

Further Study: Are you fearful of death? Why? Isn't it cool that we should have no fear? What does perfect (Christ-like) love get rid of? Are you convinced that Satan's stinger has been disarmed by Christ?

THE STEALTH BOMBER

The thief comes to kill and destroy, but I have come that you might
have life, and have it more abundantly.
John 10:10

☆ ☆ ☆

I don't think we will ever forget the night we heard, broadcast live by President Bush, that we had launched our first air-strike and started our ground troops in motion in the war called Desert Storm. One could hardly even watch a commercial or listen to a song on the radio entirely without an interrupting update on the war. I recall the unleashing and mystical use of a new age of technology assault plane called the Stealth Bomber. It had advance components, flew at great speeds undetectable by enemy radar, carried big bombs and looked like a black bat out of some video game. Its purpose was to be able to steal into enemy territory unobserved, surprise attack and return to its base without a peep. Maybe a better name could have been the "Deceiving Destructor."

Realize it or not, we as Christians are in a spiritual war every day of our waking lives. We, too, are being confronted with an enemy who is unseen and unpredictable by the naked eye. Our enemy attacks not to take survivors, but shoots to kill and destroy, taking no prisoners. How real do you think Satan is? How much time do you take each day to prepare yourself to do battle with the dark side of life? The Stealth is no different than the fallen angel, yet we continue to let down our guard and go into battle unprepared to win. Yes, we have won the war at the cross on Calvary with a single soldier, Jesus, yet a constant battle for our hearts and minds is being fought. Don't be deceived by the silence or the lack of visual evidence, because the enemy lurks in the darkness. Believe you me, when he attacks, only the faithful find freedom. Stand firm, put on your armor daily, and realize you have all the weapons you need to stay standing . . . His promise in His word.

☆ ☆ ☆

Further Study: When was the last time you had a sneak attack catch you off guard? How can you prepare to prevent another one? How sweet is a victory in Christ?

DISCIPLESHIP

THE GREAT OMISSION

Peter began to say to Jesus, "Behold, we have left everything and followed you."
Mark 10:28

☆ ☆ ☆

When Jesus walked among humankind, there was a certain simplicity to being a disciple. What it meant was to go with Him in an attitude of study, obedience and imitation. There were no "correspondence courses" when it came to being a disciple of Christ. The disciples had to be with Him to learn how He did it. The word "disciple" is used 269 times in the New Testament, while the word "Christian" is only used three times and was introduced to refer specifically to the disciples. The New Testament is a book about disciples, by disciples, and for disciples of Christ.

The problem seems to lie in our view of what discipleship is all about. We make a big deal about an endangered species like the large eastern sea turtle, yet what about "undiscipled disciples?" Our contemporary churches feel like we have substituted the Great Commission to read, "Make converts to a particular denomination, and baptize them into church membership." This is more the Great Omission than the Great Commission. Non-discipleship costs you things like abiding peace, a life infected with love, faith that sees as God sees, hope that stands tall in the midst of life's storms and power to do what is right in the face of pressure. It costs you exactly that abundance of life Jesus said he came to bring (John 10:10). It's only fitting to point out that one can't be a disciple of Christ without giving up all those "things" normally pursued in this life. To disciple (mentor) someone else you must first know what it means to count the cost and be a disciple. Give it up for God, then give it to someone else . . . true discipleship is "planting trees (investing into a life) that you'll never sit under for shade" (no hidden agendas or motives). The cost is great . . . but the reward is greater!

☆ ☆ ☆

Further Study: What does it mean to disciple someone? Read Matthew 28:19 and discuss what it means to you. Why is the cost of being a disciple of Christ so high?

RESOURCES

The following list is not intended to be exhaustive. There are many other excellent resources available through churches, ministries, and bookstores.

MARRIAGE

Books

Communication: Key to Your Marriage, H. Norman Wright (Gospel Light).

Dr. Rosberg's Do-It-Yourself Relationship Mender, Gary Rosberg (Focus on the Family).

52 Dates for You and Your Mate, Dave and Claudia Arp (Thomas Nelson).

The Five Love Languages. How to Express Heartfelt Commitment to Your Mate, Gary Chapman (Moody Press).

400 Creative Ways to Say "I Love You," Alice Chapin (Tyndale).

Getting Away to Get It Together, Bill and Carolyn Wellons (Wellons).

Growing a Healthy Marriage, Mike Yorkey (Focus on the Family).

Holding on to Romance, H. Norman Wright (Gospel Light).

Husbands Who Won't Lead and Wives Who Won't Follow, James Walker (Bethany).

If Two Shall Agree, Carey Moore and Pamela Roswell Moore (Baker Book House).

Intended for Pleasure, Ed Wheat, M.D., and Gaye Wheat (Baker).

Intimate Allies, Dan B. Allender and Tremper Longman III (Tyndale).

Love for a Lifetime, James Dobson (Word).

Love Life for Every Married Couple, Ed Wheat, M.D., and Gloria Okes Perkins (Zondervan).

Moments Together for Couples, Dennis and Barbara Rainey (Regal Books).

The New Building Your Mate's Self-Esteem, Dennis and Barbara Rainey (Thomas Nelson).

The Questions Book for Marriage Intimacy, Dennis and Barbara Rainey (FamilyLife).

Rocking the Roles, Robert Lewis and William Hendricks (NavPress).

Staying Close, Dennis Rainey (Word).

Tightening the Knot, Susan Yates and Allison Yates Gaskins (NavPress).

The Triumphant Marriage, Neil Clark Warren (Focus on the Family).

RESOURCES

Audio

"Building Your Mate's Self-Esteem," Dennis and Barbara Rainey (FamilyLife).
"Creating a More Romantic Marriage," Dennis and Barbara Rainey (FamilyLife).
"FamilyLife Marriage Conference," Various Speakers (FamilyLife).
"2=1: Why God Created Marriage," Dennis Rainey (FamilyLife).

Video

"Raising the Standard in Our Marriages," Various Speakers (PromiseKeepers).

FAMILY/PARENTING

Books

Different Children, Different Needs, Charles Boyd (Questar).
Discipline Them, Love Them, Betty N. Chase (David C. Cook).
Do I Have To? Patricia H. Sprinkle (Zondervan).
Drug-Proof Your Kids, Stephen Arterburn and Jim Burns (Gospel Light).
The Duties of Parents, J.C. Ryle (Gospel Mission).
God's Design for Sex Series:
> *The Story of Me,* Book 1, Stan and Brenna Jones and Carolyn Nystrom (NavPress).
> *Before I Was Born,* Book 2, Carolyn Nystrom (NavPress).
> *What's the Big Deal? Why God Cares About Sex,* Book 3, Stan and Brenna Jones (NavPress).
> *Facing the Facts: The Truth About Sex and You,* Book 4, Stan and Brenna Jones (NavPress).
> *How and When to Tell Your Kids About Sex—Parents' Companion* (To God's Design for Sex Series), Stan and Brenna Jones (NavPress).
Heaven Help the Home, Howard G. Hendricks (Scripture Press).
Home-Grown Heroes, Tim Kimmel (Multnomah).
How to Really Love Your Child, Ross Campbell, M.D. (Chariot Books).
How to Really Love Your Teenager, Ross Campbell, M.D. (Chariot Books).
The Hurried Child, David Elkind (Addison-Wesley).
Let's Make a Memory, Gloria Gaither and Shirley Dobson (Word).
Little House on the Freeway, Tim Kimmel (Questar).
The Little House on the Freeway Home Maintenance Manual, Tim Kimmel (Questar).
Making Family Memories: A Family Night Planner, Rich and Bonnie Skinner (Fulton Press).
The One-Year Book of Family Devotions, Volume 2 (Tyndale).
Parenting: An Heir-Raising Experience, Mary Glynn and Sam Peeples (Peeples).
Preparing for Adolescence, James Dobson (Regal Books).
Prodigals and Those Who Love Them, Ruth Bell Graham (Focus on the Family).
Raising Kids Who Turn Out Right, Tim Kimmel (Questar).

RESOURCES

WOMEN

For Better Or For Best, Gary Smalley (Zondervan).
Home By Choice, Brenda Hunter (Questar).
How to Be Your Husband's Best Friend, Cay Bolin and Cindy Trent (NavPress).
Mom, You're Incredible, Linda Weber (Focus on the Family).
The Mommy Book, Karen Hull (Zondervan).
A Mother's Heart: A Look at Values, Vision, and Character for the Christian Mother, Jean Fleming (NavPress).
Partners in Promise: Discovering Your Role in Your Husband's Spiritual Quest, Mary Jensen (Questar).
Women Leaving the Workplace, Larry Burkett (Moody).

CHILDREN

Arch Book Series, (Concordia).
Benjamin's Box, Melody Carlson (Questar).
Caution: Dangerous Devotions, Jackie Perseghetti (Chariot Books).

SINGLES

Books
Becoming a Friend and Lover, Dick Purnell (Tyndale).
Before You Say "I Do," Wes Roberts and H. Norman Wright (Harvest House).
Finding the Love of Your Life, Neil Clark Warren (Focus on the Family).
Free to Love Again: Coming to Terms With Sexual Regret, Dick Purnell (Thomas Nelson).
Passion and Purity, Elisabeth Elliot (Baker Books).
Quest for Love, Elisabeth Elliot (Baker Books).

Audio
"Before the Wedding Night," Ed Wheat, M.D. (Scriptural Counseling).
"Preparing for Marriage," Dennis Rainey (FamilyLife).

STUDY/WORKBOOK MATERIALS

The Financial Planning Workbook, Larry Burkett (Christian Financial Concepts).
The HomeBuilders Couples Series®, Various Titles and Authors (Gospel Light).
School Choice: Making Your Decision and Making It Work, A FamilyLife Resource (FamilyLife).
Understanding One Another: A Personalized Guide to Better Communication, A FamilyLife Resource (FamilyLife).

RESOURCES

Raising Money-Smart Kids: How to Teach Your Children the Secrets of Earning, Saving, Investing, and Spending Wisely, Ron and Judy Blue (Thomas Nelson).
Real Family Values, Robert Lewis and Rich Campbell (Vision House).
The Strong-Willed Child, James Dobson (Tyndale).
Tough Parenting for Dangerous Times, Andy Bustanaby (Zondervan).
The Tribute, Dennis Rainey with Dave Boehi (Thomas Nelson).
Watchmen on the Walls: Praying Character Into Your Child, Anne Arkins and Gary Harrell (FamilyLife).
The Way They Learn, Cynthia Tobias (Focus on the Family).

Audio
"A Biblical Approach to Spanking," Dennis and Barbara Rainey (FamilyLife).
"Building a Relationship With Your Child," Dennis and Barbara Rainey (FamilyLife).
"Dad," Dennis Rainey (FamilyLife).
"Guiding Your Child Through Peer Pressure," Dennis and Ashley Rainey (FamilyLife).
"Love, Sex, and Marriage," Dennis Rainey (FamilyLife).
"Principles for Effective Parenting," Dennis and Barbara Rainey (FamilyLife).
"Teaching Your Children About Sex," Dennis and Barbara Rainey (FamilyLife).

Other
"Resurrection Eggs®," A FamilyLife Resource (FamilyLife).

Step-Parenting
Living in a Step-Family Without Getting Stepped On, Kevin Leman (Thomas Nelson).
Resolving Conflict in the Blended Family, Tom and Adrenne Frydenger (Baker).

MEN

The Effective Father, Gordon MacDonald (Tyndale).
Guard Your Heart, Gary Rosberg (Questar).
How to Be Your Daughter's Daddy, Dan Bolin (NavPress).
How to Be Your Little Man's Dad, Dan Bolin and Ken Sutterfield (NavPress).
How to Be Your Wife's Best Friend, Dan Bolin and John Trent (NavPress).
If Only He Knew, Gary Smalley (Zondervan).
Locking Arms, Stu Weber (Questar).
The Silence of Adam, Larry Crabb with Don Hudson and Al Andrews (Zondervan).
Tender Warrior, Stu Weber (Multnomah).
Promise Keepers resources are available by calling 1(800) 265-6023.

RESOURCES

GENERAL

The Book of Virtues, William J. Bennett (Simon & Schuster).
The Gift of the Blessing, Gary Smalley and John Trent (Thomas Nelson).
How to Deal With Powerful Personalities, Tim Kimmel (Focus on the Family).
Knowing God by His Names: A 31-Day Experiment, Dick Purnell
    (Thomas Nelson).
The Knowledge of the Holy, A. W. Tozer (Spring Arbor).
A Passionate Commitment, Crawford W. Loritts (Moody Press).
Recovering Biblical Manhood and Womanhood, Wayne Grudem and John
    Piper (Crossway).
Right from Wrong, Josh McDowell and Bob Hostetler (Word).
What the Bible Says About Healthy Living, Rex Russell, M.D. (Gospel Light).
When Life Is Changed Forever, Rick Taylor (Harvest House).
The Wounded Heart, Dan B. Allender (NavPress).